PERSONAL VOICES
Chinese Women in the 1980's

PERSONAL VOICES
Chinese Women in the 1980's

Emily Honig & Gail Hershatter

Stanford University Press, Stanford, California

Stanford University Press
Stanford, California
© 1988 by the Board of Trustees of the
Leland Stanford Junior University
Printed in the United States of America
Original printing 1988
Last figure below indicates year of this printing:
04 03 02 01 00 99 98

CIP data appear at the end of the book

Acknowledgments

WHEN WE WENT TO CHINA to do research in the fall of 1979, we did not intend to write a book about contemporary women. One of us was studying the women cotton mill workers of pre-Liberation Shanghai; the other was investigating the growth of the working class in Tianjin. Most of our time was spent poring over archival documents and interviewing retired workers. Yet it was impossible to ignore the rapidly changing social environment of contemporary China, particularly as it affected women. Each of us shared a university dormitory room with a young Chinese woman. In talking with them and their female classmates we became aware that issues formerly considered "private"—adornment, courtship, marriage, divorce—were becoming topics of intense public discussion. We began to clip articles on these topics in the press, and watched as a full-fledged debate about gender roles unfolded in Chinese society. As we finished our dissertations, began teaching, and returned to China for periodic visits, the piles of clippings, women's magazines, and books by and for women grew.

In the past seven years many people prodded us to incorporate this material into an account of the lives of contemporary Chinese women. Foremost among those who helped shape this book are the women whose friendship allowed us our first close look at Chinese society: Li Biyu, Wang Yufeng, Zhao Xiaojian, Pan Hangjun, Zhou Guangyu, and Cora Deng. From Xue Suzhen we learned about the sociological investigations of women now being conducted by Chinese scholars. Su Hongjun was an inexhaustible source of clippings and critical commentary. We are profoundly grateful to all these women for sharing their observations, experiences, and opinions with us, though they may well not agree with our interpretations.

We are indebted to the colleagues and friends who read this book in whole or in part. Marilyn Young played midwife to the book and sometime therapist to its authors, giving every version of the manuscript as much consideration and care as if it had been her own. Christina Gilmartin pushed us to refine our analysis and helped us expurgate traces of

Chinglish from the translations. Margery Wolf, to whom we owe a great intellectual debt for her pioneering books on Chinese women, helped us place our work in the larger context of social science research on China. Lisa Rofel's careful reading made us more conscious of the dangers of our own ethnocentrism. Harold Kahn, who has read and edited every word that we have written as professional historians, gave us the benefit of his dependably incisive and eloquent comments. He was our toughest critic. Although we chose not to take some of his advice, the book is richer and more tightly written because he labored over it. Randall Stross did his best to clear the manuscript of bad grammar and sloppy thinking, all the while cheering us on. Carma Hinton provided a critical reading of the introduction and endless lore about growing up female in China. Michael L. Smith offered intriguing comparisons to the situation of women in United States history. Kay Ann Johnson helped us to refine our argument about the effects of the Cultural Revolution on women.

Several others made unique contributions to this project. Our research assistants, Lin Xiaoyun and Laipeng Rehfield, prepared draft translations of selected materials from the Chinese press. Weiguo Yu put in long hours clearing up questions of translation and interpretation. Gloria Rodriguez contributed essential childcare and Sarah Fang offered entertainment and distraction. Mary Beckman, Estelle Freedman, Susan Mann, and Christine Wong were crucial sources of moral support. Financial support and office space were provided by Williams College, Lafayette College, the Fairbank Center for East Asian Research at Harvard University, and the Center for Chinese Studies at the University of California, Berkeley. Muriel Bell, Senior Editor at Stanford University Press, encouraged us to finish the manuscript and took time out from her new duties to copyedit the result.

Finally, we would like to thank each other for the joys of coauthorship. This book is collaborative in every respect; the order of the authors' names was decided by flipping a coin.

E.H.
G.H.

Contents

PERSONAL VOICES
Chinese Women in the 1980's

Introduction

IT WAS THE LAST DAY of the exhibit, and the hall of the Shanghai Workers' Cultural Palace was crowded. Groups of women and an occasional man hurried to view the pictures and captions depicting the "Achievements of Shanghai Women, 1976–1986," even as workmen moved in to dismantle the display. The exhibit was an impressive testimony to the dedication and competence of women in many fields: science, agriculture, industry, education, athletics, and the arts.

Without ever making explicit comparisons to China's prerevolutionary past, the display made it clear just how much women's lives had changed in the twentieth century. No longer were women's roles limited, as they had been during the period of imperial rule, to domestic work, childbearing, household handicrafts, or prostitution. The options had widened considerably even since the Republican period (1911–49), when many women moved out of the home into industrial production, professions such as teaching, social work, and medicine, student activism, and politics. With the coming to power of the Communist Party in 1949, women were brought into the workforce in unprecedented numbers. They were also expected to participate fully in the political and social transformation of society. The results, we thought as we moved through the hall, were all around us: in the women of achievement portrayed on the walls, in the confident manner and lively conversations of the women spectators, and in the fact of the exhibit itself—a government-sponsored effort to promote public awareness of how much women had contributed to China's development.

Yet two aspects of the exhibit troubled us. First, an occasional display of statistical information indicated that the status of women was far from equal to that of men. Less than a quarter of the city's Communist Party members were women, a significant handicap in a nation where the Party makes policy and controls political life. Even more disturbing, in a society that has begun to emphasize education as the key to development, women were barely represented in the ranks of those currently studying for advanced degrees in Shanghai (50 of 410 Ph.D. students; 156 of 7,753 master's degree students).

Second, the exhibit conveyed a mixed message about the sexual division of labor. It showed women who were distinguished scientists, but at the same time suggested that women were by nature and training uniquely suited to tasks, such as the production of fine embroidered pieces, that tended to pay less than jobs performed by men. The exhibit focused on women's individual achievements outside the home, but it left unexamined the "double burden" of women who worked at both paid labor and the unpaid labor of housework and childrearing.

The public discourse on women's status in China is considerably more complicated than this exhibition suggested. Since the late 1970's, the press has carried lively discussions, and sometimes acrimonious debates, about everything from female adornment to the role of women in the workforce. These discussions are not confined to the pages of newspapers and magazines; they permeate private conversation and visibly affect public behavior, especially in China's cities. Not since the May Fourth Movement of 1919, when iconoclastic students challenged Confucian norms for women, has gender been so visible as a subject of controversy and a category of analysis.

This book is about the rapidly changing role of Chinese women in the 1980's. It is also about the excitement, confusion, and concern that Chinese people express as they contemplate the future of their society and women's place in it. The book begins with the socialization of young women, then moves on to explore adornment and sexuality, love and courtship, marriage, family relations, divorce, work, violence against women, and gender inequality. Discussions of these issues in China resemble, and sometimes echo, debates about women that have taken place in our own society. But they have been decisively shaped by the history of China in the twentieth century, and particularly by the role of women in the Chinese revolution.

Women and the Chinese Revolution

Throughout the early twentieth century, whenever Chinese intellectuals struggled to develop a vision of a united, strong, and free China, they criticized the oppression of women as a major obstacle to the realization of that vision. During the May Fourth Movement of 1919, intellectuals attacked Confucian thought and social organization as the major cause of China's inability to defend itself against Western imperialism. In the course of this movement they invoked the unequal status of women in the Confucian family as a symbol of everything in Chinese culture that kept the nation weak. But for patriotic young students, the subordinate status of women was more than a metaphor; their personal lives were a testimony to the struggle against Confucianism. They refused to enter marriages arranged by their parents, publicly discussed the nature of love, attended performances of Ibsen's *A Doll's House*, and generally sought to remake their private lives to accord with their image of a modern society.[1]

The young founders of the Chinese Communist Party inherited the May Fourth legacy; from its inception in 1921 the Party advocated the liberation of women.[2] After the Party shifted its focus to rural organizing in the 1930's, though, that liberation was often subordinated to other revolutionary goals. Campaigns to end wife-beating and ban arranged marriages had to be carefully weighed against the need to win the support of peasant men. Though the Party did succeed in modifying family power relationships in the rural base areas, increasingly it emphasized bringing women into the paid labor force as the key to their liberation. This narrowed definition of "the woman problem" was shaped by two factors: a Marxist theory of revolution that emphasized class far more than gender, and a social reality in which minimizing conflict and maximizing production were critical to survival.[3]

When the Communist Party came to power in 1949, its approach to the liberation of women drew on the experience of organizing in the base areas. Women's equality was guaranteed in the Constitution of 1950, and the Marriage Law of the same year gave women the right to choose their own marriage partners and to demand a divorce.[4] Women's feet were no longer bound, even in remote villages; girls were given at least limited access to education. The Women's Federation was established by the national government to safeguard the interests of women. In the post-revolutionary period, though, women were primarily mobilized not to fight for gender equality, but to contribute to socialist construction. It was widely accepted that the establishment of socialism would automatically result in the liberation of women. But even though the public discussion of gender issues became muted, conflicts over the role of women continued to shape the course of the revolution in important ways. For instance, the Great Leap Forward of 1958–59, which brought women into the workforce in unprecedented numbers, ran aground partly because men and women alike rebelled at the construction of collective kitchens and nurseries, which threatened the family unit.[5]

During the Cultural Revolution (1966–76), class struggle took precedence over all other issues, including those of gender equality. Serious disagreements among China's leaders about how to build socialism, as well as longstanding factional conflicts, combined with popular social resentments about the persistence of old elites and the emergence of new ones after 1949. The result was an upheaval that disrupted every aspect of political and social life: schools were closed, government bureaus shut down, political disagreements flared into deadly violence, and young people set out across China in groups devoted to exchanging experiences and making revolution.[6]

The history of the Cultural Revolution remains mired in controversy both in China and abroad, making it very difficult to evaluate its effect on the status of women. Slogans such as "women hold up half the sky" and portraits of heroic women workers and peasants adorned many billboards, but little official attention was given to assessing the gender inequalities that remained or designing measures to eliminate them. In fact, recognition of gender as a category distinct from class was regarded as reactionary. The Women's Federation, like many other organizations, was disbanded, and some of its leading officials were criticized for "bourgeois" attitudes. Women took on nontraditional tasks in the workplace, but their duties at home were not altered, and they were exhorted to shoulder cheerfully the burdens of the double day in the name of socialism. The complexities of courtship, marriage, and family life were reduced to the simple statement that politics should be in command in the home as well as in public.

In spite of the official neglect of women's issues, though, the lives of young women in particular were profoundly affected by the Cultural Revolution. For all its terrible destructiveness, it conferred on young women a mobility previously denied them. Freed from family control, young women Red Guards moved across the landscape more widely and in greater numbers than at any time in Chinese history. Like their male counterparts, they were encouraged to challenge parents, teachers, and officials, and to act with a confidence and enthusiasm probably never before permitted adolescent women in China. To be sure, when young urban people were sent to live permanently in the countryside in 1968, women found themselves unprotected by familial networks and vulnerable to sexual and other abuse. Yet their years away from home, and their interactions with their generational cohort, created expectations and experiences that changed their lives irrevocably.

After Mao Zedong's death in 1976 and the arrest of his wife Jiang Qing and her political allies, Cultural Revolution policies were resoundingly rejected in every walk of life. Beginning in 1978, economic reforms began to restructure the lives of women. In the countryside, agriculture was decollectivized and production was reorganized with households as the basic unit. Peasants were encouraged to engage in sideline production, private markets were permitted, and the government raised the prices it paid for farm produce. These new policies increased women's opportunities to earn income, but also placed their labor firmly under the control of the head of household rather than the collective, reinforcing familial authority. In the cities, industrial enterprises were given expanded powers to hire and fire, and were made responsible for their own profits and losses. Since urban unemployment was a problem at the beginning of the 1980's, they had a large labor pool from which to draw. Many promptly decided that they would prefer to hire men rather than women, who were considered unreliable workers because of their responsibilities in the home. The educational system was expanded, but at the same time entrance qualifications at all levels were made more restrictive. Popular belief that girls were less capable than boys meant that female access to education remained limited. In both rural and urban sectors, individual accumulation and display of material goods became much more politically acceptable than at any time since 1949. This affected the way women dressed, the kinds of labor-saving devices they used at home, and the demands for household goods that accompanied an agreement to marry. Each of these changes meant that new types of work and behavior were expected of women.

The effects of the economic reforms on women generated an enormous amount of discussion, both in personal conversations and in the press. Women's private lives became the focus of public debate in the 1980's for several other reasons as well. A number of problems that had been building for over a decade were of pressing concern to policy-makers and citizens alike. The rate of population growth mandated an increasingly strict family planning policy, which by the late 1970's was beginning to strain marital and family relations. The traditional preference for sons put intolerable pressure upon women; those who bore daughters were often abused, girl babies were sometimes killed or abandoned, and the success of the entire policy was threatened. Other problems loomed: large numbers of urban youth who had been sent to the countryside during the Cultural Revolution had delayed marriage in hopes that they would be able to return to the city, and now constituted a large, aging, single, and dissatisfied population. The problem of finding a marriage partner was particularly acute for women, who were regarded as virtually unmarriageable by the age of thirty. Numerous marriages made in the political environment of the Cultural Revolution were deteriorating, raising questions about the nature of marriage and the right to divorce. In spite of legal guarantees, the amount of control women should exercise over their marital situation was a matter of public debate. During the decade of the Cultural Revolution, attention to personal life had been regarded as "bourgeois"; in the post-Mao decade, public policy made discussion of personal life imperative.

China's opening to the West in the 1980's also influenced the debate about women's roles. As part of the Four Modernizations drive, China was beginning to study, borrow, and buy Western technology. Foreign experts, business people, journalists, and diplomats became increasingly common in China. Foreign movies and books were eagerly received by a Chinese audience that for years had been isolated from the West. What sorts of Western values would accompany Western technology, and whether those values could or should be separated from that technology, were matters of discussion and disagreement in high government circles and among ordinary people as well. Stories in Chinese women's magazines reported on the situation of women in Western nations. Western fashions, family arrangements, and sexual morality became topics of public controversy.

Old Topics, New Controversies

The situation of women in the 1980's, and the public debate over what their social role should become, was shaped by the past but was not a reenactment of it. The world of pre-1949 China, and the role that women played in that world, was gone. Although the early 1980's saw a resurgence of female infanticide, elaborate marriage rituals, and other practices that looked like a return to the past, those practices took place in a radically changed historical context. Some social problems, such as female infanticide, were unintended consequences of the economic reforms. But if state policy had caused some of these practices to reappear, it also opposed them vigorously and with more effect than any pre-1949 government could have done. Other practices, such as parental control of marriage choice, were opposed not only by the state but by a generation of young people born and brought up after 1949. Generational conflict over such issues was far more widespread than it had been even during the May Fourth Movement. Because of higher levels of literacy, advanced communications technology, increased mobility, and widened popular participation, the public debate in the 1980's involved large segments of the urban population and many rural dwellers as well. Although many women in China still suffered discrimination in working life and mistreatment in the family, they could raise questions that would have been unthinkable in an earlier era, and draw support from allies that had not existed before. Most notably, they could and did use the press to voice complaints, expose injustices, seek advice, and articulate support for or dismay at the social changes of the 1980's.

Although some of the topics under discussion had been raised first in the 1950's, the debates about women's issues in the 1980's were not a restatement of earlier concerns. Chinese publications before the Cultural Revolution had taken up such topics as the dangers of adolescent love, the appropriate time to marry, the virtues of late marriage and frugal weddings, the evils of extramarital affairs and the heartbreak of divorce, the competing claims upon women of paid labor and household duties, and even the permissible limits of fashion. The 1980's discussion picked up these interrupted conversations, using categories and language familiar to readers from an earlier era. But as the Chinese social context changed rapidly in the 1980's, the discussion was carried along with it. Revolutionary comradeship was no longer mentioned as an indispensable element of marriage; it was replaced by notions of a companionate partnership managed by an emotionally sensitive wife. Adornment and sexuality became matters of public concern to a degree undreamed of in the 1950's. Female employment became problematic in new ways because of the economic reforms. Each of these issues was more complex, and the public pronouncements on it less unified, than had been the case thirty years before.

In all these areas, public discussion in the 1980's was shaped by a decisive rejection of the experiences of the Cultural Revolution. The fervor and enthusiasm with which women beautified themselves, the widespread support for moving women back into "suitable" lines of work, the discussions of womanly virtues in the press, must all be understood in part as a reaction to Cultural Revolution norms. Conversely, it became impossible to advocate certain approaches to gender inequality because they were associated with the Cultural Revolution era. In the 1950's, the main culprit in women's oppression had been the feudal past; in the 1980's, the excesses of the Cultural Revolution were blamed as well.

To an American reader, much of the discussion in the Chinese press might sound familiar. Descriptions of fashions, advice on how to snare a man, accounts of new marriages in crisis, strategies for juggling career and home responsibilities, all could be read as Chinese variations on articles in *Redbook*, *Cosmopolitan*, and *Ms.* magazines.

Many of the conflicts faced by Chinese women in the 1980's resembled those of other societies at other times. In the United States after World War II, for instance, women were sent back into the home after a period of wartime mobilization that had moved them into roles previously reserved for men. American women's magazines in the 1950's featured articles about homemaking, adornment, and the importance of good mothering, topics that also figured prominently in the 1980's Chinese press. In both countries, a period of widespread social disruption was followed by an attempt to reestablish clear gender roles. And in both countries, this attempt was supported by large numbers of women as well as men.[7]

Yet it is crucial to understand that China was not simply passing through a series of universal stages on the way to modernity, that its history cannot be reduced to a slightly exoticized version of our own. And it would be both insulting and misleading to conclude that Chinese women were mired in an earlier stage of historical development, thirty years behind the United States. Their 1980's differed radically from the American 1950's. The ambitious modernization program devised by the post-Mao leadership sought to complete by the year 2000 the kinds of transformation that had occurred in the West over a much longer period. Chinese women found themselves trying to absorb changes and social strains similar to those brought about in the West through the industrial revolution, late-nineteenth-century urbanization, several wars, and the feminist movement—all at once. It was as though Queen Victoria, Rosie the Riveter, Helen Gurley Brown, and a host of others had appeared simultaneously on the scene, all proffering advice. Not surprisingly, Chinese women, themselves products of a complex tradition and a cataclysmic recent history, reacted with a mixture of fascination, incomprehension, and wariness that was entirely their own. They initiated some changes and acquiesced in others, but protested vigorously when they felt their interests threatened, as when changes in hiring practices made it more difficult for them to find certain jobs. Their situation was not a simple replication of the female experience elsewhere.

Sources and Scope

Each chapter in this book is devoted to an aspect of women's lives that has become a subject of controversy or change in the 1980's. At the end of each chapter are translations that convey the flavor of the discussions in Chinese publications. The study draws on the periodical press, books for women, and interviews conducted from 1979 to 1986.

Discussion about women's issues began in the late 1970's in official national publications, chief among them *China Youth News* (Zhongguo qingnian bao) and *Chinese Women* (Zhongguo funü). By the mid-1980's, a host of newly founded official, semi-official, and unofficial newspapers and magazines had taken up these issues. Most of these publications were new, and not much is known about their circulation, readership, or average lifespan. But a look at any urban newsstand, even outside the major cities, showed that these magazines continued to proliferate and sell quickly. Many, such as *Woman's World* (Nüzi shijie), *Home* (Jiating), and *Woman's Friend* (Funü zhi you), were directed specifically at a female audience.

Books devoted to private life also appeared in great numbers after 1979. Many of these were handbooks of advice to young people. In contrast to periodicals, the books spoke with a more unified and generally more conservative voice. Often they took the form of letters asking for guidance, followed by lengthy replies. Unlike the complicated, detailed letters in the press, these missives were usually simple formulaic devices. In most cases, such collections of questions and answers appeared to have been written by a single author. These books were useful to us in identifying issues that national and local authorities considered especially problematic.

China has a state-controlled press, and issues about the lives of women appeared in that press at least in part because they touched on areas of concern to the state. But official concern did not imply that government and Party officials had a clear-cut set of policies they wanted to impose. State policy in the 1980's mandated a lessening of official control over many spheres of activity, from economic planning to marriage choice to fashion. Although the newspapers were unlikely to print direct criticisms of government policies, most women's issues fell outside the sphere of topics subject to direct censorship. Articles in the official press reflected the belief that some aspects of personal life should not be regulated by adherence to a state-imposed "correct line." In addition, officials did not seem to know quite what to say about some of these private issues. Publications for women and young people stressed certain dilemmas, and frequently provided a "correct" solution to those dilemmas. Yet even though editors of state-controlled newspapers undoubtedly believed that their articles should teach a lesson, they did not always agree on what the content of that lesson should be.

Readers of the official press showed a similar variety of outlooks. They wrote to advice columnists requesting help with their personal problems. Frequently the columnists encouraged public discussion and published some of the results. In such forums, public opinion did not speak with a unified voice. The volume and diversity of public response indicated that young readers felt both great interest and great confusion about women's issues. Readers seemed to agree that some actions were socially acceptable while others were not, but they differed on where the bounds of social acceptability lay. The voices of editors and readers were too cacophonous to be orchestrated.

The debate in the press spilled over into private discourse, where it became permissible to discuss aspects of personal life that had been politically suspect or even taboo during the Cultural Revolution. Both the authors lived in China from 1979 to 1981, and have visited frequently thereafter. Our personal observations and conversations with Chinese friends revealed that the issues we were reading about were also of paramount concern to people we knew. When an author named Yu Luojin published a story describing her experiences with love, marriage, and divorce, for instance, it created a sensation among university students. They cut classes and abandoned homework when their turn came to read one of the hard-to-find copies of the magazine in which it appeared, which sold out almost immediately. As we listened to our friends fervently argue about this story, we realized that two things were happening. A debate about social and personal mores was beginning, one that was bound to profoundly affect women. And aspects of female life that had been invisible were becoming public, visible for the first time to us and to our Chinese friends.

Some of our women friends were in their twenties, educated, and unmarried; they had entered the university after passing a rigorous set of examinations in the late 1970's. Most had worked in the countryside or in factories for a number of years before becoming students. We also talked extensively to older women, educated before 1949, who had remained concerned with women's issues throughout the tumultuous years after the revolution. Virtually all these women were urban intellectuals, and their viewpoints were in some respects not typical of Chinese women as a whole. Yet even our limited survey of the concerns of individual women made it clear to us that the debate in the press was not a sterile exercise divorced from popular concerns.

Most of this book focuses on women in urban China; although there are over 100 million of them, they represent a scant one-fifth of the female population. They were the readers, as well as many of the writers, of the new women's press from which we have drawn much of our material. Every official and unofficial source available to us thus had a strong urban bias. However, several key women's issues arose overwhelmingly in a rural context, and the press relied on rural examples to discuss some of these problems. Among them were parental interference in marriage, the role of the daughter-in-law in the family, female infanticide, and domestic violence. We have included these discussions here, even though we were not able to supplement what we read with our own observations. This has left us in the awkward position of devoting the majority of the book to describing a minority of Chinese women, while giving just enough information about the rural majority to raise questions our book cannot answer. Yet given the constraints of the written sources, and the impossibility of conducting extended rural fieldwork, we had no alternative. Rural Chinese women are too important to leave out, but an exhaustive treatment of their experience will have to be done by someone who has the opportunity to live in the countryside.

A word about the prejudices of the authors, since the book was shaped by our questions as much as by the available answers. We came to the study of Chinese women as two American feminists, products ourselves of a specific scholarly training and historical era. Our analytical framework differed in some respects from that of the Chinese who were discussing women's issues. First, we owe a great intellectual debt to those Western scholars who came before us in investigating the lives of Chinese women. Some of them combed the Chinese press for clues to official policy, while others conducted interviews and ethnographic work in Taiwan and Hong Kong, as well as on the Chinese mainland. Taken together, their work has made it possible for us to place the debates and changes we witnessed in a broader historical context.[8]

Second, we have been influenced by the emerging feminist scholarship on countries other than China, which has provided us with a rich comparative context. Like feminist scholars in other fields, we look at gender as one of several basic principles around which every society is organized, and we seek to identify the relationships of power and inequality that structure gender roles in China. We employ this method not only to understand the experience of women, but also to illuminate other social problems that are central to China's development in the late twentieth century. Gender relations are a powerful key to understanding the relationship between official ideology and popular values, the social costs of economic development, and the persistence of hierarchy in a society that has tried, and rejected, some dramatic routes to egalitarianism.

We have tried to avoid an analysis that says "Chinese society is good insofar as it becomes more like our own" or (the oft-heard feminist twist on this) "China is becoming a worse place for women as it comes to embrace the forms of oppression that Western industrialized societies have imposed upon women." Yet we pretend to no Olympian detachment from the history we record. As foreigners in China, outsiders to Chinese culture, we sometimes raised different questions from the ones that shaped the public debate. Rigid sex-role socialization of children, and the very limited social autonomy of women of all ages outside the family, interested and disturbed us but did not seem subject to public scrutiny in China. Some of the new developments we witnessed were also jarring. For instance, in rejecting the puritanical asceticism of the Cultural Revolution, many Chinese women embraced a notion of femininity that American feminists would find restrictive or demeaning. Understanding the historical reasons for their enthusiasm did not prevent us from wondering about its eventual consequences.

Gender hierarchy is very much alive in 1980's China. In spite of government assurances that it is a "feudal remnant" whose disappearance is historically inevitable, it continues to appear, expressing itself in both familiar and novel forms. The subordination of women dismays us in Chinese society as it does in our own, though it does not surprise us. When we voice that dismay in this book, we do so realizing that the ideals of feminism have yet to be realized anywhere in the world. We hope this account of the lives of Chinese women will contribute to an understanding of the forms that gender inequality takes in different societies, since understanding women's subordination is an essential step toward eliminating it.

✦ 1
Growing Up Female

WHEN PEOPLE STROLL by the banks of a lotus pond, enjoying the sight of budding lotus flowers," began a 1985 handbook for young women,

they cannot help but be deeply affected by the purity, grace, and vitality of the flowers, their beauty that emerges unstained from the mire, their noble qualities. And they naturally associate this with fair, slim, and graceful young girls. . . . Girls entering the age of young womanhood (ages fourteen to eighteen) undergo great physiological changes. . . . How this stage develops, how the basis is laid, often will deeply affect their entire lives. For this reason, enabling them to grow up healthy, and not become deformed or break when they are washed by wind and rain or infested by "insect pests," is not only the urgent desire of young women themselves, but also a matter of deep concern to their elders, teachers, relatives, and friends.[1]

When a young woman reached adolescence in 1980's China, her elders regarded her as uniquely beautiful and uniquely vulnerable. She became the target of publications that sought to guide and protect her by explaining female capabilities and describing proper female behavior. The advice literature discussed the two social roles she would play as an adult: worker at paid productive labor, and worker at unpaid reproductive labor—that is, as wife and mother. This chapter analyzes the messages young women received about how to fill the first role by choosing a career appropriate to female capabilities.

Although much advice literature concerned areas of public controversy, the opinions of adolescent women themselves were heard very little in the discussion. Unlike older women, whose views on love and courtship, marriage, family relations, and divorce appear later in this book, young women from ages fourteen to eighteen were expected to listen and to ask questions, not to hold forth themselves.[2] Because most of the writing about adolescence in 1980's China was of this type, this chapter and Chapter 2 of necessity draw largely upon the words of adults to explore the experience of adolescents. They risk describing things as adults would like them to be, rather than as they are. Yet by listening to the voices of adults as they explain, cajole, chastise, and warn, it is possible to learn something about adolescents, and a great deal about adult attitudes toward the socialization of young women.

In preparing for their role in the working world, young women were offered ambiguous guidance. They were encouraged to develop their own talents and character, in spite of physical limitations and social obstacles they might meet along the way. But while exhorting young women to accomplish all they could, books of advice and articles in the press also subtly communicated the conviction that girls were inferior to boys in intellect, physical ability, and emotional stability. Only by overcoming their female weaknesses, girls were told, could they hope to achieve equally with their male classmates. This message was reinforced by the use of role models who performed well by male standards.

Female Capabilities: Is Biology Destiny?

"Is it true that girls are not as smart as boys?" young women asked in several collections of letters and advice.[3] One high school student, preparing for the university entrance exam, was told by all her girlfriends that she should not waste the effort. Girls, they said, are more stupid than boys to start with, and after they marry and have children they become so preoccupied with housework that they cannot hope to achieve much even with a college degree. When she looked around for evidence to counter their opinions, she could not help noticing that most historical and contemporary personages, in China and abroad, were men. She began to wonder, said her letter to a former teacher, whether girls were really inferior in intelligence to boys.[4]

At first glance, the answer usually given to this question appears to be "no." Girls were invariably told to remember that Madame Curie, the only scientist in the world to win the Nobel Prize for science twice, was a woman. Most replies also cited examples of other famous women, such as Han dynasty historian Ban Zhao, Song dynasty poet Li Qingzhao (whose brilliant scholar-husband tried in vain to write poems as captivating as hers), and Rosa Luxemburg. Since the founding of the People's Republic, girls were reminded, many women have become pilots, ship captains, scientific researchers, and contributors to industrial and agricultural production. With so many examples of female achievement to emulate, the advice ran, girls should be convinced that it was possible for them to achieve as much as boys.[5]

Yet these authors qualified their assertion that boys and girls are equal in a number of ways. Although they pointed out that male and female brains show no differences that might influence intelligence, they often went on to describe gender differences in ways that made female intelligence seem both different and naturally inferior.[6] In August 1982, *China Youth News* published an article entitled "The Special Characteristics of Female Intelligence."[7] The article, written in technical scientific language, indicated that a difference in brain function between girls and boys first becomes evident in childhood. Experiments showed that girls had stronger tactile feeling which made them good at fine motor activity, that they spoke and read earlier, that their hearing was more developed, and that it was easier for them to learn foreign languages. Boys, on the other hand, were stronger in spatial perception and vision. The reason for this, the author ventured, was that in boys the speaking and space perception abilities were "installed" in different halves of the brain. In girls, verbal and nonverbal abilities were spread throughout both cerebral hemispheres. "Perhaps the two hemispheres of the female cerebrum," the author commented, "do not have a very specialized division of labor." The article thus presented controversial areas in brain research as though they were universally accepted scientific fact.[8]

This author felt that gender differences in brain function had important implications for social engineering. Moving from an account of sex differences in elementary school children to a comment on adult capabilities, he concluded,

It is easier for girls to learn foreign languages, and so it is relatively easy for them to take up occupations that require proficiency in languages. . . . When girls select an area for independent study, they must take into account the special features of their brain function, to utilize female strengths. Only in this way can a girl grow up to be useful (*zao ri chengcai*). If her choice is inappropriate, twice the effort will yield half the result. Of course, this is not absolute.[9]

Clearly it was not absolute for boys, who were not enjoined from pursuing careers in languages or other verbal arts. For girls, though, childhood brain function and later occupational choice were explicitly linked. The perception that girls were inherently better than boys at typing, while boys were inherently superior at math, was expressed in private conversation with us by young people of both sexes, including women whose academic performance belied the typology.

In the advice literature, analyses of gender difference often contained an implied rating of higher (male) and lower (female) orders of intelligence. After the usual disclaimer that men and women have no great difference in inborn abilities, one author quickly added,

But this is not to say that women and men are completely alike in all respects. For example, the thinking of male classmates is comparatively broad and quick. They have wide-ranging interests, a strong ability to get to work, and they like to think things out for themselves; but sometimes they are not careful or thorough enough.

Female classmates often have stronger memory and language ability, and are more diligent and meticulous. But they have one-track minds, do not think dynamically enough, have a rather narrow range of activity, and easily become interested in trivial matters. Their moods fluctuate easily, they are shy, and they don't dare to raise questions boldly.

These differences in intellectual style, the author continued, have an adverse effect on female academic achievement:

In their study methods, female classmates are accustomed to repeat, write, and recall from memory. They tend to stress grades and are good at rote memorizing. Male classmates, on the other hand, are bold in practice, like independent thinking, and dare to doubt preexisting conclusions. In the lower grades, perhaps the achievements of male classmates cannot keep pace with those of female classmates, yet their knowledge and intelligence increase through independent thinking and practice. Therefore, when they get to the senior middle school stage, their grades often surpass those of female classmates. In the study of mathematics, female classmates often rely on imitation and mechanical memory, are poor at grasping the overall situation, and have a rather weak capacity for logical thought. When they meet difficulties in solving a problem, they often first seek help from a book or look for a similar problem in the examples, while it is more common for male classmates to think things out for themselves.[10]

What was being described was not merely gender difference; it was gender hierarchy. Male intellectual style was clearly preferable, and in fact the article went on to encourage young women to overcome what amounts to a learning disability and try to emulate their male classmates. Although it is certainly possible that girls and boys in general may exhibit some of these differences in learning style, the authors of advice to young women seldom asked where biologically based gender differences leave off and social training begins. In failing to do so, they left the field to biology and the "scientific" legitimation of a gender hierarchy based on the superior intelligence of men.

Young women were also told that their intellectual capabilities would be altered by the onset of puberty. Here again, the message was mixed. On one hand, young women were told that with adolescence, their intellectual development would reach its peak:

[The adolescent girl] is full of exuberant energy, her memory is especially sharp, her brain is like a computer that can store a great deal of information. Her powers of logical and imagistic thinking all develop greatly. This is the best time to study and amount to something. It is during this period that many girls, after rigorous training, develop into outstanding dance performers, singers, athletes, and other talented people, and bring honor to the motherland.

Even at her pinnacle of achievement, a young woman apparently was limited to accomplishments in athletics and the performing arts; no one suggested that her "powers of logical and imagistic thinking" could rival those of a young man. Furthermore, this productive period in her life was not to be of long duration. In fact, the advice literature warned, puberty might be the last chance for a girl to achieve anything of note, because "after this period, when she is confronted with love, marriage, and child-bearing, every kind of interference and burden will become heavier." [11]

On the other hand, adolescence might already be too late, for it was then that girls fell behind boys in intelligence tests.[12] Although written sources said very little about why this happens, teachers and parents often blamed puberty. Young women in middle school were told repeatedly to lower their intellectual aspirations. In one such case, a friend of ours who was preparing for the university entrance exam came home from school one day very discouraged. Her science teacher, a middle-aged woman, had called the female students together for a serious talk. Acknowledging that it was all right for the girls to take the entrance exam, she advised them not to pick a science as their preferred area of study. Girls, she told them, just did not have the mental equipment to study science. In child-hood, she continued, they might do very well in school, but "at this time in their lives" (that is, puberty), their bodies would undergo physiological changes, their brains would grow more fuzzy, and their attention would turn to matters like establishing a family. Leave science to the boys, whose brains are sharper, she advised. If you want to study something, study humanities.[13]

This kind of "guidance" was not a matter of state policy. Yet state-approved publications perpetuated the idea that girls lag behind boys in intelligence. In doing so they both reflected popular social prejudice and helped to create an environment in which it was permissible to say such things to girl students. Boys got the message, too. A woman professor complained to us that despite her efforts to convince her ten-year-old son that men and women were equal, he came home from school every day proclaiming his satisfaction at being a member of the superior sex.

In much of the advice literature, girls were reminded that their in-feriority was physical as well as intellectual. Descriptions of a young woman's physical development at puberty were often constructed so that female worth was measured by male standards. A 1982 article on "Labor and Exercise for Young Women," for instance, rather than dwelling on the capacities of the female body, proceeded almost immediately to a de-tailed series of comparisons with pubescent boys. Girls, it said, have a fine bone structure and low bone density, as well as muscles that lack the abil-ity to contract and move powerfully. Their subdermal fat makes their waists and legs heavy, and the center of the body rather low, so that they cannot rival men in strength or speed.

Compared to young men, again, young women have less blood, fewer cells, less hemoglobin, a smaller heart, and less lung capacity. They tend to breathe more quickly during exercise, and to breathe from the abdomen, increasing abdominal pressure and influencing the circulation of blood in the pelvis. This affects the reproductive organs, creating a "special physiological problem" for women. "In sum," the article concluded, "whether in functions of the kinetic system, blood, circulation, respiration, and adjustment of body temperature, or in endurance and adaptability in heavy manual labor and physical training, young women cannot match young men of the same age." [14]

Although many biological facts presented in this article are beyond dispute, it was striking for the way in which it focused on the weakness of women when compared to men on selected measures. Like other articles of its genre, it made no mention of scientific evidence about the superior endurance and flexibility of females. It outlined not sex differences, but a gender hierarchy in which male strengths were the sole standard of value.

In addition to their intellectual and physical inadequacies, young women were warned that if they did not control themselves, their emotional development also might lag behind that of men. Their "natural" sensitivity to the nuances of human relationships might become a narrow-minded concern with the shortcomings of their neighbors or an obsession with what people were saying about them behind their backs.

Two explanations were given for these female emotional defects. The first was biological, again singling out puberty as the culprit. As an adolescent girl's body matures, she becomes more sensitive and attentive to the attitudes of others. Her expectations of self and others are raised, but she often lacks self-confidence and is afraid she will not be understood or taken seriously. Sensitivity becomes oversensitivity and what one author called "suspicionitis" (*duoyibing*), "a psychological abnormality of female adolescence." [15] Puberty apparently did not have this deleterious effect on boys, and girls were told to emulate them:

In general, boys very seldom catch "suspicionitis"; why is this? Because in general, the social circle, activities, interests, and hobbies of boys are a bit broader. So many things in life absorb them that they're not inclined to turn round and round in the small circle of suspicion. Throw yourself into the rich and varied sea of life, add a little "rough-and-readiness" to your character, add a bit of boy's flavor, let yourself become lively, optimistic, and open-minded, and "suspicionitis" will not be able to find you. [16]

The second explanation of women's emotional inferiority was historical. In "feudal society," a term used in popular parlance to describe China before 1949, women had very constricted horizons. They paid excessive attention to human relationships because they were not permitted to do anything else. In a discussion of why women gossip more than men, one author explained:

In feudal society, men were respected and women were deemed inferior. Women didn't go out much, lacked a wide range of contacts, and easily became narrow-minded. Hence, the topic of conversation among sisters and sisters-in-law was often the strengths and weaknesses of their neighbors.

But after the revolution of 1949, according to this author, the social constraints shaping female personality had fallen away. "We are women of a new age, we have equal status with men, we can be as determined as men, and like them we can come into contact with society, broadening our field of vision." Under these circumstances, the author concluded, women who continued to gossip were "caught in a web of our own making . . . acting like detestable 'long-tongued women,' and thereby lowering our own status, dissipating our energy for study and work, and letting our finest hour go to waste." [17] If women failed to eradicate the scars left by feudalism—that is, failed to become more like men in their emotional makeup—then they had no one but themselves to blame for their own inferiority.

The assumption of female difference—intellectual, physical, and emotional—had social consequences that perpetuated the existing sexual division of labor. The school curriculum, for instance, reflected certain assumptions about appropriate activities for girls and boys. In 1984, pre-school girls in a Shanghai day care center performed a dance for foreigners where they fed, changed, and combed the hair of baby dolls, while their male classmates looked on from the sidelines. [18] Adolescent girls and boys were also introduced to very different types of activities in middle school. In one Shanghai school, a middle school principal introduced a rigorous new physical education program that consisted of instruction in boxing for boys and dancing for girls (*nan quan, nü wu*). A news report of his efforts extolled the virtues of exercise; the division of exercise along gender lines was not subjected to critical scrutiny. [19] After-school activities, too, were commonly expected to feature instruction in gender-specific hobbies. A male reader of *China Youth News* proposed organizing girls' clubs modeled on those run by the Communist Youth League of Romania. The reader approvingly described the range of activities offered by the Romanian clubs: talks on health education, clothing design, makeup, marriage and divorce law, how to be a good wife and mother, and cooking. "These activities are good," he commented, "because they take account of the physiology and hobbies of young women, satisfy their particular needs, and provide them with knowledge which will enable them to organize a happy family and advance toward a new life. For sooner or later young women must marry; they are future wives and mothers, and at the same time must also take on the responsibility of looking after household duties." [20]

In both rural and urban cases, the belief that girls were intellectually, physically, and emotionally inferior to boys—an old belief newly clothed in scientific garb—helped to legitimize the limiting of educational and career opportunities for girls. In 1983, girls were 43.7 percent of all primary school students nationwide, less than 40 percent of middle school students, and slightly over a quarter of all postsecondary students. [21] In the countryside the ratio was often much more lopsided. One eleven-year-old rural girl pointed out in a 1982 letter that in 1978, twelve of her fifty classmates were girls, but by 1980, when she reached fourth grade, the number of girl students had declined to five. Parents had pulled their daughters out of school to herd cows and farm, reasoning (as they had in prerevolutionary times) that since girls eventually would marry into another family, there was no point in educating them beyond simple literacy. Even the goal of literacy often was not reached; a 10 percent sampling of the 1982 population showed that almost 70 percent of the illiterate and barely literate in China were female. Even more disturbing was that in spite of overall gains in literacy among women, the gap between men and women was increasing. Only 14 percent of all twelve-year-old girls were illiterate or semi-literate, compared to 95 percent of all women over sixty. But twelve-year-old girls composed 72 percent of the illiterates and semi-literates in their age cohort, whereas sixty-year-old women were only 64 percent of the illiterate in theirs. The evidence suggests that as the population as a whole became more literate, women did not share equally in the benefits. [22] In urban areas, where a girl's connection to her natal family remained stronger after marriage and education for both sexes was more highly valued than in the countryside, parents nevertheless often piled household chores on their adolescent daughters so that their sons were free to study. [23]

Scattered voices were raised to criticize these assertions of "natural" difference between the sexes, and the assumption of female inferiority that often accompanied them. Occasional articles began to emphasize the importance of parental encouragement, rather than biology, in determining a young girl's development. One author commented, "If girls were given the same treatment [as boys], I firmly believe that a spirit of confidence and steadfast bravery would take root and sprout in the virgin soil of their pure souls." [24] As more and more families have only one child under the family limitation program and find themselves raising a daughter as sole heir, this type of thinking will probably become more common.

Some educators also wondered whether gender differences might be partly social in origin. In 1981, one group of teachers concluded that girl students did not do as well as boys in senior middle school because of problems with the teaching, not the innate abilities of the students. They set up a separate science class for girls, although the humanities classes remained coed. After three years of segregated science classes, all 46 girls in the class passed the university entrance exam, and 28 were admitted to key universities. Their average total score was 5.1 points higher than that of women in regular classes, and their average math score was 6.7 points higher. This experiment suggested that the normal classroom situation trained girls to be less competent than boys in science, a problem that some Chinese educators, like their American counterparts, are beginning to recognize.[25]

But separate classes for women, even when intended to develop women's strengths, could also reinforce the sexual division of labor. A Xi'an women's college established in 1984, for instance, enabled several hundred women a year to receive postsecondary training. Its founder, Shen Huili, was a professor of aircraft engineering at Northwest Industrial University who felt that women should have more opportunities to receive technical training. She personally solicited government support, obtained funding, and borrowed classrooms for a "new type of school appropriate to the conditions of women." The college offered three majors: industrial accounting, applied computer science, and secretarial skills. While it and other institutions like it will help to meet the expanding demand for higher education facilities, its graduates will be suited for support work in technical and secretarial positions, not for the type of scientific research that is currently dominated by men (see Chapters 7 and 9).[26]

In the attitudes and institutions they encountered every day, then, young women received a subtle but clear message that they were inferior to men intellectually, physically, and emotionally. At the same time, they were told much more directly that the Constitution of the People's Republic of China guarantees them "equal rights with men in all spheres of life, political, economic, cultural, and social, including family life."[27] They were reminded that old-fashioned thinking about women, not state-condoned policies or attitudes, was the cause of gender discrimination: "Because the prejudice of valuing men over women still has a certain amount of support in society, in your studies or in finding a job you will meet with more discrimination than a man."[28] Yet, they were told, it should be possible for them to triumph over social discrimination. The "old ideas of a minority" were said to be on the decline, merely a source of "temporary worry to women."[29] And while "obstruction is a bad thing, what counts is the person facing the obstruction."[30]

The message, like most given to young women, was ambiguous. It acknowledged and condemned the continued existence of gender discrimination, and let young women know that the attitudes they may encounter at home or at school should not go unchallenged. It also took account of the psychological damage done to young women by repeated encounters with adults who valued them less than their brothers. At the same time, it put the responsibility for challenging these attitudes almost solely on the shoulders of young women themselves, and sometimes even chastised those who let the pervasive social prejudice around them affect their sense of self. One young woman, who had just failed the college entrance exams and could not find a job because all the local work units wanted to hire men, was told by her uncle:

I remember that in elementary and junior high school you were always a top student, but after you entered senior middle school, your grades fell. I felt sorry for you, and only found out later that this was a consequence of your parents' view that boys are more important than girls. They wanted to guarantee that your younger brother would pass the university entrance exam, and so they only asked him to study hard and didn't want him to dirty his hands with housework. They pressed on you all the endless household tasks of buying food, cooking, and laundry. How could you study well? This bias of theirs did not mean that they didn't love you dearly; it was the mischief wrought by the view that boys are more important than girls.

I was about to have a good talk with your parents, to help them change this incorrect thinking. But what was your own view on how to deal with this pressure? You said, "I'll have to find a boyfriend a little sooner, and sacrifice myself in the future for my husband and child." Foolish girl, that kind of talk is too lacking in ambition. . . . You shouldn't fall apart after a single setback . . . you should leap over the barrier and hurry forward.[31]

The uncle went on to suggest that she should either continue with her studies or organize a group of young women to start their own business in a suitable line of work, such as mending, handicraft production, or childcare (see Chapter 7). Ironically, each of these activities would help to reinforce the very gender differences she was supposed to be transcending.

In much of the advice literature, authority figures took the side of young women in their struggle to advance, and exhorted them not to lose faith in themselves. "If you want to progress," a woman teacher told a girl student, "you will meet obstacles. . . . Females can encounter them, and so can males. If we . . . think that it is because females are not as bright as males and for this reason waver in our confidence, we are just psychologically laying down our arms before the battle and suffering defeat." A girl who sees her grades decline in senior middle school, the teacher continued, should not conclude that it is happening because she is a girl; if she observes carefully, she will notice that the boys' grades are plummeting too.[32] Yet although this teacher meant to encourage her girl students, her message did not prepare them to deal with the attitudes they most commonly encountered about their capabilities. No one told a boy that his grades were going down because he was a boy, and in the Chinese social environment of the 1980's the thought would be extremely unlikely to cross his mind. Girls, on the other hand, were surrounded by social messages that confirmed their sense of inferiority. Their elders told them to "consciously strengthen the training of their capacity for independent thought and logical thinking, and boldly engage in creative thinking activities"—that is, think more like a man.[33] But this type of encouragement was not likely to overcome their sense that they were starting out life with a handicap—being female.

Contemporary advice to young women in China presented discrimination against women as a remnant of feudal thought while actively disseminating modern, "scientific" messages about female inferiority. Many of these "scientific" assertions were gleaned from Western literature; in the contemporary West, as in China, they were used to perpetuate gender hierarchy. But in China, the bearers of these messages were often the same writers who asserted that gender inequality was virtually a thing of the past, needing only the courage and effort of individual young women to finish it off completely. Although their intention was to encourage young women, the authors of advice literature imparted a confusing set of guidelines. Eager to buttress their arguments with modern scientific evidence, they often did not question the assertion that gender hierarchy had a "natural" basis. Impressed by the improvement in the status of women that they witnessed after the revolution, they seldom addressed the need for concerted social action to redress the inequalities that remained. Lack of public attention to the roots of gender hierarchy contributed to a situation in which women's inferior status remained socially acceptable to many in China.

Decoding the Role Models

The message that women would be liberated through their individual efforts in the working world was reinforced by official role models. After the founding of the People's Republic (and even earlier in the Communist base areas), the Party advocated the view that women could be emancipated only through participation in work outside the home. Government publications consistently publicized role models of heroic women whose efforts were helping to build socialism and raise the status of all women. Visitors to China during the early and mid-1970's, for example, were invariably told about the Iron Girl Brigades. Along with the slogan

"Women Hold Up Half the Sky," they were probably the most frequently cited proof that women in New China had become equal participants in society.

Iron Girls were groups of young women who took on the most difficult and demanding tasks at work. Their prototype was a group of young women in Dazhai, China's model agricultural brigade. These adolescent girls had formed themselves into a work group when flood struck their brigade in 1963. Working alongside the men to salvage grain and move peasants out of homes that threatened to collapse, they earned the admiration of all who saw them work. Legends grew up about their individual exploits: one cut her finger to the bone but kept on working, another became a crack shot in the militia.[34] When Dazhai was chosen as a national model in the mid-1960's, the hardworking Iron Girls' team rose to national prominence too, as a model for young women.

The Iron Girl teams that foreign visitors saw had seemingly boundless reserves of energy. After exceeding a production quota or bringing in a bumper harvest, they were likely to zoom off for a quick game of basketball on their break time. They were frequently found doing types of work that previously had been deemed unsuitable for women, such as repairing high-voltage lines. When their achievements were written up in the domestic press, or explained to foreign tourists, the presentation inevitably included Chairman Mao's observation that "times have changed, and today men and women are equal. Whatever men comrades can accomplish, women comrades can too."[35]

The Iron Girl Brigades gave young women a clear revolutionary message: that biology was not destiny, or at least that it was possible to overcome an inferior biology and influence one's own destiny. This message was a variant of a more general Maoist formula widely applied to social problems until the end of the Cultural Revolution: that concerted human effort and will could overcome all objective constraints. Given enough revolutionary enthusiasm, young women could equal men in physical and intellectual achievements. These achievements were then to be their ticket to a new society in which the traditional constraints on women's social role would fall away. Although it is impossible to measure the actual effect of the Iron Girls and other Cultural Revolution models on the self-image of young women, some rural women were inspired by the possibilities of breaking free of old roles and taking on new types of work outside the family.[36]

The Iron Girl model also conveyed the message that a woman's worth should be measured by a man's standard. It was not suggested in the 1970's, nor was it suggested in the 1980's, that the sexual division of labor in China should be restructured, that "whatever women comrades can accomplish"—caring for children, shopping, cooking, washing, cleaning, *and* working fulltime—"men comrades can too." What was important was that women, in spite of the burden of the double day, could participate in the same ways as men in the work of socialist construction. In the future, when that construction reached an advanced stage, housework would be socialized. In the meantime, young women were encouraged to emulate the Iron Girl Brigades—in effect, to make it in a man's world. Significantly, all of the Iron Girls were young, unmarried women. It would have been difficult to find a model who could match their work achievements while managing a household.

By the late 1970's, the Iron Girl Brigades, like many other Cultural Revolution artifacts, were no longer popular. The Iron Girl concept was mocked mercilessly in 1979 in a popular crosstalk (*xiangsheng*). In the dialogue, Mr. A delivered a long-winded lecture on the achievements of a local Iron Girl. Mr. B, impressed, asked if he wouldn't like to have such a capable maiden for his wife. Mr. A, horrified, replied that he would be afraid that such a woman might flatten him with a random swing of her overdeveloped biceps, not to mention what might happen if she actually got angry. This crosstalk was received by audiences with hilarity and rueful recognition. What was occurring was not simply mockery of the notion that a woman could be strong and capable. Rather the audiences were laughing, very painfully, at one of the symbols of the political environment of the Cultural Revolution—the Iron Girl.

Commentators in the 1980's took the critique of the Iron Girls even further. The idea that women could or should behave like men was explicitly rejected as just another ill-conceived Cultural Revolution attempt to challenge human nature. In 1985, a young woman computer scientist, nationally recognized for her work and a happily married mother, dismissed the Iron Girl model as unnatural, un-Marxist, and insufficiently domestic:

Eastern women have a tradition of gentleness, capacity for deep love, and dignity. I feel that this is not a shortcoming, but a kind of beauty. I do not hope that women will all bare their fangs, brandish their claws, and become short-tempered "Iron Girls." Marx once said that the feminine virtue he most liked was gentleness. People with a strong sense of dedication to their work should also be good wives and mothers at home.[37]

A group of male scholars, in Beijing to attend a 1986 meeting on the status of women, declared themselves particularly revolted by the idea that women should "masculinize" and become "imitation boys" (*jia xiaozi*) or "iron women" (*tie nüren*). They asserted that the Iron Girl model discriminated against the very women it claimed to promote:

A woman who becomes masculine is a mutant. Capable women should be different from men. They have their own special charm, for example exquisiteness and depth of emotions, and well-developed imagistic thinking. Women's own latent abilities should be called forth. The appearance of "fake boys" and "iron women" is a disguised form of discrimination against women; it belittles them. Its basic point still is that men are better than women, and that therefore when women are strong they should resemble men.[38]

This analysis criticized the Iron Girl model for measuring a woman's worth by a man's standard. A more appropriate female standard, these scholars assumed, would be calibrated to women's innate biological capabilities. Like many of the thinkers described in the preceding section, they assumed that gender differences in behavior, including such aspects as emotional sensitivity, are biologically determined. And in emphasizing their disgust with the possibility that women might become more like them, they confirm a suspicion that at least part of the backlash against the Iron Girls was, so to speak, manmade. These highly educated men, at least, were only too eager to add their voices to the chorus of political disapproval of a model they found threatening.

The demise of the Iron Girls clearly signaled that role models for young women were changing. In the 1980's, the successors to the Iron Girls were of four types: tireless workers for economic reform, famous personages, daring heroines, and loyal wives. The first group were all ordinary working women who had learned their tasks well and gone out of their way to take on extra responsibility. Praised in 1982 articles in *China Youth News* were a bricklayer, a woman in charge of the hot-water heater in a teahouse, a panda trainer, women who raised pigs and chickens, and a coalyard worker. Each of the women, by virtue of patient and meticulous work, managed to learn everything she could about her particular trade, and some made innovations which improved production. A few won praise because they took on unusual leadership responsibilities and discharged them well. Three women in their twenties, for instance, were elected to leadership posts in a pharmaceutical factory that had been losing money. As factory director, vice-director, and Party secretary, they increased production, cut costs and administrative fat, and introduced a number of reforms.[39]

Several of these jobs would be considered nontraditional work for women in China as well as in the West. But unlike the Iron Girls, these women were not touted for doing work that challenged the sexual division of labor, or exhibiting physical strength equal to that of men. Although the articles invariably noted that the workers were women, the content of the stories did not revolve around gender-related issues. These women demonstrated virtues expected of all workers; the obstacles they overcame were the type faced by anyone new to a job. Some of the women had been warned that employment in a low-status, dirty occupation would make it difficult for them to find husbands. The teahouse worker, for instance, was jilted by her boyfriend when she persisted at her post. Where they faced social prejudice, their difficulties came not from their performance of tasks unusual for women, but from their decisions to stay in jobs that normally were avoided by men as well as women. They became models because of the lessons they conveyed about class, not gender.

The second group of model women were those who achieved renown as athletes, writers, or actresses. They too were praised for working hard, for overcoming political or professional difficulties, and occasionally for postponing marriage in order to further their careers, a decision that dovetailed with the government's promotion of late marriages. Actresses also began to appear on calendars, a practice that conveyed a clear (if nonverbal) message that an attractive appearance could contribute to a successful career. Accounts of the professional achievements of women seldom referred to the effects of gender on their work choices or career success.[40]

The third group comprised young women who took heroic actions, sometimes at physical risk to themselves, to save an individual, protect state and collective property, or prevent a crime. In May 1982 Chen Yanfei, a woman in her fifth month of pregnancy, saved a drowning man in Suzhou Creek. A month later a twenty-nine-year-old "women's work" cadre in Shaanxi forced the authorities (after more than thirty reports) to bring to justice a male cadre who had stolen state funds and poisoned his wife in order to take up with another woman. In July 1982, two female flight attendants on the national airline CAAC, along with the rest of the crew and some passengers, helped subdue a group of five hijackers by attacking them with mops, teacups, saucers, and soda bottles.[41] In each of these cases, even that of the pregnant woman, virtually no emphasis was placed on the fact that the protagonists were female. Instead, the press coverage focused on their ideals as Party and Youth League members, or their spirit of public service in an age of growing public indifference.

Unlike the first three types, the fourth group of models was cited for outstanding performance of exclusively female roles: fiancée and wife. A rural Shandong woman moved in with her future in-laws and took over her fiancé's farming and household duties, freeing him to volunteer for service in the 1979 border conflict with Vietnam. A Shaanxi woman married a paraplegic soldier and returned with him to his home in Qinghai, one of China's more rugged and remote areas. A Hangzhou woman followed her Air Force pilot husband to the cold Northeast. Recognizing that piloting a plane required a great deal of mental and physical effort, she prepared his favorite foods on Saturday so that he could enjoy them on Sunday while she went to work, and did not let him do any of the housework.[42] These women were all commended for those virtues which have traditionally been regarded as the attributes of a good wife: loyalty, unselfishness, frugality, and hard work. (For a detailed discussion of this type of model, see Chapter 5.)

The women in all four of these groups made only one-time appearances in the press. The only female role model to receive the kind of extended coverage formerly enjoyed by the Iron Girls was Zhang Haidi, whose life and thoughts were described in numerous articles in 1983 and 1984. Zhang Haidi, in fact, may be the key to decoding the role models of the 1980's. Because of the proliferation of television sets and the expansion of national programming in the 1980's, Zhang received far more extensive coverage than any earlier models for youth; she was the first role model to become a live media star.

Zhang became paralyzed from the waist down in childhood. In spite of the considerable difficulties faced by a disabled person in Chinese society, she managed to learn English, medical skills, telecommunications equipment repair, and playwriting.[43] As a health care worker, her duties included home visits to bedridden patients, acupuncture, moxibustion (the burning of medicinal herbs on the skin), electrotherapy, and writing prescriptions. In 1983 she was named an "outstanding Youth League member" by the Central Committee of the Communist Youth League. A national campaign followed, in which young people were urged to emulate Zhang. The award and publicity praised her for persisting in her studies and work in spite of her paralysis. More important, she was lauded for her belief that "real happiness comes from creating value for society through your own efforts, bringing happiness to more people." At a time when the newspapers were full of commentary decrying the growing materialism of young people, Zhang Haidi provided an inspiring challenge. A life spent "sitting on the sofa, watching color TV, listening to popular songs, opening the refrigerator to get a high-class drink would be comfortable enough," she commented, "but the soul would be empty." Her most-quoted statement was, "The significance of life lies in contributing, not demanding."[44]

Zhang Haidi was chosen as a model for the 1980's because of her optimism, her capacity for hard work, her pursuit of knowledge, and her sense of social responsibility.[45] She was, by all accounts, an unusually determined individual and an inspiration to disabled people in China. She was also, however, a gender-free role model. The difficulties she faced had little to do with her sex. Gender discrimination was not the primary impediment to her achievements, and overcoming it appears to have played little role in her development. Her success was the result of her own hard work and determination, aided by neighbors, friends, and the Party.

The publicity given Zhang's life story led to a number of open forums in women's magazines, where young women explained how her example had influenced them. One extended discussion, which ran for six months, posed the question "How Should Young Women Live in the 80's?" [46] For most, the answer gleaned from Zhang's life and the new economic policies seemed to be "through our own hard work." Many accounts focused on the problems young women faced in starting small individual businesses, an undertaking sponsored by the government to reduce urban unemployment. A tailor, a barber, a restaurateur, and a roving photographer, all in their twenties, described how they learned their skills, how they went out of their way to serve the needs of older, housebound people, and how they overcame suspicion of the new individual enterprises.

Each of these women carefully explained that her goal was not only to make a living, but to "serve the people" (a slogan from the 1940's much heard during the Cultural Revolution as well) in a polite, efficient, and moral fashion. The tailor, for instance, stayed up for two nights to make wedding clothes for a couple joining a collective wedding ceremony because she supported the government campaign to promote frugal nuptial rites (see Chapter 4). She steadfastly refused to make outlandish clothes for young people, lecturing them on the inappropriateness of such dress. [47] If these young women faced any special obstacles in setting up small businesses because of their gender, their stories betrayed no hints of them. What they learned from Zhang Haidi was that individual effort would guarantee success. In short, they were selected as models because their economic achievements and social attitudes reflected current government policy about individual enterprises. Their gender was incidental. This was true also of women employed in the state and collective sectors, who expressed their faith in hard work as the key to fulfillment. [48]

Of all the individual accounts in this series, only one touched even indirectly upon the serious structural problems preventing women from developing their talents. Liu Guiqin, a nineteen-year-old rural Henan woman, quit high school to support her family when her father died. She studied at night, completing the high school curriculum on her own. Later she used her spare time to read and tell stories to other rural girls. Gradually these girls realized that being literate would bring them certain advantages; they asked Liu to teach them. She began a class in her home which grew from eight to thirty-eight students, providing all of the supplies herself. Eventually the local government began to supply her with chalk, blackboards, and textbooks. When she wrote this article, Liu planned to continue running the school, in addition to cultivating the land and taking care of her mother and brother. The point of her story was that the problems of educating rural women could be solved if only enough people put in individual effort to solve them. [49]

The lessons that young women learned from Zhang Haidi were summed up by Li Chunli, a young woman from rural Heilongjiang. "Like me," Li wrote, "she grew up in New China; like me she is female; but I have a healthy body. Why could she achieve such great things? The comparison made me feel deeply guilty and ashamed. . . . A woman can do anything she wants to do, as long as she has a goal, confidence, and willpower. After a period of painstaking effort, she will certainly achieve something." [50] Li may have been more inspired by Zhang Haidi than the average Chinese youth. Many reacted to the political models of the Cultural Revolution by becoming indifferent or cynical about all models presented for their edification.

Although they were presented as a model for young women, Zhang Haidi and her followers had little to say to them about the problems they might encounter because they were young women. Gender discrimination was not an issue raised by their stories. Instead, they provided models of heroic individual effort against serious odds. These models had their uses. Like the messages about biology discussed earlier, however, they did not prepare young women for the obstacles they would actually face in school and at work, and did prepare them to blame themselves if they met with failure. In an era when gender was being reasserted as a "natural" and valued division in society, these role models downplayed gender issues.

Female role models in the 1980's were markedly different from those of the Cultural Revolution era (1966–76), though both groups were praised for "serving the people." Zhang Haidi and other model women of her generation differed from the Iron Girls in that they did not expect to do whatever men could do. They did not challenge the sexual division of labor, and did not encourage women to overcome an inferior biology through superhuman physical achievement. Instead, they stressed female capacities for intellectual development, and female contributions to national economic development. Often these models were used to encourage women to pursue traditionally female work, advice that one woman college teacher regarded as more practical than the Iron Girl approach. This teacher, born just before Liberation, commented to us:

It was very different when I was growing up. We were taught that women and men were equal, that women could do what men could do. And then it took me the entire Cultural Revolution, and almost ten more years after that, to realize that reality was totally different. What was the point of teaching us ideals which had no relation to reality? That's why I say that the current advice is more pragmatic. [51]

In contrast to the message their older sisters had received from the Iron Girls, young women in the 1980's were told, in both direct and indirect ways, that biology *is* destiny. Their gender, the message ran, would place certain limitations on their development. As the earlier discussion of women's physical capabilities has shown, certain crucial limitations were assumed to be biologically determined and therefore immutable. The social limitations, while acknowledged, were regarded as secondary in importance, since they were expected to wither away. At the same time, individual effort on the part of young women was expected to play a key role in changing social attitudes.

In spite of their differences, the Iron Girls and their 1980's successors had some important characteristics in common. Both suggested the possibility of a gender-free world—that is, one where both men and women are free to perform well, albeit by male standards, in the public sphere. Neither model addressed the kinds of changes that would have to occur in the home to make such a performance possible. Neither raised questions about whether it would be desirable for the universal standard of performance to be a male one.

Both models were also similar in that they were byproducts of political campaigns that had objectives other than raising the status of women. The Iron Girls rose and fell with the Dazhai agricultural model. In their day, gender equality was ultimately regarded as less important than service to the collective, and they were used to publicize the virtues of collective spirit. In the 1980's, the messages directed at young women were a subset of those given to young people about contributing to the Four Modernizations (of agriculture, industry, science and technology, and defense). The problem of reviving the national economy and reestablishing a shared sense of social purpose was very much on the minds of policymakers; female role models were employed to make points about the correct approach to these "larger" issues. And in the rare cases where the models did call attention to gender differences—as in the cases of model fiancées and wives—attitudes about female virtues remained consonant with those of the imperial era, unchallenged by the public discourse that has recently challenged so much else in new China.

Translations

Young women received a variety of messages about how they differed from young men. "Differences Between Males and Females" outlines the physiological differences in such a way that women repeatedly fall short of the male standard. "Sex Differences Between Men and Women" and "A Comparison of the Characteristics of Females and Males" lay out differences in temperament that are thought to influence intellectual performance and emotional life.

The widespread assumption that girls were inferior to boys helped to limit opportunities for girls. "Why Such a Wide Gap" explains the problem of low female school enrollments in one district of Hunan province. "Female Self-Confidence Must Be Fostered from Childhood" suggests that parents have a responsibility to raise their daughters as strong, confident citizens. Finally, "A Model Woman Worker Dressed in Gold and Jade" describes the increasingly fashionable appearance of role models for women in the 1980's.

Differences Between Males and Females

Obvious differences exist between men and women in body structure, physique, and physiology. . . .

In height and weight, men generally are superior. At the same time, the ratio between length of leg and body height is generally smaller in women than in men, and so their stride is not as long as males'. It is inadvisable for men and women to compete with one another in carrying heavy loads.

The weight of an entire female skeleton is about 20 percent lighter than that of the male. The bones of the four limbs are rather short, while the spine is rather long; the internal structure of the bones is also not as solid as that of the male. In addition, the skull of the female is 10 percent lighter and the capacity is 4 percent smaller than that of the male. The chest cavity formed by the ribs in the female is short and protrudes in front. It does not move as much when she breathes as that of a male, and so her breathing capacity is smaller. When labor is too intense, a woman may become short of breath.

As for the pelvis, a man's is thick and heavy, narrow at the top and the bottom, and suited for carrying heavy weights. A woman's is shallow and broad, big at the top and bottom, and suited for giving birth. If a woman carries too heavy a load and too much pressure is put on the abdomen, the bottom of the pelvis cannot withstand it. This very easily results in a prolapsed uterus or a change in the position of the uterus.

Men's muscles are strong and developed, but those of women are not prominent. The proportion of muscle weight in men and in women is 100 catties versus 60 catties [1 catty = 1.1 lbs.], or a 5:3 ratio. Women's muscles contain slightly more water than men's and more fat, but less sugar. These characteristics mean that women have less muscular power than men. Women's muscles not only have less power when they contract, but their movement and endurance also fall short. They tire easily and take longer to recover.

The difference in the muscle power of men and women begins to appear at about age ten, largely because of boys' secretion of testosterone. Until the age of seventy, the muscle power of the female, on average, is two-thirds that of the male. . . .

The hearts of men and women are different. Women's hearts are 10 to

15 percent lighter than men's. Men's hearts are slightly bigger. The amount of blood pumped out of the heart per beat is less in women than in men. As for blood pressure, women's is lower than men's by about 10 percent. Ordinarily, a woman's heart beats eight to ten more times per minute than a man's. As soon as she engages in physical labor, her heart beats even more rapidly. Men are different; even when they do heavy labor, they mainly rely on the added strength of the heart's contractions to increase the body's blood supply.

Women have somewhat less blood than men, and their blood is also a bit thinner. This is because women's blood has more plasma and fewer cells. Because the blood is rather thin, its ability to combine with oxygen is weak. Women's blood contains slightly fewer red blood cells and less hemoglobin than that of men.

Women consume fewer calories than men. At the age of fifteen, girls only consume 33.7 calories for every square meter of body surface, whereas boys consume an average of 38.9 calories. This difference in their consumption abilities naturally results in a disparity in physical strength.

So, looking at differences in breathing, circulation, and blood, the physical strength and endurance of women is slightly less than that of men (individual exceptions are possible). Therefore, it is inadvisable for women to engage in heavy physical labor, or they will easily become ill and develop problems. In general it is not advisable for men and women to compete, or to be treated equally in work arrangements. In tasks that involve lifting excessively heavy loads, standing for too long, or working at high or low temperatures, and in work of differing intensities, arrangements must differ [by sex].

In addition, women have special physiological burdens that men do not have; menstrual periods are an obvious example. During menstruation, if attention is not paid to health protection, it is easy for women to develop menstrual disorders that impair health.

Women also have the physiological burden of giving birth. For the sake of the health of the next generation, attention must be paid to protecting the health of women. Consideration should be given to whether or not women should engage in certain harmful occupations.

SOURCE: Xie Bozhang, *Qingqunqi weisheng* (Adolescent health), 2d revised edition (Beijing: Beijing chubanshe, 1983), 52–55.

Sex Differences Between Men and Women

In temperament, observation indicates that in men an irascible disposition often gets the upper hand. Men often react strongly. They have willpower, are resolute and steadfast, have blazing emotions, and are full of vigor. So an irascible disposition is often called a "male temperament."

Statistics show that men often exhibit more strength in direct attack, are driven by great ambitions, and at the same time are rather tenacious and able to resist brutal pressure. Women, in contrast, are naturally vivacious in temperament. This kind of temperament is characterized by flexibility, emotional expressiveness, and moodiness. Even when women's emotions are impossible to suppress, they often are directed inward, becoming implicit, unlike the emotions of men, which break out exposed into the open. Women are generally rather delicate, fragile, and gentle, although they are sometimes very stubborn. Men's character is manifested in struggle, women's in gentleness. . . .

The nervous system of females is not as stable as that of males. Thus, women's moods easily shift. The ability of women to change to another state of mind in a twinkling is greater than that of men. Women are highly sensitive, so much so that the slightest misfortune can make a woman cry. Men, in contrast, only shed tears on extremely tragic occasions. Any happy event can cause a woman to express her elation immediately, but in such situations men do not readily express their emotions. Their reactions are comparatively slow. A difference also exists in the duration of emotions. A crying woman can rather easily stop her tears and forget her pain, but a crying man finds it difficult to calm down. Women's laughter for the most part is like a light breeze; it sweeps past and is gone. The laughter of men is not often heard, but is very infectious.

Women and men also have certain differences in so-called psychological stability and "steadfastness." In life, men are more often able to stand on their own two feet, and are better able to resist the influence of the social environment. Once the framework of a man's reactions is formed, it is very slow to change. Women are the opposite, rather easily influenced by the outside world. The psychology of women continually vacillates. When the environment changes suddenly, women adjust easily to it.

Women find it easy to understand and recognize things, in keeping with their characteristically vivacious temperament. But in general, a vivacious person is quick to remember, but also quick to forget. Men are the opposite, slower than women to remember, but also slower to forget.

In life, women "pay more attention to reality." Their train of thought and actions attach more importance to the concrete. Men tend to gallop about in the realm of abstract thought. Men like to adopt a comprehensive attitude in dealing with reality, and prefer generalized skills. Women are more careful about each part, each detail of the total. These tendencies gradually begin to manifest themselves clearly from early childhood. For example, boys like to paint industrial scenes, while girls like to paint trees, flowers, and plants. When girls paint human portraits, they generally depict the clothing and hairstyle meticulously.

By nature girls have a stronger love of beauty and elegance. From childhood on, girls like to wear beautiful clothes, and take pleasure in making up and dressing up. They are compulsive about cleanliness, and are very sensitive to everything that causes disgust in people. Women are considerate, good-hearted, and compassionate. They are particular about beauty but do not stress practicality. They are oversensitive and can detect the slightest snub.

One may say that the two sexes complement each other. The differences between men and women, as it happens, determine that in life they must form two aspects of equal value that unite into a whole. Conversely, without differences, combination would be an unsuitable goal.

To sum up, in general the differences between men and women are: men's bodies are rather cumbersome, women carry themselves gracefully; men are rather robust, women are more fragile; men are rational, women are emotional; men are "bold," women are "meek"; men stress logic, women rely on direct emotion to handle matters; men are stern, women enthusiastic; men stress synopsis, women analysis; men like to struggle, women are rich in sympathy; men are fond of abstract concepts, women are concerned with concrete objects; men are steadfast, women change again and again; men are easily excited, women are controlled by their mood; men's emotions are more dramatic, women's more optimistic; men are resolute, women are cautious; men are "majestic," women are "refined"; men "dare to do," women are diligent and untiring. All of this shows that men have more male mettle, while women possess more female gentleness. . . .

This description is by no means absolute. Not every man or woman is this way. . . . Actually, in real life, real men and women differ in thousands of ways. If people are aware of the differences between men and women, in choosing a mate they can pay attention to and respect the specific characteristics of the other party, and better understand the other party. So it is important that young people have an understanding of this.

Lin Ling

SOURCE: *Yuelao bao*, 7 (July 1985), 7, 4–5. The author is female.

A Comparison of the Characteristics of Females and Males

Characteristics of the female:
1. loves to talk
2. very refined
3. understanding of other people's feelings
4. extremely devout

  5. pays a great deal of attention to her appearance
  6. very neat and clean
  7. very quiet
  8. has an extremely strong need for security
  9. loves art and literature
  10. easily expresses gentle feelings

Characteristics of the male:
  1. possesses an aggressive nature
  2. very independent
  3. seldom expresses feelings
  4. not easily influenced
  5. extremely dominating
  6. not excited by trivial matters
  7. full of vigor
  8. feelings not easily hurt
  9. daring
  10. makes decisions easily
  11. independent
  12. inattentive to his appearance

SOURCE: Sheng Ping et al., *Xiandai nüxing shenghuo shouce* (Handbook for the contemporary woman) (Beijing: Gongren chubanshe, 1985), 59–60.

Why Such a Wide Gap in the Proportions of Boys and Girls Entering the Upper Grades?

Comrade Editor:

In our Yueyang district of Hunan in 1978, more than 73,000 people took the university and polytechnic entrance examinations. Of the 3,412 people admitted, only 460, or 13.4 percent of the total, were female students. Of 340,010 people who took the university exam in 1979, 11,627 were girls. Among the 3,392 people admitted by universities and polytechnical schools, only 576, or 17 percent, were girls. Yueyang Normal School and Yueyang Secondary Normal had originally planned to admit half boys and half girls, but the result was that of 310 new students admitted by the Normal School, only 36, or 11 percent, were girls. Of 548 new students admitted by Yueyang Secondary Normal, only 78, or 14 percent, were girls.

Why is there such a wide gap in the proportion of boys and girls entering higher-grade schools? As we understand it, the problem is twofold.

One is the serious persistence of feudal thinking that values males over females, and doesn't allow girls to study. Especially in the countryside, many people believe that girls belong to someone else [because they will marry out of their natal family], and that letting them study is a waste of effort. Thus many girls are deprived of an education or drop out. The higher the grade, the more girls leave school. According to statistics from the annual report issued second semester last year, there are 651,176 peasant children attending school in the district, of which girl students make up 46 percent. Of the total, 161,700 are in junior middle school; 40.2 percent of these are girls. Of 39,518 middle school students, 33.8 percent are girls. In the middle school senior class, girl students are even fewer. Looking only at the statistics of the 19 middle schools in Gulo county, of 2,446 graduating seniors, a mere 30.2 percent were girls.

Because girls are deprived of an education or drop out, women make up most illiterates and semi-literates. According to Linxiang county statistics for the end of 1978, of 15,931 illiterates and semi-literates in the county, 11,187, or 70.2 percent, were women. Of thirty-eight young illiterates and semi-literates in the Pailou brigade, Lukou commune, thirty were female. Among them was one young woman with three brothers, two of whom had finished middle school, the other of whom was in elementary school. Yet she had not even finished the second year of elementary school before dropping out to stay home and do housework.

Second is the prejudice held by the leadership and teachers in some schools that girl students are not as good as boy students. They see that the girls' grades on one or two tests are not outstanding enough, decide that this is a sign of falling behind, and give up trying to coach them, causing this group of girl students to give themselves up as hopeless and lose their desire to do better. Last year a high school in Xiangying county was divided into a key class and an ordinary classes. When a girl student in the key class who normally got good grades performed badly on one test, the school transferred her into the ordinary class. She became so anxious that she cried, her emotional state was disturbed, and from then on her grades leveled off.

One or two girl students may spend their time dressing up, waste their energy, and lack a spirit of studiousness; this inevitably influences their studies.

The low cultural level of women is no small matter. It is a big obstacle to raising the cultural level of the entire Chinese people, and is very disadvantageous to the construction of the Four Modernizations. It is suggested that the Party, Youth League, Women's Federation, and other concerned departments at every level, as well as all educators, take this problem seriously.

Wang Jingwen, Bureau of Education,
Yueyang district, Hunan province

SOURCE: *Zhongguo funü*, 9 (September 1980), 40.

Female Self-Confidence Must Be Fostered from Childhood

People often sigh at the feelings of inferiority of some grown women, and blame them for lacking self-confidence. It never occurs to them that much of this sense of inferiority is formed in childhood. This is mainly because parents do not understand how to cultivate a girl's self-confidence. So, in order to train strong self-confident women appropriate to a new era, it is necessary to begin in childhood.

If parents pay attention to educating their girl children in self-confidence, giving them more encouragement, more support, more help, more opportunities to temper themselves, and help them to form a strong, brave character, then after they grow up they will be able to fully develop their own abilities and shoulder the heavy task of constructing the "Four Modernizations." Conversely, if parents impose on their girl children the concept that "males are worthy of respect and females are inferior," this will cause them to form a sense of inferiority and a weak and timid character. It will limit them in giving full reign to their intelligence, ability, and wisdom, constrain their creativity, strangle their enterprising spirit, and cause them to become weak people.

At present, many parents have not yet become conscious of the importance of fostering the self-confidence of girl children. Some even unconsciously undermine their self-confidence. For example, some girls are bright, like to study, and have high aspirations, but their parents don't encourage them and even say that girls have low intelligence, that no matter how hard they work it will be a futile effort, and that they are better off doing more housework instead. Aside from doing housework, girls very seldom have the chance to temper themselves in other ways. Thus a difference is created in the abilities of boys and girls, which in turn becomes a reason for deprecating girls. Then there are some parents who often say in front of their girl children that girls are not as good as boys, causing the girls to feel they are second-class citizens from birth. The result is that in all respects they become careful and cautious, and are always shrinking back. With all of this, how could a girl's newly sprouted self-confidence not come under attack?

People often praise boys for their spirit of striving hard, seeking to outdo others, and swearing not to stop until they reach their goal. But this spirit, this self-confidence, this self-strengthening and courage, are by no means innate in their minds. They are the result of social education, and more important, parental education. When a boy is easily upset and cries, his parents often say, "Why are you crying? Men don't cry." When boys retreat in the face of difficulties, parents often say, "Be brave—it's not like a boy to shrink back." This talk, these exclamations, are a form of education and encouragement. They bolster the courage and confidence of boys. If girls were given the same treatment, I firmly believe that a spirit of confidence and steadfast bravery would take root and sprout in the virgin soil of their pure souls. . . .

Zhao Bingren, Heilongjiang province

SOURCE: *Zhongguo funü*, 4 (April 1985), 34.

A Model Woman Worker Dressed in Gold and Jade

When I went to the Shenzhen Daily Use Goods Factory to gather material, I found sitting in the office a dignified, beautiful young woman. Her hairdo was done quite tastefully, two gleaming earrings adorned her earlobes, a glittering necklace hung from her neck, suspended from her wrist was an exquisite small golden bracelet, and encircling the ring finger of her right hand was a conspicuous golden ring. Ah, one look and I realized that it was Fan Liying, deputy to the provincial People's Congress and provincial model worker.

I could not help feeling stunned. So many stories about her tumbled about in my brain. . . .

Originally she was an embroiderer. Once, she embroidered a woman's blouse and broke forty embroidery needles in a row. Her fingers were covered with needle marks, yet she still delivered the blouse to the customer on time.

Two years ago, when the factory cashier was discharged, Fan gave up her monthly income of about 300 yuan without complaint, and happily took over the post of cashier, earning only a little more than 100 yuan. With great care she studied from scratch, and in the past two years has not made the slightest error. . . .

Yet I simply didn't quite believe my own eyes when I saw her. As if she saw my astonishment, she smiled gently, revealing shallow dimples, and said, "I am a twenty-three-year-old woman, and of course I like to dress up."

Suddenly I understood. Model workers of the 1980's are good at creating wealth, and they also understand how to enjoy it. This is probably the charm of our times.

A model woman worker dressed in gold and jade? The way some people see it, perhaps this is a great outrage. In their eyes, a model worker who fits the image should be covered with grease and dirt, dressed in blue and black.

But nowadays in the Shenzhen Special Economic Zone, model workers no longer have that old appearance. There, the wage system has been reformed, and anyone who works hard has a higher income. Naturally, the income of model workers is higher than that of most, and they live better lives than most. Not only do they dress in suits and leather shoes, they also have money to buy gold and jade. So why be astonished that model women workers are dressed in gold and jade? Rather we should say that if model workers live better lives than most, they will have greater appeal, and will encourage more people to work diligently. If model workers only get "a suit of blue and black" for their work, I'm afraid no one will want to be a model. From the changes in the style of dress of this model woman worker, we can catch a glimpse of the economic development of our nation and the change in people's concept of consumption!

Chang Hanqing

SOURCE: *Zhongguo funü,* 2 (February 1985), 18.

The Pleasures of Adornment and the Dangers of Sexuality

In the classroom, girls were told that they would do well if they acted more like boys; at work, young women were presented with female role models whose achievements were measured by male standards. In preparing for a socially approved marriage, on the other hand, women were told to accentuate their femaleness.

This message emerged after the end of the Cultural Revolution, and no broad social consensus existed on the proper way to present oneself as a woman. Much of the advice literature said, for instance, that beauty and personal adornment were important and natural concerns for young women. Yet the advisers also warned that good looks were not as important as good health and proper behavior, and that certain types of beautification were morally questionable. The relationship between physical adornment and female sexuality was a matter of public debate, as was the whole question of sexual morality for unmarried women. What sort of attire and makeup are socially acceptable? When women dress up, what messages do they convey about their attractiveness and availability, and who is the intended audience? Does a connection exist between adornment and female vanity, between a woman's vanity and her sexual downfall? Sexuality, young women were told, has its time (adulthood) and place (marriage), but multiple dangers awaited the adolescent girl who chose to explore it. This warning was driven home by tales that graphically described the fate of young women who strayed from acceptable codes of behavior. How should a young woman pick her way through this enticing and dangerous territory and emerge safely from adolescence as a respectable candidate for marriage? In short, how should she present and manage her sexuality? On this topic, advice for young women, much of it contradictory, abounded.

Beauty and Its Perils

In twentieth-century China, what a woman wears has not been merely a matter of aesthetic preference; it has often been an expression of a conscious political stance. Qiu Jin, a revolutionary who worked for the overthrow of the Qing dynasty, had her picture taken in men's attire to emphasize her rejection of traditional female roles. When Communists were purged by Chiang Kaishek in 1927, many young women with bobbed hair were executed because Chiang's men assumed—correctly—that cutting off one's braids indicated revolutionary sympathies. Women who joined the Communist movement during its years in the countryside adopted the military dress of their male comrades. After 1949, women dressed plainly except for a brief interval of political and social liberalization in 1956. Urban women in the early years of the People's Republic sometimes explained their austere appearance as a badge of personal liberation. As one put it, "The women of new China, especially women workers, cadres, and intellectuals, are truly able to work independently, and have completely equal status with men. We don't need to use our dress and makeup to try to please our husbands."[1] Dressing in dark, simple clothes made a statement that women no longer needed to trade sexual attractiveness for economic security.

Yet revolutionary dress had its compulsory aspect as well. From 1957 to 1976, each new political campaign brought with it a demand that everyone dress plainly to show their identification with the masses. In many cities, cadres kept a set of old, faded clothes in the closet to don whenever the political situation demanded it; with the onset of the Cultural Revolution, everyone began to wear army-style green as a sign of revolutionary zeal.[2] As in the 1920's, a woman's coiffure was thought to indicate her politics, and groups of Red Guards chopped off the braids of women on the street, accusing them of politically incorrect attitudes. In such an environment, interest in fashion and adornment was regarded as bourgeois and counterrevolutionary. One of the major criticisms leveled at Wang Guangmei, the wife of head of state Liu Shaoqi, was that she had worn low-cut and revealing dresses on an official visit to Indonesia. These political attitudes coexisted easily with the traditional belief, still current in many parts of rural China, that a woman who conspicuously adorned herself was sexually loose and morally degenerate.

Nowhere did the public messages for young women change so radically in the 1980's as in the area of adornment. Opinion about fashion, as about many other things, reacted against the compulsory austerity of the Cultural Revolution. Political slogans on every billboard came down, replaced in many cases by pictures of attractive women selling everything from industrial machinery to cosmetics. The "leftist" line of previous years was blamed for pitting revolution against the beautification of life in general and female adornment in particular.[3] In the 1980's political environment, dressing up, not down, was regarded as a liberating act. Attention to dress was considered a natural byproduct of a rising standard of living, indirect proof that the new economic reforms were successful. As one magazine article explained: "Along with the leap in development of our nation's economy and the rise in the standard of living, the demand for the beautification of life has become extraordinarily urgent among the broad masses, especially women. To make oneself up in daily life, to improve one's looks, is regarded by people as a sign of respect and courtesy toward comrades and friends."[4] Young women, who were generally thought to "love beauty to a greater extent than others,"[5] were encouraged to pursue what one magazine called "the new health and beauty craze."[6] At the same time, newspaper and magazine articles warned young women of the dangers of paying attention only to how they looked, rather than their physical and moral health.

A series of new magazines guided the nascent connoisseur of fashion through the uncharted territory of style at home and abroad. Chief among these publications was *Fashion* (Shizhuang), a Beijing quarterly that began publication in 1980. The Winter 1983 issue was divided between introductions to Parisian fashion and descriptions of new clothing collections being produced in Northeast China. Sultry blonde models showed off coming attractions in women's attire, while European men with smoldering expressions, leather jackets, and striped pants sulked their way across the pages of features on men's clothing. A photo essay on Paris street dress contained such captions as "A family of large and small jeans," "Both men's and women's clothes can expose the back," and "Shorts can expose more of the vigor and grace of the leg."[7] The stories on domestic clothing included men in corduroy suits, bow ties, and letterman's jackets, women in silk frocks and yellow pants suits, and two features on the traditional Chinese gown or *qipao*, a fitted garment with high side slits.[8] Many articles showed how to lay out patterns for ski outfits and winter coats, and a special feature explained, with illustrations, five ways to wear a scarf draped across the shoulders.[9]

A year later, while the basic format of the magazine had not changed, it had become bolder in the poses struck by both Chinese and foreign models. A young woman leaned provocatively against a pillar, sucking a stick of candied haw fruit; women in leather outfits nestled against men in matching togs, and an Asian man and woman flanked a blond couple, the

Left: Cover of the 1985 book *Handbook for the Contemporary Woman.* Sheng Ping et al., *Xiandai nüxing shenghuo shouce* (Handbook for the contemporary woman) (Beijing: Gongren chubanshe, 1985).   *Right:* Cover of *Fashion* magazine, 1985. *Shizhuang* (Fashion). Beijing.

sportswear-clad shoulders of all four touching daringly.[10] Japanese companies placed advertisements for sewing equipment in most issues. In early 1985 a Japanese hospital took out an ad demonstrating the beneficial effects of cosmetic surgery on an Asian woman's receding chin, complete with before and after pictures.[11] These magazines, like their counterparts in the United States, had two aims: to give practical guidance in how to dress, and to satisfy readers' taste for glamour and (if only by innuendo) romance. Soon the connection between fashion and romance was taken up explicitly by other women's magazines, which began to run articles on such subjects as what a young woman should wear on her first date.[12]

Magazines were only one means of publicizing new styles. Fashion shows became popular by the mid-1980's; special troupes of models were organized in the major cities. As some of these troupes began to model fashions by Pierre Cardin and Japanese designers, an article in *People's Daily* made a halfhearted attempt to distinguish fashion shows in China

Left: How to apply makeup. *Zhongguo funü* (Chinese Women), 6 (1985), inside front cover. *Right:* Cover of *The Young Generation* magazine, 1986. *Qingnian yidai* (The Young Generation). Shanghai.

from those in the West: "There [in the West], the performance of fashion models is purely commercial, but in our country most take artistic performance as the dominant factor, while doing a commercial performance at the same time. Performance not only reveals the beauty of the clothing, and attracts consumers, but also leads people to love beauty, understand beauty, and attain beauty (*hui mei*)." Although many in the urban population found the clothing of Cardin and other Western designers incomprehensible, the job of fashion model was highly coveted. When one troupe opened its ranks to newcomers in late 1984, the applicants included not only workers, peasants, childcare workers, service workers, and unemployed youth, but also college graduates and graduate students.[13]

Hairstyle and cosmetics also garnered their share of attention. Newspapers and women's magazines offered instruction on the appropriate hairdo for each facial shape, and provided tips on how to preserve a permanent as long as possible (keep it out of the rain, use moderate amounts of hair cream, wear curlers while sleeping, and learn to "push, pull, and press" the hair into shape).[14] Illustrated magazine stories featured pieces by a Hong Kong cosmetologist, who described with illustrations the ten steps in applying foundation, powder, eyeshadow (purple and blue), mascara, eyebrow pencil, blusher, and lipstick.[15] The new magazine *Chinese and Foreign Women* (Zhongwai funü), introducing an article by a professional makeup man, explained, "Our readers have sent us numerous letters saying: Before we thought of beauty but did not dare to be beautiful; now we want to be beautiful but don't know how. We hope you will carry pieces that introduce in detail knowledge about makeup for everyday use." The purpose of the article was to teach readers "how to make themselves up to be more beautiful, how to conceal worrisome wrinkles," as well as to provide them with "knowledge about redoing the contours of the facial features and eyes without surgery."[16] Lest makeup prove insufficient to conceal nature's flaws, however, the magazine *Chinese Women* also published a list of thirteen hospitals nationwide that performed cosmetic surgery.[17]

Personal adornment was not only of concern to young women; it was also encouraged and justified by middle-aged female political authorities. In 1984, the chairperson of the Shanghai Women's Federation, Tan Fuyun, appeared at a tea hosted by a beauty parlor and endorsed the use of makeup. Later she told a reporter that on an official visit to Hong Kong, she and the other woman delegates looked better and were better received after they began to wear light makeup. Her assertion that makeup enhanced a woman's job effectiveness was echoed by eighty-seven women teachers at a Shanghai teachers' college, who expressed desires for permanents, makeup, and removal of facial hair. One of them, a political instructor, explained that using cosmetics to improve her appearance would enable her to teach more energetically.[18]

This interest in beautification of the face was frequently coupled with advice on how to achieve a more attractive body. At a Beijing elementary school during evening hours, young and middle-aged women combined a "beauty boxing" exercise routine designed to take off excess pounds with lectures on hair care and makeup. Their instructor, a forty-two-year-old gymnastics coach, was preparing to publish a book of her exercises, Jane Fonda–style, with accompanying music cassettes.[19] Other publications, like the book *Wishing You a More Healthy and Beautiful Youth*, offered young women instruction on such diverse topics as how to dress, what to do about bad breath and body odor, and how to exercise muscles in the face, arms, chest, stomach, and legs.[20] Regular columns in national and regional youth magazines dispensed advice to young women readers worried about facial hair (see a doctor and use a depilatory cream) and excess weight (exercise regularly and limit sugar intake).[21] In another magazine feature, an exquisitely attired model with long wavy hair touted the importance of good posture, demonstrating twelve graceful ways to stand,

Left: Husband-and-wife champion bodybuilders, Shenzhen, 1986. *Jinse nianhua* (Golden Years). Nanning. *Right:* Advertisement for a bust enhancer. *Zhongguo funü* (Chinese Women), 5 (1985), inside back cover.

walk, and sit.[22] But as with facial beauty, more drastic remedies were suggested for those female bodies unresponsive to diet, exercise, and correct deportment. In 1985, for instance, a Guangzhou factory began to market a device resembling a length of garden hose attached to a turkey baster on one end and a brassiere cup on the other. Its pumping action was intended to restore sagging breast tissue and enlarge the bust.[23]

Beauty had thus become a socially approved concern for women of all ages by the mid-1980's. The cultivation of an attractive appearance was regarded by many as an assertion of personal identity that had been impermissible during the Cultural Revolution. Women enthusiastically made use of the freedom to adorn themselves, sometimes describing their new modes of dress as an explicit attack on "feudal" notions of behavior that required women to make themselves as inconspicuous as possible. But the movement toward gender-specific adornment reestablished old values even while seeming to reject them. The idea that a woman should "look like a woman," not strive for a unisex appearance, was part of the reassertion of gender as a natural and valued division in society.

Even though the move toward fashionable dress was restorative of pre-

vious gender roles, many observers regarded it as subversive of proper behavior for Chinese women. Articles in the press cautioned young women
in particular that single-minded pursuit of beauty could be dangerous
to their physical well-being, their national identity, and their personal
morality.

The warnings about health hazards were couched in scientific terms,
and they included almost every accoutrement of 1980's fashion. Heavy
makeup was criticized for interfering with the excretion of wastes through
the skin and burdening the kidneys and lungs. Gold and silver jewelry
were pinpointed as a cause of contact dermatitis. Shoes with heels higher
than three centimeters were faulted for cutting off circulation to the toes
and leading to toe deformities. Tight-fitting jeans were identified as a
source of pressure on the nerves of the lower back and pain or numbness
in the thighs. Young women were also cautioned to avoid excessively
strict dieting, lest they end up in the hospital attached to an IV. One of the
more extreme cases of damage incurred in the pursuit of beauty involved
a young woman who secretly used industrial glue from a factory to stick
on false eyelashes. She inadvertently glued her eyelids shut, and after
many unsuccessful trips to the hospital finally unglued them with a sol-
vent obtained from the manufacturer.[24] In several of these cases, authors
invoked the authority of foreign researchers. Presumably the foreign scientific evidence was meant to show that the criticisms were not a result of
national prejudice, that even in the fashionable West people were not willing to sacrifice health to the demands of beauty.

Yet foreign standards of beauty also came under criticism, especially in
the early years of the fashion explosion. Young women workers and students were sent home in some places for wearing "bizarre clothing."
Their elders frequently reminded them that beauty had national character. It would be inappropriate, one writer commented, for young Chinese
women to follow the custom of the African tribe who found long necks
beautiful, and lengthened them by fastening copper rings around them.[25]
Similarly, writers discouraged young women from slavishly copying Western adornment. One author poked fun at an adolescent girl who "often
took 'foreign' as the standard, and the peculiar and odd as beautiful,"
dyeing her hair blonde, wearing "provocative colors," and generally
dressing in a way the author characterized as "not in keeping with our
nation's customs."[26]

As fashion magazines increasingly featured foreign models in avant-
garde clothing, however, these warning voices became easier for young
people to ignore. After all, even a top woman official like Hao Jianxiu,
alternate secretary in the secretariat of the Central Committee, dismissed

objections to fashionable dress. In a time of rapid social change, she said, not everyone would think alike. Some comrades would exhibit unliberated thinking. But dressing up should be regarded, she felt, not as an expression of bourgeois lifestyle, but as an indication of the flourishing development of socialist production.[27] Although the term "bourgeois" often had been used to castigate those who hankered after foreign material goods and foreign thinking, in 1980's China, fashionable clothing, both Western and Chinese, began to be cleansed of its bourgeois taint.

Aside from its danger to health and its effect on national identity, fashion was sometimes suspected of posing a threat to the personal morality of young women. Women were demeaned and trivialized, some writers felt, when female appearance was commodified. Sounding very much like critics in the United States, these authors decried the use of images of attractive women in product advertisements. In an ad for a tire factory, for instance, a miniskirted damsel in high-heeled shoes swung in a tire, her bare legs dangling seductively. *China Youth News* reprinted the ad with a sardonic caption:

> A rubber tire and a fashionable woman
> Like a horse and a cow in heat, have nothing to do with each other,
> But form a "pleasing contrast." . . .
> When an ad features a woman,
> Do the goods become glamorous?
> Probably the author wracked his brains to come up with this ad.
> Since "the price is reasonable" and the maker honest,
> Why have a girl
> Make eyes at the customers?[28]

Even more dangerous than the use of women to sell commodities, these authors said, was the commodification of women themselves. In rural western Zhejiang, for instance, young women wearing heavy makeup and attractive clothing literally hurled themselves in front of trucks on the area's single highway in order to persuade drivers to stop and eat at local roadside diners. At the instigation of the restaurant owners, one newspaper reported, some of these women had even "acted in ways that offend public decency," presumably by making sexual advances to the drivers.[29] Other young women, writers warned, had begun to deck themselves out for sale—through marriage—to men who could pay the price. An advice handbook linked the pursuit of fashion with the onset of moral decay and personal ruin:

Some girl students . . . are fond of wearing perfume and high heels, and after school they dress even more elaborately and saunter through the streets. They feel that the more fashionably they dress the "higher" their social status. Some don't study, and busy themselves finding a boyfriend. A few don't give a thought to personal or national dignity, and try to ingratiate themselves with overseas Chinese businessmen or foreign travelers they don't even know, hoping to use the "superiority" of their youthful good looks to "marry up." Some among them meet scoundrels and traders in human flesh, who use color TV's, tape recorders, and the promise "I'll take you out [of the country]" as bait to seduce ignorant girls. . . . After these girls are ruined, some are discarded like a banana peel; others . . . are sold abroad as prostitutes and lead a wretched life far from home. . . . A self-respecting young woman would never treat herself as a piece of merchandise, waiting for the highest bidder.[30]

Thus young women who traded on personal appearance to gain access to "the dazzling world with all its temptations" were courting moral disaster.[31] Their moral failing, as described by advice books, was vanity. Vanity led them to pay too much attention to their appearance, crave the praise of men, and eventually relax their vigilance and fall into the clutches of tricksters. One author invoked the fable of the fox and the crow to illustrate this point. The crow had a piece of meat in his beak, which the fox coveted. The fox flattered the crow with compliments about its beautiful voice, and when the crow opened its beak to sing the fox made off with the meat. Lest the comparison be too subtle for adolescent readers to grasp, the author added, "In order to satisfy its vanity, this crow lost a piece of meat. In order to satisfy their vanity, some girls go so far as to lose their virginity, causing themselves lifelong regret."[32]

The best protection against the perils of physical attractiveness, writers of advice literature said, was to cultivate "inner beauty." In a piece entitled "What Is Female Beauty?," a young man reacted with trepidation when he heard his family praising the good looks of his girl cousin. He urged her not to be content with her physical beauty, but to develop three characteristics even more important than a pretty face: gentleness, steadiness, and resourcefulness. A woman should avoid "crude, shrewish, obstinate, and unruly" behavior, maintain a calm and poised demeanor when she saw an attractive man, and display her "natural inborn talent" of resourcefulness, a female attribute described by Rousseau. These characteristics would help her protect herself, get along with others, and successfully fill the roles of wife and mother.[33]

Even if a woman was well-dressed, another piece in the same advice book warned, immodest public behavior would cause her to seem unattractive to others. The author decried the actions of a group of schoolgirls who shouted, laughed, pushed, cracked vulgar jokes, and ate melon seeds on the trolley. In contrast, he described a relative's daughter who nodded politely when she met acquaintances, rose to welcome guests at home and pour them tea, never interrupted in conversation, listened earnestly, and made suitable replies when others spoke.[34] This, the author concluded, was true maidenly beauty.

Although contemporary authors of advice cited Rousseau rather than Confucius, their list of desirable feminine attributes often was compatible with traditional Chinese womanly virtues. The advice they gave young women was profoundly conservative, no doubt because they perceived cherished notions of proper gender behavior as threatened by new fashions and the values suggested by them. The dismay of these advisers was certainly increased by the enthusiasm with which young women adorned themselves, and their fervor in equating adornment with personal freedom.

The detractors of the new trends in fashion were not much heeded by young urban Chinese. In the environment of the 1980's, the charges that women were trivialized by excessive adornment, or that they stood to lose their Chinese essence if they copied foreign modes of dress, were dismissed as the old-fashioned mutterings of those who would limit China's contact with the rest of the world. In this context, even their critique of the commodification of female images—one that would be shared by many Western feminists—was discredited as a disguised attempt to bring back the *status quo ante*. Though most young urban women in the 1980's undoubtedly pursued their interest in fashion without much thought to its social significance, others regarded dressing up as a positive means of asserting their identity as individuals and as women.

Nevertheless, the advent of elaborate attire and makeup did not in itself suggest much about the changing status of women. What looked like an increased scope for self-expression and individuality in women's attire may merely represent a new standard of conformity, one geared to pleasing men. As the example of numerous industrialized nations shows, female adornment and even the open display of female sexuality that the authors of advice columns feared so much are perfectly compatible with female subordination.[35] Even if these authors lose the battle over high heels and low-cut clothes, the traditional female virtues whose demise they deplored may continue to feature prominently in the socialization of young women for some time to come.

Adolescent Sexuality

To Talk or Not to Talk

During the Cultural Revolution, no public word was spoken about sexuality. Even marital sex was a taboo subject, an aspect of private life and therefore a "bourgeois" concern. Yet the silence on the subject also reflected a much older tradition of reticence. Chinese parents were not in the habit of providing their children with sex education. Like parents in many other times and places, they avoided the topic out of embarrassment and ignorance, reassuring themselves that "After they grow up, they'll become aware of it naturally," and "There is no need to talk about it; that's how I grew up."[36] As one commentator put it in a 1985 article: "For many years in our nation, sex has been something that could not be explicitly explained. Sometimes, even though there was no alternative to talking about it, it was discussed in an ambiguous manner, as though whoever spoke of it in clear language was offending public decency and acting uncivilized."[37] Sex education for young women traditionally was limited to warnings that they must guard their chastity until marriage and after the death of their husbands. On subjects like the physiological changes of puberty, sexual self-awareness in adolescence, and the social channeling of sexual desire, individual reticence reinforced official silence.

In the early 1980's, this situation began to change. The voices of parents, teachers, and occasionally young people were heard in the press, debating whether, when, and how to talk about sexual physiology, activity, and morality, who should do the talking, and what they should say. This discussion concerned the nature of sex itself. It acknowledged that sex was a matter of concern to unmarried adolescents as well as married adults, and that since sexual impulses influenced the private lives of young people they had best be acknowledged in the public discourse as well.

Those who broached the subject of sex were motivated, in part, by a concern for the physical and emotional health of adolescents. They spoke of young women who were frightened by the changes happening to their bodies but too embarrassed to seek adult guidance, causing themselves unnecessary psychological suffering and even physical harm.[38] The writers also expressed concern about new sexual mores among adolescents. In allowing increased contact with the West, they argued, China had opened the door to Western notions of "sexual liberation"; at the same time, domestic economic reforms and liberalization of the arts were widening the scope of permissible activity within China. Adolescents had begun to pursue in their own lives the kind of romantic scenes they encountered in books, on TV, and at the movies. Exasperated high school teachers wrote of their attempts to teach in classrooms where the students were passing notes and making eyes at members of the opposite sex. More ominously, they pointed to an upsurge in cases of young women who had been "tricked"—that is, lured into premarital sexual activity and then abandoned.[39]

In terms reminiscent of recent debates in the United States, some Chinese commentators blamed the increase in adolescent sexual activity on the public discussion of sex. In an article entitled "Doubtful 'Guidance,'" Jiang Yuanming deplored the availability of articles like "The Wedding Night" and "A Good Sex Life" in contemporary magazines. This information might be appropriate for newlyweds, he felt, but its widespread publication ensured that young students would see it too, and interpret it as a license to act. Anticipating that others might find his reaction "feudal," he countered that it was not his views, but "the serious chaos in relations between the sexes in Western society," that represented "a giant step backward in human progress."[40]

Unlike Jiang, most of those active in the debate agreed on the need to provide "widespread, scientific education about puberty to high school students."[41] They were particularly concerned that young women be given correct information about sex, not merely exhorted to preserve their chastity. In a scathing critique of the concept of chastity in old China, Xu Jin described it as a "rope around the neck of women," which imposed strictures on their behavior while men were free to take multiple wives and concubines. Although chastity remained a desirable goal that could "promote the constancy and purity of love," Xu wrote, "under current conditions, when the remnants of feudal thought are rather widespread, an overemphasis on chastity education often actually becomes an invisible rope binding the spirit, and in the end it is still young women themselves who suffer."[42] Chastity education was not only oppressive to women, Xu felt; it was also ineffective in preventing premarital sexual activity. Far more useful would be an approach that demystified sex, talked about a sexual morality appropriate to a Communist society, and clearly explained the harmful consequences of "sexual liberation" for young people and society as a whole.[43]

Out of this social imperative to provide sex education to adolescents came a dual message aimed at young women in particular, and delivered to them at home, at school, and in the press. On one hand, they were told that the physiological and emotional changes they experienced at puberty were natural, that they should learn to understand these changes and feel comfortable with them. On the other hand, they were warned that sexual feelings, if not properly managed, could lead to physical harm and social ruin. Young men were also told about the dangers of unrestrained sexual activity, but the advice literature overwhelmingly stressed what it said was the special responsibility of young women: to channel and control the sexual desires of young men as well as their own, and to defer acting on those desires until they reached the socially appropriate age for courtship and marriage. This message was reinforced by the use of cautionary tales graphically illustrating the consequences for women of yielding to their "natural" sexual feelings.

Acceptable Questions

The message that sexual development was natural and not to be feared was disseminated largely through the press. In 1981, for instance, the magazine *Chinese Women* began to run a regular physiology column for teenaged girls. The editors explained that their decision to include this feature came in response to letters from young women:

In front of us is a stack of letters from girls. Puzzled by some physiological phenomena, they have become extremely anxious, but their girlish sense of shame makes it difficult for them to bring the matter up with relatives, friends, or even their doctors. They "control their thumping hearts, screw up their courage," and send inquiring letters to the "understanding sisters and aunts in the editorial department": "What is having a period all about?" "Will painful periods influence future childbearing?" "Why do some young women have mustaches?" "Why do freckles appear on the face?" "How can I slim down?" . . . They often end with "Please answer soon," or "Hoping for a sincere reply" and quite a few exclamation points. Their eagerness fairly leaps off the page.[44]

Other periodicals directed at women or young people instituted similar features, and a number of books describing adolescent physiology were published or reissued.[45]

These publications offered detailed information about menstruation, the development of male and female sex organs, secondary sex characteristics, hygiene, and assorted aspects of female appearance such as breast size, facial hair, and excess weight. The physiological explanations did not differ dramatically from what one might find in Western sex education books, but some of the commentary addressed specifically Chinese social conditions and beliefs. A typical article about menstruation described its cause, appearance, and duration. With conditions in rural China in mind, the writer advised young women to keep themselves scrupulously clean when they had their periods, and to use sanitary paper towels rather than the rags or raw cotton often used in rural areas. She also warned women to avoid heavy exercise and spicy or raw foods and not to go out in the rain or wade in water while menstruating.[46] Adolescent girls were instructed to watch for signs of gynecological infection and get treatment promptly.

Anticipating that many young women would be embarrassed to seek medical attention, the editors of one magazine added a word of advice to gynecologists: "Young women are not easy to examine for gynecological diseases, and so a minority of gynecologists and nurses are impatient and not conscientious with the patients. This is one of the reasons why young women hang back at the gynecologist's door. We hope that medical workers will examine their own attitudes and treat these ailments in a conscientious manner." [47] Such articles touched on the emotional aspects of puberty in order to reassure young women that their periods were nothing to be afraid of. [48] Unlike similar publications intended for newlyweds, they did not include descriptions of sexual intercourse, and referred to sexual desire only in order to warn young people away from masturbation (discussed below). Young people who took these publications as their guide could learn a great deal about the clinical aspects of adolescent physiology, but they would hear little about the psychological component of adolescent sexuality. That was regarded as a moral question, to be dealt with at home, in the schools, and in articles devoted to ethical guidance.

Sex Education at Home and School

Parents were encouraged by the official press to break their traditional silence and help disseminate the second message: that sexuality should be managed carefully. A 1985 investigation at one school showed that only 24 percent of all mothers discussed "adolescent hygiene" with their daughters, while a mere 5 percent of all fathers raised the subject with their sons. [49] This situation had to change, said the writer of a series of articles on parental responsibility for sex education. She advised parents to do three things. First, they should establish a "unified, healthy, harmonious, and civilized" atmosphere at home. In such a setting, adolescents would experience "the warmth of the family," and would not feel compelled to seek sympathy and emotional support from members of the opposite sex. Parents were told that if family conversation touched on a situation where relations between the sexes had not been proper, they should be sure to adopt an attitude of "condemnation and disdain," rather than merely describing a "scandal of vulgar interest." Adults should also avoid using foul language, since the sexual connotations of many curses demeaned "the mystery of sex." [50]

Second, parents should encourage their children to develop friendships with both boys and girls, but teach them not to become too close to members of the opposite sex. Parents who discovered that their children were experiencing "first love" should distract them—that is, "patiently and meticulously educate, guide, and supervise them"—to concentrate on their studies and on "healthy scientific, literary, artistic, and athletic activities." [51]

Third, parents should give their children a rational education about physical and mental health. In the physical realm, they should provide information about the physiology and hygiene of sexual maturation. As for mental health, they should make sure that their children engaged in planned activities outside of school, rather than loitering on the streets looking for trouble, or lying in bed "letting their imaginations run wild with love scenes from TV, movies, books, and magazines."[52] Parents were thus advised to be confidants and teachers as well as disciplinarians.

Increasingly, these nascent parental efforts were supplemented by formal and informal sex education in the classroom. The effort began in 1982 in some institutions of higher education. Classes for women at a mining institute, for instance, "let them receive information it was not easy for them to hear from parents, teachers, and friends."[53] But attention soon shifted to the high school level, where beleaguered teachers were unsure how to deal with the burgeoning phenomenon of "premature love."[54] As one advice handbook described the problem,

Some high school students are very interested in books, periodicals, and movies that reflect love life. Some girl students are particular about how they dress, and keep a special lookout to see who likes to cast sidelong glances at them or hang out in their vicinity. Some boy students secretly write notes to a girl student, setting a place for a lovers' rendezvous. Third parties then treat this "news" as an opportunity for mischief and ridicule, broadcast it about, and discuss it endlessly.[55]

While the writer of this piece did not find the outbreak of "premature love" surprising, he cautioned young people that they should not sacrifice their valuable study time for the sake of emotions that were fleeting and changeable.[56] He warned:

While others are wholly absorbed in class lectures, those who are preoccupied with love cannot help thinking of how to pour out their hearts on their next date; while others are full of zest for collective activities, those who are preoccupied with love want to avoid the collective, and restlessly seek their own small universe. As time goes on, this necessarily influences their studies, and it is easy for their thinking to become narrow.[57]

Some teachers confronted the epidemic of note-passing, eye-batting, and pairing off among students by delivering informal lectures in which they tried to guide and persuade rather than condemn and forbid. One advised his students to take their newfound attraction for the opposite sex and "bury it deep in your heart; store it like a treasure for a long time. Because now it is just a seed, and it needs pleasant sunshine, clean air, and a piece of fertile soil where it can send forth shoots and grow." Since high school students were in no position to provide optimum conditions for the growth of love, he explained, they should use these new feelings as a spur to self-improvement. He observed that "premature love," when properly sublimated, could inspire personal growth: "In order to win the good opinion of the girl he has in mind, one day a boy suddenly begins to realize: My grades must stand out from the rest; I can't let her think I'm a blockhead. In order to win the respect of the boy she has in mind, a girl may, without realizing it, make demands of herself: that she treat people gently, carry herself with grace and poise."[58] In other words, boys in love become smarter, while girls in love grow more feminine—all desirable traits, he felt, that would be lost if teachers forbade their students to fall in love rather than teaching them to channel their emotions properly.

In addition to this type of informal guidance by teachers, school systems undertook an ambitious program of formal sex education. Educators and family planners from throughout the nation met in the summer of 1985 to plan for the founding of a China Sex Education Research Association.[59] On the municipal level, political instructors in the Shanghai school system conferred with specialists on adolescence to design a sex education curriculum. It was to begin in the upper elementary grades and include physiology, psychology, hygiene, morality, the place of sex in society, and the prevention of sex crimes. The curriculum designers agreed that the program should not merely disseminate information, but also offer students individual guidance on how to deal with menstruation, seminal emission, and masturbation.[60]

An intriguing glimpse of one such program in action was provided in a newspaper report on puberty education for girl students at the Shanghai Number 3 Middle School, a junior high school in the Zhabei section of the city, a rough neighborhood where "school spirit and school discipline were rather lacking." Physical examinations of the first- and second-year classes revealed that 70 percent of the first- and second-year girl students (aged thirteen and fourteen) had already reached puberty, and conversations with them indicated that they were interested in the opposite sex. When teachers and political instructors held discussions with the students, they found that boys and girls in the first-year class were pursuing, teasing, and writing notes to one another, while second-year students had progressed to hugging and kissing. Teachers declared themselves particularly worried about the girls, whose ignorance and emotional nature made them vulnerable: "Because they did not understand enough about physiology and hygiene, were good at imitating the actions of others, easily became emotionally excited, and were unable to deal with sudden sexual incidents, they often made mistakes or were seduced and cheated."

To deal with this distressing situation, the school began a course of lectures and films about physiology for all the students. Boys and girls then met separately to discuss sexual morality. The report did not mention what went on in the boys' class, but the girls were taught to practice the "four selfs": self-esteem, self-respect, self-possession, and self-strengthening. They were told to maintain a sense of propriety in dealing with all males, including classmates, teachers, brothers, and fathers. They were also instructed how to protect themselves if they met with "special circumstances," a term that apparently meant sexual advances rather than outright assault.[61] A report on a similar program in another school defined self-protection as the ability to manage the sexuality of both parties: "When the occasion warrants it, they should maintain their feminine restraint and seriousness; when they suddenly encounter a rash action, they should be able to respond with a sense of propriety and not become panic-stricken."[62] As part of the Shanghai program, mothers were also invited to the school for a special forum on educating their adolescent daughters.[63]

According to the news report, the program was a great success with the girls and their parents. Many girl students expressed gratitude at being saved from wandering into error, and parents thanked the school for "sounding an alarm for us." Best of all, commented the reporter, "the girl students' sense of right and wrong has been heightened, and when they discover irregular relationships between boys and girls in the class, they all take the initiative to report them to their teacher. They also have increased their awareness of how to deal with certain situations."[64] Ultimately, the prescription given to teachers dealing with "premature love" was the same as that given to parents—distract your students, encouraging them to divert their attention with classes and extracurricular activities, and to refuse advances from would-be sweethearts until a later time.

For their part, students were instructed to learn the importance of controlling their impulses. The sex drive was natural, they were told, but unlike other biological drives, it could be controlled, weakened, and adjusted. Although humans and animals alike felt the urge for sexual activity, only humans understood when, where, and under what conditions they should satisfy their sexual needs. Adolescence was a particularly dangerous period because young people felt sexual desire but lacked a mature outlook on love, morality, and human life. They were forced to confront what one writer called the "fanatical period" of interest in the opposite sex, but as yet lacked the will to consider the consequences of their actions. Much of the literature on adolescent sex was intended to steer young people through this troubled stage so they could safely reach late adolescence, the end of fanaticism, and the beginning of "formal romantic love."[65]

However, the kind of guidance and supervision provided by parents and teachers did not always meet with an enthusiastic response. In letters to youth magazines, students often complained that adults applied feudal standards of behavior to the social lives of adolescents. Misinterpreting the content of innocent friendships with members of the opposite sex, parents and teachers forced young people to give up nascent romantic relationships, moves that were much resented.[66] By the 1980's, the battle over adult interference in courtship, long an issue among people in their twenties (see Chapter 3), had spread to the secondary schools, to the dismay of parents and educators. It was not at all clear that adult supervision would be able to channel adolescent sexuality or make it disappear from public view. Initially, at least, the attempt to do so had exactly the opposite effect: sexuality among adolescents became visible and in some ways legitimate to an extent unprecedented in the People's Republic.

Sexual Danger

Young people who strayed from the correct handling of sexuality as defined by their elders were warned that a bleak future awaited them. To begin with, excessive attention to sexual desire could lead to the habit-forming practice of masturbation, which was said to damage the nervous system and permanently impair one's health. Young people of both sexes were told to get plenty of exercise, refrain from sleeping in tight pants or under heavy covers, and get out of bed to study or wash their faces in cold water if they became sexually aroused.[67]

But not all the perils of sexuality could be avoided by leaping out of bed. Suggestible young women in particular also were told to beware of reading novels too uncritically. Losing oneself in fiction like *Wuthering Heights* or *Dream of the Red Chamber*, some writers felt, could cause adolescent girls to identify too closely with romantic heroines. Their imaginations befogged by novels, girls might lower their vigilance and be taken in by swindlers or worse.[68]

The next step on the continuum of sexual danger was addiction to pornography. The definition of pornography in 1980's China was a broad one: popular music from Hong Kong and Taiwan, hand-copied novels describing romantic and erotic scenes, and videotapes smuggled in from abroad were all regarded as pornographic. An official of the Ministry of Culture, interviewed in 1982 about how to identify pornographic songs, defined them as "decadent songs that give an undisguised description of sex. Their lyrics advertise sex and their tunes are degenerate and vulgar, giving people morbid sensory stimulation." He classified songs from Hong Kong and Taiwan into three categories: low-class and filthy, "pure

Pornographic music entraps a young man. *Gongren ribao*
(Workers' Daily), Dec. 6, 1983, 3.

love songs," and songs about ordinary life and homesickness for the
mainland. He regarded only the last category, the one whose subject
matter did not touch on any aspect of sex, as completely acceptable.[69]

Much "pornographic" material came under attack in 1982. Public discussion abandoned the language of gentle guidance and persuasion in
favor of more strident warnings. A commentator for *China Youth News*
sounded the alarm in a front-page article in 1982:

A very poisonous corrupting influence is in the process of invading the bodies of
some young people, requiring our serious consideration and vigilance. We mean
pornographic publications. In some places at the present time, obscene and dirty
pornographic publications are increasingly running rampant. Young people who
have been poisoned by pornographic publications have suffered serious physical
and mental destruction. Some of them fall into a trance, neglect their studies, and
even sink into a life of crime, destroying their youth.[70]

The writer expressed particular concern about the appearance of "obscene
tapes" and magazines in the schools; he saw this as an invasion of the
"rotten thought and life-style of foreign bourgeois culture." He called for
a public effort that would treat these materials like "rats crossing the
street—everyone should cry out and hit them, and utterly annihilate
them from our socialist Chinese soil."[71]

Three steps were taken in 1982 to combat the influx of pornography.
First, a series of well-publicized arrests were made of people who smug-

gled pornography in from Hong Kong, sold pornographic books and showed pornographic tapes, or printed and sold home-grown pornography. Every effort was made to brand the traffickers as degenerate elements in search of high profits, which indeed were there to be made: in one Guangdong city, 1,700 showings of videotapes netted an estimated 221,000 yuan.[72]

Second, high schools took up the anti-pornography crusade. School authorities discovered that both male and female students were perusing "extremely obscene" hand-copied books, as well as listening to, singing, and dancing to dubious songs. In response they organized meetings to "clear away spiritual garbage," encouraged students to turn in salacious material, and beefed up their program of extracurricular activities. They ordered new books and magazines for the school libraries, encouraged athletic activity, and began music classes to teach revolutionary songs, presumably so that young people could satisfy their desire to sing without resorting to licentious tunes. In several schools, the move against pornography was accompanied by new regulations forbidding students to wear "outlandish clothing." Boys were told not to grow their hair long or to curl it, and girls were lectured on the value of female chastity.[73] What was at issue here was not simply pornography, but the entire code of youthful behavior that celebrated adornment and "premature love."

The third measure was the publication of articles and short stories warning young people of the danger of pornography and encouraging them to help eliminate it. In one story, "Older Sister Was Stared Down," a young girl turned in her older sister and the sister's boyfriend for copying tapes of pornographic music. As the older sister was escorted to the police station, she was too ashamed to meet her younger sister's unflinching gaze; hence the story's title.[74] A cartoon in *China Youth News* featured a long-haired, bell-bottomed, mustachioed young man reading a pornographic book. Over his shoulder loomed a skeleton, pointing a bony finger down a road labeled "Degeneration and Crime."[75]

A life of crime was guaranteed to all readers of pornography, male or female, but other warnings were gender-specific. Young men were told that exposure to pornography would cause them to commit sex crimes, such as charging into a women's public bathroom.[76] Young women were told, at much greater length, that absorption in pornography would lead them to lower their vigilance and fall prey to male seduction. In a fictionalized advice piece, an aunt found some "unhealthy" books by her niece's bed. She warned her niece that a study done at a reform school showed that many young girls who had gone astray had begun by reading hand-copied pornographic works, and had "gone down the slope and even fallen into the water." Lest the niece misunderstand, the aunt elaborated:

Hand-copied pornographic books often present young girls whose sexuality is not yet awakened with something unabashedly tantalizing, causing them to move from curiosity to yearning to wallowing, so that they want to go try it. Quite a few innocent and uncorrupted girls have been led astray, had their dispositions changed and their entire lives ruined, by a slim hand-copied volume. That is why people call them "deadly poison."[77]

This homily and others like it gave young girls in particular a message about pornography: women were coming of age in an increasingly dangerous world. To cope with this situation, young women were told to resist the road to seduction, whether it came in the form of premature love or pornography.

The criticism of pornography intensified during the campaign against "spiritual pollution" in the fall of 1983. The issues raised in that campaign went far beyond concern about pornography, extending to a high-level debate about the wisdom of opening China to Western influence and pursuing economic reform.[78] But official denunciation of pornography and its effect on young people both preceded and outlasted the discussion of spiritual pollution. In summer 1985, a year and a half after the end of the campaign, the State Council issued updated "Regulations Strictly Forbidding Obscene Goods." The regulations forbid the importing, reproduction, sale, and broadcast of obscene goods, defined as "videotapes, audio tapes, movies, TV movies, slides, photographs, drawings, books, periodicals, and hand-copied books that concretely describe sexual activity or undisguisedly advertise lascivious images; toys or other articles with this kind of picture printed on them; aphrodisiacs and sexual equipment." In contrast to the practice during the spiritual pollution campaign, the 1985 regulations specifically exempted works of art showing the beauty of the human body, as well as medical and scientific works. They reaffirmed particular concern with the effect of pornography on young people.[79] The pornography discussion should not be interpreted as merely a disguised metaphor for all Western influence, as a code used by one government faction to attack another over reforming the Chinese economy. It reflected, in part, deep concern with the changing sexual mores of young people, and the desire to promote a return to the simpler, more conservative code of sexual behavior that had characterized the early years of the People's Republic.

Cautionary Tales

In 1985, a popular magazine for young people carried the following story: A young woman from rural Yunnan, desperate to escape the dreariness of life in her home village, finds a job as a temporary laborer in a railway station. She likes to admire her beautiful face and figure in the mirror, and aspires to use her good looks to make a marriage that will free her forever from her rural origins. She is introduced to a very modern-looking young man with long hair, a colorful shirt, and pointed leather shoes. He tells her that he is a college graduate and a traveling salesman dealing in Chinese medicine. But unbeknownst to her, he is a "sex wolf" who specializes in "tricking, seducing, and having illicit sexual relations with many girls from good families."

The naive young woman takes him home, and her parents are charmed by him. He asks for permission to take her to Fujian to meet his family; on the way he persuades her to sleep with him and takes her with him to several cities. Eventually he reveals that he already has a wife and child; when his horrified sweetheart threatens suicide, he promises to divorce his wife. When they reach Fujian, she discovers that he lives in a small earthen house, not, as he originally told her, in an eight-room mansion equipped with TV and refrigerator. After he abandons her, one of his friends then "rescues" her and seduces her in turn. Later both men are arrested and she is sent home. Her story concludes with a warning:

Remember, young women friends, when someone caters to some need of yours, fawns upon and flatters you, open your eyes, differentiate between true and false, and give him careful scrutiny. Under no circumstances should you readily place your trust in him, much less lose your senses, get carried away, and give up everything to someone. Is not the bitter experience of this young woman a lesson in blood and tears? Friend, beware of those "sex wolves" who surround you, staring with blood-red eyes! [80]

In the mid-1980's, virtually every issue of the many newspapers and magazines for youth and women carried at least one cautionary tale like this one. Cautionary tales, a genre of popular literature intended specifically for adolescent girls and young women, laid out in merciless detail the consequences for women who gave in to their own sexual feelings and suffered the depredations of men. The treatment of female chastity in the cautionary tales differed greatly from a parallel discussion about whether it was permissible to sleep with one's steady boyfriend, an issue discussed in the next chapter. The latter discussion was carried on in advice columns and surveys, and represented a genuine social dialogue between adults and young people about a controversial issue. Cautionary tales, in contrast, offered verities rather than ambiguities. Right and wrong were perfectly clear, the heroes and villains were starkly drawn, and no woman who gave up her virginity met with a happy ending, although she might achieve a measure of satisfaction when her seducer was brought before the law for forced seduction, rape, or indecent behavior. A typical tale read like a novel even when it was based on a real incident. It was embellished with dramatic descriptions of the physical setting and the tear-stained faces of the fallen heroines, and enriched with reconstructed dialogue and illustrations.

The theme of the cautionary tales was always the same: the world is full of tricksters, and a young woman must be on her guard against the loss of her virginity. But the specific plots were full of variety and ingenuity. They conveyed a number of messages about fatal flaws in female character, and about the nature of male and female sexuality. Although their tone was moralistic, their prose was often sexually explicit, satisfying prurient interest while at the same time decrying scandalous behavior.

The character flaw that brought most of these unfortunate women to ruin, according to the cautionary tale formula, is vanity. Like the woman in the story recounted above, they spend an inordinate amount of time admiring their own good looks. They go beyond beautifying themselves to meet the requirements of "the new health and beauty craze," and seek to use their appearance to make upwardly mobile marriages. One woman, for instance, became involved with the son of a cadre household, whose social status was high enough to "satisfy [her] vanity." She had sexual relations with the man under duress, and they registered their marriage, but before they could hold a ceremony his family made it evident that they regarded her as too low-class for them. Her erstwhile sweetheart then threw her out, commenting that "these days I can buy a girl for ten dollars." She prepared to drown herself, to "let the anguished past and regretful tears, along with my sullied flesh, be forever submerged in the calm waters of the lake." But she was rescued and recounted her story as a warning about the perils of giving in to a man's sexual desire, and the dangers of seeking material gain through marriage.[81]

The message is delineated even more graphically in cases where the woman's vanity leads her to marry in order to leave the country. One such protagonist married a Hong Kong man twenty years her senior. When she reached Hong Kong, her husband turned her out as a prostitute, then abandoned her when she contracted tuberculosis. She returned to China and committed suicide.[82] Another young woman, influenced by the hugging, kissing, and dancing she saw in foreign movies, let her boyfriend seduce her and tried to flee with him to the USSR. Sent back by the Soviet militia, she found herself pregnant and facing criminal charges.[83] In each of these stories, the women not only cross a national border, but transgress the boundary between acceptable and unacceptable behavior. Ultimately they find that prevailing social mores are not so easily discarded, and they are pulled back—literally, to Chinese territory, and figuratively, to the consequences of their actions.

A second flaw exhibited by women in the cautionary tales is extraordinary credulousness. One young woman allowed herself to be picked up at the gate of a Shanghai park, and provided her new sweetheart with 200 yuan to buy them each a set of clothes. In return he gave her a false home address, a bogus workplace address, and a gold necklace that her vigilant mother got appraised; it proved to be aluminum. The entire story, from meeting through gift exchange to his final arrest, unfolded within a space of five days.[84] A second ingenue, whose chief talent was the ability to dance the tango, was so eager to become a fashion model that she obeyed the interviewer's order to strip so that he could obtain accurate body measurements. He recorded her vital statistics on an English-language form, as follows (spelling as in original):

Lenth of booy	1.67 m
Width of waite	0.60 m
Highth of nipples	0.30 m

She further agreed to pose in the nude for him, and only began to suspect that something was awry when he demanded that she dance naked with him, in order to see how well she used her legs. After his arrest for forced seduction, she learned that he had sexually assaulted a number of women over a two-year period.[85]

The men in these stories are usually portrayed as little better than rapists, using a mixture of sweet talk and coercion to get what they want. The women, in contrast, are weak, sexually inexperienced, and frightened—quintessential victims. A typical seduction scene reads: "The young man moved closer to her, caught hold of her hand, and put out the lamp. He held her close, and kisses fell like rain on the young woman's face. She felt dizzy from this sudden heat wave, and was at a loss what to do. She tried with all her might to dodge him, but the young man's arms gripped her waist and limbs like a pair of iron pliers. Thus she gave up her most precious virginity." [86] Women are able to enjoy sexual pleasure only by becoming less than human. When a woman has sexual relations with her boyfriend, the author comments: "How sad! Merely to satisfy another, merely to satisfy herself, she completely exposed her body and soul, and so lost a young woman's most basic sense of dignity and shame. Ah, young woman, when lust is all that remains of 'love,' isn't it time to regain consciousness? . . . Between them nothing was left but a bit of animal instinct." [87] The view of both male and female sexuality in the cautionary tales is uniformly negative. Men are predators; women are vain and foolish, either passive prey or wanton degenerates.

Yet the cautionary tales also describe erotic scenes that, if presented under a less moralistic rubric, would have been banned as pornography. As long as the author places the sexual activity in a context of moral disapproval, it is possible to include scenes of surprising explicitness:

> She boldly caught hold of his hand, and moved her body toward his. Jia Hui exploited her motion, pulled her into his embrace, and kissed her lightly. Then he slipped his feminine hand inside Chen Hong's underwear. Chen was instinctively startled, and gazed at him, but saw only that his expression was self-possessed. She could not see the slightest hint of lewdness or evil. . . . She immediately had a feeling of safety and peace of mind. Her gaze changed from surprise to stiffness, and then from stiffness to softness. She lay happily in his embrace, smiled slightly, and put herself at his mercy. [88]

Secure in the knowledge that the man will eventually be brought to justice and the woman will suffer for her surrender (in this case, by undergoing three abortions), readers can relax and enjoy this erotic interlude.

Ultimately, however, the message of the cautionary tales differs little from that of traditional chastity education. True, in the cautionary tales, it is not only women who suffer; men who engage in illicit sexual activity invariably feel the wrath of the law. But the stories emphasize at much greater length the broken hearts and ruined lives of women who yield to men before marriage. They make it clear that virginity, the ticket to a legitimate romance and a respectable marriage, is to be squandered only at the risk of becoming a social outcast. And they leave no doubt that the responsibility for preserving female chastity, and indeed for managing the sexual desires of both men and women, lies with young women alone. Chastity is redefined as a socialist goal: "Our concept of chastity is an expression of the spirit of communist civilization in the realm of love and marriage. Unmarried women must preserve their purity; married women must be loyal to their own husbands. This is the social morality that women must observe in a socialist society." [89]

When it is understood that the woman is expected to regulate sexual conduct, the dual message young women are given about sex—that it is natural and understandable on the one hand, dangerous and uncontrollable on the other—becomes comprehensible. Young women must be given adequate information about sexual physiology and psychology *in order to better suppress* their sexual desires: "If you understand your own physiological development, then you can go a step further and control yourself, for instance regulating your mentality, consciously controlling your mood, associating with the opposite sex in a reasoned and unaffected manner, and cultivating a good character."[90] Or, as another article more succinctly put it, women must "remain cool, think of the consequences, be on guard, and . . . not pour oil on the fire" of male sexuality,[91] all the while keeping their own fires contained as well. The cautionary literature portrays women as emotionally vulnerable and easily led astray, a description consonant with the female personality traits described in Chapter 1. But it also assigns them unprecedented responsibility as guardians not only of their own chastity, but of the morality of men.

Women coming of age in 1980's China received messages about how to prepare themselves for marriage that were less consistent than those heard by their elder sisters. Unlike women in the Cultural Revolution years, they were encouraged to make themselves sexually attractive, even if doing so required major alterations in the shape of their bodies and faces. At the same time, they were expected to hold themselves aloof from sexual activity until safely married. The evidence suggests that young women enthusiastically followed the first dictum while responding to the second in lukewarm fashion.

Increased attention to adornment and increased discussion of sexuality makes it seem that China is becoming more like the West—perhaps the United States of the 1950's or of the 1980's fundamentalist revival rather than the West of the sexual revolution. The dubious comfort of finding that the Chinese are looking and talking "more like us," however, should not obscure the difficulties of growing up female in a society, Chinese or Western, that communicates such mixed messages about sexual attraction and activity. It remains to be seen whether the changes in China in recent years will help make it possible for women themselves to have more say about the use and abuse of their own sexuality.

Translations

Fashion was regarded as a natural and legitimate concern of young women in the 1980's. "Methods of Wearing Rings," "China Pioneers a Bust Enhancer," and "The First Date" all offer instruction in the adornment of face and body. "Young Women Who Love Beauty" warns that the rash pursuit of beauty can lead to disaster. Still, the dominant message young women received was that those who opposed female adornment were old-fashioned or downright backward. "Getting a Permanent and Losing a Life" and "Is This Outlandish Clothing?" criticize parents, employers, and teachers who try to prevent young women from making themselves prettier. In "It Is Not Permissible," however, readers of one magazine protest that images of beautiful women, especially those that emphasize their sexuality, should not be used to sell products.

Young women were encouraged to take a matter-of-fact attitude toward puberty. "The Consequences of Being 'Shy'" encourages them to overcome their embarrassment and seek regular gynecological care. Where sexuality was concerned, however, knowledge was not supposed to lead to action. "Is This True Love?" warns of the dangers of early dating. "I Hope You Will Learn a Lesson from My Mistakes" is a young woman's account of her seduction and subsequent suffering. "Worries Brought by Songs on Campus" and "My Corruption by Pornographic Publications" describe and condemn sexual themes in popular culture. "Young Woman, Be Vigilant!," the story of an attempted rape, cautions young women against being flattered or cajoled into sexual activity.

Methods of Wearing Rings

The significance of wearing a ring is different for each finger. This is a kind of silent language, a message or symbol.

Worn on the index finger: would like to marry; indicates a marriage proposal. Worn on the middle finger: already in love. Worn on the ring finger: already engaged or married. Worn on the little finger: I am single.

In general it is the custom not to wear rings on the thumb. Wedding rings cannot be made of an alloy; they must be made of pure gold, platinum, or silver, to show the purity of love.

SOURCE: *Zhongguo funü*, 4 (April 1985), 36.

China Pioneers a Bust Enhancer: Remarkable Results in Attaining Rapid Healthful Beauty

The Silver Star Plastics and Color Printing Factory of Jiangmen City, Guangdong, . . . in the interests of eliminating flaws in female development and promoting the development of healthy women's bodies and healthful beauty activities, has prepared and manufactured the "Rapid Healthful Beauty Bust Enhancer."

This bust enhancer is made in accordance with the principles of physiology. Through strengthening the movement of the muscles of the chest, it stimulates the secretions of the pituitary glands in the chest, expands the elasticity (*haimianti*) of the breasts, and causes flat breasts to become full and protruding (*fengman, tingba*) in a short period of time. It causes the limp, sagging, or drooping breasts of postpartum women to return to their original shape. According to the letters from some users, the bust enhancer not only can add to the curvaceous beauty of a woman's appearance, but can also promote blood circulation in the breasts, prevent breast cancer, guard against neurasthenia, make both breasts a uniform size, and cause freckles on the face to disappear naturally. . . .

Our factory handles mail-order and contract purchases (*chenggou*). All those sending remittances to our mail-order department should clearly write their name, address, and size. Mail-order price: for the large and medium sizes, 17 yuan; for the combined large/medium size, 19 yuan, including postage, packing, and miscellaneous fees. . . .

Our factory wholeheartedly and enthusiastically serves the women of the whole country. We welcome letters and will do business with commercial departments, trading companies, licensed individual enterprises, cosmetology centers, and individuals. Detailed material available upon written request.

SOURCE: *Zhongguo funü*, 5 (May 1985), inside back cover.

The First Date

On the first date, of course you hope to make a good impression on the other party. That which meets the eye, your dress and makeup, are all very important.

First of all, makeup should be simple and elegant, as though you don't have it on but you do. When your date sees that you have painstakingly dressed up for him, he will feel that you take him seriously. This can help develop the as yet indistinct and undecided feelings of both parties. But when you dress up you must by all means avoid plastering on thick and gaudy makeup, or you can ruin the atmosphere of the entire date and give the impression that you are false and affected.

As for clothing, you should choose according to the kind of activity in which you are participating. If you are strolling in the park, then a fitted (*heti*) blouse, matched with a knee-length skirt, will add to your elegant demeanor in the reflection of the setting sun. If he invites you on an outing, then a pair of navy jeans and a loose, full-sleeved sweater will be enough to allow you a range of spirited, youthful activities.

If it is a group activity, you had best ascertain first what kind it is. If you are immaculately dressed but your friends are all wearing everyday clothes, then you look too serious. But if you attend a formal dance, you should meticulously plan your hairdo, makeup, and attire. You absolutely cannot go casually dressed in work clothes, or it will not only make you seem out of step, but will also be discourteous to others.

SOURCE: *Zhongguo funü*, 4 (April 15, 1985), 25.

Young Women Who Love Beauty Should Be on Their Guard

Gao X, a young woman worker at the General Textile Mill in Puni, Hubei, felt that the bridge of her nose was too low and short, and hoped to raise it through plastic surgery. One day an old man who claimed to be a renowned surgeon came to the factory. He carried letters of introduction affixed with all kinds of official seals, as well as certificates from several hospitals saying that he specialized in plastic surgery. She was easily convinced and gave him 8 yuan to perform surgery on the bridge of her nose. After the old man took the money, he used a knife to cut a one-inch incision on either side of her nose without even using an anesthetic. He put medicine in each of the incisions, bandaged them up, and said that the operation was finished. After more than ten days, the young woman happily pulled off the gauze and looked, only to find that the bridge of her nose was not the least bit higher, while two ugly red welts were left on her face. When she went looking for the old man, he had long since disappeared.

Mao Lihui, General Textile Mill, Puni, Hubei

SOURCE: *Zhongguo qingnian bao*, March 2, 1982, 3.

Getting a Permanent and Losing a Life

On November 28th last year, Wang Bixia, a nineteen-year-old woman from a village in Sichuan province, went with two other young women from the same production team to the market at Jianyang county seat. Because Wang felt happy after buying a new piece of clothing, she decided to go to a beauty parlor and have her hair curled. When Wang's father saw that his daughter had gotten a bouffant hairdo (*paohua tou*), he became angry and began to curse. He said that a village girl who wore her hair that way simply showed bad upbringing, and that her parents would not be able to face people. He ordered his daughter to have her hair cut at once, and threatened her, "Making a fool of yourself like this—should I die or should you?!" Wang Bixia was both angry and frightened. She cried all night, and the next day before dawn, full of hatred, she actually took poison and killed herself.

SOURCE: *Zhongguo funü bao*, February 13, 1985, 2.

Is This Outlandish Clothing?

Comrade Editor:

I am a 23-year-old woman shop employee. In May of this year I bought two summer outfits in Wuhan. When I wore one of them to work, one of the people in charge of our unit said that this clothing was no good and I couldn't wear it. So I changed into the second outfit. To my surprise, he told me not to wear this one either. He said they were outlandish clothes, that I was not allowed to come to work, and that even if I did he would count it as an unauthorized absence. I am very worried about this, and write to ask your help in solving the problem: are these two items of clothing outlandish or not? Awaiting your reply.

Li Lanling
Enshi city, Hubei province

Comrade Editor:

This suit is a school uniform made by our class. We wore these outfits when we participated in the May 4th district singing contest, and received favorable comments from many teachers and students. But after the event, some people criticized us for wearing outlandish clothes. We are mailing you one of the girls' uniforms, and ask you to give us an appraisal as soon as possible.

Youth League Class Committee, English Class of 1982,
Ankang District Teachers' College, Shaanxi

Comrade Li Lanling and Classmates of the English Class of 1982:

After we received the clothing and letters you sent us, we immediately paid a visit to the relevant unit at the Ministry of Light Industry, and consulted experts in clothing design and research. In their judgment, these items of clothing are not outlandish. The pattern and color of Xiao Li's two blouses are actually quite tasteful and pleasing to the eye.

Beauty and ugliness are two completely different concepts. The problems that you report in your letters just illustrate that some people cannot differentiate clearly between beauty and ugliness in clothing, and call beautiful things ugly. As far as the style of clothing is concerned, as long as it does not expose too much of the chest or back, does not appear bizarre or give people a sense of ugliness, then it cannot be called outlandish. If only you explain your argument clearly, sooner or later the leadership and your classmates will understand.

. . . In a sense, clothing reflects the level of development of a nation's civilization, and embodies the traditional style and spiritual features of a nation. When young people focus on beauty in dress and personal adornment, they should first understand what true beauty is. Some young people blindly pursue clothing that is "tight, revealing, and transparent," thinking it beautiful. But this seems frivolous to others and makes them uncomfortable. We should use persuasion and guidance on these young people; simply adopting administrative measures is inappropriate.

Also, the clothing designers we consulted feel that the class uniform is rather tight in the seat. This style is not completely appropriate for a student uniform. Furthermore, it is pink, a warm tone, rather delicate. Of course one can wear it to perform on stage, but for a student uniform, it would be better to use more solemn, sedate, cooler colors.

SOURCE: *Zhongguo qingnian bao*, August 1, 1982, 1.

It Is Not Permissible to Defame Woman's Image

Comrade Editor:

Recently, we have discovered that many advertisements, product announcement posters, calendars, New Year pictures, and displays in photo studio windows feature women in every sort of pose. On the street one can often see people hawking various pictures of women in outlandish clothing, striking affected poses. Even more infuriating is that some people have the gall to use pictures of nude women to drum up business. This is an extremely abnormal phenomenon. Its source is the valuing of men over women in feudal society. The spread of the pernicious habit of regarding women as a commodity is also an expression of the influence of capitalist society, which treats women like a flower vase or a toy provided for people's enjoyment. We strongly oppose this, and hope that the relevant authorities will give this problem their attention.

We do not oppose the use of photographs or portraits of women on calendars, advertisements, or the cover of some publications. . . . But we must not allow women to be defamed or insulted. We also are not in favor of some periodicals carrying images of women on their covers merely to emphasize and publicize a woman's good looks, causing people to pursue interests that are senseless and devoid of meaning. We should publicize the true beauty of women. A proverb says: "A person's beauty lies in the soul, a bird's beauty in its feathers." Under the socialist system, Chinese women are a great reserve of labor power, an important force in socialist construction, consistently celebrated for their virtues of diligence, thrift, honesty, and kindheartedness. We suggest that the press do more to publicize images of women working energetically for the Four Modernizations on every front. . . .

Wang Yingzhao, Wang Junying, Xu Shuhan, Luo Zhiling,
and twenty-four others

SOURCE: *Zhongguo funü*, 5 (May 1981), 41.

The Consequences of Being "Shy"

I am a thirty-year-old woman. In my adolescence I had an extremely regrettable experience.

I remember when I was thirteen, one time in gym class one of the older girls got her period and stained her pants. Our classmates didn't help her out and made her feel ashamed and disgraced. From that time on, I thought that periods were "dirty," "unlucky," something to be ashamed of. But very quickly, unavoidable physiological phenomena occurred in my body. I was scared to death but too embarrassed to go tell my mother, and didn't know how to deal with the situation. So I hurriedly found several pairs of pants to wear, and had to change and wash them many times each day. When my mother questioned me, I still maintained that I hadn't gotten my period. Later, when my period came I quietly used rags and sewed a thick cushion into my pants. Because these rags had not been sterilized and were very unhygienic, they eventually caused an inflammation of the uterus and fallopian tubes. But I was a young girl and embarrassed to see a doctor, so it got to the point where I suffered from a chronic uterine inflammation, tuberculosis of the fallopian tubes, and other gynecological diseases. Now I have been married five or six years, but I still have not been able to bear a child and I often suffer pain in my midsection and abdomen. This disease has brought me mental and physical suffering, and has influenced my personal life and work.

Young women friends, please take a lesson from me. You must pay attention to routine menstrual hygiene; if you get a gynecological disease, you must ask a doctor to treat it immediately. At such times, shame and prejudice can only bring bad consequences.

Xie Hua

SOURCE: *Zhongguo funü*, 8 (August 1982), 47.

Is This True Love?

To the Editors:

I am a fifteen-year-old girl who graduated from junior middle school this year. I have a problem I don't know how to handle.

A boy several years older than I am approached me and said that he wanted to be friends with me. At the beginning, I consented because I felt it was very interesting. We often met behind our parents' backs, and as time went on I gradually fell in love with him. He also really loved me, and we were very happy together. But eventually someone found out about it and told my parents. My mother told me that I am too young to talk about such things. When I told him, he was unwilling [to break off], and said that if I didn't keep seeing him, he would kill me, and we could die together. Actually, I don't want to break up with him, and he loves me so, really! Loves me so much!

But there is lots of talk about us, and I wonder whether there is something wrong in our being this way? If we are both loyal to our partner, is it all right to talk about such matters [as love] or not? This is why I am writing this letter. I hope that the editors can help me.

Your reader, Sisi

Dear Sisi:

Reading your honest, frank letter, I understand your longing for help. As a teacher, I wish to talk to you confidentially. . . .

At first you began to go out with that young man because you "felt it was very interesting," and afterward fell in love with him. This is not at all surprising. It is an experience that adolescent girls love to have. During this period, people who are not yet adults undergo a stage when their body grows rapidly and their sexual physiology gradually matures. They begin to feel a vague curiosity about the opposite sex. The young shoots of first love sprout in their hearts, and they have the desire to experience sexual love. But because their knowledge of sexual love is at a hazy or even ignorant stage, they don't understand what real love is. Out of curiosity, they often conduct secret investigations of love. They are fond of reading romances, copying passages from love poems, watching the sex scenes in movies. They try out love by making dates, writing love letters, presenting keepsakes, making pledges, kissing and hugging, and even engaging in improper sexual relations. They think that this is true love.

You have only been meeting secretly with this young man, behind the backs of your parents, for several months. It is not possible that you have a deep understanding of one another, yet you think that you share a faithful love. This is really an immature deduction. When this young man heard that you wanted to break off relations in obedience to your parents' advice, not only did he not agree, but he wanted to kill you; yet you still thought, "He is so in love with me." One can see that you two do not understand what love is, and further that you are out-and-out "legal illiterates." If he sincerely loved you, could he stand to kill you?! If one pursues so-called love by fair means or foul, without care for the consequences, ultimately one will sink from "the net of love" into "the net of the law." This kind of tragedy is not uncommon. Because people who are not yet of age have a strong sense of curiosity but lack social experience and the ability to distinguish right from wrong, because their moods fluctuate easily and their emotions are easily stimulated, because they do not know how to correctly pick a mate, and also have no fixed source of economic support, premature love often leads to bad consequences. Young people get married rashly, and rashly divorce; or they readily believe sweet words and are tricked; or they don't succeed in love and strike out violently; or, to satisfy the material demands of the other party, they turn to theft and robbery, and go down the road of crime. Of course, I believe that you have not yet gone that far. But the powers of reason of fifteen- and sixteen-year-old youths are not completely mature, their self-control is rather weak, and without realizing it they can fall into love's net and have no means to get free.

In the Number 1 class of second-year students I once taught, there was a Study Committee member (a member of the Youth League). When she was a first-year student, her grades were among the best in the class, and she was very enthusiastic about social work. But later she acted very strange. In class she became absent-minded, and she just went through the motions of her work as a class officer. When I sought her out for a heart-to-heart talk, she didn't tell me the truth. Only after the final exams, when she got failing grades in two courses, did she come to her senses. It turned out that when she had participated in a math contest, she had developed an attraction to a boy from another school. The boy wrote to her, proposing that they study together. At first she too thought they could help each other. But with frequent contact, her power of reason could not control the feelings of first love. Nominally the two of them were studying together, but in reality they were distracted, casting glances at each other, to the point where they even would hug each other at his house, and wallow in talking about their love for each other. Study and work naturally went from bad to worse. It is clear that for middle school students to start courting does a lot of harm and no good. The middle school years are a time when you should increase your knowledge and learn some skills. Whatever you do, you shouldn't disperse your energies and waste your time. Afterward it will be too late for regrets.

Sisi: Your mother's advice is correct. You should break off your relationship with him, and clearly explain to him the harm of premature love. I believe that he can understand your reasons and your actions. At the same time, you must inform your parents and teachers, and let them take the necessary measures to protect you, to prevent him from harming you if he becomes overwrought and loses his reason. I believe that you can leap out of the whirlpool of love, and that after this you will treasure your youth for study and work, and go on to even greater achievements. Of course, this will take courage, willpower, and reason, and it will also take some time. I wish you success!

Chen Yi

SOURCE: *Xiandai jiating*, 1 (January 11, 1985), 27.

I Hope You Will Learn a Lesson from My Mistakes

Dear Sisi:

When I read the letter that you wrote to *Modern Family* asking for help, and Teacher Chen Yi's instructions, I was overcome by my feelings and could not calm down for a long time. I will tell you my own bitter lesson; take it as a warning.

When I was fifteen, I was in junior middle school. From childhood I loved to read and liked to play and do sports. But my thinking was too simple, and I didn't understand much about the world. By chance I got to know a boy four years older than I, and he pursued me. I didn't know what to do. Because I didn't have a good relationship with my mother and had no way to discuss it with anyone, I became confused and believed his sweet talk. He often asked me out, and I felt very happy. Later, he invited me over for a meal and took me by force. Then he tricked me again, saying that he would be good to me, would never abandon me, etc. He said that if I didn't keep on seeing him, he would say bad things about me to our classmates and make things hard for me. I was afraid and worried, so I went along with it. After I got pregnant he secretly gave me an abortion, and I almost lost my life. At that time I was bitterly regretful, but again I could not resist his enticements and threats, and could not break free of him. He always said to me, "You are mine. No one else would want you. I'll treat you well," etc. My parents also hated me for letting them down, and often cursed me. There was no way out; I could only go back to him. Later I had a child. I thought that if I had a child he would always be good to me, but to my surprise he just didn't love me. He deceived me, and used me as a tool to vent his animal desires. Once he had had enough he threw me aside and went off, caring only about his own pleasure. He seduced another young woman and arranged for her to have a secret abortion. At that time I still secretly hoped that he would change his views. But he not only didn't change, he intensified his threats, and forced me to yield to him as before. It was only then that I fully understood his evil nature. When I didn't want to submit to him anymore, he invented slanderous stories about me and spread them around, ruined my reputation, and kept me from going to work. I really wanted to die and put an end to it, but I gathered my courage and sued him in People's Court, requesting a just settlement under the law. . . .

Looking at my experience, Sisi, I don't know what you think. Will my lesson cause you to be more careful? I hope that you will concentrate on your studies, and strive for a bright future. Good luck.

Xiao Ming

SOURCE: *Xiandai jiating*, 5 (May 1985), 13.

Worries Brought by Songs on Campus

Innocent, pure high school students raise their clear, melodious children's voices in the classroom, and in unison loudly sing this kind of popular song: "You come to my side, smiling slightly, bringing such worries to me. In my heart is already a 'she,' ah, she came before you to me." How would their parents feel if they heard this?

This scene has become quite common in recent years in our high schools, and even in our elementary schools. As I understand it, the weekly music class in many junior high schools has long since existed in name only, because of a lack of qualified teachers and teaching material. Thus, popular songs have rushed into the breach. The content of these popular songs is all about sweethearts and other such topics. With the aid of modern sound equipment, which is becoming more common every day, these songs have gradually occupied the long-neglected territory of high school and elementary music teaching. School leaders and Youth League cadres, concerned about the present open policy in literature and the arts, want to take charge but don't dare, and so they let matters drift. Young students have always liked to listen to music and to sing, but now good songs suitable for them to sing are really pitifully few. No wonder that, under the "compulsory" education provided by radios, tape recorders, and TV, like "a hungry person who is not choosy about his food," they learn without teachers (*wushi zitong*). As a teacher and a parent, I feel vaguely uneasy about this.

To be sure, we cannot categorically reject popular songs. Among them are some that truly are full of charm, and there is no harm done if adults listen to them in their leisure time. But objectively speaking, a considerable number of today's so-called popular songs are ambiguous, and a small number are even pornographic. These things first originated in Western capitalist society and in the bars and dance halls of Hong Kong and Taiwan. They are full of the howls and moans of decadence, extremely low-class and vulgar. The main purpose of composing and singing them is to provide listeners with sensory stimulation, and thereby to attract business. . . . Junior high school students, whose thinking is hazy and unclear, are imperceptibly influenced by what they hear, see, and sing every day. "Nurtured" by these songs and unable to tell good from bad, as they gradually grow older and mature, their characters will be subtly influenced for the worse. This worries those of us in the parents' generation.

Yan Chengsheng, Yinshan Middle School,
Zizhong county, Sichuan

SOURCE: *Renmin ribao*, December 30, 1985.

My Corruption by Pornographic Publications

By chance I got hold of some hand-copied pornographic reading material. Some of the thinly veiled descriptions in the book caused me, a youth without any defenses, to become more and more involved, and I read it three times in one sitting. After that, on Sundays I would close the door and read it, and when I went to political education class I would stick the hand-copied book in my study material or notebook and read it.

In the process of reading pornographic material over and over again, I became a different person without realizing it. Many strange things happened: at night, as soon as I closed my eyes I would go off into wild flights of fancy; during the day, I had no heart for study or work. I became listless and apathetic, as though in a trance. Before, when I saw a woman I got red in the face, but now I would stare at people and even think about making a move. I became lean and haggard. In order to seek even more stimulation, I went around buying and borrowing more than forty books and magazines dealing with sex, spending more than 70 yuan in less than half a year. Gradually, I went from feeling that sexual knowledge was new and strange to yearning to try it. In the end, that which I had not even dared to think about happened.

One day at dusk, I passed a public women's bathroom and heard someone inside. Immediately I had an evil thought. The obscene plots of the pornographic publications caused me to lose my senses, and I rushed into the women's bathroom. Because a crowd gathered immediately, my crime was prevented.

I am grateful to the Party for patiently educating me. I cannot bear to look back at this crooked path. I have learned that pornographic publications are really spiritual opium that do great harm. Today I have resolved to make my shameful actions public, as a warning to pure young people. Remember my bitter lesson. Don't let yourself be tricked and mess up your youth!

Oral account by Cheng Xuliang,
edited by Xu Tianyou and Xue Xiban

SOURCE: *Zhongguo qingnian bao*, March 21, 1982, 1.

Young Woman, Be Vigilant!

The curtain of night was gently falling, and the number of people walking along the mountain road became fewer. Wei XX, a youth in his twenties, was driving a truck toward the N county seat.

A walking figure appeared in front of the truck, and he sped up to overtake it. Ah! A gentle and graceful young girl! He was unable to restrain a moment of mad glee, and abruptly slammed on the brakes as he reached the young woman's side.

"Hey, miss, where're you going?"

"I'm going to the suburbs of N county seat."

"Hop in—I'm going the same way."

The young girl was secretly delighted. She thought, "My family told me to come home right away. The last bus already left, and I was just worrying about what to do!" So she quickly said, smiling, "Sorry to cause you trouble." Then she climbed up on the running board and into the cab of the truck.

After the young woman sat down in the cab, Wei cast a series of rapacious sidelong glances at her. Unable to restrain the flames of his desire, Wei said teasingly, "Miss, you are really beautiful!" The young woman blushed, but was secretly pleased to hear that she had a beautiful face. The truck turned one corner and then another, the flames of Wei's desire burned more and more fiercely, and finally he stretched his evil right hand toward the young woman's thigh. The young woman instinctively pushed his hand away, and he said brazenly, "Excuse me, I was really attracted by your beautiful face. . . ." The young woman had seen little of the world. Not only did she not become vigilant, she actually felt a little smug at his praise.

Wei began to boast about how he often drove by himself to Guangzhou and Shanghai, about how he was attending TV University (*dianda*) and had also published several articles in the press. Surprisingly, the young woman was fascinated by his nonsense, and began to look up to him.

In a deserted spot on the mountain road, he stopped and said, "The truck's broken down." Then he made a great show of fixing it. The young woman, still in the dark, believed he was telling the truth, and so she handed him first the pliers and then the wrench. But he was seeking an opportunity to hatch a sinister plot. Just as he was about to commit a crime, a jeep drove by in front and disrupted his actions. After that several people passed by on foot, and so he had no choice but to be patient and wait. The next time he was about to make a move, another truck drove by, and he had to restrain his evil thoughts temporarily. After fiddling with the truck for a while, he said to the young woman, "It's fixed." The young woman once again climbed into the cab.

When the truck reached the county seat, it was already seven o'clock in the evening. He politely told the young woman, "It's already late. Let's have dinner together, and then I'll see you off." The young woman didn't know this was a ruse and agreed. He ordered food and liquor, and the two of them sat down to eat. When the young woman saw how sincere and attentive he was, she drank one cup of wine after another. How could she imagine that she might meet with misfortune? He poured her one glass of wine after another, and gradually she got drunk. Thereupon he rapidly dragged her to a concealed place in the backyard of the warehouse, like a hungry wolf pouncing on a sheep. Just as he was giving vent to his animal instincts, he was discovered by the warehouse night patrol, and seized on the spot. At that point the young woman woke from her drunken stupor and shed bitter tears, regret mingling with self-reproach. But how could beating her breast and stamping her feet bring back her maidenly virginity?

Young women friends, by all means be vigilant! Don't let your capacity for clear thinking be muddled by sweet talk. Don't be tricked because you hanker after convenience and petty gains!

Chen Huoxiang and Lin Jun

SOURCE: *Yuelao bao*, 7 (July 1985), 6.

3

Making a Friend: Changing Patterns of Courtship

Courtship in China, usually referred to with the euphemism "making a friend," became visible to foreigners in the 1980's. Tourists often returned from Mao's China wondering about the hidden rituals of love and marriage. But in the post-Mao era, returning Americans were more likely to comment on the hundreds of people lined up two by two in the evening along the Bund in Shanghai, or the amorous couples hidden behind every bush in Beijing's Purple Bamboo Park. The change in courtship patterns was not entirely in the eye of the beholder. Young Chinese in the 1980's became more public in their displays of affection, reflecting a general liberalization in public mores with the end of the Cultural Revolution. This liberalization extended beyond daily street behavior to the realm of public discussion in the Chinese press.

Courtship, love, and marriage in 1980's China were probably talked about more, and agreed about less, than at any time since the May Fourth Movement of 1919. The discussion was no longer limited to daring intellectuals and students, as it had been during the May Fourth era. It extended to most sectors of the urban population, and on some issues to the countryside as well.

The discussion included a wide range of issues: the role of the matchmaker, parental participation in the choice of a partner, the problem of finding a mate appropriate to one's social status, the emotional perils of courtship, and even sex and the public parks. Conflicting sets of priorities—economic, emotional, and social—made these issues every bit as confusing as they are in the West, though for somewhat different reasons. Some conflicts resulted from generational differences, as young people moved toward more control over their own marriage choice. The issues that the Chinese reading public found most troubling, however—changing marital criteria, growing numbers of single people, and premarital sex—reflected differences in gender as well as generation. Men and women brought divergent expectations to courtship and faced differing perils in concluding a successful match.

Courtship as a Community Affair

Before Liberation (the Chinese term for the 1949 revolution), when marriage was unambiguously an alliance between families, the match-maker or go-between had a crucial role to play. It was her job (matchmaking was generally a female occupation) to unite couples whose economic and social status were compatible, to check discreetly but thoroughly on the character of the groom and the beauty of the bride (or her capacity for hard work if the family she would be marrying into was poor). It was not considered necessary for the matchmaker to arrange for the couple to meet, much less to concern herself with sticky questions of emotional compatibility. Whether the matchmaker was a professional or a friend or relative of the family, her responsibilities were clear. If she was successful she could expect a material reward.

In the decades after the revolution of 1949, this practice began to change. By the post-Mao period, marriage in urban China was no longer an arrangement between families, based upon economic and social alliances that took little account of the personal preferences of the young couple. The right to choose one's own spouse was guaranteed by the Marriage Law of 1950, although in the 1980's, more than thirty years after the law was first passed, it was still often flouted (see below, "Parental Participation"). Since it was a widely shared assumption that everyone would marry, finding the proper spouse was a major concern of young people in their early and mid-twenties.

Yet more than thirty years after the Marriage Law guaranteed the right to find one's own lifetime partner, the role of the matchmaker was still crucial. To some extent the continuing activity of matchmakers bespoke a society in which members of the opposite sex still found it extremely difficult to meet or interact casually. From grammar school on, powerful cultural factors constrained male-female interaction.

Among the many cultural constraints was the fear of gossip among classmates or co-workers. Students might be interested in each other at age sixteen or even younger, but they were well aware that people who gave open expression to such interests at that age were regarded as "hooligans." The restraint required of schoolgirls was particularly pronounced. They were expected to deny any interest in affairs of the heart, and to react with appropriate embarrassment or even disgust when the subject was broached. Failure to rebuff the advances of boys, as discussed in the previous chapter, often led to censure from parents and teachers. Some groups of young people, like university students, were discouraged by the school authorities from courting and forbidden to marry while they were in school.

Yet as young people approached the socially appropriate age for marriage, new behavior was expected of them; thus the same authorities publicly lamented their inexplicable shyness and lack of social skills in dealing with the opposite sex. Even the more socially adept young men and women found few opportunities to meet eligible mates. Some were lucky enough to experience what was called "same window love"—that is, to find a partner in their place of work. An increasingly common phenomenon in Chinese factories, "same window love" gave young people the opportunity to become acquainted slowly, rather than making snap judgments about a prospective spouse on the basis of superficial characteristics. But commentators pointed out that courtship on the job also distracted young people from their work, and contributed to a complicated and ingrown social atmosphere in the workplace. Ultimately, they hoped that young people could be given more occasions to meet one another outside of work.[1]

Given the paucity of such opportunities for social contact, however, matchmakers continued to play a role in bringing young people together. A survey of people married in 1982 in Beijing showed that 60 percent of them had been introduced by matchmakers.[2] No longer commissioned explicitly by the family, these new-style matchmakers were motivated by friendship with one of the parties, a long-standing relationship with the family, or a public-spirited sense of duty. Some simply brought young people together informally by introducing neighbors, relatives, and friends. Others helped to direct the work of the Communist Youth League, and they regarded matchmaking not as a remnant of feudal marriage, but as a type of political work, a natural extension of their concern for the well-being of youth. Their zeal was endorsed by the highest echelons of Chinese officialdom. Disturbed by the increasing numbers of people over thirty who failed to find spouses (see below, "Old Maids"), Communist Party Secretary Hu Yaobang and ranking economic planner Chen Yun in 1984 encouraged Party, women's, and workers' organizations to assist young people with marriage introductions.[3] With the enthusiasm formerly reserved for political campaigns, local newspapers established prizes for outstanding matchmakers, reporting the accomplishments of successful go-betweens in language reminiscent of that describing model workers. One sixty-year-old woman, for instance, was praised because she made tireless efforts to pair people up, ignoring her own frail health and forgoing sleep as she worried over particular matches.[4]

Like all political work, matchmaking required both a correct attitude and a certain amount of skill. When a Youth League cadre wrote to *China Youth News* in 1981, asking for advice on how to be a good matchmaker, the answer made it clear that she should strive to be sensitive to questions of emotional compatibility, as well as concerned with questions of status and economics. She was first directed to investigate the character of both parties: their levels of learning, morals, temperament, family circumstances, previous romantic experience, and criteria for choosing a mate. If she felt that all these elements were compatible, then she should describe each person to the other, neither exaggerating their good points nor concealing their weak points.

Her next responsibility should be to set up a meeting for the couple, help them start up a conversation, and remind them to exchange phone numbers and addresses. When the meeting was over, she should talk to each party separately and, if they liked each other, should help them arrange further meetings. If either one or both had no interest in pursuing the matter, she must explain the situation clearly to both of them.

But her responsibilities did not end there. "You must also help both parties establish the correct view of love and marriage," the editors told her. "Remind them that only beauty of the soul can bring long-term happiness. Some people go after material enjoyment; help them recognize true love. . . . If they run into interference from family or society, help them find ways to deal with it. If one of them is too picky, urge that one to see the 'big picture.'" If they did decide to get married, the article concluded, the matchmaker should urge them to have a simple wedding and not waste money (though it is unclear how many matchmakers actually became involved in such decisions).[5]

In short, a good matchmaker should both promote the Party line on marriage (free choice, frugality, high ideals), and involve herself in questions of personal preference and compatibility. Although most matchmakers still stuck to the old role of matching economic and social status, it was considered progressive to attend to these other criteria as well.

Finding a mate was still a community affair in the 1980's, but the scope of the community had broadened beyond the immediate circle of family and neighbors. The matchmaking efforts of relatives and friends were supplemented by a variety of institutions. In some factories and offices, Youth League cadres took the initiative in organizing cultural activities at which young people could meet one another.[6] The Communist Youth League and Women's Federation in one innovative township even published an advertisement in a national magazine, promising preferential treatment in work assignments to women who married any of the township's 178 aging bachelors (that is, men older than twenty-six).[7] But as early as 1980, letters to newspapers in various parts of China began to suggest that the government establish institutions devoted exclusively to matchmaking. After all, one letter commented, the main duty of communes and factories should be production, not introduction.[8]

By the end of 1980, marriage introduction bureaus (*hunyin jieshaosuo*) had opened in Shanghai, Beijing, Tianjin, and a number of smaller cities. By 1984 they numbered fifty-three. These bureaus were sponsored locally by the municipal government, and run by the unions, the Communist Youth League, and the Women's Federation. Additional bureaus were established by umbrella economic organizations such as the Tianjin Textile Bureau. Their money came from the social welfare funds of the city government, and those who used the bureaus' services paid only a small registration fee.[9]

Although the bureaus set no formal limits on who could use their services, their main clientele comprised people in their late twenties or older who had not yet made a successful match. Each marriage introduction bureau developed its own procedures. Usually people were required to fill out a sheet giving information about their background and indicating the characteristics they desired in a mate. Then the bureau staff would adopt various means to match people up. One Beijing bureau, for instance, filed the registration forms by sex and age. Three days a week, women who had registered were permitted to read the men's applications, and to write down their registration numbers on the cards of men whose files appealed to them. On the other three working days, men were allowed access to the files, but were only allowed to read the applications of women who had expressed interest in them (no reason was given for this difference in procedure). The bureau staff arranged meetings for aspiring couples; after three such introductions, a person was required to fill out a new application and pay a new fee.[10]

The marriage introduction bureaus were given a rousing public welcome. A few days after the Tianjin office opened, the local newspaper printed a plea that young men stop loitering outside the door of the bureau hoping to catch glimpses of eligible young women entering to fill out their applications. If this behavior continued, the paper warned, it would be necessary to set up two offices—one where men could register, and one for women. Enthusiastic factory managers in Tianjin registered their entire cohort of young workers for introductions, while bureau cadres in Guilin took registration forms to young women who were too embarrassed to come to the office.[11]

As they gained matchmaking experience, the more innovative bureaus expanded their activities from simple introductions to organized social events where young people could make one another's acquaintance in a relaxed atmosphere. Institutes in Beijing sponsored day trips to the Great

Wall and New Year's parties. On these occasions, staff members stationed themselves at strategic points to make introductions of young people who expressed interest in one another.[12] A Beijing organization even provided a computer at one such mixer; it could match someone with several marriage prospects in a matter of seconds.[13] *Family* (Jiating) magazine reported on a party for older singles sponsored by a subsidiary of the Guangzhou People's Radio. The evening began with a trivia contest organized to break the ice. Seating was arranged at each table by the participants' age and marital criteria. Hosts circulated, asking questions designed to help people get to know one another, such as "If you only had ten dollars and your mother's birthday and a friend's wedding were both coming up, what would you do with the money?" and "What would you women say if a friend came to you and asked if she should keep seeing a man only four inches taller than she was?" Each of the hundred people who attended was issued a list of the names, ages, and occupations of all participants, to facilitate individual followups.[14]

At a national conference in 1985, bureau representatives agreed that their future work should concentrate on expanding such social activities and sponsoring ongoing groups for young people with common interests. A Guangzhou representative recounted the success of the local bureau in organizing parties, cultural groups, day trips, and even poker parties.[15] Only by broadening the social circle of young people, several analysts argued, could the bureaus change the prevailing social practice of choosing a marriage partner on the basis of a rigid set of predefined material criteria rather than mutual understanding and affection.[16]

Initially, the marriage introduction bureaus seemed to promise a modicum of success in helping young people who had difficulty finding spouses. Between October 1980 and October 1981, more than 12,000 young men and women registered at Beijing's six bureaus. Of these, *China Youth News* reported hopefully in 1981, more than 600 couples were now dating, and 150 couples had already married.[17] But several years of operation did not result in a rising rate of nuptials. A 1984 report found that nationwide, the bureaus had handled 120,000 registrations, with a success rate (that is, a marriage rate) of about 10 percent.[18] But other investigations found success rates of between 2 and 3 percent, and potential success rates (people currently in love as a percentage of registrants) of about 20 percent.[19]

Commentators offered a variety of explanations, some of them contradictory, for the mixed performance of the bureaus. Inadequate funds, personnel, and office space were all cited as constraints. Some critics called for increased government support, whereas others stressed the need for the Youth League and workplaces to take on part of the burden of organizing social activities introducing young people. Some commentators felt that the bureaus were not given enough publicity. But others argued that the problem was unbalanced media coverage that dwelt on success stories, encouraging a flood of applicants that the bureaus could not handle. Bureau workers, observers agreed, needed to be trained in psychology and not depend only on their enthusiasm for making matches.[20] But even the best-trained matchmaker could not be expected to solve all of the problems caused by demographic squeeze and applicants whose standards were too high to be met by the available pool of young people (see below, "Marital Criteria").[21]

Young people themselves voiced additional criticisms of the bureaus. In Shanghai, several hundred youths began to organize what they called "spontaneous marriage introduction bureaus" in local parks, meeting several times a week to listen to music, talk, go boating, and play badminton. Park authorities and the police complained that they were obstructing traffic, disrupting social order, and attracting hooligans. But they replied that they had taken their social activities to the streets because the official bureaus were expensive, their activities often short-lived and uncomfortably stilted. One young man interviewed at a "spontaneous bureau" ruefully described his attendance at an official mixer:

Each of us took a form and filled in our name, work unit, education, income, housing, etc. Several dozen young men and women were admitted with this form. As the activity began, if you saw someone you liked, you handed over your form. If the other party was interested, then she gave you her form to look at. If both parties were interested, they sat down to talk, the bureau staff stapled your two forms together, and the "pairing up" was regarded as complete.

The situation that day made one unsure whether to laugh or to cry. The beautiful girls were surrounded by young men who handed over their forms one after another. The surrounded girls found themselves in an intolerable predicament, and some were so scared that they simply fled. It was calmer around the average-looking girls, but the plain ones were left out in the cold—no one cared to ask about them. Quite a few people went there full of enthusiasm and had cold water poured on their hopes.

These young people expressed their determination to continue meeting until the authorities established a regular place, perhaps a designated section of an urban park, where they could go to enjoy social activities and meet other eligible singles.[22] Meanwhile, in spite of their shortcomings, the marriage introduction bureaus provided a service that many young people felt they needed, at least until such time as society could provide them with more natural ways to meet.

Another matchmaking effort with official endorsement was the publication of personal advertisements in national magazines, under the head-ing "Marriage Solicitation Announcements" or "Magpie Bridge" (named for a legendary bridge of birds that spanned the sky and enabled two lovers to meet). Personals began to appear in the mid-1980's in staid government publications like *Chinese Women* as well as semi-official tabloids. A typical personal ad gave the applicant's gender, age, height, marital status (never married, divorced), health, a stock phrase or two describing appearance, level of education, occupation, and occasionally income level or hobbies. It then briefly described the qualities sought in a mate. Women usually specified the height and occupation they looked for in men:

Female, 33, unmarried, 1.69 meters tall, healthy, college graduate, at present a college English teacher, regular appearance, refined and sedate. Conditions for making a friend are: honest and upright, healthy, college level education, taller than 1.7 meters, under 40, engaged in scientific and technical, cultural, or educational work in this city (Beijing).[23]

Some women put forward extremely exacting requirements, then hinted at their willingness to negotiate:

Woman teacher in middle school in Chengdu, Sichuan, 27, 1.52 meters tall, healthy, cheerful disposition, honest, wants to give her love to a frontier guard defending the highlands or the Gobi Desert. Required conditions: an unmarried soldier (cadre) on active duty, about 30 years old, about 1.6 meters tall, possessing a junior middle school education, who likes to study and is honest. If it is a comrade working in the vicinity, no limitation as to type of work.[24]

Men, on the other hand, spent more time describing desirable female personality traits, seldom mentioning occupation or education:

My nephew, 31, unmarried, regular features, healthy, upper middle school graduate, works as fourth-grade fitter, loves literature. Desires to seek as a close friend an unmarried woman, with regular features, about 1.6 meters, suitable age, gentle and good, cultured, healthy, with urban residence registration, no restriction as to district, nationality [i.e., ethnic group], or whether employed or unemployed.[25]

Although the tone of the personals was usually matter-of-fact, occasionally an applicant would wax poetic:

Qiumin, female, 34, 1.57 meters tall, unmarried graduate of institution of higher education, with rather good literary abilities, at present a government cadre in Beijing. She is lively and cheerful, gentle-sounding (*yinyun wenrou*). Contained within her dignified appearance is a blazing, intense emotion. She possesses the pure, candid temperament of a young girl. Desires to seek as companion a cadre, scientific researcher, or army cadre working in Beijing, of good character, healthy, unmarried, under 40, taller than 1.65 meters, of straightforward and good-natured disposition, with a high school degree or better.[26]

Men could be lyrical as well:

I am 25, unmarried, a junior middle school teacher of Chinese, over 1.6 meters tall, healthy, industrious, and plain, like to inquire into all branches of knowledge, possess masculine beauty. At the age of 18 entered into a happy marriage with literature, and at present have published items in nine national publications. Dear girl, if you are under 27, no matter how far apart we are, or whether your heart has been wounded, I will truly love and respect you. Hand in hand, let us build a new life! Those interested, please converse by letter.[27]

Like the marriage introduction bureaus, personals were often a method of last resort for people in their late twenties or older who had difficulty making a match through conventional channels. Far more men than women placed ads, indicating both that more men had difficulty finding mates and that women were more reluctant to publicly solicit marriage partners.[28] A practiced reader of the personals could usually discern the reason an individual had been unsuccessful elsewhere. Many of the men had some physical infirmity: they were partially deaf, had eye trouble, were disabled in one leg, had lost fingers in a work accident, been disabled by polio, or had facial burn scars.[29] Another category of men who had touble finding wives were those with low salaries, like rural schoolteachers, or those from poor districts, like this frank young man: "Because my school is located in a remote mountain district, I have not yet found a girlfriend. This year I am 26. I wish to seek as my wife an honest and upright girl whose all-round demands are not too exacting, and who has an urban residence registration card."[30] Some men expressed their willingness to wed divorcées with children, or slightly disabled women. The women who placed personals, on the other hand, usually had difficulty marrying because they had a high level of education, filled a work position of unusual responsibility, set exacting requirements, or were considered too tall or too old. In general, the men who placed personals would not have considered marriage with the women who did so, and vice versa.

The gender mismatch in marital criteria must have affected the success rate of the personals, yet the demand for the ads was great. Unlike the bureaus, personals drew from a nationwide pool of singles. Compared to other matchmaking efforts, they had two additional advantages: they enabled interested parties to contact each other quickly and without intermediaries, and they preserved the privacy of such contacts.[31] Although the fee for one-time publication could be as much as 20 yuan,[32] half a month's salary for beginning workers, the magazines were inundated with ads. By February 1985, *Chinese Women* had such a backlog of unpublished personals that the editors gave notice they would accept no more until July. In June they announced their intention to get out of the business altogether, because the volume of mail was exhausting their staff. They also asked that young people stop writing, phoning, and visiting their offices to importune a staff member who had offered to act as an intermediary for young couples but now found that her health was being ruined by the rigors of the work.[33] In addition to their normal editorial tasks, members of the magazine staffs had to verify work or residence identification from each person placing an ad, in order to prevent people from using the personals column for fraudulent purposes.[34]

In spite of this safeguard, one critic warned, people who replied to personals ran several risks. First, someone placing an ad could use the replies he received as an opportunity to "dally with women." Second, many people replying to the ads were so eager to find a mate that they revealed intimate details of their history unknown even to their own parents. This, too, could lead to their being "insulted" (a euphemism for seduced) and harmed. Third, the person placing the ad often had as many as one hundred replies to choose from. Pursuing several prospects at once could lead to conflicts. Although this critic did not explicitly say so, his choice of language made it clear that in all these respects, women were more vulnerable than men.[35]

Like the marriage introduction bureaus, personals were criticized for treating people as commodities, and encouraging marital decisions based on superficial knowledge of characteristics rather than in-depth knowledge of character.[36] Yet they were also touted as a move toward more individual control over marriage choice.[37] Most Chinese commentators hoped that as society created more opportunities for people to meet one another directly, the need for private and state-sponsored matchmaking would diminish.

Parental Participation in Marriage Choice

In spite of the increasing social opportunities for young men and women to meet one another, sometimes the right to choose a mate was itself an issue. Before 1949 most marriages had been arranged by parents. Although youthful cultural rebels challenged parental authority over marriage as early as the May Fourth Movement of 1919, their rebellion affected only a tiny minority of elite city dwellers. In 1950, the Marriage Law promulgated by the government of the People's Republic extended freedom of marriage choice to the countryside, but the law proved difficult and sometimes even dangerous to enforce because of widespread resistance.[38] The Marriage Law of 1980 reiterated that marriage must be completely voluntary, with no third-party interference.[39] Nevertheless, well into the 1980's parents usually participated in the marriage decisions of their children, and their right to do so, while not guaranteed by law, was accepted by many young people in both city and countryside. A sociological survey released in 1986 asserted that nationwide, only about 30 percent of all marriages were fully free of family influence. Fifteen percent were arranged outright, a common practice in rural areas. Another 55 percent were "half-free," that is, marriages in which families played an important role.[40]

In 1980's China, it was still widely expected that children would listen to the opinions of their parents and let parents arrange introductions for them.[41] In many urban families, parents took the initiative in arranging matches for children who were too shy or socially inexperienced to meet partners on their own, but who felt that they had reached the correct age for marriage and should "solve their personal problem," as finding a spouse was called. Participation became interference only when a young person opposed the choice of mate made by the parents.[42] Even if a young person found his or her own match, parents often held informal veto power. The parents of one woman university student we knew, for instance, dismissed a prospective spouse because he was in the merchant marine and would not be home for long periods of time. Our friend did not regard this as parental interference, but as a natural expression of her parents' concern for her future happiness. Interference usually came to the attention of the state and the press only when it turned violent, or led to the suicide of one of the young people concerned.[43]

In the early 1980's, a number of articles about parental interference in marriage choice were published as part of a campaign to publicize the new Marriage Law. The usual pattern in these cases was that parents wanted their children to choose a spouse on the basis of family political or economic background, whereas the children held out for a marriage based on love. Press commentators objected to two aspects of parental behavior: desire to use marriage to gain political or material advantage, and interference with freedom of choice as guaranteed by law.

Parents who obstructed marriages for political reasons came in for particularly thorough criticism in these articles. The most famous urban case of parental interference involved a young woman named Sun Jing, a typist in the city of Baoji, Shaanxi province. When she decided in the late 1970's to marry literary worker Shang Ziqin, her father, Sun Linsheng, objected vehemently. His reason: Shang's father was a former member of the Guomindang, the ruling party defeated in the 1949 revolution. Although Shang's father was long since dead, Sun Linsheng felt that the son of a counterrevolutionary must himself be politically suspect. He called his daughter a "traitor to the poor peasants," turned her siblings against her by telling them that she would ruin their chances to obtain a security clearance, and threw her out of the house. Still not satisfied, he plastered her workplace with posters denouncing her as a "wild chicken" and a "broken shoe," two epithets for prostitute. Not deterred, Sun Jing married Shang in 1978. For the next two years, her father continued to harass her, causing scenes at her workplace and attacking her on the street, until in desperation she wrote to *Chinese Women*, the magazine of the Women's Federation, asking for official help in getting her father to leave her alone.[44] Eight months later she wrote again, expressing her feeling of despair and threatening suicide if her situation did not improve.[45]

The Women's Federation eventually conducted two investigations of Sun Jing's case. It found no basis for the father's many accusations that his daughter's actions were immoral. Further, it found that Sun Linsheng had used his status as a Party member and head of the district cultural and education bureau to pursue his vendetta. Contacting an old classmate in the city construction bureau where his daughter worked, he had been successful in blocking her promotion.[46]

Chinese Women ran an open forum on Sun Jing's case for four consecutive months in 1980–81. Readers of the magazine, as well as officials involved in the case, pointed to several crucial problems highlighted by her situation. First, they criticized Sun Linsheng's interference as an example of "feudal patriarchy"; that is, he saw his daughter's marriage as a way to enhance his personal power and regarded her as his private property to dispose of as he pleased. Second, they faulted him for "upholding the theory of blood lineage" in blaming Shang for the political sins of his father. Though such thinking had been common during the Cultural Revolution, one reader commented, Sun had no excuse to think that way four years after the fall of the Gang of Four. If Sun Linsheng judged a man on the basis of his class background, another wondered, how could he help the Party work together with people who were not Party members, much less help bring about the reunification of the mainland with non-Communist Taiwan? Third, readers censured him for his belief that the daughter of a cadre should only marry someone from a similar background—a viewpoint that betrayed his feeling of superiority to ordinary families. Finally, readers castigated him for using his official connections to persecute his daughter, and reproached other officials for either actively assisting him or looking the other way. All these attitudes were characterized as remnants of feudal thinking.[47] Conversely, the struggle of young people for freedom of marriage was praised as an officially sanctioned assault on such thinking and on the social relationships that supported it.[48]

Under mounting pressure from Party and Women's Federation authorities, and under fire at his own place of work, Sun Linsheng finally admitted he was in the wrong and ceased harassing his daughter. Sun Jing and her husband expressed their gratitude to the Party and their belief that young people in their situation should fight back, not commit suicide.[49] But in cases that received less official attention, suicide was not an uncommon dénouement. A rural couple from Baodi county in Hebei province, for example, committed a dramatic double suicide in 1977 when their families opposed their marriage because the woman was from an ex-landlord family. As with Sun Jing's situation, press coverage of the case devoted a great deal of attention to criticizing the political atmosphere of the Cultural Revolution, in which family political background was considered more important than personal character.[50] The pervasiveness of such thinking was portrayed as a tragic and wrongheaded mistake that had already cost the nation a great deal and was still destroying its young people. In this context, freedom from parental control of marriage choice was linked not only to the elimination of feudal remnants but to repudiation of the Cultural Revolution, and by implication to the creation of a sphere of private life detached from national politics.

Even as the political practices of the Cultural Revolution faded and marriage choice became depoliticized, parents continued to intervene in the marriages of their children for economic reasons. In a 1981 Tianjin case, for instance, the parents of Liu Fengmei opposed her romance with Zhang Baoyi because his family was poor and he was not handsome enough. Later he got a job with the Tianjin sea transport company, brought back gifts from abroad, and won her parents over. But after the couple became engaged, the parents again grew dissatisfied with the match. They beat their daughter, on one occasion hitting her on the head with a chamber pot, and physically attacked her fiancée as well. Liu moved out of her parents' home and successfully brought a legal complaint against them for interfering with her freedom of marriage.[51] But not all young women were so resourceful or so lucky; many officials were reluctant to intervene in what they saw as domestic disputes, particularly if it meant taking a stand against the parents.[52]

Some of the advice literature in the 1980's press instructed young people on how to deal correctly with parental interference. Most parents were motivated by genuine concern for their children, one 1986 article argued, and children should listen to them and heed whatever was rational in their arguments. But some parents paid too much attention to economic and social advantages in making a match for their children.[53] Others, having grown up in another generation, did not understand the desire of young people for free choice. They were also unwilling to admit mistakes to their children, and were sensitive to outside social opinion. One writer advised young people to exploit this last characteristic by mobilizing respected elders—grandparents, other relatives, Party and workplace cadres, Women's Federation workers—to intercede with parents.[54] Another approved technique was to quietly win over the parents or future in-laws by displaying the model qualities of a prospective spouse. One widowed mother, for example, initially feared that her son's girlfriend was "too capable" at her job and would not be a devoted wife and daughter-in-law. She relented when the young woman exhibited continuing concern for both mother and son.[55] If all else failed, young people were encouraged to rely on the law to win freedom of marriage. Since the legal system was growing stronger and more effective every day, they were told, there was no need to resort to suicide or to violence against others.[56] Young people were encouraged to emulate the example of the musicians Clara and Robert Schumann, who brought several legal suits to gain the right to marry despite the opposition of Clara's father.[57]

Parents, too, were offered advice in the press. An article in *Modern Family* (Xiandai jiating) commented that sensible parents did not interfere with marriage choice on the basis of economic status. However, because of their greater experience, they were apt to foresee problems of incompatibility that their lovestruck progeny could not. If they pressured their sons and daughters, the article warned, they might actually drive them closer to the objectionable mate. Far better to keep their misgivings to themselves, be polite, and wait for their daughter to realize that her boyfriend was a spendthrift and an indifferent student.[58] Such articles looked ahead to the time when the cruder manifestations of parental interference would wither away, to be replaced by subtler, more modern forms of guidance.

This advice was basically directed at an urban readership; it had little relevance to marriage practices in the Chinese countryside. Rural parents continued after 1949 to play a larger role in their children's choice of partners than did urban parents, reflecting the more conservative social mores and slower pace of change in the countryside. Where urban parents might object, even violently, to choices made by their children, rural parents often arranged their children's marriages outright. The 1980's press reported extensively on abuses of this parental authority. Parents were found, for example, marrying off their daughters in payment of debts to the groom's family, refusing to allow their daughters to marry into a rival lineage, opposing matches with exemplary young men from poorer households, and promoting marriage between first cousins, in violation of the law. Mothers as well as fathers took an active role in forcing their wishes upon their often unwilling progeny.[59] None of these practices was new. They showed the persistence of attitudes, on the part of officials as well as parents, that often made rural marriage choice a matter of parental fiat.

In addition, alarmed observers of the 1980's rural scene began to report disturbing dimensions in parental control of marriage. In the villages, they said, childhood engagements, early marriage, child daughters-in-law, and "exchanging relatives"—all common pre-1949 practices—were beginning to reappear in force. In one Guizhou village, a 1985 investigation revealed that twenty-nine of the village's thirty-two young women had been engaged by their parents during childhood, some as early as the age of one.[60] Many of these women must have become engaged well before the 1980's, giving rise to the suspicion that such practices never disappeared in remote rural areas after 1949, but were ignored in public discussion. The Women's Federation in a rural Fujian county found in 1984 that 80 percent of all children born between 1974 and 1978, and 20 percent of those born after 1979, were already engaged.[61] A Gansu man who returned to his home village at Spring Festival in 1983 discovered that most marriages taking place at that season involved people who had not yet reached the minimum legal marriage age (twenty for women, twenty-two for men).[62] Marriages of women in their mid-teens were reported on the rise in rural areas, with brides as young as twelve in some locales.[63]

The reappearance of these practices, explicitly illegal since 1950, was related to the rural economic reforms of the 1980's. The reforms replaced collectivized farming with a system in which families contracted to farm the land on a household basis. This had several immediate effects: rural prosperity increased, heads of household obtained more control over the labor power of family members, and families with more labor power began to employ it in a number of lucrative entrepreneurial ways. In short, the reforms expanded the economic functions of the rural family, enhanced the authority of the household head, and indirectly promoted the return of a traditional preference for large families, in spite of a state birth control policy that mandated fewer children.[64] At least one article linked the resurgence of early engagement and marriage to the desire of rural families to find brides for their sons and produce grandsons as soon as possible,[65] a practice that would increase the household's total labor pool. Although the full effects of the reforms on rural marriage are as yet unclear, the desire to procure spouses for one's children early apparently contributed to an increasingly competitive marriage market in the countryside. Rural parents told investigators that it was their duty to arrange marriages for their children, and that if they did not do so well before their offspring reached marriageable age, the children would not be able to find mates. Young women likewise felt that waiting until age twenty-one or twenty-two would make them undesirable partners.[66]

If some households promoted early betrothal and marriages because they wanted more male children, others did so in order to divest themselves of unwanted daughters. A 1983 report decried the reappearance of "disguised child brides," a practice in which four- and five-year-old girls were sent to live with a boy's family, with the intention of marrying the two as soon as they came of age (sooner if possible). This arrangement had been common before 1949.[67] As in pre-Liberation times, in the 1980's the practice was called "adopting a daughter." But in actuality the girls were "little daughters-in-law," expected to "handle heavy household duties in the house of their mother-in-law."[68] Parents who disposed of their daughters in this way could then try to give birth to sons. Parents of sons, on the other hand, saved the considerable brideprice they would have to pay if they waited until the girl grew up.

Another traditional way to avoid brideprice in the 1980's countryside was to "exchange relatives"—that is, to marry the daughter and son of one family to the son and daughter of another. In such cases the families merely had to pay the cost of a banquet and household equipment; they saved the brideprice. Many other families married off daughters to the highest bidder in order to make enough money to pay for wives for their sons. For hard-pressed rural households, this was one way to cope with the rising cost of brides (see Chapters 4 and 8).[69] Young women who resisted the strategy were often ill-treated, and some chose suicide rather than comply.[70]

Needless to say, all these practices involved near-absolute control by parents over the marital choices of their children. One young rural woman complained in a letter to a women's magazine that teenaged girls who wanted to pick their own partners were objects of social ridicule. Parents and matchmakers made the arrangements, and local rural authorities declined to interest themselves in the question of freedom of marriage.[71] Ironically, it appeared that one of the unintended side effects of the rural reforms was to give new support to assorted "feudal remnant" marriage practices. Ensuring that rural marriage was free from parental control was of concern to the state for several reasons. First and most obvious, parental interference violated the Marriage Law, one of the state's major attempts to guarantee equality for women. Perhaps even more important to the state, parental control generally resulted in early, arranged, reproduction-oriented marriages. Compared with city practices, one commentator noted, these marriages shortened the period of time a generation took to reproduce itself by almost a decade. This, of course, increased the rate of population growth.[72] In such marriages, family interests prevailed not only over individual choice, but over state family planning policy. The state interest in free-choice marriage was formed not only by an abstract commitment to women's rights, but by a desire to break the cycle of family-controlled marriage with its early and uncontrolled reproduction. State concern resulted not only in growing press coverage of rural parental interference in the 1980's, but in pressure on local Party and Women's Federation cadres, and on the legal system, to combat such practices.[73]

Marital Criteria: In Search of Happily Ever After

Young people in 1980's China came to their quest for a mate armed with criteria from a variety of sources. Beginning in the late 1970's, an unprecedented outpouring of films and fictional works explored the theme of love. Even the advice columnists of *China Youth News* waxed eloquent on the subject, referring to love as a "complex and delicate feeling" and urging young people to seek a mate with shared ideals, commitment to work, common hobbies, and compatible temperament.[74] A 1983 survey of a thousand young workers in nine factories found that in choosing a partner, the vast majority valued quality of thought, compatible disposition, and common goals as the most important factors.[75]

Yet the same young workers who expressed their desire for shared goals and temperament commented that what they saw happening around them in society was quite different.[76] Common ideals were not the whole story; economic and social considerations were very much present when young Chinese began courting. In a society where changing residence or jobs was extremely difficult, marriage offered a unique opportunity to improve one's living quarters or enhance one's social status. Through the end of the Cultural Revolution, the most reliable way to attain this goal was to find a mate of good class background, preferably one with ties to officialdom.[77] But with the economic reforms and changing political climate of the 1980's, concern with political criteria waned. Some young people filling out applications at marriage introduction bureaus noted specifically that they were not interested in Party members, because they were "seeking a mate in order to live, not in order to make class struggle."[78] Attitudes that formerly had been celebrated as politically correct also fell into disfavor. In the Henan countryside, it was reported that several women had turned down marriage offers from a man who spent too much of his time doing good deeds for others; they feared that he would not devote all his energy to the welfare of his family.[79] Scrutiny of political status and attitudes was supplanted by attention to occupation, educational level, and income of a potential spouse, as well as the economic and social status of his or her family—criteria similar to those of pre-1949 China. In the 1980's, attempts to match the individual and family backgrounds of the couple, and to gain maximum material advantage for each party, competed with and often overshadowed emotional considerations.[80]

Marital Materialism

The tendency to tie "love" to more mundane considerations was summed up in two cartoons in *China Youth News*. The first pictured a young man carrying a slip of paper which read "three-part melody." He was leaping from one circle to the next: the first was labeled "good work unit," the second "good job," and the third "good woman." It was necessary to pass through the first two steps to get to the third.[81] The second cartoon was even more explicit. Two men inspected a dollar bill through a magnifying glass.

> A: Do you know who that person on the dollar bill is?
> B: I don't know.
> A: That's my matchmaker. My love affair with my girlfriend depends completely on him![82]

One reflection of the materialistic rider on courtship was that certain occupational groups, long considered pariahs, continued to have trouble finding mates. Nobody wanted to marry a street-cleaner, for instance, a mortician, a coal miner, or a woman pedicurist in the public baths.[83] None of these groups was highly paid; more important, all performed work that was dirty, dangerous, or popularly regarded as demeaning. Though these workers may well have had problems in courtship throughout the postrevolutionary period, it was only in the 1980's that their plight was made public. But news reports that praised a woman university graduate who married a coal miner, or extolled the contribution of pedicurists to the public good, apparently did little to ameliorate their difficulties.[84] And in a nation that had long taken as its heroes the worker, the peasant, and the soldier, many women factory workers hoped to marry someone who was "more than a worker,"[85] while the desire of men from the countryside to marry—or remarry—into the city caused several major social scandals in the Chinese press in the 1980's.

In the 1980's, women continued to try to marry up the social scale, but the scale itself began to change. In the cities, the rising status of intellectuals made a university degree a prime asset for a man. Male workers, as well as cadres who had not attended college, complained in several surveys that women would not consider a suitor without an advanced degree.[86] Even some women university students had this goal: an opinion poll at Beijing University found that more than one-fifth of the women students surveyed wanted a partner with more education, ability, and income than themselves.[87] Failing this, women hoped at a minimum to match their own educational background. Among women over thirty who registered with the Guangzhou Marriage Introduction Institute, for instance, more than 80 percent were looking for men with an equivalent level of education. These women were disinclined to consider prospective mates less educated than themselves, fearing they would have few interests in common.[88]

Since men with college degrees were in high demand among women at every educational level, apparently a shortage of them developed on the marriage market. For example, almost half the women registering at a Beijing marriage introduction bureau had a college education, whereas only 6 percent of the men did. Some institutes even refused to let women with college degrees register.[89] Commentaries in the press also discouraged women from their single-minded pursuit of an educated husband. One news article editorialized that a degree was no guarantee of character, and pointed out that Engels, after all, had married a textile worker.[90] This formulation missed the point that Engels, the male partner, was the more educated of the two—exactly the situation that many Chinese women hoped to attain.

As our discussion of personal ads suggests, women also had certain requests about the work they would like their mates to do. In Tianjin, 63 percent of the female registrants at a marriage introduction bureau wanted a partner who did scientific and technical, cultural, or medical work; at one institute in Shanghai, the figure was 83 percent. Yet the male registrants who met these requirements came to only 7 percent in Tianjin and presumably a similar percentage in Shanghai.[91]

Men did not share women's concern with their future spouse's educational or occupational level. Male university graduates, rather than seeking women of similar attainment, looked for women who possessed beauty, poise, gentleness, loyalty, honesty, and the ability to run a household.[92] Some stated grudgingly that strong women were acceptable, as long as they were also gentle, like Madame Curie. But men generally agreed that they were not looking for women whose ability was greater than their own, and that their wives must be willing to do more of the housework and take care of details, while deferring to the husbands in important decisions.[93] Their indifference to a woman's education was shared by men without a university degree. Famous soccer player Zhao Dayu, for instance, stated in 1986 that a woman's appearance, education, and occupation were of secondary importance to him. What he looked for were enthusiasm, unaffectedness, docility, and support for his soccer playing; additionally, he would prefer a southerner about 1.5 meters tall.[94]

In the Chinese countryside as well, educated women—that is, those with a high school degree—found themselves at a disadvantage if they insisted on a match with someone of equivalent education. In a 1984 national survey of several thousand peasant men, only 40 percent of the rural men with a high school degree cared about the educational level of their mates, and those with less schooling evidenced even less concern about whether their future wives were educated. Among all the men surveyed, 70 percent wanted a wife of good character, a good-tempered, healthy woman who would respect her mother-in-law.[95]

Men seldom demanded a specific occupation from a potential spouse. Of 190 men picked at random from among those registering at a Guangzhou institute, four wanted to marry a cadre or technician, two sought to wed an accountant, twenty wanted a worker spouse, and the rest did not specify any occupation.[96] In fact, a woman with a good job often had problems finding a partner. An investigation of several textile work units found that 4.5 percent of the women aged thirty to thirty-five were unmarried, but for women Party members and cadres in the same group the proportion rose to 14.2 percent. One woman Party secretary was introduced to a factory director, but because neither of them wanted household affairs to infringe on their work time, they gave up the idea of marrying. Successful women also suffered from the popular belief that they would dominate their husbands, leave the housework to the men while they attended to their careers, and lose their female charm because of their work and political commitments.[97] In despair, a young woman named Ye Hong wrote in a 1985 letter to *Liberation Daily* (Jiefang ribao) that she had always believed in the complementarity of love and work. But all the men she met disdained career-minded girlfriends, saying "eagerness to do well is a strong point in a man, and a weak point in a woman." Ye cited the counterexamples of Margaret Thatcher, Madame Curie, and the members of the highly lauded Chinese women's volleyball team; all were outstanding workers and good wives as well. But many who wrote in to respond to her letter expressed skepticism that women could carry this double burden successfully.[98]

By the mid-1980's the economic reforms had begun to affect rural marriage choice in new ways. Whereas women had previously sought to marry out to more prosperous districts—from the mountains to the plains, from the plains to the suburbs, even from the suburbs to the city—more women were now content to marry within their home districts, if those districts were growing wealthier thanks to the reforms.[99] In one Shanghai suburb, it was even reported that forty-four men from a city-run factory had chosen to marry peasant women, attracted by the high incomes their wives could earn, the superior housing conditions, and the opportunity to make money by moonlighting at commercial enterprises.[100] These changes did not represent a move away from marital materialism, but rather a shift in the areas that promised the most materially advantageous matches.

Marriage choice, both rural and urban, thus remained firmly tied to socioeconomic criteria, even though the criteria themselves were in a state of flux. At the same time, the urban popular press also reflected a new interest in romance and mutual attraction as components of courtship. As one reader of *Family* magazine wrote in a 1985 forum, love and marriage were becoming important elements in the enjoyment of life among contemporary youth. Young people cared not only about external criteria, but about whether they could talk and enjoy themselves with their sweethearts (*tandelai, wandelai*).[101] Along with this attention to emotional compatibility came a public discussion about the character traits an ideal lover should possess. In a woman, as discussed earlier, gentleness seemed to be the characteristic most desired by men. Men, on the other hand, were told to display courage, self-confidence, and other attributes of a "manly temperament" (*nanzihan qizhi*).[102] As one woman put it, "If a man is only capable of prostrating himself at a woman's feet, he is not worthy of my love." One author described a "real man" as one possessing three traits. First was firmness, which men needed more than women because men still played the main role in society. Second was strength, and third was devotion to work, again more crucial for men than for women.[103] Although the manly temperament remained vaguely defined, it excited a great deal of social attention among both sexes, even giving rise to a magazine called *Real Man* (Nanzihan) exclusively devoted to its elaboration. Just as women were told to make themselves pretty and act gentle in order to be suitable marriage candidates, men were instructed to "act like men." Discussions of the ideal man and the ideal woman helped to legitimize tightly defined sex roles in a society that a few years earlier had dismissed such differences as bourgeois indulgence.

Criteria in Conflict

Young people, caught between these evolving romantic ideals and serious material considerations, often found themselves in real emotional anguish. One young woman named Xiaofeng wrote to *China Youth News* in late 1981 from Changsha, Hunan, declaring that she was "standing at ·the crossroads of love." A student at a technical school, she was about to graduate and be assigned a job. Three men were courting her. The first was a classmate whose father was a high government official in Changsha. Xiaofeng had no deep feelings for this classmate, but he promised that if she married him, his father would arrange for her to stay in Changsha. Her second suitor was a cadre in the factory attached to her school. Originally it was he who had arranged for her to come to the school from the mountain district where she grew up. He was nine years older than she, an unusual age gap among contemporary couples. He promised to secure her a good assignment in the factory if she married him. Sweetheart No. 3, for whom she had the deepest feelings, was a classmate she had known since childhood. He was a worker in a small factory in her hometown; his parents were ordinary workers with no social clout. Her parents, who in an earlier era would have been the arbiters of this decision, had told her to make her own choice. Traditional authority having failed to guide her, she turned to modern means—the advice column of the newspaper. What, she asked, should she do? [104]

In a scant two weeks, her letter and another like it elicited more than one thousand replies from readers of the newspaper. The editors printed a selection of these responses, which included the following advice:

A reader from Beijing pointed out that in choosing a spouse, some people use the criteria of morals, character, age, health, compatibility, and hobbies, whereas others look only at appearance, family background, job, wages, and status. In a society where special privilege still exists, the letter continued, those who have it may attain happiness, but not true love. Gather up your courage, the letter concluded, and seek pure, true love, for as a poet once said, a marriage without love is a "life sentence" of bitterness. A reader from the countryside of Anhui concurred, advising Xiaofeng to marry her childhood hometown classmate. The two other suitors, this letter said critically, had offered to use special privilege for her in ways that were not completely correct.

A woman from Nanjing wrote that she once had been in a similar situation. Two men wanted to marry her: the son of her factory director, and a classmate from an ordinary worker's family who lived with his parents, grandmother, and siblings in cramped quarters. After much thought, she concluded that since women now have a choice about whom they marry, she should pick the man who could provide more comfortable material conditions. So she married the factory director's son. She had not suffered any spiritual retribution for her frankly materialistic stance. Rather, she had worked, successfully, on developing feelings of affection for this man after she married him. On the basis of her experience, she advised Xiaofeng to marry the son of the government official.

Finally, a writer from Jiangsu combined the moralism of the first two letters and the practical advice of the third. Xiaofeng should consent to marry one of her powerful suitors, the letter said, but after her job assignment in Changsha was settled she should break the engagement. That would teach these people not to use their public position for private purposes; at the same time, she would be able to stay in the city. [105]

China Youth News never ran a follow-up story, and so Xiaofeng's ultimate choice was not revealed to an eager readership. But the number of responses indicated that this type of problem was commonplace, while the variety of advice clearly showed that there was no social consensus— nor even an editorial consensus—on how to reconcile the conflicting claims of emotion and practicality.

On some issues, however, the social consensus was clearer. For instance, a person who was too frankly calculating about the practical side of marriage could expect public disapproval. In September 1982, a desperately unhappy young woman in Shanghai wrote to *China Youth News* with the following problem. During her college years she and a classmate had fallen in love. But since university students were actively discouraged from dating by the school authorities, they had never done anything about it. After graduation he was assigned a job far from the city. The two of them decided that since they had no hope of ever living in the same place (work transfers to Shanghai are virtually unobtainable), they should not pursue their romance.

At her parents' urging, she was introduced to another young man, and although she was not deeply involved with him, they quickly registered their marriage so that they could apply for housing. Now, to her delight and dismay, her first love had passed the graduate school examinations and returned to Shanghai. She wanted to break off her first marriage, and many friends advised her that, since she had not yet lived with her husband, doing so would not require a "real" divorce. After registering one's marriage, she asked, is it possible to go back on one's word?

Possible, but hardly laudable, came the stern reply from the editors. (This case was not thrown open for public discussion.) "You have handled this business in a rash manner," the editors scolded her. "How could you be in such a hurry to get a marriage license when you hadn't attained a sufficient degree of mutual understanding and didn't yet have deep feelings for each other? Registering one's marriage is a very serious legal procedure. Once you have obtained a license, whether you are living together or not, you have established yourselves as husband and wife in the eyes of the law. If you go back on your word . . . you will have to go through divorce procedures as stipulated in the Marriage Law regulations." The editors warned her that she should only seek a divorce if she and her husband really had no basis for mutual affection and if her first love still cared for her and had not yet found another girlfriend. But if her true love had made subsequent commitments, or if, the editors added sententiously, "he sees how hasty you are about marriage and no longer wants to marry you, then you will have to make other plans."[106]

This editorial homily never explicitly addressed the questions that got the young woman into trouble in the first place. Faced with a job assignment system and a housing shortage that often made it inconvenient or impossible for young couples to be together, what was a young person to do? A conservative 1985 estimate placed the number of couples forced to live separately for work reasons at five million nationwide. Under these circumstances, many students graduating from university took work assignments into account when making marital choices.[107] Access to housing also greatly influenced courtship. A 1984 survey showed that 40 percent of 3,738 unmarried Shanghai dwellers over thirty could not find mates or had lost sweethearts because they had no housing.[108] Ignoring the emotional complications engendered by these constraints, the editors implied that the young woman had only two correct choices: stick with her first love and resign herself to seeing him once a year, or find someone more convenient to marry and then set about the business of developing "mutual affection." What was not permissible, apparently, was to waver between notions of "true love" and "the best marriage possible under the circumstances."

Some abuses of the courtship process for material gain were cynical and premeditated. Many cases were reported where someone was tricked into marriage by a suitor with ulterior motives. In mid-1982, for instance, a woman electrical worker named Zhao wrote that an army cadre named Song had hoodwinked her into marrying him. His sole purpose in this was apparently to secure a permanent job assignment in Shijiazhuang, a provincial capital where Zhao worked. After they had known each other for only a month, Song persuaded Zhao to obtain a letter from her work unit indicating that they had permission to marry. Since he was a Party member, she never thought to question his motives. He then announced to his fellow workers that they were married, gave out marriage candy, and accepted presents, all without informing her. When some suspicious officials came to investigate, he hastily went with her to register their marriage, falsifying the date on the marriage certificate to cover up his previous actions. The night after his Shijiazhuang job assignment was approved, and still before they had moved in together, he demanded a divorce. As a result of Zhao's letter to the newspaper, an investigation was initiated, and many readers wrote in condemning Song and telling of similar scoundrels in their own areas.[109] Although these actions drew an unusually unified chorus of disapproval, they represent only the most extreme end of a continuum along which marriage was used as a means of social mobility.

The Problem of "Old Maids"

In the 1980's, the assumption that everyone would marry was still widely held in Chinese society. Yet in spite of the matchmaking efforts described earlier in this chapter, large numbers of men and women failed to meet the marital criteria put forth by others, or to find someone who satisfied their own requirements. Statistics showed that most of these unmarried people were rural men. A 1983 investigation of 128 rural locales showed that 15 percent of the men aged twenty-five to thirty-five had trouble finding mates, while only 0.9 percent of the women had such difficulty. These men, one analyst argued, were victims of a lopsided sex ratio in the countryside, a problem aggravated by their low economic status. If their problems were not addressed, the author warned, more rural parents were apt to resort to arranged marriages and outright purchase in order to obtain brides for their sons.[110]

In the cities, the situation was reversed. A 1983 study found that in the preceding decade, one in nine Beijing women, or a total of 50,000, were "surplus" women unable to find a mate. Using the same method of calculation, another study found more than 16,000 "surplus" women in Guangzhou. Two reasons were given for this: men tended to marry women who were several years younger than they, and a baby boom had taken place in the late 1940's and early 1950's. Together, these two facts created what demographers call a "marriage squeeze" for women; that is, men born in 1944–53 had more women born in 1946–55 to choose from. The ratio of women aged thirty to thirty-one to men aged thirty-two to thirty-four, for instance, was 1.5 : 1. The study predicted a reversal of this trend and a marriage squeeze for men in the 1990's, because a drop in the birth rate in the early 1960's meant that a future cohort of men would be seeking mates from among a reduced number of women. In the short run, however, many women who wanted to marry were out of luck. Of women between the ages of twenty-eight and thirty-seven, the Guangzhou study calculated, 6 percent could expect not to marry.[111]

Top government and Party leaders expressed their concern about the marital plight of both rural men and urban women.[112] It was the unmarried urban women, however, who caught the imagination of the press and the public. Single women over thirty were known colloquially as "old maids" (*da guniang*), a term reflecting the popular social perception that a woman, whatever her age, was a child until married. They were seen as victims not only of demographic squeeze, but of changes in popular attitudes as well. Most often it was the women who had taken seriously the political slogans of an earlier era, who had postponed marriage in order to make revolution or pursue an education, who now found themselves squeezed out of the marriage market.

Their situation first came to public attention in the early 1980's. In January 1981, the director of Communist Youth League work at Tianjin University wrote to the local paper about his New Year's resolution. He had resolved, he said, to find husbands for ten "big sisters"—older women, aged thirty-one to thirty-five, who had not yet married. He explained that these women had come of marriageable age during the latter part of the Cultural Revolution. Young and full of idealism, they had heeded the call of misguided local Party leaders to put their work first, and not to fall into the "bourgeois mudpit" of courting. They had spurned with revolutionary speeches all offers of love and marriage. Two of the women, scornful of men who were not as revolutionary as they, had established requirements for a mate that were too strict for any of the local bachelors to meet. Now they were not only aging, but were suffering as well from a backlash toward Party members. They were also victims of the popular belief that women who took on leadership responsibilities were apt to be uppity at home. Worse, they might be targeted in the next political campaign and get their husbands into trouble, too. This dedicated cadre, in resolving to find them husbands, declared, "Although I am not the Monkey King [a legendary folk hero with magical powers], and cannot blow on a hair and produce myriad appropriate people, if we can mobilize enough people to be concerned about the marriages of these 'big sisters,' the problem can be solved." [113]

Many single women joined this well-intentioned cadre in deploring the fact that their most marriageable years had been spent making revolution. Whereas some had consciously chosen to devote their attention to politics rather than romance, others had found themselves caught in a situation beyond their control: sent down to the countryside, or unable to find a mate because of their parents' political troubles. [114] Nor did the end of the Cultural Revolution era resolve their plight. As discussed earlier, many found that men were uninterested in their educational attainments and intimidated by their accomplishments at work. The result of the differing demands made by men and women was that women had a more difficult time finding spouses who met their requirements. The older the woman, the more constrained her choices and the less desirable she looked to men.

Commentators offered additional reasons why in the cities more women than men remained single. Increasing numbers of women, said one author, were demanding that marriage offer companionship, not just sexual relations and shared economic arrangements. [115] Women were "more deeply affected by emotions than men" and made "more persistent emotional demands." [116] Many older singles were women of "personality, attainment, and strong dedication to their work, with their own unique understanding of love." In search of true love, they refused to marry men who did not please them just to "make do." [117] Some were career-minded and did not wish to spend their spare time waiting on a husband and children—although authors usually hastened to add that such women might change their minds if they could find the right men. Still other women had been hurt by bad relationships or previous marriages, and felt that they had "seen through men."[118] Since women in new China had political and economic equality with men, commented one author, they could contemplate living independently if they did not find a match that suited them.[119]

Some authors saw the single state of these women as a choice, not a plight. Yet unmarried women repeatedly encountered two problems. One was unintended but widespread social discrimination. Single women were given low priority in housing assignments, assigned unfavorable work schedules, and passed over for raises in favor of those with a family to support.[120] The other was the psychological pressure brought to bear on them by friends, relatives, and workmates, pressure so great that they often married only in order to end it.

In letters to women's magazines, single women voiced vehement objections to this situation. One older nurse described how younger colleagues mocked her when she faulted their work, saying that her unmarried state made her crotchety.[121] A thirty-year-old woman worker complained that gossip about her caused her to feel that she was "a head shorter than others."[122] A third woman invented an imaginary suitor to stop her parents from pressuring her. Pretending to meet him several times a week, she actually spent her time reading at her place of work. A year later, she wrote to an advice columnist in a panic when her parents demanded to meet him.[123]

In a passionate 1984 essay, Tang Liqin, a single woman, eloquently described her situation. She had been introduced to a series of men with whom she was incompatible, including one who wanted to marry her so that she would care for his aunt when he emigrated, in return for his house and a lifetime of remittances from abroad. When she declined to marry any of these prospects, she encountered ridicule from those around her:

[People say that] I am too picky, that I have too pure a view of love and marriage, and cannot tolerate a little shadow, sham, and inadequacy. People discuss me when they are passing the time of day. They feel sorry for me, casting curious glances my way. They say that I am a "high-priced girl," that I am old, psychologically abnormal, physiologically incomplete, possessed of a shameful secret that cannot be told, a person with a history of numerous losses in love, an "old biddy" who has fought and lost in the arena of love. It seems that I have become a beggar seeking food, a criminal publicly exposed. . . . I have become the target of public criticism: the deprecating descriptions and sentimental sighs in novels; the sighs of emotion from matchmakers in the marriage introduction bureaus who are willing to help this kind of woman but are unable to do so, and are at their wits' end;

the caustic, unbridled ridicule and richly imaginative rumors and gossip of those around me.

Yet Tang defended her right to be left alone to make her own choices, indicting as she did so the quality of many marriages:

Society can tolerate couple after couple who share the same bed while dreaming different dreams. It will conduct countless mediations for families in which the couple has just married and the relationship is verging on collapse. Faced with the grim reality of marriages made carelessly with no emotional basis, where each party takes what he or she needs, to the point where husband and wife divorce or a third party gets involved, society will go to great lengths to censure them in the "court of morality" or punish them according to law. Yet it cannot understand and tolerate older women who hope for a congenial lifelong companion, who take preventive measures and are slow to marry.[124]

Single women also spoke of the internal pressures they felt living in a society where most needs for intimacy were met by a spouse and a family. Several described how they dreaded watching love scenes on television and at the movies, and hid from public view on holidays.[125] One described her lonely existence:

I keep on waiting. I do not want to use pretty words to mask the pain I feel, like "satisfaction from work" or "pleasure from study." These don't work for me. I do my best at my job and study very hard. But to be frank, whatever pleasure I might get from work or study is overwhelmed by my loneliness. . . . People always say that "old maids" have strange temperaments. Am I going to change from a person whom others consider easygoing and nice to a "queer-tempered old maid?"[126]

Single women felt that their problems would be partly ameliorated if society acknowledged the legitimacy of being single and adjusted its attitudes and policies accordingly. They asked for an end to gossip and pressure, equal access to housing, singles' clubs where they could relax after work and on holidays, and the right to their own residence registration, so that they would not be considered forever subordinate to their parents.[127] Above all, they asked for tolerance. As Tang Liqin put it:

There is no need to advocate being single. It should be like religious belief—not promoted, but with freedom of belief [guaranteed]. If a person is willing to remain single, is it like graft and embezzlement, posing a potential social threat? And under the present national policy of fewer and better births, how does it impair the national economy? Looked at from this angle, what is reproachable about not marrying unless one finds an ideal mate, remaining single all one's life? I go so far as to feel quite at ease about doing so. Perhaps this will be seen as the reflection of psychological abnormality, but I hope I can gain social recognition and support.[128]

More and more voices were heard in the 1980's recognizing the inevitability that many women would remain single for life, and demanding their right to be treated as full adult members of society rather than "old maids." Yet mainstream social opinion still held that marriage was more natural than, and superior to, singlehood. Responding to Tang Liqin, one reader commented: "Since nature caused humankind to have gender differences, embracing celibacy obviously runs counter to the laws of nature. If everyone were to remain celibate, human society would have no means to continue. Clearly marriage and love are not only in accord with reason, but also fulfill a social duty." [129] Another author pointed out that suppressing sexual desire might adversely affect one's work and study. Since sex outside of marriage was regarded as immoral in China, he continued, singles faced long-term sexual deprivation, unlike their counterparts in the West. While he believed that unmarried people deserved sympathy rather than censure, he felt that the ultimate key to their psychological health lay in providing them with more marriage opportunities. [130]

Accompanying concrete efforts to marry off singles (see above, "Courtship as a Community Affair") was an attempt to use the press to change the attitudes of both sexes. Men were told that older women would make excellent wives, in spite of the old sayings that "She's three years older? The roof will falter," and "Four years instead? A thorn in your head" (*Nü da san, wuji tan; nü da si, tou chu ci*). Older women were touted as mature, better at home management, and more constant in love than their flighty younger sisters. One article described a woman three years older than her husband who remained loyal to him after he lost his legs in a work accident. Another model older wife was excellent at managing money, and could sew, wash, cook, mend, starch, and produce sumptuous meals for surprise guests even when her husband thought the cupboard was bare. No evidence existed, the article said, to confirm the popular fear that an older woman might product a defective child. The writer called for an end to local regulations that said women must be twenty-three and men twenty-five to marry, so that a twenty-five-year-old woman could not wed a sweetheart two years her junior. [131] Arguing that older women made better wives, commentators like this one left the traditional standards unquestioned in their rush to advertise the virtues of "old maids."

Women, for their part, were instructed to be less choosy about their preferences in a mate. A woman who had graduated from college in the 1950's, for instance, wrote an article describing how she "became enmeshed in a web of her own spinning" when she decided that she wanted a good-looking, learned spouse with a high-paying job. The result: she rejected one man because he had crooked teeth, spurned others for similarly trivial reasons, and reached the age of forty without marrying. Only then did she realize that the conditions she had set were no guarantee of happiness. She finally married a widower with four children, a man who, though he had graduated only from primary school and earned less than she, was good-hearted and well-read. External conditions were no guarantee of happiness, she argued, and being finicky about them in the name of companionate marriage was not a progressive attitude.[132] Other authors carried the criticism further, saying that women who desired mates with attainments superior to their own were exhibiting feudal thinking.[133]

Ultimately, the discussion of the "old maid" problem confirmed the desirability of marriage as a social arrangement. Unmarried women felt that they had the right to remain single if the alternative was a loveless marriage. Yet they criticized the quality of contemporary marriage rather than rejecting the institution outright. "Old maids" spoke approvingly, even longingly, of marriage based on companionship and common interests rather than political or material criteria. They regarded themselves as casualties of an era in which demographic factors were against them and social attitudes lagged behind. But even as they defended singlehood, they continued to aspire to companionate marriage rather than unwedded bliss.

The Correct Handling of Courtship Among the People

Manners and Morals

"Love is a state of transition to marriage," intoned one author in a 1985 discussion of courtship. "The object is to become husband and wife, and develop your love in the long-term form of a household."[134] Most of the advice offered to young people about how to handle the emotional perils of courtship reminded them that they were involved in a serious, goal-oriented enterprise, not a casual recreational pastime. Therefore, they were told, they should conduct themselves carefully and sincerely at all times.

Young people apparently took this admonition to heart, writing frequent letters to newspapers and magazines asking for advice on love. One column on the subject became so popular that in 1982, the China Youth Publishing House brought out a collection of thirty-five of the most common questions asked about love, with the correct answers. The anthology was entitled *What Kind of Love Is Happiest?* Its purpose was to guide young people through emotional territory that had not been publicly discussed since before the Cultural Revolution, and to give them clear guidance about the correct attitude toward love and courtship:

serious, honest, emotional yet balanced, anti-feudal but definitely not bourgeois.[135]

The advice ranged from manners to morals. When visiting the family of a prospective spouse for the first time, young people were instructed to dress neatly, bring a simple present, knock before entering, receive an offered teacup with both hands, listen politely to the parents of the house without interrupting, avoid bragging, and not stay too long.[136] But good manners were not enough; honesty and emotional sensitivity were important as well. It was considered immoral, for instance, to pursue more than one sweetheart at once. When a young man who had courted six women argued that finding a wife was like conducting an experiment, and one could not expect success on the first try, he was publicly rebuked. An advice columnist told him that it was wrong to accumulate experience or lovers as one might accumulate capital.[137] And a woman who asked how to refuse advances from a young man who did not interest her was advised not to treat him in a careless manner. More than 2,000 readers contributed to an open forum on the subject, telling her to be honest, point out his strong points, help him to recognize his weak points, and make her refusal clear. She was warned not to make fun of him, gossip behind his back, or treat him as though he were "a toad lusting after swan's flesh."[138]

If care and restraint were called for, timidity was definitely not encouraged. When a young man wondered how to win the heart of his true love from a rival, the editor replied, "It is like a hotly contested soccer match. To win a victory, you must use your skill, tactics, and will," as opposed to bribing the referee or purposely injuring the opposing players.[139] Women, too, were urged to boldly express their interest in men.[140] In the past, one reader commented in a magazine forum, women had taken a passive role in love because of traditional attitudes that condemned female initiative as an offense to public decency. It had become a point of pride for women to be inept at social interactions. Thus many women spent the best years of their lives waiting for men to approach them, and ended up taking whatever match could be arranged for them so as not to remain single.[141] In the 1980's, in contrast, semi-fictionalized stories in many magazines showed young women how to take the initiative. The heroine of one such story approached her true love by arranging to sit next to him at a movie, asking him to fix her bicycle, watering his plants, and obtaining tickets to a flower show for both of them. Finally, she declared her love outright and quieted his worries that her family background was better than his own. This tale was accompanied by an approving editorial note saying that young people should learn how to express their feelings for potential sweethearts.[142]

Nevertheless, women entered the world of love and courtship at the risk of provoking gossip that might mar their reputations. The magazine *Chinese Youth* (Zhongguo qingnian) in 1984 printed a collection of letters from young women whose lives had been damaged by gossip. One young peasant woman had broken up with her boyfriend; an unknown person then forged two letters to him in her name, cursing his subsequent girlfriend. She reported that the entire village was now criticizing her. Another woman rejected a suitor, after which he spread rumors that she had slept with him and had an abortion. The talk ruined her relationship with her current boyfriend; even her own father believed the rumors. A third woman, a nurse, was accused by a coworker of sleeping with a doctor. A fourth woman, whose nephew often visited her, became the subject of neighborhood gossip about their relationship. She suggested acerbically that people with time on their hands should read or listen to music rather than gossiping. A fifth woman was dogged by rumors that her work supervisor had raped her, and that she had forced him to pay her 200 yuan to hush the matter up.[143] The public discussion of gossip universally condemned its deleterious effects, but the coverage also showed that gossip was difficult to counter and impossible to ignore. Although the romantic activities of young men also became the subject of gossip, the love lives of young women seemed to be subjected to closer scrutiny and harsher judgment.

One situation in which men seemed to suffer more condemnation than women, however, was that of broken engagements. Engagement was considered tantamount to marriage, especially in the countryside. A party who sought to end the relationship had to extricate him- or herself from a complicated family exchange of betrothal presents, and to brave village opprobrium as well. In the press, a man who broke an engagement was usually portrayed as an opportunist who dumped his fiancée because he hankered after higher status. A man from rural Hebei named Wang, for instance, joined the army after his engagement to Liu, and was away from his village for several years. While Liu assumed the duties of a model daughter-in-law—caring for Wang's sick mother, making clothes for his sister, doing fieldwork for his family—Wang become convinced that he deserved better than a peasant wife and persuaded his parents to end the engagement.[144] Cases like this reported from around the country all had several things in common. The woman had dutifully fulfilled the unwritten expectations of a future daughter-in-law. But the man, eligible for mobility opportunities unavailable to most women, eager to leave rural life behind him, was no longer willing to keep his half of the bargain. This phenomenon was called "loving the new and rejecting the old," and it was criticized in the press as socially harmful and immoral.[145]

When it was the woman who sought to break a rural engagement, both the reasons and the moral issues were typically somewhat different. Young peasant women complained in letters to the press that the men they met through matchmakers often turned out to have nothing in common with them. Frequently, by the time the young couple had seen enough of each other for the woman to figure this out, the two were already engaged. These women were pressured by their families and neighbors to go through with the marriage. But the advice they got in the press was quite different from what they heard at home: they were told that breaking an engagement was perfectly legal, and that refusing to enter into an arranged marriage was a politically progressive thing to do.[146] For rural women, unlike men, roads out of the village and away from family control of courtship were few. In condemning men who broke engagements while praising women who did so, advice columnists sought to redress the balance of power in rural courtship and ensure women some freedom of choice.

Premarital Sex

"Love," said an article for young people in 1985, "is not only of the spirit, it is also of the flesh."[147] In the mid-1980's, the question of physical intimacy between unmarried urban people became a new and controversial topic of public discussion. Most people acknowledged that some degree of sexual activity was a normal feature of courtship. When a young woman wrote to an advice columnist that she had rebuffed a suitor's "uncivilized actions," for instance, she was told that it was natural for people in love to become sexually stimulated, and that she should have dealt with her sweetheart calmly rather than losing her temper.[148] A reader of *Family* magazine further spelled out the permissible limits of sexual activity in a letter:

After a young man and woman enter the stage of "hot love," aside from expressing their feelings in a conscious and civilized way, on appropriate occasions they may use hugging, stroking, kissing, and other such actions to express the love between them. This form is already a common occurrence in some places, given tacit approval by society, suitable to our country's degree of civilization, and permitted by the demands of our country's social morality.[149]

Yet although some physical affection on the part of courting couples was widely accepted, public disagreement flared about the acceptability of premarital sexual intercourse. This was almost exclusively an urban discussion; virtually nothing was said in the press about sexual behavior in the countryside, and foreign observers had very little opportunity to make their own observations. Urban and rural sexual mores might well have been diverging dramatically, but because public discussion on the subject omitted mention of the villages, it was impossible to tell how rapid or significant the divergence was.

Among city dwellers, it often seemed that the primary difference of opinion was generational: elders advocated premarital abstinence, whereas young people asserted their right to sleep together before marriage. But the advice young people received and the opinions they held were deeply gendered as well. Both the older generation and the youth of the 1980's agreed that the risks of premarital sexual activity were greater for women than for men, particularly if the relationship did not culminate in marriage.

Chinese social commentators believed that sexual activity among urban young people had become an issue in the 1980's for both biological and social reasons. Because of improved nutrition, young people were reaching sexual maturity about two years sooner than their parents' generation. At the same time, the legal and socially approved age for marriage had been delayed. The long period of sexual abstinence between early puberty and late marriage caused a "psychological imbalance among young people." It had more measurable consequences as well: a 1986 newspaper quoted reports that in Beijing, 27.9 percent of all abortions were performed on unmarried women, 90 percent of whom were already engaged.[150] Couples who could not obtain permission to marry—because they were too young, because their work units had set an age limit even higher than that of the Marriage Law, or because they were close cousins—sometimes chose to cohabit without legal sanction.[151]

Changing attitudes among young people in the urban areas were also responsible for new sexual mores. Three-quarters of the university students questioned in a 1985 survey believed that Chinese were too conservative on the question of relationships between the sexes. Half of them felt that traditional sexual morality was stifling of human nature. Only one-quarter asserted that it was immoral to cohabit before marriage in the context of an established relationship.[152] As attitudes changed, so did behavior. Cohabitation among college students, rare in the early 1980's, was discreet but increasingly noticeable in the years that followed. In university dormitories, it became common for couples to arrange to stay together on weekends, asking their roommates to vacate the room for a night. One young teacher at a major university found that among his students, several couples would stay together in the same room at the same time. In the summertime, mosquito nets around each bed provided a modicum of privacy. Other young couples arranged meetings at home when their parents were away on business. Although much of this behavior was new, it quickly became acceptable among young people. Classmates declined to report such trysts to the school authorities.[153] As one participant in a public discussion of premarital sex put it: "If we try to say what the difference is between young people in love in the 1980's and those in the 1950's and 1960's, I think that it is probably just that 1980's youth are bolder about it, more daring in what they do."[154]

This particular commentator, an older person, believed that adults should not worry themselves about sexually active young people, or assume that "if their life does not resemble ours then they cannot live it."[155] But most adults were more dismayed by the rapid change in urban sexual behavior, fearing that premarital sex among established couples would soon lead to widespread sexual promiscuity. One columnist deplored the spread of what he saw as a Western concept of sexual behavior, in which people switched partners "like cats and dogs," and threw "people away like plates, razor blades, or old cars."[156] Commentators often characterized Western thinking about sexual liberation as "decadent" and "bourgeois." They reminded young people that China had a long history, that it was now in the socialist period, and that the form taken by love should be appropriately civilized and socialist.[157] One 1984 article reported that even American youth were rejecting the notion of sexual liberation. It quoted with approval a *Playboy* survey that found young Americans returning to traditional attitudes toward love, sex, and marriage. "Sexual liberation," the article said, was a product of the 1960's: "It took the 'self' as central, fanatically pursuing selfish desires, taking drugs and despising the traditional family, ridiculing marriage and doubting its value, calling marriage and the establishment of a household a 'secret suicide contract.'" This concept had "poisoned almost all of American culture," leading to a rise in venereal disease, unnecessary pregnancies, abortions, and even cancer.[158] The article's central message was unspoken but clear: Chinese youth should not emulate a bankrupt concept that even Americans had begun to reject.

These admonitions in the press were accompanied by attempts to regulate sexual activity among young people whenever it came into public view. Excessive public displays of physical affection were denounced as uncivilized and a bad influence on children.[159] A 1982 cartoon depicted an old peasant whose neck had become permanently twisted when he turned his head away in embarrassment at the sight of a young couple entwined on a public bus.[160] University authorities sometimes punished cohabiting students by giving them undesirable job assignments when they graduated.[161] In an attempt to control premarital encounters as well as extramarital affairs, people traveling together were required to show their marriage registration certificate and photo identification in order to stay together in hotels and guest houses. In one case a married couple in their sixties was harassed for failing to carry a marriage certificate.[162]

The main combat zone where public regulation met youthful sexual desire was the public parks of Chinese cities. Security patrols were organized in urban parks to reprimand, and if necessary arrest, unmarried couples found making love behind bushes and under raincoats. (One such patrol also found it necessary to spend a fair amount of time hauling in voyeurs of all ages who gathered to watch the action. A thirteen-year-old boy in Beijing explained that he was just trying to "learn something," while a grizzled older man protested that he had been told to come to the park to "see one of the sights of Beijing—we don't have sights like this in the Northeast!")[163] On a less coercive note, young people were advised in a 1985 article that the park on a summer's night offered numerous dangers to physical health. They were reminded that the body's resistance to disease is lower after 10 o'clock at night, and that courting in the late hours might lead to colds or headaches. They were also told that lying on the grass for long periods was harmful, because at night plants could not conduct photosynthesis and the carbon dioxide they emitted could influence the health. Finally, the article waxed eloquent on the discomfort caused by mosquito bites and rheumatic joints inflamed by prolonged contact with wet grass. Most of these hazards, the author concluded, could be avoided if young people alternated periods of sitting and walking around.[164]

While some of the attempts to discuss and regulate premarital sex emphasized its immoral, illegal, and unhealthful nature, most of the literature directed at young people consisted of practical advice on how to handle problematic situations. Both the problems and the solutions varied greatly by gender. Young women were counseled on how to deal with troublesome male sexual advances, and whether to confess their previous sexual activity to a marriage prospect or partner. For men, the main issue was whether or not to forgive a wife or sweetheart who had slept with someone else, even if the event had occurred years before the current couple met. Underlying the discussion, sometimes stated explicitly, was the message that loss of virginity was a woman's problem: that although premarital sex was immoral for both parties, only the woman paid the cost. Among the same university students discussed earlier who stood ready to jettison traditional Chinese sexual morality, 62 percent believed that "the chastity of a virgin is sacred." The survey showed that the men in the group demanded chastity of women, and the women guarded their chastity from men.[165] A woman who had lost her virginity was referred to as a *shishen nü*—literally, a woman who had lost her body. Premarital sex entailed no such loss for a man, who was only asked to be enlightened enough to forgive his partner for something he himself might have done.

In the popular press, advice columnists labored mightily to describe the deleterious consequences of premarital sex so that young women would recognize danger when they saw it. One article, entitled "Please refuse loveless sexual love," instructed young women how to recognize several situations where their suitors wanted only sexual relations, not love. A man who sought sexual relations with a woman so that she would not be able to leave him for someone better, the article said, was interested only in possession, not love. So was a man who felt compelled to conquer a woman who was unusually beautiful, learned, or wealthy. Implicit in both these cases was the assumption that a woman could be permanently captured if she gave up her virginity since she would find it difficult to move back onto the marriage market. Men who were motivated by overpowering sexual desire (described as "insane lust") were also suspect. Finally, a man who was overstimulated by a woman's provocative appearance or actions might desire but not love her:

When the man and woman are on a date, the woman's blouse is light, frivolous, and transparent, exposing the shoulders, back, and chest, easily causing the man to feel stimulated by the sight of it and put forward the request for sex. The woman snuggles up to the man's body, ear to ear and temple to temple, and kisses, hugs, and strokes him, easily causing the man to feel stimulated by the warmth and put forward the request for sex. The woman uses language with sexual implications, also easily causing the man to feel stimulated by the sound of it and put forward the request for sex. All requests for sex that men make because of these "three feels" are without love.[166]

Though these situations did not portray male sexuality in a very flattering light, they presented male motivations as somewhat more complex than those attributed to men in the cautionary tales discussed in Chapter 2. As in the cautionary tales, though, women were reminded that they stood to lose more than men from premarital sex, and that they should neither provoke sexual advances nor accept them before marriage.

For some women, this advice came too late. A woman with a sexual history found her marriage prospects forever shadowed, no matter how virtuous her subsequent behavior. In a 1985 letter to *Chinese Women* entitled "Can this tattered love still give me happiness?," a twenty-seven-year-old man described his sweetheart, a beautiful woman who treated him well and had spent a year caring for his chronically ill mother. When she confessed that she had had sexual relations with a previous boyfriend, he was devastated. Although he could not imagine life without her, he also feared that he would be publicly jeered and belittled for staying with her.[167] Over a two-month period, more than 600 readers wrote

Advice to a young man who discovers that his fiancée had a previous sexual involvement. "Jiaru wo shi Xiao B . . ." (If I were Xiao B), *Zhongguo funü* (Chinese Women), 8 (1985), 10–11.

in to offer him their advice. Most letters reprinted by the editors advised him to ignore public opinion and find the courage to marry her, but all of them acknowledged that he faced a difficult choice. And although the discussion paid more attention to the young man's psychological torment than to that of the woman, one letter from a female college student poignantly described the damage done by a premarital affair to a woman's self-esteem. This woman described herself as "beautiful, bright, good, an excellent cook, able to sew, filial to my parents, loving to my siblings, caring of my classmates"—in short, a model candidate for a wife. But because one of her classmates had forced his sexual attentions upon her and then deserted her, she avoided all further relationships with men for fear of being found out and rejected. Feeling that she had "lost the right to love and be loved," she also had lost the "courage to love" and saw no personal solution other than to eschew marriage and bury herself in her work.[168]

The moral hammered home in most of these tales was that loss of virginity was tragic for a woman and her future suitors and should be avoided at all costs. But in another public forum on this issue, it was acknowledged that women who slept with their boyfriends before marriage suffered social ostracism only if the marriage did not take place. Therefore, one writer advised, a woman should carefully calculate her chances of marrying someone before she became involved in a sexual relationship:

A woman should understand something about the skill of self-protection. For the sake of her future happiness, she must act prudently. I am not saying that women should all guard their bodies like jade, not even allowing anyone to touch them. I am saying, rather, that before someone touches you, you should have planned it out. If you hope to marry, you should think about whether or not the other party would make a suitable lifelong mate. Another important point is whether or not the other party wants to be your lifelong mate. These two conditions are very important, and neither must be missing. If the former is missing, you may enter into an inappropriate marriage. If the latter is missing, then why do you want to waste your time getting tangled up with him![169]

Perhaps more realistic than the admonition to avoid premarital sex altogether, this advice nevertheless made the point that marriage was the ultimate purpose of courtship—and perhaps also the purpose of dispensing sexual favors, carefully, of course.

A woman's sexual history would follow her all her life, she was told, even if she later succeeded in finding someone to marry. If she told her husband about her past history, she might be thrown out. When one magazine ran a forum on how honest a wife should be with her husband about previous sexual experience, two men offered accounts of how they dealt with their wives. Both wives had had previous sexual relations when they were sent down to the countryside as teenagers. In both cases the women intended to marry the men they slept with; in both cases the men subsequently broke off with them. One wife did not tell her husband before marriage because she was afraid of losing him, and did not tell him after marriage because she was afraid of hurting him. After a year of married life, she finally decided she trusted him enough to divulge her secret. He decided to forgive her because it was a good marriage, and he felt that to do otherwise would be to fall victim to the feudal concept of chastity. But the second husband decided to divorce his wife after she confessed, feeling that he had lost face, that her history could not be erased, and that the sympathy he felt for her plight was not enough to sustain a marriage.[170]

Even if a woman married, was honest about the past, and obtained the forgiveness of her husband, she might later find that he or other relatives would hold her previous sexual activity against her. In a harrowing 1985 account, one such woman, married nine years, was slapped by her husband and cursed by his family when she stayed at work late so her factory could complete its contracted production. The husband referred insultingly to her premarital history, and when he saw her talking to a male ex-classmate on the street, he slugged the other man and called his wife a whore. Later he whipped her with a rope and beat her with a club. Even more astonishing than his behavior was the reaction of her factory leadership: they tried to force her to write a self-criticism, yet refused to intervene when her husband left her, saying that domestic disputes were outside their jurisdiction. Ultimately she filed for divorce.[171] Although the commentary accompanying this article criticized her husband for his feudal attitude toward female chastity, it underscored the point that a woman with a sexual past was vulnerable to continuing abuse.[172]

The most obvious danger for a woman who lost her virginity before marriage was an unwanted pregnancy, which would force her to marry hastily or confront public disgrace. Although contraceptives were available in drugstores and an unmarried couple could also obtain them through married friends, many did not use contraception.[173] Several magazines in 1985 mentioned the rising incidence of abortions among young unmarried women. Abortion was both legal and socially accepted for married women, but out-of-wedlock pregnancy was neither, and some young women used pseudonyms and went to great lengths to keep their parents and coworkers from finding out. Other women, reluctant to go to an abortion clinic for fear of discovery, sought back-alley abortions and risked their lives.[174] Some bore children out of wedlock, who subsequently faced ostracism and were a "heavy burden to those concerned."[175]

Given such serious consequences for young women with a history of sexual involvement, it is not surprising that many chose to keep their past secret. One woman who had slept with her cousin many years before her marriage decided for the sake of her family's happiness not to discuss the relationship with her husband. Why, she asked, should she cause her husband pain and bring disaster upon her current household because of a mistake she made in her youth?[176] Other women, like the college student described above, carried lasting psychological scars. Some chose to avoid men altogether, while others gave themselves up to either loveless marriages or indiscriminate promiscuity:

Some women feel that [once they have had sexual relations, they are bound to their partners for life, and that] no matter what their spouse is like they absolutely will not divorce, to the point where it causes some tragedies, and brings them very great pain. [In other cases,] after a young woman has this type of experience, she herself feels that she is not whole, is one grade below others. She writes herself off as hopeless. She smashes the pot to pieces just because it's cracked. Her moral viewpoint completely collapses, and she becomes cynical and runs wild. She does not understand that after you are wounded, you may still uphold the integrity of your character.[177]

Some advice columnists encouraged women not to give themselves up for lost because of a single mistake. One article cited the example of the heroine in the Soviet movie "Moscow Does Not Believe in Tears," who gave birth to a child out of wedlock, yet went on to become a nationally famous factory director.[178] Another pointed out that many nonvirgins later married and led happy lives. Women should regard the loss of their virginity as unfortunate but not catastrophic, and certainly should not contemplate suicide. The article concluded: "Is it worth it to die for a heart-less man who defies morality?"[179]

Authors of articles like these were at pains to distance themselves from the traditional Chinese concept of chastity for women. Some explicitly attacked it, pointing out that in old China memorial arches were erected to honor chaste women, while men were free to take multiple wives and concubines and visit prostitutes as they pleased. Excessive attention to the technicalities of female chastity, said one author, sometimes led to a situation where a woman who did not bleed on her wedding night was regarded as unchaste, or a woman who had been raped was discarded by her boyfriend.[180] A second commentator speculated that the one-sided de-mand for female chastity had resulted from the fact that it was more diffi-cult for women to hide the loss of virginity. Alternatively, it showed that men had the long-standing habit of making demands upon women. The demand that only women be virgins, she said, was a remnant of the think-ing of a polygamous society, not a product of women's free choice. "Equal-ity between the sexes," she concluded, "should be embodied in sexual morality."[181]

Nevertheless, these authors concluded, the social reality in 1980's China was that women who had lost their virginity faced social discrimi-nation and lack of adequate legal safeguards.[182] This situation, they ar-gued, called for a new concept of chastity, one that would make equal demands on women and men. In a socialist society where men and women had equal rights, if a man and woman had sexual relations before marriage and then broke off the relationship, it was unjust to regard the woman as besmirched while nothing happened to the man.[183] One author even proposed that the terminology be changed from *zhencao* (chastity), which had traditionally referred only to women, to *zhongzhen* (loyal and steadfast), which would be a quality required of both sexes.[184] In short, premarital sex would become taboo for both men and women—a situa-tion, these authors argued, that would preserve social stability, protect women and the next generation, prevent pregnancy, and generally be ap-propriate to the demands of communist morality. The alternative of aban-doning chastity requirements for both sexes was rejected as a degenerate Western notion. These authors argued that China should not reject the feudal moral viewpoint only to fall prey to the dictates of bourgeois morality.[185]

The proposed formulation, though admirably egalitarian, did not seem likely to have much effect on actual social arrangements. Premarital sex was demonstrably on the rise in urban 1980's China, and appeals to com-munist morality were far less persuasive to young people in the wake of the Cultural Revolution than they had been thirty years before. In a so-ciety where sexual practice was changing far more quickly than articulated moral beliefs, young women who engaged in premarital sex continued to take greater risks and face more social opprobrium than their male partners.

Young Chinese who set about "making a friend" in the 1980's juggled economic, social, and emotional priorities, not always very successfully. This juggling process was not unique to China, nor was it a new phenomenon in Chinese society. But after more than ten years of silence on affairs of the heart, the complexities of the courtship process emerged more clearly than at any time since Liberation. At the same time, public discourse expanded the vocabulary of love and courtship, drawing on many sources: the Confucian moral code, the language of Western romantic love, the idiom of the advice column, the terminology of psychological and social analysis. The use of the press as the main forum for this discussion meant that young people could seek advice on intimate affairs of the heart in the anonymous public sphere, professing beliefs and describing behavior that might bring them censure or ridicule in their own communities.

As public debate on these issues developed, many of the participants— young people and their elders—seemed uncertain of their positions. Young people in 1980's China courted and married in a society that did not speak with a unified voice about love. Matchmaking and "free love," material and emotional criteria, compulsory marriage and singlehood by choice, moral conduct and physical desire, all involved values that co-existed uneasily. The choices that young people faced, and the possible actions open to them, varied by locale and by gender. But in city and countryside, among young people of both sexes, these choices and actions began to change rapidly in the 1980's. The experiences of their parents and the Cultural Revolution slogans of their elder brothers and sisters were no longer a sufficient guide, but it was not clear when or whether a new social consensus would emerge to replace them.

Translations

Young people often lacked social opportunities to meet potential spouses on their own. "How to Make Friends with Young Women" suggests some ways that young men could approach young women without appearing disreputable. "Clear Away the Old Custom" and "Exchanging Relatives" describe rural situations in which parents continued to interfere in marital choice to a degree that their children, raised since the revolution, no longer found acceptable.

Now that parents had ceased to hold absolute sway over the marriages of their children, a variety of voices advised young people on how best to choose a mate. "My Well-Intentioned Words," written by a matchmaker, urges young men to be realistic in their demands and not to place undue emphasis on looks. In "My Views on Selecting a Spouse," a male university student explains why beauty and gentleness are his primary criteria, and why he is put off by career-minded women. This latter point elicits several angry replies in "A Woman Who Has Her Own Goals Is Preferable" and "Please Listen to the View of a Woman University Student." In "Where Is the Real Man of My Heart?" a young woman sharply criticizes contemporary attitudes among young men that she finds unattractive.

Economic criteria still played a prominent role in marriage choice. "Chronicle of a Marriage" describes an extreme case, in which a man married solely for the material advantages he hoped to gain. But criteria of personal compatibility were socially recognized as well, and much advice literature instructed young people how to develop them. "How to Tell If a Girl Likes You" is typical of this instruction. "Do Not Disturb Others When Courting" comments on courtship etiquette, offering indirect testimony to the problem of finding privacy in a crowded society.

How to Make Friends with Young Women

A young woman from Beijing told me of the following incident: One evening, she rode the No. 10 bus to attend a party. Not many passengers were on the bus. As the bus neared the Xidan station, a young man walked over to her and said in a low voice: "Let's be friends." The young woman answered coldly, "Go away! I don't know you." Thereupon the young fellow, looking very embarrassed, got off the bus. Actually, the young man's desire to make friends with young women is understandable, as is the young woman's refusal. So how can a young fellow successfully get acquainted with a young woman?

Generally speaking, other than at dances and other social occasions, . . . it helps to have an "introducer" whom both parties know rather well. You should find an honest and upright person to play this role, as this will lead the other party to trust you. When the "introducer" introduces you to the other party, you should nod your head in a refined and courteous manner; if the other party offers her hand, you must shake hands with her naturally and gracefully, but make sure not to shake her hand too hard in order to display your strength, or shake it too long and show excessive enthusiasm. If you discover the other party is not interested in you, you should leave politely, without showing displeasure. At the first meeting, be sure to adhere to a sense of propriety in speech and manner. It is best to be neither obsequious nor supercilious, but affable, sincere, and believable; never be frivolous, arrogant, or discourteous. Otherwise, your first meeting may be your last.

If you want to get to know a girl, and there is no one around who knows the two of you, what should you do? There is no need to be disheartened, but you must seek and create an opportune time. A refined and courteous bearing, and actions where you help others out, can decrease the difficulty of social intercourse and eliminate the psychological barriers between men and women who are strangers to each other. For example, helping a woman pick up something she has dropped, and saying something appropriate, will often provide an opening for you to become acquainted.

Generally speaking, it is inappropriate to talk to girls you don't know on the street or on a bus. But there are exceptions. For example, on the way to or from work, riding a bicycle or taking the bus, you always encounter a certain young woman, and you look very familiar to each other. Or you sit next to a girl on a long-distance train. Under these two circumstances, you can initiate a conversation. If the other party seems indifferent and restrained, then use a bit of tact. If she does not look unhappy, you may first introduce yourself in a natural way. If the girl also introduces herself to you openly and sincerely, then obviously you two have become acquainted. Perhaps this will be the starting point of your friendship.

In the times in which we live, young men and women all seek to understand the other party and to gain a friendship. This is a sign of social progress. We hope young men and women will meet openly and sincerely so that this kind of interaction can develop in a healthy manner along civilized and courteous lines.

SOURCE: Jin Jian, "Zenyang jiejiao nüqingnian" (How to make friends with young women), *Qingnian zixun*, 1 (May 1985), 25.

Clear Away the Old Custom of Arranging and Interfering in Marriage

I Became the Payment for a Debt of Gratitude

I am an eighteen-year-old village girl. Last winter I became engaged to a youth from my village who I don't like at all.

If I don't like him, why become engaged? The past two years, my family fell on hard times. Our housing was tight, and with the help of this young man's father (the head of the production team), we built a new house. Last summer the house collapsed, and our fellow villagers again helped our family to build once more. During both construction periods, this young man put in the most effort. After the house was built, his father asked my father about marriage. Out of gratitude, my parents readily agreed. In this manner I became engaged. At the time of the engagement I made a big fuss, but it was no use. After the engagement I made a fuss again, but my father said, "We accepted someone's kindness, and we must repay it; you are engaged, you belong to someone else, and no matter how much you carry on it is no use!"

Now I am outnumbered and powerless. I never thought that just as my life was beginning, I would become a payment for my parents' debt of gratitude.

He Fangdi, Zhejiang

My Mother Wants Me to Fulfill My Filial Duty

I am a young woman worker who works in the county seat. Half a year ago, I got to know a young village man. He is willing to bear hardships, eager to learn and advance, and exceptionally honest. The two of us get along well in terms of interests, hobbies, thinking, and emotions and have already reached a point where we can hardly tear ourselves away from each other.

But when my mother found out about this, she was strongly opposed, for just one reason: his village residence registration [i.e. his peasant status]. No matter how I explained or begged, it had no effect. Finally, my mother went on a hunger strike, saying I was an "unfilial daughter." I was scared out of my wits. My mother was widowed in her youth and brought me up with great difficulty. If anything happened to her, I would regret it bitterly all life. So I could only promise to break off with him. My mother's sorrow turned to joy, and she said, "Doing this makes you a filial child." But when I explained the situation to my boyfriend, he looked like he had been hit with a club. His suffering face made my heart want to break. Only at that moment did I truly understand how much I love him. But what should I do? If I keep on with him, I really fear that something will happen to my mother. If I break off with him, both he and I will find it extremely hard to bear.

I know my mother can go on a hunger strike at any time. This worries me a great deal. I want to be a filial daughter, but is it possible that one must sacrifice one's own love in order to "fulfill one's filial duty"? It is such a pure love!

Li Hong, Peng county, Sichuan

I Can Only Keep Delaying

I am a high school graduate who did not pass the university admissions exam, so I contracted out twenty *mu* of fishpond to work at home. This year my father said that work was busy in the fishponds, and asked my "fiancée" to come help out. He wants us to get married at New Year's.

This "fiancée" is the result of an engagement arranged by my parents when I was in school. From the beginning, I have had a premonition that this marriage would be a tragedy, because we are relatives (her father is my mother's brother). The Marriage Law contains a regulation forbidding marriage between cousins, and the newspapers and magazines have also explained the harm caused by marriage between close relatives. But my family pays no heed to such considerations. In addition, the girl has not attended school and can't even read one character (right now she is sitting at my side knitting, and we are sharing an oil lamp). In future how can we have a common language?

I attempted several times to break off this marriage. But as soon as I revealed my feelings, my father scolded me severely, and my mother threatened suicide several times, saying, "Breaking off this marriage will damage the feelings between relatives, and afterward we won't be able to face people. . . ." Because of this business, I often can't sleep and my mental burden gets heavier and heavier. Now whenever my father urges me to go register the marriage, I always decline on account of my age. My plan is to delay and delay this marriage, and never marry. But can this plan work?

Bi Xinming, Jiangli, Hubei

SOURCE: Excerpted from "Qingchu baoban ganshe hunyinde jiu xiguan" (Clear away the old custom of arranging and interfering in marriage), *Zhongguo qingnian*, 12 (December 1983), 14–15.

Exchanging Relatives, Forced Marriage, Jumping the Wall, Rescue

Jieshou County, Anhui, Deals with a Case of Feudal Marriage

At dusk one day not long ago, Chen Suying, a young woman from Small Chen village, Fanzhai township, Jieshou county, Anhui province, fleeing for her life, in desperation ran into the women's bathroom in the courtyard of the Guangwu township government offices. When she found a middle-aged woman in the bathroom, Chen Suying burst out, "Could you give me a boost over the courtyard wall?"

"Tell me what kind of trouble you are in!"

"My mother is going to marry me off in a 'relative exchange' to get a wife for my second elder brother. I am to be married to Zhang Zhiye, of Big Zhang village in this county. He is seventeen years older than I am. His younger sister will marry my second elder brother. The day before yesterday, my family forced me to go to Zhang's house. I didn't want to marry him and ran back home. But my two elder brothers forced me back to Zhang's house. I tried to run away from them, so they beat me. Now my two elder brothers are guarding the gate of the township offices, and I have no way out. Help me, quickly!" Chen Suying spoke in a panic-stricken way, shedding tears.

The middle-aged woman was the wife of a cadre in Guangwu township. She said to the girl, "First hide in the bathroom, and I'll go find Chairwoman Huang of the district Women's Federation to support you!"

When Huang Aixia heard the news, she went to the gate of the township government to check out the situation. Sure enough, she saw two robust men, one on the left and one on the right, squatting on either side of the gate. Chairwoman Huang made a prompt decision. She took Chen Suying to the district office, related the situation to the court, and then temporarily placed Chen Suying in the home of Duan Hui, a woman cadre in the township.

The judge of the district court at once sent a cadre to summon Chen Suying's two elder brothers to the court.

The next morning they arrived. The district court judge explained the relevant articles of the Marriage Law to them, and informed them that no one had the right to force Chen Suying to marry Zhang Zhiye against her wishes. Then he let them take Chen Suying home.

Unexpectedly, one evening a month later, Chen Suying fled her home once again. It turned out that her mother and elder brothers had not abided by their pledge. Under pressure from Zhang Zhiye, they beat her, cursed her, and forced her to go to Zhang Zhiye's home. On this day, as she was being "sent under escort," she ran away to the home of Chairwoman Huang.

Chairwoman Huang expressed deep sympathy with the girl's plight and kept her in her house that night. Early the next morning, she contacted the court, which immediately sent someone out in the rain to talk to Zhang Zhiye. Zhang was ordered to come to the district court on the following day. The next day the court announced: Although Chen Suying and Zhang Zhiye conducted a "marriage" ceremony, the law does not recognize this "marital relationship" because it was counter to the wishes of Chen Suying. Furthermore, they have not registered their marriage with the government. In future, if Zhang Zhiye tries to force Chen Suying, he will be held legally accountable. The mother and elder brothers of Chen Suying must abide by their pledge. If they violate the right of Chen Suying to freedom of marriage, they will be held legally responsible.

SOURCE: *Xinmin wanbao*, March 25, 1986.

My Well-Intentioned Words

At a party for young singles, I am happy to see young people talking seriously and warmly two by two. Yet I also see people in need of help, but unwilling to accept it.

Look, here he comes again. This is the fifth time tonight! I look in the direction of his pointing finger and a slender girl, wearing a beautiful skirt and blouse, comes into view. I can't help but dissuade him: "She is only twenty-six, but you are already forty-eight!"

"May I trouble you to ask for me again, perhaps. . . ."

I can only brace myself and go meet with the fifth rebuff on his behalf. When the girl follows my gaze and casts a sidelong glance at him, dark and old, she shakes her head. Probably he has already seen her reaction from afar. When I approach him, he says, "You always say that I am too picky, but see? It is always they who refuse me!" Since his wife left him during the Cultural Revolution, he has lived a lonely bachelor life. Wrinkles have impolitely crawled all over his face, much of his hair has quietly fallen out, but he knows his current worth: employed in a scientific institute, with several achievements in scientific research, relatives overseas. . . . Everything that his wife disdained in those years is now highly valued. His current objective is to find a beautiful woman under thirty, . . . a modern type, 1.65 to 1.70 meters tall. . . . Looking at his feverish quest, I really don't know how I can make him understand that the perfect goddess does not exist. And even if she did, would she love him?

——Look at that fellow. He will go home disappointed again tonight. He is 1.62 meters tall. At the last party he said to me, "Although I am a bit short, I am a university graduate, with a good family background. I have to find someone taller than 1.6 meters—I don't care about anything else."

I wanted to help him get acquainted with a girl. "Look at that girl, 1.58 meters tall. In high heels she looks even taller than you, and she is gentle and quiet. Shall I have a word with her for you?"

He answered obstinately, "No way! Didn't I tell you? I want someone taller than 1.60 meters—that is my only principle."

I was stunned. One must buy clothes according to size; if they are too big or too small they will be uncomfortable. But love is the joining of heart with heart, and finding a sweetheart means seeking in the crowd a heart that beats in harmony with your own—can you depend only on a ruler?

——That thirty-five-year-old, 1.78-meter-tall reporter is really terribly busy. He has hardly missed one of these parties. At every event he always wants to find a girlfriend. At present, aside from conducting "love diplomacy" with seven or eight girls simultaneously, he is also unwilling to give up any dance or party. I urge him to pick a girl that he finds satisfactory and deepen his relationship with her, develop some affection. He looks at me disapprovingly: "That will hold things up! Only by comparing can one distinguish. What if a better one comes along later?" I don't know which girl would give her heart to him if she heard him talk like this. Who can guarantee that she is the "best" girl? Who wouldn't worry that in the future he will meet a better one, and then what will happen?

As a "matchmaker," I want to build bridges and act as a go-between. I hope that everyone will find a satisfactory companion. But you must put yourself in a suitable place.

A "Matchmaker," Guo Shangnan

SOURCE: "Wode hua shi shanyide" (My words are well-intentioned), *Zhongguo funü*, 11 (November 1984), 24.

My Views on Selecting a Spouse

What are the ideal criteria men use to select spouses, from the point of view of a male university student? I often discuss this with my classmates, and have found the most common answers to be beauty, poise, gentleness, and good breeding.

Between the sexes, first of all, there must be mutual attraction before love can emerge. The beauty and refinement of women moves men's hearts more directly than anything else. A beautiful appearance often arouses beautiful visions in people's souls and causes a favorable impression to take hold. If a man has a beautiful woman companion, not only does he himself feel proud, but he also becomes the object of envy and imitation on the part of other men. For example, a young man accompanies a beautiful girl walking down the street, and people walking along repeatedly gaze at them. The young man naturally can't help feeling pleased with himself, as if his status had been raised.

Men admire the gentleness and virtue of women, just as women adore the fact that men are open and aboveboard, resolute and steadfast. Gentleness accords with woman's nature. Especially after all the ultra-left jargon of the past, people want very much to distance themselves from the Fang Haizhen type of woman. [Fang Haizhen was a woman Party secretary in the Cultural Revolution–era opera "On The Docks."] I often hear girls say, "At least I must find a real man." By the same logic, men also want to find a gentle and virtuous wife.

Of course, if you can naturally get to know such a person in the course of your life and form a profound attachment, there is certainly no greater happiness. In that case, it is not only because the other party is beautiful that you feel she is lovable, but because she is lovable that you feel she is beautiful. But at present the social activities of young people are few, and they produce this kind of opportunity only by chance. Currently, men and women mainly make each other's acquaintance through the channel of introductions. Having no way of reaching a deep understanding of the other party, they accord outward appearance and age the first importance. Thus, to reproach males for stressing nothing but outward appearance, without analyzing the whole situation, is inappropriate.

Why do some men avoid career-minded women? I do not want the woman's status and capabilities to surpass my own. After struggling with all my might in society, when I return home I hope to obtain relaxation and pleasure. If I still have to talk about work and ideals, it is really a hardship. I certainly do not want the woman to pursue career goals, but rather want her to be well brought up. If, in addition, the woman has a bit of cultivation in music and the arts, that is all one could wish. Besides, at present the economic conditions of most families are not good, and household tasks are onerous. It is not possible for both people to put their entire effort into the pursuit of careers. "Two maintaining one" is a social reality.

What I have said above represents only my own observation, and it is hard to avoid bias. I hope everyone will air his own view; I wish to probe the subject further with everyone.

Yang Tong, Beijing

SOURCE: "Wode ze'ouguan" (My views on selecting a spouse), *Zhongguo funü*, 7 (July 1984), 14.

A Woman Who Has Her Own Goals Is Preferable

I am a single man, and after reading Comrade Yang Tong's article "My Views on Selecting a Spouse," I would like to air my own view. I believe that a woman who has her own goals is better.

Of course, the beauty, gentleness, and virtuousness of women is without doubt lovable. But if a woman has no career goals, and is merely a "family-style" "virtuous wife and good mother," in the 1980's one must say that this kind of woman is lacking in something. If a strongly goal-oriented man marries this kind of woman . . . it is not certain that their future life will be rich and happy. I have a classmate named Xiao Yi. In college, when we would discuss this question in our spare time, he forcefully maintained that "if a woman is beautiful and gentle, that's enough; nothing else is important." After he graduated from college and worked for a year, his wish was fulfilled, and he found a beautiful and virtuous "family-style" girl. For a time after they married, the young couple were quite lovey-dovey. They truly got along well, but after a few years Xiao Yi began to feel that his life was not complete. He was a writer in the cultural center, very career-minded. In the evenings he would read and study. He wife would always silently take up her endless knitting and sit soundlessly by his side, keeping him company, right until bedtime. When he would write something and bring it home to read to her, she always would respond "Uh-huh, uh-huh," never expressing any opinion. If he wanted to talk a bit about literary and artistic trends, his wife would merely respond with the "Uh-huh" that often hung on her lips. The two had no common career language, and their life slowly drifted toward mediocrity. Last month he wrote in a letter to me: "For a woman not to have talent is definitely not a virtue!" [This is a play on the words of the traditional Chinese saying, "A woman without talent is virtuous."] True, for a woman not to have talent is definitely not a virtue. Women need to have a bit of career-mindedness, especially in today's civilized society.

Fellow countrymen, when you pick a partner, don't forget—a woman who has her own goals is preferable.

Xie Xue, Hunan

SOURCE: "Haishi you suo zhuiqiude nüxing hao" (A woman who has her own goals is preferable), *Zhongguo funü*, 11 (November 1984), 24.

Please Listen to the View of a Woman University Student

Comrade Yang Tong believes that it is inadvisable to pick a career woman as a wife. It seems that once a woman is career-minded, she will lose the womanly disposition of gentleness and virtuousness, not understand how to live, and be unable to manage household affairs. Is it possible that things really are this way? I wish to talk about this from the perspective of a woman university student.

My classmates and I believe that only people who truly love their work can love life and understand its value. We have ideals, we have aspirations, but we are by no means the ethereal bookworms that some men imagine us to be. We not only have a certain degree of specialized knowledge, but also have a strong desire to master every kind of knowledge, including music, art, literature, cutting out garments, cooking. . . . Each of us has an individual personality and individual interests, and we hope to design our individual lives from different points of view. Perhaps some people will ask, is it possible to have both a career and a rich and varied life? We feel it is possible! This is because a career trains us, forces us to adapt to a fast-paced life, and to arrange our time compactly and efficiently. We are different from other women in that we have learned to dispense with the meaningless time spent strolling on the street and chatting idly, and use it instead for work, study, and beneficial activity. We wish to and we firmly believe that we can in future assume the duties of a wife in the home, like Madame Curie and Prime Minister Thatcher, who have both careers and a private life. We certainly do not want our own husbands to be like Fu Jiajie [the husband of a woman eye surgeon in Shen Rong's story "At Middle Age"], so encumbered by housework that he cannot advance in his career. We have only one request: we hope that with our husbands we can engage in mutual encouragement in work and study, and mutual aid in housework.

We despise those men who do not want a "woman strong in status and ability." They are not "real men." They do not dare or wish to compete with the strong, but want merely to treat their wives as nursemaids or dolls and to wallow in lovers' talk. True love is found in mutual consideration and caring. A person who can only make demands, who does not wish to make contributions or to fulfill obligations to others, cannot win true love.

Wang Shaoxia, Sichuan

SOURCE: "Qing ting yige nüdaxueshengde kanfa" (Please listen to the view of a woman university student), *Zhongguo funü*, 11 (November 1984), 25.

Where Is the Real Man of My Heart?

I am twenty-six this year, and have already passed the age for late marriage. I want to find a real man to be my lifelong companion. I have tried five times, but each attempt failed.

The first was a university graduate who worked in a company engaged in foreign trade. At our first meeting, he wore a well-pressed Western-style suit, his hair was so shiny it almost dripped oil, his face looked like it had been made up, and the smell of perfume assailed my nostrils. His affected and bashful manner differed too greatly from my mental image of a real man.

The second was a teacher, sincere and honest. But when we talked, he always said "Yes, yes," "Right, right"—too obsequious. It really seemed as though he had no opinions of his own.

The third was a young manager. In conversation he often displayed "crude behavior," always bragging how high his income was, that he had an uncle who was a boss in Hong Kong, etc. I disliked this behavior, since I was not seeing him in order to pursue such things. Furthermore, I feel that someone who uses these things as capital to brag about is not a real man.

The fourth was a factory technician. We had seen each other two or three times when he took liberties with me. I was very angry—he was too disrespectful. What did he take me for?

The fifth was a government functionary. We saw each other for a relatively long period and had some feelings for each other. But once when we got on a crowded bus together, I gave up my seat to a woman carrying a child. Later he said to me, "You are really dumb. Why couldn't you just pretend not to see them?" His words hurt me, revealing some of his hidden characteristics. So in the end we parted.

After these failures some friends asked, "Just what kind of man are you looking for? What are your criteria?" I can't spell them out, but I know that these five were not real men. Ah, where is the real man of my heart?

Xu Li

SOURCE: *Xinmin wanbao*, March 12, 1986.

Chronicle of a Marriage Fraud by a "Person Who Craved Office"

It was May 1st, International Workers' Day, and in a meeting room of the National People's Committee Guest House, where forums were commonly held for the nation's model workers, a solemn, lively, extraordinary marriage ceremony was taking place.

The groom, Zhao Chuansheng, was a soldier of the People's Liberation Army and a probationary Party member, of sound body, with regular features. The bride, Ji Yaqin, was a model worker of Jilin province, a Party member, vice-secretary of the Party branch of Siping City Machine Factory, a half-blind disabled girl.

The marriage celebration continued until dark. The guests who had come to congratulate the bride and groom on this happy occasion escorted them to the bridal chamber. As the sounds of their footsteps were dying away in the corridor, Zhao Chuansheng, who moments before had been bashfully rubbing his hands together as he answered the questions of guests, changed his facial expression: "After I am discharged and go to Siping, can you arrange for me to become a cadre?"

The bride was panic-stricken and had a premonition of trouble to come. But she gently and tactfully tried to persuade him: "Originally you were a village soldier. To arrange an urban job for you would require the local party to defy regulations. How could . . ."

Zhao Chuansheng glared at her and cut her off in a stern voice: "What nonsense! You are an important person there. If you can't even arrange a cadre position for me, what use was it for me to marry you?"

That night was the most painful of Ji Yaqin's entire life.

It could well be asked whether Zhao had married Ji reluctantly. Actually, before the marriage Ji Yaqin had fully considered her own physical handicaps. Three months earlier, Ji Yaqin had received a letter from a stranger in Beijing. Because she could not read the characters clearly, she had to have someone read it to her:

> Ji Yaqin:
>
> How are you?
>
> I read a report of your achievements in the *Jilin Daily*. It impressed upon me the beauty of your soul. I was deeply moved by the way you try to bring happiness to others. I'll say it directly, I love your way of thinking and I love you. I have never loved anyone before. I am not an impetuous person who carelessly takes up his pen, and have no other motives but am doing this out of a soldier's sincere aspirations. . . .   *Zhao Chuansheng*

After she heard the letter, Ji Yaqin did not speak for a long time. The person who read the letter offered to answer it for her, but she refused. When her parents, family, and friends found out about it, they all encouraged her to correspond with Zhao Chuansheng. But Ji Yaqin flatly refused. Her parents had her younger sister write an answer to Zhao Chuansheng falsely using her name, and another goodhearted person also wrote to Zhao. The two letters both truthfully described Ji Yaqin's situation. Later, after many solemn vows and entreaties from Zhao and repeated urging from her parents and many enthusiastic people, Ji Yaqin reluctantly promised to consider the matter. Her letter replying to him talked candidly about her physical handicaps, the great difference in their ages, her inability to live independently, and other weak points, and urged Zhao to seriously reconsider. But Zhao wrote several times, each time stating his determination to marry her. Even so, Ji Yaqin did not consent.

After more than two months, Ji Yaqin was sent to a national forum for model workers in Beijing. When Zhao heard the news, he immediately went to the place where the delegation was staying. The two had their first face-to-face conversation. Zhao began by describing his deep sense of longing for Ji Yaqin, saying he was so agitated that he had not slept for many days. Faced with this impromptu meeting, Ji Yaqin was temporarily speechless. She remained silent, pondering how to answer.

News of their meeting quickly spread among the conference delegates. Several days later, Zhao Chuansheng brought over someone who said the army leadership was taking the matter very seriously, and wanted them to give some thought to when and where the marriage might take place.

At this point, Ji could only silently nod her head.

The day after their marriage, Zhao put his plan into operation. He rented a camera and bought a thick new notebook. He used every opportunity to have his picture taken with famous delegates attending the meeting, and asked them for their autographs as a memento. He said to Ji Yaqin: "I want to rise to power and will pull these people up with me to be my righthand men. If they climb to power first, I will take the pictures I have had taken with them, the letters we have exchanged, and their autographs, and find them so they can pull me up with them. Only by relying on contacts can one become an official, a high official."

From the night of their marriage, Ji Yaqin passed almost every day in tears. During the conference she fainted several times, and her eyesight rapidly deteriorated. But Zhao Chuansheng did not relent. Aside from using his marriage to Ji Yaqin to go everywhere, swindling and bluffing, he constantly tormented and played with Ji Yaqin, presenting her with difficult, almost preposterous demands: 1. Arrange for him to be a cadre at the bureau level or higher after his arrival in Siping. 2. Apply for good housing. 3. Mail him 1,000 yuan before his discharge. 4. Permit him to see other women. 5. Give birth to a boy, not a girl. . . .

Ji Yaqin really was driven beyond the limits of forbearance. She wanted to reveal the truth to the press and expose his plot. But Zhao said without the slightest concern: "Our marriage has caused a sensation throughout the country. The newspapers are not going to slap themselves in the face, especially when you don't have any witnesses. So who is going to be rash enough to publish it in the newspaper?"

Innocent Ji Yaqin was temporarily intimidated. She racked her brains and couldn't think of a way out. Finally a relative made a suggestion, which she accepted. At the same time she filed for divorce from Zhao Chuansheng, she reported the true story to his army unit. Following a conscientious investigation by the army Party branch, the shameless trickster Zhao Chuansheng was relieved of his standing as a probationary Party member and was sent back to his home in Liangshan county, Shandong province.

SOURCE: "'Guanmi' pianhun ji" (Chronicle of a marriage fraud by a 'person who craved office'), *Baokan wenzhai*, February 11, 1986.

How to Tell If a Girl Likes You

—Does she often find excuses to be with you?
—Does she often ask others about you?
—Is she especially sensitive to your words and actions?
—Has she intentionally asked you some questions about love?
—Does she earnestly take to heart things you say casually?
—Is she interested in your past, your future, and your family affairs?
—Are her interests becoming more like your own?

—Is she jealous when you are with other members of the opposite sex?
—Is she happy to introduce you to her workmates, friends, and relatives?
—When she receives a message from you asking for her love, does she give any straightforward sign?

Selected by Huang Mingzhan

SOURCE: Huang Mingzhan, "Zenyang zhidao guniang xihuan ni" (How to tell if a girl likes you), *Dangdai qingnian*, 5 (May 1985), 22.

Do Not Disturb Others When Courting

I live in a dormitory room with a young worker from my workshop. We used to haved a good relationship. We helped each other in study, supported each other at work, and looked after each other in life, just like brothers. Late last year, he began to see a girl, and often brought her to the dormitory. Every time his girlfriend came over, I would take it upon myself to leave, to make things as convenient for them as possible. Almost imperceptibly, this became standard practice. At the beginning of February this year, I began to prepare for the exam for TV University. I wanted to make the best use of my spare time to review and broke with this "standard practice." My roommate was very unhappy. After work, I would read in the dorm room, and he would bring in his girlfriend. He turned the radio up as loud as it would go so they could talk in private. It made so much noise that I was terribly upset and had to pick up my books and go to another dormitory to study. They often engaged in lovers' talk in the dorm room until 11 or 12 at night. Once I was on night shift and should have gone to sleep at 8 in the evening, but he and his girlfriend were in the dorm room laughing and making noise until after 10. I really couldn't take it any more, and said to them, "It's late and I have to work night shift—please break it off for the night." But he took exception to this, and answered me: "No one's stopping you from sleeping." Just think, how could I take off my clothes and go to bed in front of his girlfriend? Since there was no alternative, I reported this problem to the workshop leadership, who talked with each of them separately. This added to his dissatisfaction with me, and behind my back he said that I was "jealous of him," a "hypocrite." I don't know whether to laugh or cry.

I want to offer a word to young men and women in love: when courting, do not disturb the work and study of others.

Dong Bing, Jiangxi

SOURCE: "Tan lian'ai shi buyao yingxiang bieren" (Do not disturb others when courting), *Zhongguo qingnian bao*, April 20, 1982, 3.

❈ 4
Marriage

IN PRE-LIBERATION CHINA, weddings were the occasion for as much festivity and extravagance as a family could afford. After the passage of the 1950 Marriage Law, however, the Chinese government encouraged its citizens to simplify weddings. It hoped to minimize the economic exchange involved, making marriage a union between equal individuals rather than a complex economic and status transaction between families. In addition, the government aimed to make legal registration replace weddings as the primary marriage ceremony, thereby asserting a degree of state control over marriage that did not previously exist. Despite intense propaganda, extravagant weddings continued to prevail until the Cultural Revolution, when celebrations were toned down for fear of attracting criticism (as either feudal or bourgeois, depending upon who and where one was).

The late 1970's witnessed a revival of extravagant wedding celebrations. The festivities, though in part a backlash against the spartan practices of the Cultural Revolution, were primarily an expression of the increased prosperity resulting from the post-Mao economic reforms. Whether a marriage was based on romantic love, compatibility, status, wealth, or convenience, weddings once again became an occasion for conspicuous consumption and display. No matter how much freedom parents might have given their children to select a mate, they rarely remained uninvolved in arranging the wedding itself. As consumerism became a more prominent part of life in the post-Mao era, wedding festivities were increasingly seen as an opportunity for families to display their wealth and status in the community.

If marriage offered a unique opportunity for women to achieve upward social mobility, then weddings were the occasion to begin collecting the benefits. All aspects of a wedding—engagement presents, goods provided by the bride and groom at the time of the wedding, and the wedding feast itself—symbolized both the groom's economic status and the value accorded the bride.

Government officials, perhaps disturbed by the return to traditional nuptial practices, frequently issued pleas that marriage ceremonies be kept simple. Yet since the government was gradually reducing its regulation of private life, the control it exerted over wedding celebrations was limited. Moreover, weddings were so much a family affair that even young couples who responded to government pleas to plan simple celebrations were often overruled by their parents.

Legal Versus Social Marriage

In pre-Liberation China, a marriage ceremony not only involved, but actually required, extensive public celebration. Only then did the marriage have legal validity.[1] In the eyes of the Chinese Communist state, though, marriage was strictly a civil bureaucratic procedure, requiring nothing more than a license from the marriage registration bureau. Marriage registration involved no ceremony, fanfare, or celebration. Before going to register, both the bride and groom had to have a physical examination and then secure marriage registration certificates from their respective work units. In the case of urban youth who were waiting to be assigned employment, this certificate was issued by the neighborhood residence committee. The certificate stated the person's full name, date of birth, ethnicity (Han or minority), previous marital status (never married, divorced, etc.), state of health, and the name and workplace of the person's spouse-to-be. The work units were responsible for ascertaining that the couple met the requirements of the 1980 Marriage Law. Replacing the Marriage Law of 1950, this law stipulated that marriage be voluntary on the part of both the bride and groom, that the groom be at least twenty-two and the bride at least twenty years of age. It prohibited marriage between immediate blood relatives and between collateral relatives within three generations, as well as marriage in which one partner suffered from "leprosy or any other disease that is deemed by medical science to render the person unsuitable for marriage." Finally, the law required that the prospective bride and groom appear at the marriage registration office themselves—no one could go as their substitute. These regulations were designed to ensure that marriage was truly the free choice of the couple, and not an arrangement made by their families.[2]

After the bride and groom had each secured the required certificate from their work units, they were supposed to go to the city marriage registration office within three months. At this time they were required to present their residence and work cards. The official at the marriage registration office would ask them how they met, who introduced them, and whether or not they were both entering the marriage of their own free will.[3] Whether the marriage was actually based on love or mutual convenience, on the desire of the partners or of their parents, as long as the marriage registration official was satisfied that the couple met the requirements of the law, they would be given a marriage license. Henceforth they were considered husband and wife.

Marriage in the eyes of the state, however, was not tantamount to marriage in the eyes of society, which continued to demand a ceremony or celebration.[4] In many cases, several years intervened between the marriage registration and the final wedding ceremony. This was primarily so the couple had time to acquire their own apartment or room, and the material goods with which to establish a household, before they proceeded with the wedding ceremony.

The status of a couple's relationship in the interval between marriage registration and wedding ceremony was ambiguous in many ways. It was generally assumed, for example, that the marriage would not be consummated until the wedding. However, many couples engaged in sexual relations as soon as they registered for marriage, often to the dismay of their parents. In one extreme case, a young man's father was prepared to report his son to the local police office for this "offense," abandoning the idea only when his daughter convinced him that there was nothing illegal about her brother's actions.[5]

Housing was one of the most urgent problems facing all urban residents in China. For young couples the problem was especially distressing, since they could not even put their names on the list for housing until they had registered their marriage. In Shanghai, plagued by the worst housing crisis of any Chinese city, many couples who had long since completed the marriage registration procedures were not able to marry until they were in their mid-thirties, simply because neither partner had access to housing.

A couple could obtain housing in several ways. One was through the family of the bride or groom. If the family had a house with more than one room, one of the rooms could be given to a married child. Often, though, especially in Shanghai, families had only one room. They could then build a partition, allocating the newly created room to the first child to marry. Since sons almost always had priority over daughters, a bride commonly moved to the groom's home, although it was not unheard-of for a newlywed couple to move in with the bride's family.[6] Needless to say, in families with several children competing for the limited housing stock, tension over the few available rooms frequently led to bitter conflicts. The problem was particularly acute because most people reaching marriageable age in the early 1980's were products of the "baby boom" of the 1950's, and typically had four or five siblings.

Liu Xinwu's story "The Overpass," a fictional examination of urban life published in 1981, describes the competition between siblings for the scarce housing space of their family after marriage. In this story, Hou Yong, the second brother of a Beijing family, marries the daughter of a middle-ranking cadre, hoping that this marriage will permit him and his wife to transfer back to Beijing from the countryside. But the wife's brothers do not want her to return and occupy a room in their parents' spacious apartment, since they plan to bring their own brides there after marriage. They are, after all, the sons of the household, and their needs come first. Meanwhile, Hou Yong's family lives in a crowded Beijing courtyard, with two aged parents, an elder son, his wife and child, and an unmarried sister sharing two small rooms. Hou Yong spends most of his time scheming to get his elder brother and sister-in-law transferred out of town and his younger sister married off so that he can return to Beijing and claim the room he feels is rightfully his.[7] Another fictional treatment of the housing problem is "The Destination," by Wang Anyi. The protagonist of this short story is Chen Xin, a young man who has just returned to Shanghai after ten years as a "sent-down youth" in Xinjiang. After his return his brother, hoping to secure the room in their parents' home for himself, pressures Chen Xin to marry a woman whose only merit is her family's spacious dwelling.[8] Both these stories enjoyed widespread popularity because they were among the first portrayals of an acute problem that often poisoned family relations and even influenced choice of a marital partner (see Chapter 3).

Another method of securing housing was to rely on the city housing bureau. Since this usually involved a wait of many years, during which the applicant had to visit the bureau frequently, ply the staff with gifts, and try to find contacts who had personal connections with the staff, it was not considered a particularly fruitful route. More commonly, young couples relied on their work units to assign them housing, which they could apply for once their marriage was registered.

Although in theory both men and women could join the pool of housing applicants, many urban work units gave priority to men. The situation was sufficiently extreme that some women publicly complained. Chen Yuexiang, a worker at a diesel engine factory in Weifang, Shandong, was only one of many women throughout the nation who wrote letters about housing allocation to the national women's magazine, *Chinese Women*, in 1980–81. "Several years ago I submitted a request to our factory leadership for housing," Chen reported.

My factory has plenty of housing, but it is only assigned to the male workers. It is not distributed to women workers, and in fact there is a regulation that women workers are not entitled to have housing assigned to them. The Constitution of our country stipulates that "in political, economic, cultural, social, and family life, women have the right to enjoy equality with men." Nevertheless, we do not have the right to enjoy equality with men in access to housing. What is this all about?[9]

Similar letters from women in Shenyang prompted the local Women's Federation to conduct a small-scale survey of housing assignments in thirty work units in the city. The Federation discovered that only one of these units treated men and women equally in assigning housing. Thirteen gave priority to men and special consideration to women in particularly difficult predicaments; the remaining sixteen units assigned their housing to men only. This was even true, the Federation found, of work units such as textile mills, where the overwhelming majority of workers were women. In units with no housing shortage, all newlywed men were assigned housing immediately upon request, whereas newlywed women, even if they had no alternative housing, were not eligible.[10] The same situation prevailed in textile factories in the city of Shashi, in Hubei province. Until 1985 the rule was, "Housing will be assigned to male workers who have worked for five years and to women workers who have worked for fifteen years; men who have worked for two years and get married can be assigned housing, but women [who get married] will not be eligible."[11] Factory officials most likely did not regard this as discrimination, but rather as allowing the man to fulfill his responsibility to provide housing for his family. Women, it was assumed, would inevitably have access to housing through their husbands.[12] Thus, it was most commonly the groom who had to secure housing for the couple before they could finally hold a wedding celebration.

Housing was only one—albeit the most important—of several items necessary before a couple could establish a household. While waiting for housing, both partners were usually busy collecting the goods they were expected to contribute to the new household. The expectation that each would provide certain goods was reminiscent of the exchange of brideprice and dowry that characterized marriages in pre-Liberation China: formal negotiations about the brideprice to be paid by the groom's family and the gifts to be included in the wife's dowry were crucial to any marriage agreement. Although the exchange of brideprice and dowry was attacked by the Chinese government after 1949, it persisted clandestinely in many rural areas, becoming explicit once again in the late 1970's. In large cities, though, payment of brideprice was rare, and discussions about gifts to be provided by the bride and groom were often casual.[13] Occasionally, the goods to be exchanged were negotiated at a formal engagement ceremony; more often, though, they were determined informally.[14] As in earlier times (and as in the countryside in the 1980's), however, many urban families understood the exchange of gifts at marriage as symbolic of the value and social status of the bride and groom.[15] In the 1980's, the cost of goods to be provided by the groom usually far exceeded that contributed by the bride.[16]

In most cities the husband provided the so-called hardware. This consisted primarily of furniture, referred to as the "forty-eight legs"—a bed (4 legs), two bedside stands (4 legs each), a dining table (6 legs), four chairs (4 legs each), a wardrobe (6 legs), and two chests of drawers (4 legs each). (It was considered desirable, but not essential, to provide a sofa as well.) In addition to the "forty-eight legs," the hardware provided by the groom ideally included a "whole chicken" (an expression derived from the fact that the Chinese word for chicken—*ji*—is a homonym for the word for machine, and these items were all thought of as machines): a sewing machine, radio, tape recorder, television set, electric fan, watch, desk lamp, and camera. The bride's family was responsible for the "software": four to eight cotton quilts (and preferably one down quilt as well), bed sheets and pillows, kitchen utensils, a washbasin, and toilet articles. In addition, the bride was expected to own a set of new clothes. No rigid rules governed the exchange of goods, and there was a great deal of variation from city to city (and even within cities). Furthermore, as new items became available, the components of the "hardware" and "software" continued to change. According to a 1982 survey, for example, it had become common for men living in major urban centers to supply (or be expected to supply) a washing machine and a refrigerator.[17]

Most of these items reflected the increasing availability of modern consumer goods in Chinese cities. But gift preparation also suggested the persistence of traditions that had been brought to cities such as Shanghai and Tianjin by rural migrants during the late nineteenth and early twentieth centuries. In Tianjin in the early 1980's, for example, when a young woman planned to marry, her female neighbors helped sew at least one ritual stitch on the quilts her family made for her wedding. It was believed that bad luck would befall those whose quilts were made by only one person. A peanut and a date were sewn into the corners of each quilt to encourage the production of offspring. (The Chinese word for peanut, *huasheng*, is a homonym for the words "varied" and "to give birth," while *zao*, the word for date, is a homonym for "early." Together they expressed a wish that the couple would give birth to many different kinds of children as early as possible: *sheng gezhong geyang de haizi, yue zao yue hao.*)[18]

Purchasing and preparing these items was as difficult as arranging housing. The first difficulty was the expense, which could be upward of two or three thousand yuan. A survey of the cost of marriages in Shanghai in 1981–82 showed the following breakdown of expenses for an average wedding: [19]

	(yuan)		(yuan)
furniture	750	radio	340
two trunks	90	washing machine	200
eight quilts	300	lamps	200
sewing machine	150	vase and tea set	40
television	400	TOTAL	2,620
electric fan	150		

By 1985, goods for a marriage ordinarily cost 3,300 yuan, and some couples spent as much as 5,000 yuan—several times the average urban worker's annual salary, which in 1985 was about 1,000 yuan.[20] Unless their parents helped, young couples often exhausted the savings they had accumulated over three or four years of work in order to get married. Having sufficient funds, however, did not guarantee that the bride and groom would be able to purchase the goods they desired. Many goods were in short supply and required coupons for purchase. To obtain the coupons for goods such as furniture or television sets, the bride and groom could enter their names on the waiting list at their work unit. The amount of time they had to wait was unpredictable. Most tried to hasten the process by going through unofficial channels, a process known colloquially as "going through the back door."

A young man's experience in Shanghai in 1980 illustrated the problem. He had registered for marriage and was waiting for his work unit to assign housing to him and his bride-to-be. In the meantime he started to look for the furniture he would have to purchase. First he went to various furniture stores in Shanghai, but discovered that a wait of several years would be required to buy the goods he wanted. Furthermore, no one in his family had personal connections with any of the furniture stores. His sister, though, had spent several years working in a town in Jiangxi province, one of the few areas in China where wood is plentiful. Relying on her connections in Jiangxi and on her family's personal relationship with someone who worked for the railway, the groom's family was able to purchase and transport a supply of wood from Jiangxi to Shanghai. Since government policy permitted small-scale independent businesses in the cities, his family was able to hire a carpenter to build the furniture. For several months, the carpenter came to their home (a single room) every day to work. At the time the furniture was completed, the young man still did not have housing. His family had no choice but to store his furniture in their room, making their already cramped quarters even more crowded.[21]

To some extent, it became easier to secure goods in the early 1980's. As more consumer goods, such as refrigerators and washing machines, became available in department stores, it became possible for those who had enough money to purchase the items without lengthy delays. Nevertheless, accumulating the items required for the wedding continued to be a troublesome burden for young couples.

For many young couples, then, preparing for the wedding was a long, trying process. Marriage registration was only the first step. Only after they acquired the material goods necessary to establish a household—sometimes as much as four or five years later—could they finally begin to plan a wedding celebration.

The Wedding

Once a couple secured housing and all the agreed-upon items, they could plan the wedding celebration, paid for by the groom's family, that would mark their actual marriage. In contrast to the situation in pre-Liberation China, when wedding rituals symbolized the passage of the bride from her natal family to that of the groom, wedding ceremonies in urban China in the 1980's reflected the increasingly conjugal nature of marriage.

Several rituals were performed by the couple just prior to the wedding celebration. The wedding photograph was the most important. This was taken at one of the many studios found in the downtown districts of most cities. The studios provided a choice of "costumes," ranging from traditional Chinese gowns (*qipao*) to American-style lacy white wedding dresses with veils for the brides and tuxedos for the grooms. Often these outfits consisted of only the top portion—from the waist up—since that was all that would appear in the photograph. Prior to the wedding it was also customary for the bride and groom to select and purchase a matching pair of stone chops (signature stones). The figure of a legendary animal was sculpted on top; the bride's name was carved on the bottom of one, the groom's name on the other. They would use these chops for any official transactions that required a signature.

Many aspects of the wedding ceremony as practiced in Chinese cities in the early 1980's were modernized versions of customs that were widespread before Liberation. In early twentieth-century Shanghai, for instance, it was customary for the groom's family to send a sedan chair to pick up the bride at her family's home. After she was carried to his home, the couple bowed to his parents and knelt in front of a table holding the ancestral tablets, with candles and incense alongside. The groom's family hosted a wedding feast, to which numerous friends and relatives were invited, and which often left the family heavily in debt.[22]

In the 1980's, sedan chairs were replaced by bicycles, or more commonly by automobiles or vans, known in Chinese as "breadloaf cars" (*mianbao che*) because they look like loaves of bread on wheels. A van and its driver could be rented or, with the proper personal connections, borrowed.[23] On the day of the wedding the younger female relatives of the bride and groom piled into the van, which was decorated with red rosettes and ribbons, and were driven to the bride's house. There they had tea and chatted with the bride's family. Then the bride joined this group, and they returned by van to the house of the groom, or sometimes to the bride and groom's new apartment. As the bride stepped out of the car, it was customary for friends or relatives of the groom to set off firecrackers. This was partly to create a festive atmosphere, but also represented the continuation of a traditional belief that evil spirits had to be frightened away from the bride. The same purpose was also served by requiring the bride to throw her shoes out the car window. The Chinese words "to throw shoes out" (*qu xie*) are a homonym for "getting rid of evil."[24]

In large cities such as Shanghai and Tianjin, it was most desirable to hold a wedding feast at a fancy restaurant, where newlyweds could reserve seven or eight tables (each seating ten guests) for their party.[25] A restaurant banquet was not only expensive but often difficult to arrange, and it was usually necessary to use personal connections to secure a reservation. During the peak wedding season at the time of the Spring Festival, the popularity of this practice made it almost impossible for individual patrons to dine in restaurants; wedding parties reserved every table virtually every day of the week.

Even if the wedding feast were held at the home of the groom instead of in a restaurant, the family still had to use all its connections to purchase the necessary foodstuffs and borrow enough kitchenware for the guests. Some families even hired a cook for the occasion. The proliferation of free markets after 1978 made it much easier, although also more expensive, to procure an impressive array of foods: chicken, beef, peanuts, noodles, and vegetables, as well as large quantities of hard liquor. In northern Chinese cities, where most people lived in rooms around a courtyard, neighbors usually offered their courtyard space to the groom's family to use for the festivities. The rooms and courtyard were decorated with "double happiness" symbols cut from red paper and pasted on the walls.

Wedding dress for the bride and groom reflected the influence of Western styles on Chinese youth described in Chapter 2. Both the bride and groom dressed in Western-style slacks and jackets. The bride often wore a blouse of pink or red, traditional nuptial colors, although by the mid-1980's it became more common for brides to wear a wedding dress or gown. Wearing red roses in the lapels of their jackets, they would stand near the entrance to the restaurant, greeting the guests as they arrived.

In contrast to practices in pre-1949 China, and in some rural areas up through the 1980's, the banquet guests at urban weddings included the bride's relatives and friends as well as the groom's. During the feast, the bride was expected to pour wine for the guests, and to see them to the door when they departed. The bride sometimes had an additional duty: as relatives arrived, her new mother-in-law would introduce them, saying, "This is your husband's second uncle." The bride was then to say "How are you, Second Uncle?" This ritual, perhaps a modification of the bows to the husband's relatives expected in traditional rituals, signified that she had taken her place in the family and that the groom's relatives were now her own.[26]

Part of the expense of the wedding feast was recovered by the family, it being customary for each of the guests to give the married couple a gift. At the feast, a list of those who had given gifts in advance was sometimes posted on the wall. Other guests brought money in a red paper envelope, which they discreetly pressed into the hand of the bride as she poured their wine. Thermos bottles, bed sheets, art work, spittoons, and lengths of cloth were common wedding gifts. Some gifts were explicitly given to the family of the groom, while others were intended for the young couple themselves.

During the feast, guests teased the young couple and played practical jokes on the bride, such as forcing her to light their cigarettes, then refusing to inhale so that she had to repeat the procedure again and again. The bride and groom were exhorted to tell the story of how they fell in love. Sometimes an apple was dangled on a string before the young couple, and the guests would order them each to take a bite. At the last moment the pranksters would jerk the apple away, leaving the surprised couple kissing before the assembled visitors. Many of these jests were the legacy of traditional wedding customs. In rural areas, they were carried on in even more extreme forms that usually made the bride the victim of the pranks.

After the wedding feast many of the guests would accompany the bride and groom to their home or room. As the evening progressed, some of the male guests could be expected to make suggestive comments to the groom or even to sing suggestive songs. In the countryside, friends of the groom, ostensibly to "loosen up" the bride, engaged in a custom known as "disturbing the bridal chamber," which in extreme cases was tantamount to gang rape.[27] In one tragic incident, friends of the groom hid a microphone connected to the commune's broadcast system under the newlyweds' bed. Humiliated, the bride committed suicide the next morning.[28]

In the cities, friends and colleagues would visit the newlyweds for several weeks after the wedding, and for such occasions the bride and groom purchased "happiness candy." According to one survey, a couple with an average income in Shanghai had to purchase approximately 100 *jin* (1 *jin* = 1.1 pounds) of candy, at a cost of 200 yuan.[29]

"Make Your Weddings Frugal, Civilized, and Lively"

Wedding celebrations had become increasingly extravagant in the late 1970's, with the increasing availability of consumer goods and the reopening of elegant restaurants closed during the Cultural Revolution. A survey of marriage-related costs in Shanghai in 1981–82 reported that families spent an average of 1,200 yuan for the wedding ceremony—including everything from the wedding photo to the happiness candy.[30] This was more than the annual income of many workers. Weddings were one of the few occasions when families could display their wealth and generosity, and thus they often vied to outdo one another, for instance in the number of tables they reserved for the weddings of their children.

The extravagance of wedding feasts varied with a person's social status. At one extreme were intellectuals—the boldest in departing from traditional customs—who often skipped the feast entirely and instead invited a few friends for a simple dinner. Factory workers tended to hold more elaborate celebrations. A factory in Shenyang reported that of the 165 couples who married in 1981, 80 percent hosted banquets of more than ten tables.[31] Many urban families, not satisfied with using one car to pick up the bride, arranged long caravans of cars, or even used their personal connections to hire a bus.[32] By far the most extravagant weddings were those involving sons or daughters of high-level officials, some of which were the subject of well-publicized scandals. One such case involved an official in Beijing who, for his son's wedding, invited six hundred guests to feast for three days at a famous restaurant. The vegetables alone reportedly cost 400 yuan.[33]

As the extravagance associated with wedding presents and celebrations increased, the government stepped up efforts at control. Newspapers and magazines published numerous descriptions of marriage arrangements and wedding feasts, designed either to warn people of the dangers of extravagance or to provide models of thrift that could be emulated.[34] Although the articles were directed at everyone involved in marriage arrangements—the bride, the groom, and their respective parents—a careful reading suggests that women, in particular, were held responsible for the extravagance.

This portrayal of women as the culprits began with articles about engagement presents. Not all couples became formally engaged, but when they did, the groom-to-be was often expected to give presents not only to the bride, but to her mother as well. An article entitled "Too Expensive to Visit the Future Mother-in-Law" reported the complaints of male factory workers in Shanghai that the increasingly elaborate gifts expected by the bride's mother had become an intolerable burden. Whereas a few years earlier, simple presents worth 10 or 20 yuan had sufficed, by 1982 young men had to spend 50 or 60 yuan, the equivalent of a month's wage for many. A common warning was that a man should not cross the threshold of his future mother-in-law's home without a "machine gun" (a whole ham), two "packages of explosives" (two boxes of cakes), 400 "cartridges" (twenty packs of cigarettes), and four "grenades" (four bottles of top-quality liquor).[35] The Youth League Committee of the Shanghai Light Industry Bureau attributed this problem to "mothers-in-law competing with one another for the most expensive presents from their sons-in-law," and to "young women compet[ing] with one another for the 'richest' fiancé."[36] The problem, in other words, originated with women.

The same analysis was applied to the discussion of wedding gifts. Beginning in the early 1980's, articles in *China Youth News* criticized young couples for requiring too many goods when they married. Tragedies resulting from unreasonable demands, invariably attributed to the bride-to-be, were publicized in order to warn young people of the dangers of being excessively materialistic. In some cases the difficulties attendant on securing the wedding goods led young men to theft. Stories such as the following were repeated in scores of newspaper articles: A young man in Shanghai was planning to marry and his wife had "demanded" that he provide an imported watch, woolen clothing, modern-style furniture, etc. Unable to purchase these items, and afraid that if he did not buy them she would refuse to marry him, he decided to try his hand at stealing. First he stole some small toys, just to make sure he could do it without being caught. As his confidence increased, he tried stealing the more expensive items he needed for his wedding, as well as things he could sell for cash. By stealing and then selling leather handbags and electric fans, he was able to accumulate several hundred yuan. Unfortunately he was caught while trying to sneak onto a boat and steal the passengers' belongings—a trick he had successfully performed on three previous occasions—and was subsequently turned over to the Public Security Bureau.[37]

In the countryside, where the groom's family commonly had to pay a brideprice, the consequences were often even more tragic. In one case, an enlightened young woman insisted that her fiancé did not have to pay the expected 2,000 yuan brideprice. Her parents, however, felt the absence of a brideprice was an insult. They refused to recognize their daughter's marriage, disowned her, and attempted to beat her; when she escaped, they threatened to beat her to death if they ever saw her again.[38] In another case, the brideprice demanded by a woman's family drove the family of the groom-to-be to poverty and near-starvation. Just as they had finally saved enough money, the bride's family raised the price. The young man, already plagued by guilt for the hardship his marriage had inflicted upon his mother and brothers, committed suicide.[39]

Lest these cases seem too extreme to be applicable to most families, the press also published numerous stories with slightly less tragic, but equally instructive, endings. A woman in a Zhejiang village, unusually pretty and a high school graduate, considered herself a "golden phoenix," and figured that she deserved a substantially higher brideprice than ordinary women. Therefore, on every holiday she demanded a gift from her fiancé's family. When they became engaged, she requested eight sets of clothes, three pairs of leather shoes, and 100 yuan. Before the actual wedding, she required that her fiancé provide a wardrobe, sewing machine, bicycle, and sofa. In addition to insisting on an elaborate wedding feast, she requested a 50 yuan gift for "passing through the [groom's] gate." She reveled in luxury until she had to face the reality of married life. Then, the debts her husband had accumulated to meet her demands became her debts as well. To repay the debts they had to sell the bicycle, sewing machine, and sofa. Two years after the wedding, they still owed 300 yuan. "I, who used to be a 'golden phoenix,' have now become an 'ugly duckling,'" the woman lamented. She deeply regretted her previous belief that a high brideprice was necessary to confirm her value, and warned readers of *China Youth News* to learn from her mistakes.[40]

In each of these cases as they were portrayed in the press, the tragedies would not have occurred had the bride or her family not demanded gifts. The underlying message was that it was incumbent upon women to regulate the material aspects of marriage. This analysis was extended to the public discussion of wedding feasts. Although the groom's family was responsible for the banquet, writers commonly portrayed the degree of extravagance as a response to demands made by the bride's family. A number of news articles reported the potentially catastrophic consequences of ostentatious weddings. Although the tragedies themselves often had little to do with demands by the bride's family, authors of these accounts often went to great lengths to establish a direct connection.

For example, an article entitled "Unreasonable Demands for Extravagance Resulted in a Deadly Auto Accident" related the story of a young couple in rural Jiangxi. For a year prior to their wedding, the bride's family had continually demanded presents from the groom. As the wedding day approached, her family insisted that a car be provided to deliver the bride to her new home. The groom's proposal that he use a mini-tractor was unacceptable to the bride's family, so he rented a truck. When the groom went to the bride's home on the day of the wedding, her family, "determined to squeeze something out of them for the last time," insisted that the groom give them yet another sum of money. Presumably because so much time was spent negotiating this final gift, it was already dark when the truck finally set out to deliver the bride's family to the banquet. The driver, drunk and pressured to drive fast, crashed into a tractor. The truck was demolished, the bride suffered broken bones in her hand and leg, and her brother was killed. Local observers concluded that "the bride's family really deserved what they got!"[41] The editor of the newspaper apparently agreed, for the article's title implied that their materialism was the direct cause of the tragedy. Readers not convinced of the connection might have drawn a slightly different, though equally instructive, conclusion: individuals guilty of excess materialism in wedding celebrations would eventually be duly punished, not by Party or government officials, but by fate.

Such incidents were not confined to the countryside. In Shanghai, for instance, one young man who could not afford to have an elaborate wedding banquet was forced to borrow 800 yuan when "the bride's family insisted on having one." The burden of the debt caused the newlywed couple a great deal of hardship: to earn more money, the husband worked overtime until he finally became ill and collapsed; the wife developed problems during her pregnancy. "Comrades," the young man concluded, "having a big wedding banquet has caused me so much grief! I have not been able to even taste the happiness of the first month of marriage. Instead I have been scorched by hardship."[42] Nowhere was it implied that the groom or his family had any responsibility for the extravagance; they had simply complied with the wishes of the bride and her family.

This ascription of guilt to women has several possible explanations. Women's families may truly have been the primary advocates of extravagance, reflecting a desire to obtain their money's worth for the daughter they had raised, as was the case in traditional Chinese society. The demand for gifts might thus be understood as a disguised version of the traditional brideprice. The increasingly extravagant demands made by women's families may also have indicated the enhanced economic value of women that resulted from their employment outside the home. More than economic value was at stake, however. A woman was seen as a piece of "second-rate goods" if she did not have a collection of expensive gifts at her wedding. Wedding gifts reflected a woman's status and value, and by extension that of her entire family, who by showing off the presents to neighbors and friends made a statement about their status in the community. Weddings were perhaps the only time in a woman's life that she and her family were the beneficiaries of custom, and it is thus not surprising that they would exploit the occasion for all it was worth.

Criticism of extravagant weddings and reports of their dire consequences were coupled with a campaign to "make weddings frugal, civilized, and lively." The press published numerous accounts of model weddings, in which the participants scaled down their wedding feast to two tables, used a bicycle to fetch the bride, and still had a good time. In a typical story, a rural couple was praised for resisting parental and social pressure to have a big feast. When the bride's family warned that "a girl who moves into her husband's family without a wedding violates customs and poisons the air," she and the groom simply took their marriage license and lived together. The money that would have been wasted on an elaborate celebration enabled them to live comfortably:

After their marriage they used the money originally intended for the wedding feast to repair their house, and to buy furniture, fertilizer, farm machines, and books on agricultural technology. They also raised chickens, rabbits, and bees. As a result of sowing seeds and applying fertilizer as the books directed, the wheat in their field is the best in the village this year. Now when people see Cai and Zhao living happily with love and respect for each other, they all say that Cai was wise in using the money on these needs rather than on a wedding feast. Her parents also admit that she took the "right step." [43]

Stories such as this were intended to convince couples that any short-term hardship they faced by defying the wishes of their parents would be more than offset by long-term happiness.

The editors of *China Youth News*, hoping to encourage less extravagance, also cited the examples of the modest weddings held by famous people: "When the famous French physicist Madame Curie got married, she did not tell any relatives or friends; nor did she have a celebration. She and her husband just bought two bicycles and went bicycling through the countryside for a month." Or: "When Lu Xun [a revered Chinese writer of the 1920's and 1930's] and Xu Guangping were married, all they had in their new home was a wooden bed, a desk, two tea tables, and four square stools." [44]

Even the wedding ceremonies of some of China's minority groups were heralded as models of frugality. One article in *China Youth News*, for instance, described the customs of the Yao people in Guizhou: "On the evening of the wedding day, the boy goes to the girl's home with a pair of new shoes and socks. He presents his request to marry the girl to her parents, has a very ordinary meal with them, and then takes the girl home for the wedding. There is no feast, no guests, and no specially furnished wedding chamber."[45] Although the article's author refrained from editorial comments, the simplicity of the wedding was implicitly endorsed. This description of Yao weddings was presumably published not to satisfy readers' curiosity about China's ethnic minorities, but rather to suggest a commendable alternative to extravagance.

Cadres and Party and Youth League members were exhorted to "take the lead" in making their weddings simple. In Zhejiang province they were told that to inspire others they should not ask for gifts or have banquets when they or their children married; when their friends and relatives married, they should not send gifts or attend their banquets. In the city of Hangzhou, a Party directive ordered units not to provide cars for weddings (in Lanzhou it was made a crime), and instructed restaurants that, in general, they should not allow newlyweds to reserve more than two tables for wedding feasts.[46]

In addition to criticizing elaborate celebrations, the government also proposed several alternative, more frugal, forms of wedding celebration. The press, in turn, provided its readers with reports of ways in which people all over the country devised more economical wedding ceremonies. The most popular were the "collective wedding" and the "travel wedding."

Collective weddings (first organized by the Guomindang government in the 1940's) were sponsored by the city as well as by individual work units, and were usually held at the time of the Spring Festival, when the largest number of couples planned to get married. Sometimes, to lend prestige to this form of wedding ceremony, local dignitaries were invited to attend. When the city of Tianjin sponsored a New Year's collective wedding in 1982, both the second Party Secretary of the city of Tianjin and the Mayor attended. Altogether 696 couples participated. Those who had canceled plans for elaborate wedding parties in order to participate in the collective wedding received special attention in the newspaper. In the Tanggu district, for example, two brothers were both originally planning to marry—one at New Year's and the other during Spring Festival. Their parents had already planned a banquet of fifteen tables for each. "But when they heard the city was sponsoring a collective wedding," the newspaper reported, "they held a family meeting and decided to cancel the banquet and participate in the collective wedding. At the meeting the eighty-year-old grandmother said, 'This time we will rely on our children's proposal and have a new-style wedding.'"[47] It appears that most of the couples who chose to participate in collective weddings were Party members, members of the Youth League, or model workers.

A more popular alternative wedding celebration promoted by the government was the "travel wedding." Instead of renting a car and hosting an expensive wedding feast, the couple simply went on a short trip, usually for three or four days. Those who lived in Beijing or Tianjin frequently went to the seaside resort of Beidaihe, while couples from Shanghai headed for the famous scenic cities of Suzhou and Hangzhou.[48]

The major problem faced by couples planning travel weddings was finding hotel space. This was a problem for all Chinese tourists, and usually a letter of introduction from one's work unit was necessary to secure a hotel room. In Shanghai, the room shortage was so severe that many visitors had no choice but to spend the night in barber shops and bath houses. To solve this problem for couples celebrating a travel wedding, one letter to the editor of *China Youth News* suggested that special "newlywed dormitories" be established in the areas most commonly visited.[49] In the meantime, many couples stayed with relatives who happened to live in the cities they decided to visit for their travel wedding. Another possibility was to take advantage of one of the "package" group travel weddings offered by numerous travel agencies.

The travel weddings generated their own forms of abuse and extravagance. The press complained of young couples competing with one another to see who could go to the greatest number of cities or the most scenic resorts. It was not uncommon for couples to stay away longer than the vacation time granted by their work units. And many couples used travel weddings as a post-wedding-party honeymoon, rather than as the substitute for the wedding party that the government intended it to be.

Even those couples who preferred simpler arrangements such as collective weddings or travel weddings often found it difficult to resist social pressure. A letter written by a young woman to *China Youth News* in 1981 expressed concerns shared by many others. "My boyfriend and I have freely chosen each other, have been in love for one year, and plan to get married next year," wrote Xiao Feng.

We are both Youth League members, and therefore, in accordance with the Party's call, we must conduct our marriage in the new way. In addition, considering the fact that my boyfriend's family is not very well off, I have not requested any presents. I will only receive two sets of clothes from his family. But my parents do not agree, and some of my girlfriends laugh at me. They tell me, "Take a look at Xiao Ying. She did not ask for any gifts, and everyone started gossiping that she was a 'piece of second-rate goods.'" . . . "Look at Xiao Hua—the gifts she requested filled three big cars. That is really glorious!" Hearing them talk like this, I cannot help but waver in my thinking. Is it possible that women who do not request elaborate gifts are "second-rate"?[50]

Another woman Youth League member, originally determined to set an example by refusing to accept gifts from her colleagues at the factory where she worked, began to have second thoughts. Her friends reminded her that she had already sent a total of several hundred yuan to various factory colleagues when they married, and that it was now her turn to collect her share. "Hearing this, I cannot help but think they are right," she wrote to the newspaper editor.[51] Even couples who felt pressured to participate in "collective weddings" sometimes returned home and had an elaborate celebration anyway.[52]

Rural couples determined to have simpler weddings faced even more severe social pressure. The account written by a young soldier, entitled "I Was a Bridegroom Four Times," illustrated the pressures a couple could expect to confront in the countryside. Lu Limin and his bride, opposed to extravagant weddings, simply gave their soldier friends candy and cigarettes. Thus married, they went on a month-long trip to Hangzhou and Suzhou. Before returning to work they stopped at his home village and then at that of his wife's family. When they arrived at his family's home, friends and relatives came to congratulate them and brought gifts. It would have been ungracious not to hold a feast in return, and before they knew it, the couple was involved in a second wedding. When they arrived in the village of his wife's family, Lu had to confront angry relatives who warned him, "You waited a month before entertaining guests; that is already bad enough. But if you still refuse to entertain guests, then it is really shameful. Here if a girl does not have a feast, she is not considered married." Thus the third wedding celebration. The fourth and final wedding celebration took place when they went to his wife's work unit, where her colleagues had decorated her room with flowers and gifts (including a name list of gift givers and their gifts), and came to engage in the ritual teasing of bride and groom their first evening there. Lu himself commented on the typicality of these experiences when he concluded, "But perhaps none of this is really news, since so many people in the countryside do things this way."[53]

As Lu's story suggests, social pressure in the countryside tended to be more extreme than in the cities. Nevertheless, in the cities, as in rural areas, the nature of weddings was often not dictated by individual choice on the part of the bride and groom, nor by state policy. Young couples planning their weddings were likely to find themselves subjected to social pressure and the desire of their families to "have face." Despite the official directives to make weddings more modest (and suggestions about how to do so), marriage remained the major event in the lives of young women and men. It was the occasion for as much extravagance as families could afford and officialdom would tolerate.

Although the festivities surrounding wedding celebrations in the 1980's involved a revival of some traditional practices, significant differences existed. A much larger sector of the population could aspire to accumulation and consumption than had been the case before. The goods to be exchanged in a wedding, some of them products of the post-Mao revolution in consumer durables, obviously differed. Although the extravagance of wedding celebrations was primarily a reflection of the new-found prosperity of many families, women and their families were singled out for blame in government campaigns. Women, as noted above, were quite possibly the primary advocates of extravagance. It is also possible, however, that the responsibility attributed to women reflected popular belief that women were the arbiters of consumption and guardians of the domestic sphere. As our examination of married life in Chapter 5 will suggest, the wedding itself was only the beginning of a woman's responsibility in regulating the moral and material life of the family.

Translations

"Love Soaked in Tears" describes how the pressures felt by a young man to prepare adequate gifts for his wedding led him to crime. The increasingly elaborate nature of wedding banquets in the 1980's produced a range of new tensions. In "A Family Quarrel," a couple's imminent marriage is almost destroyed when the taxi arranged by the husband fails to appear at his fiancée's home. Another couple, whose plight is recounted in the story "An Extravagant Marriage Mired Me in Hardship," have to live penuriously after their wedding in order to pay back the money borrowed to finance a wedding feast. The feasts were a burden not only to the bride and groom but to their guests, who were expected to provide cash presents. One young man angrily left a wedding when he realized that guests were seated at tables according to the value of their gifts, as recounted in "Why I Left the Banquet."

To attempt to convince couples they should resist social pressure to exchange expensive gifts and plan lavish wedding celebrations, the government launched a campaign to simplify weddings. In addition to promoting alternative forms of wedding celebrations, the government publicized accounts of couples who had insisted that their marriages be simple. "Shicong Is a Clear-Thinking Girl" is an example.

Love Soaked in Tears

It was noon, August 20, 1981. Inside a police station in Nanning City, a young man sat motionless and expressionless. Suddenly, a slim girl rushed into the room and, grabbing the shoulders of the young man, asked, "Xiao Lu, what has happened to you?" Trying to evade her eyes, the young man said, "Yalin, I have done something shameful. . . ."

So it was true! Yalin's hands dropped weakly from Lu's shoulders. What a cruel reality! About fifteen days before, Lu had stolen a savings account book with a 900-yuan deposit from a worker in his factory. Since it was the first time he had done such a thing, he was frightened and did not dare cash it any of six times he entered the bank. Then one day he finally made up his mind to do it, and he was caught right on the spot.

"I'm sorry, Yalin, I'm really sorry. It's all over between us. You can have all the things we have prepared for our wedding. . . . I was afraid that when it came time to have a wedding banquet I would have no money to give you."

"What?" Yalin felt as though she had been struck on the head, and she bit her lips. She slapped Lu's face twice and ran out of the police station, tears in her eyes.

"Everything is finished." Lu closed his eyes painfully.

The moonlight was shining in front of the bed. Unable to fall asleep, Yalin began to recall the love that had brought so much happiness to her and Lu. . . .

Yalin was twenty-six and a driver in the same factory where Lu worked. She was tall and charming, with deep, large eyes and a high nose. Several young men had courted her and they were all quite all right by conventional standards. But she rejected them all. When the young men in the factory found out that Lu was dating her, they all said, with a certain sarcasm, that a fresh flower had been planted in a heap of dung.

Actually, although Lu could match Yalin in both age and height, he would be "graded" very low by conventional standards. Yalin's entire family lived in the city and everyone had a job. Lu's wages were lower than Yalin's, and his family was in the countryside. His father was too old to work. Therefore his family always had a difficult time making a living. Yalin thought, however, that what the conventional standards said was not so important. What really mattered was whether he was a good man. Lu was, in fact, the best turner in the factory and although he did not look very smart and was not very articulate, he learned things very fast: he had taught himself carpentry and tailoring, as well as bicycle and watch repair. Every time he got his pay he would buy a few professional manuals. He would really make an ideal husband!

But there was something else that had attracted Yalin to Lu. Once, while taking a walk, they suddenly heard someone shouting, "Thief! Thief!" Lu immediately turned around and grabbed the thief by the arm. He would not let him go no matter how hard the thief hit him. Only after the thief was taken away did Lu notice that his arm was swollen with bruises. . . .

Lu had proposed several times that they register their marriage right away. But Yalin insisted that they wait until they had finished all the furniture and bought all the things they would need for their marriage. Thus, at night Lu would do his carpentry in his room while Yalin would come to help. The sounds of the tools created a true Symphony of Happiness. Yalin was drunk with this happiness, and would talk to Lu about their plans for a sweet and comfortable family life.

Lacking experience, the young girl Yalin was not aware that the seeds of misfortune could be sown in a garden of happiness. She failed to notice the anxiety hidden in Lu's eyes. With no money in the bank and nothing but his muscles, he was disturbed to think that one day Yalin would say to him, "Whatever sum of money you have, take it out for our wedding." It had never occurred to Yalin that the longing for happiness could become the motive for Lu's becoming a criminal.

How could an innocent girl marry a thief? With tears, Yalin sent the official approval for their marriage back to the factory's political affairs office. But the honest girl was not to finish the business by removing herself from it. She wrote a long letter to the court, claiming her own responsibility: "When we discussed our marriage we thought it was a very important event in our lives and therefore we would have to spend a great deal of money to celebrate its significance. We preferred to postpone it than do it without enough money. I never expected that this would lead him to his crime! I should not have demanded so many material goods from him. . . ."

In the middle of November last year, the court announced that because it was Lu's first offense and because he had a good attitude, he would be sentenced to one year of supervised labor outside the prison. When he walked out of the custody room, he was astonished to find Yalin outside, waiting to take him home. . . .

After walking for a while in silence, Lu said in earnest, "Yalin, I don't want to ruin your future. Find yourself another boyfriend. I deserve my lot." But Yalin stopped abruptly and said, "Go in." They were at the door of a barber shop.

After a haircut, Xiao Lu looked like a new person. Yalin's heart was beating fast, and her feelings for Lu suddenly changed again. "I want to do everything to help him," she thought.

When he returned to the factory, Xiao Lu worked hard all day—cleaning the toilets, carrying garbage, etc. He would work until he was completely exhausted. He wanted to use hard labor to wash away the guilt in his heart. Yalin would often point out flaws in his work, and would also give him a great deal of support.

Xiao Lu was still very capable. Other workers would often ask him to fix clocks and watches, or to sew clothes for them. He would work long into the night doing these things. But through this work he was able to restore his self-respect. Yalin encouraged him, and she, too, often gave him things to do. . . . She gradually began to feel that he was still the sincere and honest person he had been in the past. She did not believe he would commit a crime again. It seemed that her feelings for him had returned to the passion of their original love.

Not long ago they formally registered their marriage. After they returned to their room in the dormitory, they put the two marriage certificates on the table. There was no smile, no kisses; instead tears dripped onto the two sheets of paper.

Such is their tear-soaked love. They have not had their wedding yet, since they have to wait until it is their turn for an apartment. They promise to invite us to their wedding celebration.

SOURCE: *Zhongguo qingnian bao*, June 24, 1982.

A Family Quarrel

On the eve of Labor Day in 1981, as an effect of harmful social practice and in response to the request of the bride's family, Xiao Li, the bridegroom, being rather ostentatious and extravagant himself, had reserved eight tables for a banquet at the Kaifu Hotel. In addition he had rented three limousines for the bride's family—one for himself and the bride, a second one for his parents-in-law and the bride's grandmother, and a third one for the bride's siblings.

It was already 5:15 P.M., and only fifteen minutes were left before the feast was to start, but the bride's limousine had still not arrived. Xiao Xing, the bride, went to the outer room, for she was too anxious to wait in the inner room any longer. Xiao Li, the bridegroom, was so worried that his forehead was streaming with sweat.

Friends and relatives asked, "What time have you reserved the limousines for?"

"Four-thirty this afternoon!"

"Why haven't they shown up then? Read your rental contract more carefully."

Xiao Li took the contract out and looked at it, and he couldn't help being stupefied. The time specified on the contract was from 4:30 to 5:00 P.M.; furthermore, the location for meeting the cars was at the corner of xx and xx streets.

"You see, here it states that you should wait at the intersection, yet you have been waiting at home. No wonder the cars haven't shown up. You didn't even write down the address of this place!"

As soon as the bridegroom heard this he ran to the crossing in one breath. And there really was a sky-blue limousine waiting on the road-side. Xiao Li, still out of breath, asked the chauffeur, "Sir, we want three cars. Where are the other two. . . ." Without waiting for Xiao Li to finish, the chauffeur Xiao Zhou replied, "The other two cars already waited too long. Since you didn't come they left to pick up the next clients."

Xiao Li explained hastily, "A friend rented the cars for me, and I forgot to read the rental contract. You have to help me, no matter what!" In an imploring tone the bridegroom continued, "A few days ago my mother-in-law asked me for 300 yuan to buy candies and hold a feast. But I'm already 700 yuan in debt because of this wedding, and I couldn't get an-other three hundred. My mother-in-law is already very unhappy with me. If something goes wrong with the cars now, everything will be even worse."

Xiao Zhou deeply sympathized with the bridegroom and immediately started making some phone calls for him. Since it was the time of day when there was the greatest demand for cars, it was impossible to find one.

What should he do now? The bridegroom had no alternative but to go home to discuss the situation with the bride. He thought that the bride, the bridegroom, and the best man should ride in the limousine to the hotel. The other guests should all go by bus. But as soon as Xiao Li ex-pressed this thought, the bride and her family, who had been deeply in-fected by old customs, became very unhappy. The bride objected, "I'm not even out my parents' door yet, and you're already asking me to cast off my grandmother and my parents. You're too heartless!"

The bride's mother immediately continued, "I've raised six children and this is my only daughter. If her wedding is not properly ceremonious, it will be difficult to explain our loss of face. According to our custom the bride's parents and brothers must ride in a car. I hope you can respect our custom."

The eldest of the bride's brothers said, "Our sister is already thirty-two. She's marrying at such a mature age. And now you want to just leave us. You two can go without us!" He then told his mother to cook dinner.

At this point the bride's father also started to speak. "I can get to the hotel without the car. I don't even care what the neighbors will say. But we just can't let our seventy-one-year-old grandmother ride with the bride as if she were an usher."

Confronted with all this, the bridegroom was getting impatient and unhappy. Bewildered, he said, "I just don't understand. Before Liberation you didn't have limousine service and you managed to get married very well. Why do you have to force me to rent cars today?"

The father-in-law's face sank when he heard this, and he said, "You think it's so easy to get a wife? If there are not enough cars we are not going to the hotel. Dinner is being cooked anyway."

Xiao Li saw that there was no end to this scene and he urged the bride, "We may as well take a bus and let them have the car." But the bride's parents would not permit this and they blocked the bride from leaving.

While the Xing household was inextricably caught up in the dispute, the warmhearted chauffeur Xiao Zhou arrived with two other cars that he had finally managed to get from the North Station taxicab service center. Thus, the dispute should have ended. But the bride's parents still refused to let the matter drop; instead they shouted and cried, "How can we eat and drink now that we're so upset?" They were determined not to go.

The bridegroom, Xiao Li, really could not hold back any longer. He pulled the bride and said, "If they don't want to go, let's leave it at that. I've never seen such a family before. If they don't come, we'll go alone!"

This only further infuriated his father-in-law, who now approached him and said, "I've finally learned about the real you." His mother-in-law also ran from the inner room and yelled, "Don't ever step into our house again!"

At this point Xiao Li was so enraged that his face had turned white and his legs felt like jelly. He had no choice but to drag the bride Xiao Xing into the car. The bride was reluctant to get in. Some of her five brothers were pulling her back and scolding the bridegroom, while others were pacifying and pulling the bridegroom. Both sides refused to give in. Even the pocket on the bride's gown was torn. Finally the neighbors came out to mediate, and only then were the bride and bridegroom, who were in tears, able to get into the car. The bride's family was determined not to go, and they let the two taxicabs go, with no passengers.

It was already 7:15 when the bride and the bridegroom arrived at the hotel. The bridegroom couldn't help bursting into tears when he saw that more than five tables of guests at the eight-table feast had already left. Meanwhile the bride, in front of the relatives, endlessly criticized the bridegroom for being an idiot and not knowing how to conduct himself. The bridegroom, on the other hand, was now wiping away his tears and complaining that the bride's parents were deliberately trying to make things difficult for him just because he had not been able to get the 300 yuan for the candy. This being the case, he wondered how they could be happy after their marriage. He thought he might as well kill himself. It was only after repeated attempts at pacification by relatives and friends that this stormy episode came to an end.

At this point the reader may ask, "What happened to Xiao Li and Xiao Xing after their marriage?" We visited Xiao Xing's parents on the day of the Mid-Autumn Festival in 1981. We found that Xiao Xing and Xiao Li were happily married and that they got along quite well with Xiao Xing's family. Both Xiao Xing's parents regretted what had happened on the wedding day and felt they should not have made such an unnecessary scene. Fortunately, the timely intervention of relatives and friends had prevented an even greater tragedy. The problem was all due to ostentation, extravagance, and vanity.

Indeed, to be ostentatious and extravagant reflects poor taste, and is despised by the noble-minded. To feast, ride in fancy cars, and distribute candies on one's wedding day are all extravagant and wasteful bad habits that should be opposed. What is worse is to quarrel over these things. When it comes to these questions, the parents of both parties should have the correct attitude, and they must set their children's thinking straight. Let us all be promoters of progress who handle weddings in a fresh, new way. Even when a difference of opinion arises, both parties must remain civilized and courteous so they can talk over and resolve their differences. They must not allow temporary anger to cause them to behave badly, further complicating the situation and creating serious consequences.

SOURCE: Liu Jinbao, "Chaojia ji" (Record of a family quarrel). In Wang Fuchu, ed., *Daode fating* (The court of morality) (Shanghai: Shanghai wenhua chubanshe, 1983), 71–74.

An Extravagant Marriage Mired Me in Hardship

My name is Zhao Chunfu. I am a worker at the main sewing machine factory in the city of Benxi. My father has already retired. For many years my family lived very frugally. For the marriages of our family's six brothers, everyone in the family "tightened their belts." Each time a daughter is married, our parents "lose a layer of skin." By the time my third brother married, our family was already in debt. When it was my turn to get married my mother had to borrow money right and left in order to put together an "engagement present" of 300 yuan. We also made the bride a set of wool clothes, a wardrobe, and two sets of bedding.

As our January wedding date approached, my mother tried to persuade me not to have a wedding feast. But the bride's family insisted on having one. At that time I thought that when my friends married, I had sent fairly big gifts. So if I held a feast I would be able to get some money and pay back my mother's debts. Therefore, I borrowed 800 yuan in order to arrange a festive wedding banquet.

On the morning of January 1, firecrackers were popping and guests kept arriving. We had to rush around taking care of the forty-plus guests we had invited; everyone was crammed in together. My wife and I ran back and forth pouring wine and lighting cigarettes. I was so exhausted that my back and legs ached and my eyes were red. We were busy until the middle of the night, when finally the wedding was considered over. After we added everything up, we had received 750 yuan as gifts. I used it to pay off the bill, but that still left me a debt of 140 yuan. At the time I figured that a debt of just over 100 yuan was not so terrible; I could slowly repay it. In February my wife and I together earned over 80 yuan. We deducted 25 yuan to pay back our debts, and we spent over 50 yuan to express our gratitude for four gifts we had received. Deducting money here and there, we were only left with 7 yuan for our living expenses. For many days we ate nothing but pickled vegetables. At night I could not sleep. I looked at the list of presents again and again, and realized that not many were given us in return for presents we had given others. Of the 700 yuan, 500 yuan could not really be counted as presents. In other words, in the future [when they invited me to a party], I would have to return the money. I felt like I had woken from a dream: in a single day I had accumulated a debt of 640 yuan!

Each month I earned fifty-plus yuan. My wife works in a collectively owned enterprise. Because she became pregnant, she left her job in March. Even if I did not eat or drink anything for a year, I thought, I would still not be able to pay back the 640 yuan!

In order to pay back our debts, we never spent more than 15 yuan a month. Our parents felt sorry for us. My parents bought us coal; my father-in-law's family bought us grain. When we needed a spoonful of sauce, we had to go to my mother's house to get it. My brothers often helped us out a bit. Because of our debts, my wife was in her eighth month of pregnancy and I still had not even bought her a single egg or a pound of fruit. Before we married, we never kept track of who spent money on cigarettes or wine, but now we calculate very carefully. . . . I work as hard as I can. Every day I hope there will be a shortage of workers, so that I can do extra work. One day in July a number of workers in my workshop did not show up. I was very happy—I worked on until day became night, and then night turned into day once again. I worked four shifts straight. I was totally exhausted, but just gritted my teeth and kept working, as I thought about the debt of several hundred yuan that we had to pay back. I worked until I was dizzy and finally collapsed by the machine. Other people helped me up, and said, "Little Zhao, you're too much!" I couldn't speak a word, and sweat and tears were dripping down my body. . . . Unless I worked that hard, how else could we make it?

One day I got sick and really could not keep on. I leaned against the wall, and eventually made it to the clinic. It turned out I had a temperature of 41 degrees [105.8 degrees Fahrenheit]. I waited until it had gone down to 38.2 [100.8 degrees Fahrenheit], and then secretly went back to work. Just at the time that I had my high fever, a friend informed me that he was going to get married. First of all, I could not get out of bed, and second, I had no money, so I did not go. When I had recovered from my illness and returned to work, he refused to talk to me. To be honest, some people want gifts just for their own purposes. If they get what they want, then they'll be nice to you, but if they don't, then they'll turn on you. I was also like that. Having big wedding feasts distorts people's feelings. Any sense of friendship or goodness is all squeezed into the eyes of the dollar bills.

A few days ago I went with my wife to the hospital for a check-up on her pregnancy. The doctor said that my wife was not in good health, that the fetus had some abnormalities, and that she should return in a few days for another examination. Comrades, having a big wedding banquet has caused me so much grief! I have not been able to even taste the happiness of the first month of marriage. Instead, I have been scorched by hardship. . . .

The tragedy resulting from a big wedding banquet not only taught my wife and me a lesson, but also taught both our parents a lesson. This May my twin brother is getting married. He earns 80 yuan a month, and his fiancée earns 50 yuan a month. They don't have much money, yet they wanted to have a big wedding banquet. My father refused to go along. Neither could persuade the other. One day my brother invited me to come drink wine in honor of his engagement. I lifted the winecup, looked at the wine, and remembered the tears and sweat of my bitterness. I couldn't drink the wine. Weeping, I said, "Brother, we were born on the same day. When you marry, I will feel happy for you as your brother, but I will not be able to spend a cent. This makes me miserable. Where should I direct my anger? Isn't it at the trend of having elaborate wedding parties that I should be angry? I cannot give you anything else, but I will give you these sincere words: No matter what, do not have a big feast when you marry. Don't follow my example, causing our parents to keep worrying." Seeing how I looked, my brother felt very uncomfortable, and immediately said he would not have a banquet. He and his wife went on a travel wedding, and spent a total of 100 yuan. Afterward, some friends and relatives sent presents. I led my brother from house to house to return them.

This July my younger sister was engaged. Her fiancé's family sent 700 yuan as a gift, but my parents refused to accept it. His family was shocked and thought that perhaps wedding customs had changed. I went to their home to explain, and I told them what had happened to me. I told them that my family was not wealthy, and that it was not that the 700 yuan was nothing in our eyes, but that we had just one request: "We hope that my sister, when she marries into your family, will not suffer the hardship endured by her sister-in-law." My sister's fiancé's family was deeply moved, and guaranteed that my sister would live happily in their home.

At present the trend of having fancy wedding banquets is becoming increasingly serious. Some people are on the verge of leaping into a fiery pit of suffering. I hope that young comrades who think that way will learn from my example. No matter what, do not have fancy wedding feasts!

SOURCE: *Zhongguo qingnian bao*, December 5, 1981, 2.

Why I Left the Banquet

Some time ago I was invited by a colleague to the wedding of his brother. At the appointed time, I arrived with my wife.

What a spectacular sight! We entered the home of the new couple as if we were peasants first setting eyes on the city. According to custom, we presented our gift—10 yuan—and were led by one of the ushers to a table.

At this moment another of the ushers rushed to my side, and asked in a whisper, "Any gift?" "Yes," I nodded. "How much?" I showed the amount with my fingers. He smiled warmly and, in spite of our hesitation, dragged us to the inner courtyard. "That place where you were just sitting," he explained in a friendly way, "is for those guests whose gifts are worth no more than 5 yuan."

We took our seats in the east room, feeling miserable. Who would expect that 10 yuan should make us important guests! Then I saw an acquaintance greeting me from across the yard in the north room. I went to his side and, seeing an empty seat next to him, sat down. This was a big blunder, for immediately I was dragged back to the east room by the same person who had seated me before. Seeing my perplexed look, the people sitting at the same table explained, "The north room is for those who gave gifts worth 20 yuan!"

My whole body felt awful. The friendship between the host and me was being turned into a farce. Or, to put it more precisely, it was sacrilege. At my signal my wife left the table with me, and together we found our way out through the hierarchy of tables and fled. On our way home I felt bitter and hurt. It is reasonable for friends to celebrate someone's wedding, to give them gifts, or to gather together for a dinner. But to turn friendship into such a naked cash deal only pollutes the atmosphere of our society.

Not that I am strong enough to challenge feudal customs. But my action is at least a counterstrike, one within my power, against the vulgarity that turns human relationships into a cash business.

SOURCE: *Zhongguo qingnian bao*, December 15, 1981.

Shicong Is a Clear-Thinking Girl

The twenty-four-year-old girl Mao Shicong is the assistant company commander of the people's militia of the Tuhe brigade in Jinghai county. She is good-hearted, healthy, and a good worker. According to a proverb, if there is a daughter in a family, one hundred families will ask for her. Naturally there were quite a few potential mates for a girl as good as Shicong. Through the introduction of the secretary of the production brigade's Party branch, Zhang Zhiming, Shicong met and fell in love with Liu Junbiao, the head of the people's militia of the Sanjianfang brigade of this county.

The custom in the countryside is that when a man and woman become a couple the woman must go to the man's family to eat an "engagement meal." Junbiao was of course no exception. He rushed to Shicong's house to arrange a date. He never expected that the moment he opened his mouth, Shicong would raise objections. Shicong said, "If we want to be a couple, then let's just be a couple. Why do we have to do something fancy? Is it possible you are afraid I will fly off if you don't do it?" Junbiao, embarrassed, said, "But everybody in the village has this custom. Furthermore, everyone in my family wants to have a look at you." Shicong said, "What family has that custom? We are both members of the Communist Party. Why don't we destroy the custom!" Ultimately she told Junbiao that she was willing to visit his home, but she would not set a date in advance and did not want any preparations made. "I'll just pick a time to go myself and let your parents look me over. That will take care of it."

Not long after that she went to their home. When Mother Liu saw Shicong, she looked her up and down. The more she looked at her the more she adored her, and she was as happy as if she had a jar of honey in her hand. She thought to herself, the first time a future daughter-in-law enters the door you must do something. She thought it over, and finally took out 300 yuan to give her as a "meeting gift." She insisted that Shicong accept it. One of them insisted on giving the gift while the other refused to accept it. Shicong understood that if she did not accept the gift the old woman would be unhappy. Having a sudden inspiration, she said, "Mother, I accept your intentions. Give me the money!" When the old woman heard this she was very happy. After taking the money, Shicong said, "You suffered great pain and endured hardship to raise Junbiao and his brothers. I am giving you this money back, to be considered an expression of my respect."

"If she won't accept the 'meeting present' then we must get Shicong two sets of clothes!" After a great deal of pressure was applied, Shicong reluctantly agreed to go with Junbiao to the department store. In the store were all kinds of things, and a wide variety of clothes, but Shicong was not in the mood to look. Junbiao said, "Shicong, take a look and decide what you like." Shicong said, "It seems to me that everything in the store is nice. You decide what to buy." He didn't know what he had done wrong. Finally Shicong got him out of his predicament by spending 2 yuan on a hat for him.

The next day Shicong wanted to return to her home. Mother Liu thought that she had not managed to give Shicong anything, so she secretly gave Junbiao 300 yuan and told him to find an opportunity to give it to Shicong. On the way home, there were several times when Junbiao thought he might raise the subject, but he was afraid of her reply. When they arrived at Shicong's home, Junbiao thought that if he took out the money, her parents would definitely refuse to take it; but if he took it home, he would have let down his mother. At the last minute he put the money under the quilt on the hearth. Despite his efforts, Shicong found the money. This made her think more deeply about the situation. She thought, "Why is it that they are so determined to give me the gift? The main reason is that they still do not really understand me." A few days later she went to Junbiao's house again. She explained her views to him and he understood. He said, "You are so broad-minded. What could I possibly say?" The two of them went to Mother Liu, and Shicong said, "Junbiao and I are engaged because we share the same ideals. Why would we ever need your 'down payment'?" She thereupon took the 300 yuan and returned it to Mother Liu.

SOURCE: "Shicong guniang sixiang hao" (Shicong is a clear-thinking girl), *Tianjin ribao*, January 12, 1981.

Family Relations

Nowhere is the contrast between pre-Liberation and contemporary China more obvious than in the circumstances under which a young bride enters her new home. In pre-Liberation China, ties to her natal family and village networks were severed when a woman married. For a young woman, having no protection, vulnerable to abuse by her mother-in-law, the only hope of finding allies, as anthropologist Margery Wolf has suggested, was to bear children.[1] In post-1949 China, the increased possibility of free-choice and companionate marriage, particularly in the cities, made the husband a potential ally. And while a bride still had to forge relations with her husband's family, she was no longer expected to break off ties with her natal family. Women also enjoyed the protection of a marriage law that guaranteed them the right to divorce.

These dramatic changes obscured more subtle continuities. Although most marriages in the 1980's were based on free choice, a woman was still marrying not just a husband, but an entire family as well. Even if she and her husband lived in an apartment of their own, she was considered a member of his family, and was expected to establish congenial relations with his parents and siblings. As in the past, she was the new, potentially disruptive family member, and was therefore often considered the cause of any domestic conflict. Although a woman could maintain ties with her own family, marriage still marked a passage from one set of social networks to another. As constructing a relationship with her husband and his family became more central to a woman's life, she was likely to find herself increasingly excluded from her former circle of female friends. When one of us accompanied a classmate to visit a friend of hers who had just married, the classmate remarked, "She won't be going out with us anymore. Now that she's married, it wouldn't be appropriate to ask her to join us when we plan to do something together." She assumed—and feared—that the same fate was in store for her. And in fact when she did marry several years later, one of her first complaints was that she felt cut off from her former network of women friends. "People treat you differently when you're married," she observed. The social circle of women who were married and responsible for managing a family of their own was quite separate from that of unmarried women.

The dramatic changes in family life after 1949 also obscured change of a much more subtle nature. In contrast to the past, when a woman was expected to ensure domestic harmony by being subservient and obedient, she was now required to assume a much more active role as a skilled emotional manager. It was incumbent upon her to resolve in a sensitive manner the conflicts that inevitably arose between her mother-in-law and herself. She also had to acquire expertise in handling the practical, emotional, and sexual aspects of the relationship with her husband. Only by developing these skills could she effectively fulfill her responsibility to manage family relations.

Being a Good Daughter-in-Law

In pre-Liberation China, the paramount concern of a young bride was what her husband's family would be like, how well she could fit into her new household, and how cruel or abusive her mother-in-law would be. So central was this last question to her future life and well-being that it was reflected in one of the most common ways of referring to marriage: not "to wed a husband," but rather "to find a mother-in-law."

In the early 1980's, a young wife had far more legal protection and social independence, and a mother-in-law less power, than would have been the case fifty years earlier. This was partly because political campaigns of the early 1950's targeted for criticism mothers-in-law who abused their sons' wives. In addition, by the 1980's many young urban couples lived in apartments of their own, and saw their in-laws only once a week.[2] Finally, many women worked outside the home, providing them independent incomes as well as social networks of their own.

Yet handling the relationship with in-laws still demanded the attention of young women, especially in the countryside, but to some extent in the cities as well. The urban housing shortage frequently left a couple little choice but to live with the husband's parents, although sometimes they moved in with the wife's parents instead. The inadequacy of childcare facilities meant that young parents often depended on the mother-in-law to take care of their child. Sometimes a mother-in-law was even expected to shoulder the burden of household chores while her son and daughter-in-law worked. Conversely, the lack of welfare facilities for the elderly in rural areas often made them dependent on their married children. The 1980 Marriage Law reinforced social custom by requiring children to assume responsibility for their aged parents.

Thus, the age-old conflict between mothers- and daughters-in-law, far from being resolved, assumed new dimensions. The myriad anecdotes reported in the media in the early 1980's not only attested to the new forms the problem took, but suggested new solutions as well. In contrast to the 1950's, almost no stories exposed the abusive or unreasonable behavior of a mother-in-law and suggested that she reform. Instead, the literature focused on the disrespectful, if not downright evil, behavior of daughters-in-law. The younger woman, it was assumed, was the cause of the disharmonious relationship. As the author of a book on family problems stated, "it is the daughter-in-law who is the primary cause of these contradictions," and "she has the primary responsibility for resolving [them]."[3] Advice literature aimed to persuade women to do what the traditional family system had formerly forced them to do—respect their mothers-in-law, take care of the elderly, and preserve domestic harmony.

A movie popular in the early 1980's, "Xi Ying Men" (Happiness Knocks at the Door, sometimes translated as The In-Laws), represented the most dramatic presentation of the consequences of unfilial behavior on the part of the daughter-in-law. Two sons and one daughter lived in a family with their mother and grandfather. The eldest son was married and had two children. When the second son took a wife, the elder son's wife tried to form an alliance with her and accused the mother-in-law of favoring the daughter. Behind her behavior was a desire to avoid caring for her aging mother-in-law and her husband's grandfather. Her machinations eventually forced the extended household to split up and the mother-in-law to become ill, and brought the woman herself to the brink of divorce from her hapless husband. But the pleading of her younger sister-in-law (a model wife), and her own guilty conscience, led her to have a nightmare one night as she slept at her parents' house. In the nightmare she returned to her house, only to discover that the pigs and chickens were dead because no one had fed them. She looked for her husband and children, but her husband told her that she was no longer the children's mother, and with a wave of his hand caused her to shrink until she was only a few inches tall. Her husband's sister then towered over her and scolded her. Chastened and terrified, she awoke from the nightmare and returned home to reunite the household and mend the relationships she had strained.

What was most striking about this movie (aside from its use of fantasy, a relatively new departure in Chinese film), was that its heavy-handed symbolism underscored both the promise and the threat of family life. If the daughter-in-law was cheerful, industrious, and considerate, the family would prosper. If she turned her back on her prescribed role and put the family relationships at risk, then she herself would shrink in stature (liter-

Actions of a good daughter-in-law. Jiang Yuanming and Li Tangzhen, *Xifu yu popo* (Mother-in-law and daughter-in-law) (Taizhou: Jiangsu renmin chubanshe, 1983), 2, 5, 9, 26, 35.

ally, in this case), risking not only her own happiness but her very existence. A review of this film in the English-language magazine *China Reconstructs* explained that the author of the original story wanted to criticize the tendency to treat the elderly in a cavalier manner.[4] The story did something else as well: it put the responsibility for a harmonious household squarely on the shoulders of the daughter-in-law.

Apparently the lesson was taken to heart in some quarters. A letter to *China Youth News* in January 1982 from a peasant youth in Hebei explained that after viewing "Xi Ying Men," three village women reformed their behavior and began to treat their mothers-in-law more kindly, so they would not resemble the daughter-in-law in the film.[5] A soldier wrote that his wife, after seeing the film, returned home and ran into her mother-in-law's arms, begging forgiveness for the more than seventy quarrels they had had in her first six months of marriage. She also apologized to her sister-in-law and brother-in-law for bickering with them. The author of the letter commented that the film was the first to portray the long-standing village problem of mother-in-law/daughter-in-law relations, and that he hoped for many more films like it.[6]

The message of "Xi Ying Men" was reinforced by a booklet entitled *Xifu yu popo* (Daughter-in-law and Mother-in-law), published in 1983 as part of a series of village readers.[7] The booklet contained anecdotes and essays advising young wives how to handle the potentially traumatic relationship with their mothers-in-law. Its main message was underscored by the illustrations, which consistently depicted a "good" daughter-in-law devotedly caring for her mother-in-law. Officials in some rural areas adopted more aggressive means to encourage women to be good daughters-in-law. In one village all daughters-in-law were called to a series of meetings cosponsored by the Party committee and Women's Federation. The purpose of the meetings was to publicize the responsibilities of young people—stipulated in both the Constitution and the Marriage Law—to take care of their elders. Although the law applied to men as well as women, the meetings were specifically for daughters-in-law.[8] Women were also warned that abuse of their mothers-in-law was a crime for which they could be tried in court and punished. In an extreme case, a woman from the Tianjin suburbs named Jin Xuerong was sentenced to two years in prison for having physically abused her mother-in-law, with whom she lived. Jin's use of a club to beat her mother-in-law eventually drove the older woman to attempt suicide. Neither frightened nor deterred, Jin continued to curse and beat her mother-in-law, forced her to live in a shack for ten days, and withheld food and medicine from her. After repeated criticism by local officials failed to change Jin's behavior, her mother-in-law finally took the case to court, where some 1,200 people reportedly cheered the verdict.[9]

The conflict between mothers- and daughters-in-law was particularly serious in the countryside, where several generations usually lived together in a single household, and where fewer institutional facilities existed for care of the elderly outside the family. But many of the problems rural women faced in handling their relationship with a mother-in-law were shared by their urban counterparts, and writers of advice columns often directed their messages at the presumably more independent-minded young urban women.

Women who married into a difficult family situation and did something to help ameliorate it were commended. A sidewalk poster display in Shanghai in 1985 praised a model daughter-in-law named Chen. She had married Xiao Wu despite the fact that his parents were ill and had financial difficulties. Furthermore, Xiao Wu had made it clear that he was so busy at work that he really did not have time to take care of his parents, and therefore hoped to marry a woman who would be able to assume this responsibility. According to the poster display, Xiao Chen got up early every day to prepare breakfast and lunch for her in-laws. When she returned home from work in the evening, she cooked and cleaned the house. Every day she bathed her in-laws, and even scrubbed their backs and washed their feet. When her mother-in-law lost her temper because she felt ill, Xiao Chen maintained her pleasant disposition. Because of her diligence, she was finally selected as a model daughter-in-law.

Another woman praised for marrying into a difficult situation was Zhang Guihua, a young wife in the eastern suburbs of Tianjin who became the senior female member of the household after her mother-in-law's death. She asked that her father-in-law take charge of the family finances and never spent a penny without his permission, made sure that her father-in-law and the rest of the family had good food and clothing, and eventually saved enough money to finance the weddings of her husband's younger siblings—all tasks that would normally have fallen to her mother-in-law.[10] And one extraordinary woman, widowed in the 1976 earthquake, was praised for continuing to care for the retarded uncle of her dead husband.[11] In each of these cases, women combined the roles of skillful household manager and nurturing wife and mother.

The conflict between mother- and daughter-in-law sometimes had less to do with actual responsibilities than with competition over emotional loyalties. For example, a woman from Nanjing attributed her husband's refusal to help with housework to the fact that he had been spoiled by his parents, with whom the two of them lived. "The old couple was feudal-minded and believed that a woman should be an obedient wife," the woman complained. "When they were home they sided with my husband, as did his sister." Her hostility toward her in-laws eventually made it necessary for her and her husband to move to an upstairs room. But then, her mother-in-law invited her husband—but not her—to eat dinner with them every day. To retaliate, the woman refused to give her mother-in-law 20 yuan that she had earlier promised, provoking her husband to beat her.[12] Another woman identified the emotional conflict more directly when she greeted her husband every evening with the question, "Which of us do you want—your mother or me? If you want me, you had better find a separate home for us immediately!" [13]

This competition for emotional loyalty was so common a problem that in some cities the Women's Federation organized classes to help young couples contend with it. A young man from Beijing, whose marriage was marred by tensions between his wife and his seventy-year-old mother, described how such a class had rescued him from what seemed a hopeless predicament. His wife refused to comply with his mother's wish that her daughter-in-law greet her immediately upon returning home each day; she also refused to cook food the way her mother-in-law wanted it. "My mother frowned upon Xiaohan and complained to me," he reported at a forum on family relations held in Beijing in early 1986.

But when I mentioned anything to my wife, she would say that I was siding with my mother, and that I must choose with whom I wanted to live. I was at a loss and often wandered the streets after work because I was reluctant to go home. I even spent one night in the railway station. One day I learned from the newspaper that an evening class for newlyweds was being offered by the Beijing Women's Federation. I signed up immediately and asked my wife to attend as well. I tape-recorded the class for her when she was working the night shift. The class was very helpful to us. Xiaohan told me later that we young people should respect our elders and their habits.[14]

Among other things, these cases suggest that a young couple's own relationship was often developed in the context of an extended family unit. While marital problems were given a great deal of public attention, a marital relationship was often a subordinate part of a larger household. Handling conflicts with her in-laws was often as much a part of a woman's married life as dealing with her husband.

Being a Good Wife and Mother

A good wife and mother, like a good daughter-in-law, saw her role redefined in the early 1980's. In both cases, forced subservience was replaced by voluntary acquisition of emotional management skills. A woman no longer became an ideal wife through blind obedience to her husband, but rather by learning to protect the relationship from the tensions of married life. The traditional Confucian ideal of "virtuous wife and good mother" (*xianqi liangmu*), attacked during the Cultural Revolution, was revived and adapted to the 1980's.

Much of the discussion about the applicability of the Confucian notion of virtuous wife and good mother revolved around the prize-winning movie "Xiang Yin" (literally Sounds of the Country, but commonly translated as Country Couple). The movie portrayed the life of a rural woman, Tao Chun, and her husband, Yu Musheng. Tao Chun was a virtuous wife and good mother in the most traditional sense. Taking care of her husband and children was the unquestioned priority in her life; she never dared challenge the wishes or wisdom of her husband. To the consternation of younger women in the village, Tao Chun sought her husband's permission to use money earned through her own work raising chickens and pigs to buy herself new clothes. When her husband objected, she silently surrendered her desire. Ultimately, obedience to her husband caused her premature death: when she developed severe pains in her liver—which proved to be symptomatic of liver cancer—she followed her husband's advice to simply take some painkillers and continue her work.[15]

When the editors of *Chinese Women* asked their readers, "Should we be like Tao Chun?" a heated debate evolved. Although the scriptwriter had intended the film to criticize the persistence of feudal values in rural areas, some urban women viewed Tao Chun as a model of virtuous behavior whom they should strive to emulate. A woman worker named Zhu Ying declared that like Tao Chun, and like her own mother, she was dedicated to the ideal of being a virtuous wife and good mother. Although she had her own job, her main satisfaction came from catering to her husband's needs and maintaining harmonious family relations. She proudly described how she would scurry from one store to another after work to find beer for her husband, who desperately needed to relax after a trying day on the job. Sometimes, she reported, he was so upset by problems at work that he would lose his temper, and occasionally even beat her. "Ordinarily," she said, "I silently tolerate this. Sometimes I cry, but when I think of the praise his colleagues have for him at work and look at the merit certificate in our home, I believe it is only because I am his wife and he is able to let off steam at home." She continued, "I used to have a great deal of determination to advance and wanted to study more."

Several days ago I was listening to a Japanese lesson on the radio. When my husband saw me, he said, "What is the point of your doing that? It would be more useful to spend the time doing some more housework!" At first I persisted in my determination to study, but gradually I came to realize the logic of what my husband had said. Women's minds are not very focused and as soon as they study something new they forget what they previously learned. So it makes more sense to spend the energy at housework and handling domestic affairs well. Let the strong male comrades be able to devote all of their concentration to their jobs. That can be considered my indirect contribution to the Four Modernizations![16]

Zhu Ying concluded that were there more women like Tao Chun (and presumably herself as well), fewer marital problems would exist.

Several urban women agreed with Zhu Ying's admiration for Tao Chun, but most took offense. "I was shocked by Zhu Ying's essay published in *Chinese Women*," wrote one woman.[17] The Vice-President of the All-China Women's Federation, Luo Qiong, complained that Tao Chun "does not represent the new women in China's socialist countryside of the 1980's. She is the victim of feudalism and male chauvinism."[18]

Although Tao Chun's critics vehemently opposed women's blind obedience to their husbands, they did not dispute the belief that a woman should be a virtuous wife and good mother. For them it was simply a question of how that ideal was to be interpreted. As a woman worker named Sun Honglin explained, "'What's so bad about being a virtuous wife and good mother?'"

This statement is logical. The fierce-browed female "daring generals" that were propagandized during the ten years of chaos were unbearable to our male compatriots, and even we women found them distasteful. Mother Nature has determined the distinction of our sex. Naturally we must assume the responsibility of being wife and mother. Furthermore, we must be good wives and good mothers. Therefore, the question is not whether or not being a virtuous wife and good mother is a good thing, but rather, what, in the 1980's, are the new criteria for being a virtuous wife and good mother?[19]

Sun's answer suggested only the broadest outlines of the new ideal: a wife should be a tender and compassionate partner for her husband, should support him in his work and point out his shortcomings, and, most important, should have knowledge, skills, and ideas of her own.

More concrete notions of how a woman should become a modern-day virtuous wife and good mother were spelled out in a variety of articles on how a woman should handle married life. These dealt with the problems young people were likely to encounter immediately after marriage, and advised women of the specific skills they would need to maintain successful relationships with their husbands.

Many writers referred to the first five years of marriage as the "dangerous period." The problems described by young couples in letters to popular magazines ranged from the mundane to the philosophical. For some newlyweds, simply adjusting to a spouse's daily habits was trying, as it was for a woman from Hangzhou who married a man from Shandong. Her husband, following the custom of people from Shandong, loved to eat food seasoned with plenty of garlic. The smell on his breath was so awful, she complained, that she could not bear to be near him. Eventually her husband "learned to control himself and eat less garlic," and whenever he ate garlic he immediately rinsed his mouth.[20]

More commonly, women complained that once they were married, their relationship with their husband was robbed of its former glamour and romance. He "gobbles his food and goes to work, leaving the room a mess," one woman complained to her elder sister. The more she compared the past with the present, the more depressed she became. The sister described her younger sibling's sentiments as follows:

It seems he no longer understands her the way he did when they were courting. They are no longer so close in spirit. His heart is like a kite that has been blown by the wind, and is gradually flying away from her. For a long time he has not gone out to stroll in the evening, listened to music, or played badminton. Either he is at his work unit or sitting home at his desk, writing. If she asks him a question he either does not react at all, or blankly looks at her and says "Huh?"[21]

Recalling romantic evenings spent in his embrace, watching the moon shine on the Songhua River, she felt disillusioned with married life. "She had never imagined it would be like this," reported her sister.[22] A woman with similar frustrations noted that before marriage she had imagined "sharing a desk and sharing a lamp," studying together after work every day. Instead, married life was consumed by rushing to buy food every day, going to work, cooking, and cleaning the house.[23]

Women who encountered these problems were advised to remember that being sweethearts was different from being husband and wife, that "to get married is to suddenly become an adult—you leave your parents and establish your own family life." Once a couple married, material life became as important as spiritual life, and as two people attempted to live together they would inevitably discover many shortcomings in their partners that they had never noticed before.

In general, when two people are courting they are very polite toward each other. Because everything is colored by emotions, it is difficult to discover the other person's shortcomings. Even if you do notice them, you usually forgive them. But once you are married . . . and establish the most intimate of relations, you will gradually discover shortcomings in your mate that you had not noticed before. At first you will be bothered by this. That is common. But so long as it is not a problem of principle, then by discussing the problem and trying to understand each other, you can solve it.[24]

Successfully weathering this "dangerous period" did not mean that a wife's problems had ended. In fact, still more ominous dangers awaited her, for once a couple had adjusted to living together it was possible that a husband would become bored and lose interest in his wife. To win her husband's continued loyalty, and thereby ensure a harmonious marriage, it was incumbent upon a woman to study the fine art of husband management. Advice columns in women's magazines sketched out in some detail the skills required to fulfill this role as emotional manager, many of which might sound familiar to readers of American women's magazines.

Essays such as "The Influence of a Wife" and "The Attraction of Women" described both offensive and defensive measures that a woman could adopt. Taking the offensive, she had to cultivate traits that would appeal to her husband. Physical attraction should not be overlooked, women were told. "It is necessary to adequately adorn yourself," one writer advised. "Do not let your husband see you with messy hair and a dirty face."[25] More emphasis was placed on a woman's temperament. "You must not have a bad temper or change your mood frequently or for no apparent reason," women were instructed. "Otherwise your husband is likely to get tired of married life very quickly and will try to break away from it. On the other hand, if you are gentle and civil, considerate and dignified, and always radiant with smiles, then your husband will feel that he is respected. He will be anxious to see you every day, and he will walk faster than usual to get home when he thinks of you."[26]

Equally important was a wife's ability to be her husband's companion. As one author pointed out in an essay entitled "Become a Modern Virtuous Wife and Good Mother":

In the traditional society, being a "virtuous wife and good mother" meant giving your husband blind obedience. But in modern society, family relations have changed, and husbands no longer simply want blind obedience from their wives. They now hope that they can achieve a harmonious relationship through spiritual support. Therefore, to be a wife you must also continually improve and revitalize yourself so that you can march forward in unison with your husband. Only this kind of marriage is truly stable.[27]

During the courtship process, a woman who was too career-minded or who had too "strong" a personality was undesirable as a mate (see Chapter 3). But ironically, once married, those who had no interests or personality of their own risked boring their husbands, potentially driving them to seek more stimulating companionship with other women.

To illustrate this point, one women's magazine reported the story of an American woman concerned that her husband was attracted to his young female assistant. The woman had erroneously concluded that her fading beauty was the problem, and therefore had undergone cosmetic surgery. Only when this failed to win her husband's affection did she realize that spiritual, not physical, beauty was the issue. "She began to change her life by renewing her independence and individuality in her career and pursuits. Naturally she regained her husband's respect and love." From this story the author concluded that "one should be continually striving to better oneself, making a husband realize that you have many precious qualities that he had never noticed before." [28] This advice was taken to heart by a Chinese woman whose husband had fallen in love with a woman at work. Self-critical of her initial anger at him, she eventually realized that "if my husband had taken a wrong turn in life, it was partly my fault. I always just followed whatever he said, and I never expressed my own ideas. Now that there is a problem I should not just get angry; instead I should reach out and grab him." [29]

These aggressive measures to ensure a husband's continued loyalty, women were advised, should be combined with defensive tactics. To prevent her husband from falling in love with someone else, a woman had to skillfully tread the line between permissiveness and strictness. If she allowed her husband too much freedom, he might abuse it; if she constrained his social activities too rigidly, he might rebel. Thus, one author advised a distraught woman to be understanding of her husband's need to get together with male friends. "Because he knows them well, he may find them more interesting than he finds you in some areas, such as card-playing, car-driving, horseback-riding, and maybe even other not-so-healthy activities." (Under what circumstances these men drove cars or rode horses is not explained by the author.) On the other hand, the wife was instructed to "pay close attention to all these events," to "actively inquire about your husband's friends," and even to accompany her husband to social gatherings. [30]

These articles shared the assumption that it was a woman's responsibility to preserve her attractiveness to her husband. A "virtuous wife" who "continually improved and revitalized herself" could expect a stable marriage; women who did not do so had only themselves to blame for being cast off by their husbands.

Men were also sometimes beset by fears that they might be abandoned by their wives, but they were advised to handle the problem somewhat differently. For example, many husbands were alarmed when their wives continued to socialize with male friends after marriage. A man from Changchun expressed this concern to the editors of the provincial youth magazine *Jilin Youth* (Jilin qingnian). "My wife and I were married on the basis of love," began his letter to the editor.

But after we got married, she continued to like to get together with men friends, just as she did before our marriage. She often goes out walking on the street with young men, or to see movies with them. There is a constant flow of male visitors in our home. I reminded her to be careful, but she said I was interfering with her normal social activities. At present I cannot say there is any abnormal relationship between her and them, but I always feel worried, and am very unhappy about this situation. I do not know how to treat this problem. Please give me advice.

Based on the number of similar queries he had received, the editor began his response by observing that "social intercourse with persons of the opposite sex after marriage seems to be a sensitive issue." He reminded the young man that "people need both friendship and love," and that so long as his wife's relations with male comrades were "normal" (i.e., not sexual), he should not interfere. The husband's major task was therefore to learn to observe whether his wife's relations had transgressed the boundaries of "normality."[31] Nowhere was it suggested that he should make himself more interesting or attractive so that his wife would stay at home and remain devoted to him.

While a wife was expected to assume responsibility for preserving a stable marital relationship, she was not supposed to become more powerful than her husband in the home. In fact, failure to handle domestic power relationships sensitively could result in marital problems. A wife's independent income, for example, sometimes inadvertently put her in a seemingly more powerful position. A secondary school teacher complained that his wife, a factory worker, not only earned much more than he, but that this had caused a "subtle change in our status as husband and wife in the home." She made decisions on her own, and even had the audacity to insinuate that since he earned so little he should do more of the housework. Eventually he convinced her that a teacher should not be judged by his salary, but rather by the importance of his work.[32] Another woman realized that by controlling the family purse she had wounded her husband's pride, and perhaps even damaged his sense of masculinity. A harmonious relationship was achieved when she transferred her economic power to him, thereby restoring his sense of "face."[33] In yet another case, a woman who controlled the family purse complained that her husband secretly withheld part of his wages each month, instead of turning it over to her, as was expected. The newspaper editor had little sympathy for her, chastising her for attempting to dominate her husband. "Under the socialist system, relations between people are to be equal and comradely. . . . A husband and wife are partners in a shared life, oarsmen in the same boat. How can you make the relationship between a husband and wife into an oppressive one?"[34]

Superficially, these articles insisted upon equality between husband and wife. Yet they invariably reflected situations in which the balance of power had tipped toward the woman. No articles expressed the frustrations of a wife who was not receiving the equal treatment she felt she deserved. The concern of these authors was to restore marital harmony by warning women not to dominate their husbands. Being a virtuous wife required responsibility and skill, but not the direct exercise of power.

The 1980's ideals of a virtuous wife were extended to a woman's role as a good mother. In both roles, women were expected to be modern and scientific. For a mother, this meant mastering the skills that would enable her to guide the psychological development of her child sensitively. One writer explained the new demands of motherhood as follows:

In the past an uneducated mother could raise a troop of children with almost no effort. . . . This was because in traditional society, raising children was primarily a matter of feeding and clothing them. But in today's society, that kind of mother would probably not be considered a good mother because she has not assumed the responsibility of educating her children. . . . Actually, because of the special connection of flesh and blood between a mother and children, a mother can be considered the child's first teacher. Especially when a child is very young, the mother seems like a deity. In the past, maternal love and tenderness were enough to qualify someone as a good mother and to win a child's respect. But in today's society, in which the level of knowledge is constantly being raised, children already know what calculators and computers are. If we are still like mothers of the past and only take care of feeding and clothing our children, and buying them toys, then we will not be able to guide their intellectual development . . . and our image will quickly fade in their eyes.[35]

Since the family planning program instituted in the late 1970's allowed urban families to have only one child (see below), parents devoted increasing attention to the art of childrearing. Having only one chance, they did not want to err in their methods. Responding to this concern, magazines offered their readers abundant instruction in how to become modern, scientific parents. A plethora of articles answered questions such as how to handle a child who was slow to begin talking, how much pocket money to give a child, what to do if one's child skipped school or was teased by classmates, and what kinds of food were most nutritious for a child.

Although the literature was ostensibly directed at both parents, it appeared primarily in women's magazines, suggesting women's particular responsibility for mastering these skills. An occasional article more explicitly underscored this attitude. One article, entitled "Promote the Superiority of Mothers," articulated for readers of *Chinese Women* a politically progressive rationale for the popular belief that a mother's role in childrearing was more important than that of the father. "Family relations in a socialist society are of a new type," the author began.

They are equal and harmonious. They have replaced the feudal family relationships that were based on the power of the husband and father. . . . [Now] both the father and mother shoulder the glorious task of raising children to contribute to the Four Modernizations of the motherland. Looking at the current condition of families in our country, mothers play a more dominant role than fathers in providing education for an only child.

The article then listed the reasons for the dominant role of mothers. First, the fetus grew within the mother's body, and its first sensations were responses to the mother's mood, habits, and health. Second, while both parents are a child's first teachers, "the role of the mother in educating a child is more outstanding." This is because the mother played a dominant role in taking care of the child's daily necessities, such as eating, washing, and resting. "It is therefore through the mother's arrangements that the child's habits develop, and this can be considered a part of education." Not considering the possibility that the father might play a more active role in taking care of the child's physical needs, the author proceeded to the third reason: since a peaceful, harmonious family environment was critical to a child's successful upbringing, and since women "play the crucial role in establishing harmonious family relations," it followed that the mother was more important than the father in raising the child. This logic extended to the fourth reason: "From the perspective of the present division of labor of family members, the husband is usually more active in his job outside the home than is his wife. Therefore, a child spends more time with its mother than with its father." Finally, the author pointed out that "women in our country are traditionally endowed with maternal love. . . . They treat the job of educating their child as a major part of their life." The author concluded that these factors "determine the dominant position of mothers in providing family education for an only child." [36]

Essentially, then, women made superior mothers simply because they did most of the work associated with childrearing. The modern, scientific aspects of motherhood that were advertised in the 1980's may have made the job more prestigious and attractive, but the basic sexual division of labor in the family was left untouched.

Sexual Relations Within Marriage

Sexual relations were perhaps the single aspect of a marriage that husbands were expected to assume primary responsibility for handling "properly." Sex was regarded as a natural and normal part of married life, at least until the age of about forty. The quality of marital sex was a topic on which there was very little discussion, however, and since both of us were unmarried during our stay in China, it would not have been considered appropriate for married people to discuss it with us, or for us to show excessive interest in attitudes toward it. Our information, then, came from a few stories gleaned from friends, the contents of several sex manuals published in the early 1980's, and our own observations of certain family arrangements.

Speaking to an American expert teaching in China, a young woman teacher who had just married confessed that many of her friends thought her odd. Among a group of newly married women who often gathered to talk, she was the only one who enjoyed sex and was interested in it. To the others, sexual relations were a "duty" from which they expected little pleasure. While intercourse was no longer painful as it had been at first, they said, they found it uninteresting and did not understand what all the fuss was about.[37] One woman described to a doctor her lack of interest in sex with her husband. Each evening, she complained, they would lie down in bed. She would then say, "Go ahead. . . . Are you done yet?"[38]

The dissatisfaction expressed by these women was probably at least partly a result of incompetent and ignorant partners. It was not unheard of for a husband not to know even the most basic facts. For example, in a letter to the magazine *Family Doctor* (Jiating yisheng), a recently married young man, enrolled in a sex education course, complained that "my wife is very shy and also I don't know where the vaginal opening is. Several attempts at intercourse have failed. Could you please tell me where the opening is?" The magazine's Dr. Ke responded as follows:

The question you have asked is not at all strange. In my daily work it is not at all rare to see couples fail at intercourse on their wedding night. This is primarily because the newly married couple does not have any sexual knowledge and is shy or nervous. I have seen a peasant who was married for a year and came to me because [his wife] couldn't get pregnant. After a careful examination, it appeared that when he had intercourse he was mistakenly putting his penis into his wife's anus, and furthermore believed that the anus was the vagina. Obviously she could not get pregnant. His wife felt that he was entering her anus, but she was too shy to tell him, so he was never informed.[39]

To add to the problem, many women themselves knew little, if anything, about sex at the time they married. One sociologist, critical of the widespread lack of sex education, reported that among the couples he interviewed, there were some who had been married for several years and were still "unsure as to whether or not they had really had sexual intercourse." He discovered that some men who complained that they were unable to ejaculate did not know (nor did their wives) that the penis had to be rubbed, not just inserted into the vagina. Some ignorant newlywed brides, he learned, were terrified by the sight of their husbands' enlarged penises and refused to have sex thereafter.[40] One of our unmarried classmates recounted being visited by recently married women friends who were bewildered and in some cases horrified by the sexual expectations of their husbands. Some, like the man described above, were not sure which orifice was to be used for sexual intercourse, and the pain the women experienced made them fearful of continued sexual activity. They sought the advice of our classmate because she had spent a year studying in the United States and had a copy of *Our Bodies, Ourselves* (a popular book about women's bodies and sexual behavior published by a feminist health collective in the 1970's).[41]

The dissatisfaction and frustration caused by the lack of information about sexual activity often became the cause of serious marital problems. A Beijing doctor observed that "the number of family problems caused by sex is not small."

If someone were to write a Chinese counterpart to the "Kinsey Report" prepared in the United States in the 1940's, the results would surprise most people. Most people who go to the courts to petition for divorce say that it is because of political or economic problems. But do you know how many of these are actually because of a problematic sex life? Do you think that when a husband and wife fight it is really because of coal, rice, oil, or salt? Of course not! It's just that they can't say what the real problem is. Many people fight and fight, but they do not really understand what the problem is: they don't know about sex. There are also some people who know in their hearts what the problem is, but their mouths remained sealed. They just let the days pass.[42]

The official press, perhaps responding to widespread reports of this ignorance and the problems engendered by it, began in 1980 to publish a number of sex manuals for the newly married.[43] Books such as *An Informal Discussion of Sexual Knowledge* and *Required Reading on Newlywed Hygiene* sold out almost as soon as they arrived at the bookstores. They were so popular that they were sold on the black market for several times their original price. The author of one of the books received quantities of fan mail, in which many readers thanked him for being their "savior."[44] These manuals were straightforward and full of useful information. While they differed in some significant respects from current medical wisdom in the West, they were candid and flexible in their descriptions of sexual desire and sexual intercourse. They were very much a modern innovation in the context of Chinese society. They were not, however, how-to books; their tone was clinical. And they were written for an audience that appeared to be both ignorant about many aspects of sexual activity and ambivalent about the appropriateness of discussing it.

An Informal Discussion of Sexual Knowledge began by stressing the need for sex education and the importance of a proper attitude toward sexual relations in the context of marriage:

We do not want to regard the question of sex as mysterious and unfathomable, nor as insignificant, and still less as a means of individual pleasure-seeking. Instead it should be recognized that this is a human biological phenomenon, one that touches upon the prosperity of the nation and the prevailing customs of society. We must recognize that sex is an indispensable part of the life of a husband and wife. But sex life is not the whole of life. The major part of life is still our cause, the cause of socialist construction.[45]

With that point clarified, the book got down to business. After a description of the appearance and function of the genitals, and the rudiments of sexual intercourse, the book advised the couple about the wedding night.

On the wedding night, the newlyweds were told, the woman might bleed or experience pain when the hymen was punctured, and intercourse should be avoided for several days following so that it would have a chance to heal. If a woman who had previously engaged in strenuous labor or athletics did not bleed on her wedding night, however, her husband should not entertain doubts about her past sexual experience—it was just that the hymen had been broken in the course of these activities. Men who experienced premature ejaculation were advised that the problem would get better with time and experience.

The book then explained, in some detail, the stages of sexual arousal and the differences between male and female sexual desire. Men's sexual desire was comparatively strong, and women's relatively weak, couples were told. Men's sexual impulses were concentrated in the genitals; men were more quickly aroused and could reach orgasm in a few minutes. Women's sexual impulses were more diffuse; moreover, it often took them more than ten minutes to become aroused.

Given these differences, the book stressed the importance of foreplay in arousing the woman: men should spend anywhere from ten to thirty minutes stimulating their wives. The clitoris is particularly sensitive, men were told. Since the woman's clitoris is stimulated during intercourse, men should try to prolong intercourse after their ejaculation, in order to give the woman more pleasure. How, when, and where a woman experiences orgasm were not covered in the discussion.[46] Finally, the author of *An Informal Discussion of Sexual Knowledge* enjoined husbands not to roll over and fall asleep immediately after intercourse, but to spend some time talking to their wives.[47]

During the first few months of marriage, the author continued, the couple might want to have sexual relations quite often, but after a while they would probably settle down to a frequency of one or two times a week, and as they got older this might decrease to once every week or two. The main criterion was whether one or both partners were tired the following day—if not, then two or even more times a night was acceptable. This lenient attitude about the appropriate frequency of sex was not universal. Some of our friends, when they did talk about sex, expressed the opinion that there was something abnormal about making love too often, and if they did so themselves, they felt that it was because they had temporarily taken leave of their senses.

An Informal Discussion of Sexual Knowledge instructed couples that at certain times they should refrain from sexual intercourse. It was medically unwise to have intercourse during the woman's menstrual period, during the first and last three months of pregnancy, and for the six to seven weeks after the birth of a child. Intercourse after menopause, on the other hand, was permissible, for though it was no longer possible for a woman to conceive, her past sexual experience would have made a deep impression upon her cerebral cortex, so that she might still experience sexual desire.[48]

The book warned couples that problems in sexual relations could cause a breakdown in their marriage, and that they should take these problems seriously. The most fundamental problem, the book said, was that men were more interested in sex than women. One solution proposed by the book was that the man should stimulate the woman more before intercourse, to increase her interest. If his sexual desire was too potent, he and his wife should sleep separately to avoid sexual stimulation. Additional exercise and washing his feet before sleeping were also recommended as ways to suppress his sexual desires. Women who were consistently uninterested in sex were advised to have a medical examination, for many problems that influenced sexual pleasure, such as a dry vagina, could be treated medically.[49]

Even with this abundance of advice, it was often impossible for couples to devote extensive amounts of time to sex, particularly once they began having children. Most urban couples in the 1980's lived in one-room apartments that functioned simultaneously as dining room, living room, study, and bedroom. Even at night, parents could not expect much privacy from their children, and in many instances this limited the opportunity for sexual activity between husband and wife. However, some parents devised ways of coping, as Liu Xinwu describes in his short story about a Peking family, "The Overpass." "When Hou Yong and Hou Ying started senior primary school, a curtain often had to be drawn across the middle of the room. But then a curtain was no proper solution to the problem. In this very room in the heat of a summer's night, Hou Yong had wakened and been startled by the sight of an act that his parents, who were still not that old, should rightfully have kept from him."[50] The curtain was clearly a less-than-ideal solution to a problem faced by many couples. In at least one case, doctors traced a man's problem of premature ejaculation to the fact that only a curtain divided the room that he and his wife shared with his brother and sister-in-law. Whenever he and his wife had the room to themselves, the doctors learned, they were able to have successful sexual relations.[51]

Many older couples, especially those living in crowded urban quarters with their children, often elected to sleep separately, each sharing a bed with the children of the same sex. Arranging a room for a newlywed couple was a priority for families allocating what little space they had; arranging for a middle-aged couple to continue to sleep together was not. Lack of privacy, the demands of work and running a household, and a popular belief that sex was not really necessary after the onset of middle age all contributed to this pattern.

Planned Parenthood

Shortly after marriage, most couples began to contemplate forming a family of their own. For newlywed couples in the 1980's, this took place within the context of a government-sponsored family planning program. China, as has often been noted, has close to one-fourth of the world's population. Improved health care and living conditions in the 1950's, combined with a state policy that actually encouraged families to have more children, resulted in one baby boom, followed by another in the late 1960's and yet another in the early 1970's. A 1980 census counted over a billion people.[52] Population pressure was evident everywhere in China, but especially in the urban areas, where shopping districts were mobbed with people every day, bicycle jams tied up commuters for hours, and housing and other public services were taxed beyond capacity.

In 1972 the government began a belated but vigorous campaign to limit further population growth. After a period during which two children were considered the ideal number, the official slogan was changed in 1979 to "one couple should have only one child." The slogan was supported both by moral exhortation emphasizing the importance of population control for socialist construction, and by hard economic incentives. Couples with one child who signed a pledge not to have more were granted lucrative cash bonuses as well as preferential access to housing, daycare, and other services in the cities. Couples who violated the one-child pledge faced penalties such as having their salaries substantially reduced, or being denied grain rations and free medical care for the additional child.[53] Largely because of peasant resistance to the policy, local authorities gradually permitted rural families a second child in so many cases that the unspoken rule in the countryside became "preferably one, two are all right, but never three." [54]

Because of the family planning program, the government made extensive efforts to disseminate birth control information. Booklets such as *An Informal Discussion of Sexual Knowledge*, as well as other marriage manuals, included detailed discussions of birth control techniques. A variety of birth control methods were recommended, depending upon the health needs of an individual. Women were encouraged to use an IUD or take birth control pills, depending upon their health history. Warnings about the side effects of these methods were usually not stressed. If these methods were inappropriate (because of a history of liver disease or problems with accepting the IUD), then condoms were recommended. Men who suffered from premature ejaculation were encouraged to use condoms. Couples who lived separately and saw each other only on holidays were advised to use condoms or a special oral contraceptive called the "visiting-relatives contraceptive medicine." [55] *Coitus interruptus* was mentioned as one method of birth control that was not reliable and also inhibited the sexual pleasure of both men and women. [56] Diaphragms were not mentioned and did not seem to be widely used, although they were available in Beijing. Finally, if other methods of birth control failed, abortion was an option, albeit an undesirable one. A stigma was attached to women who had an abortion, because it meant they had failed to use birth control properly. The manuals described vacuum abortions, dilation and curettage, and what they called "induced abortions" for advanced stages of pregnancy. [57] The actual incidence of abortion, however, was not at all clear.

It was commonly assumed that birth control was a woman's responsibility. When asked how he and his wife had obtained information about contraception after they were married, a young man we knew replied, "Oh, my wife went to the clinic at her work unit and they gave her some sort of medicine to take. I don't really know much about it." Perhaps in response to this type of situation, a writer in a popular Shanghai newspaper instructed his readers that "contraception is a matter of concern to both husbands and wives. It must not only be suitable to both at the time of use, but at the time of choosing which method to use, both must discuss it. Neither the husband nor the wife should simply consider his or her own pleasure and ignore the hardship of the other." He cited the possibility that an IUD or the pill might cause discomfort for the woman, in which case her husband should offer to use a condom, even if it decreased his enjoyment of sex. [58]

Notwithstanding the family planning program and its requirement to secure permission from one's work unit to become pregnant and have a child, many newlyweds and their parents continued to share the assumption that marriage meant children, and that as soon as people married they would begin trying to have a child. Those who delayed having children were the objects of gossip, ridicule, and even criticism. One young couple had been married for two years and, because both were still studying, wanted to postpone having children. They wrote to the editors of *Younger Generation* (Qingnian yidai) about the social pressure to which they were subjected. First the husband's mother expressed her concerns: "I'm getting older and I want to help take care of your child while I am still young enough to do so." Then colleagues at his work unit took an interest in the couple's apparent deviation from what was expected. Some speculated that his wife had a disease that made it impossible for her to bear a child. Others theorized that the husband was "too weak" to impregnate his wife. At work he had to contend with well-intentioned friends who would pat him on the shoulder, gaze at him sympathetically, and say, "I understand your problem. Let me recommend some medicines that will help you." "You could explain until your tongue is dry and your lips burn, and still only get a 'mysterious smile,'" the young man complained. "Plus, there are so many people to explain yourself to." [59]

In another case, a couple decided to postpone having children because the wife suffered from a heart problem. Female co-workers at the textile mill where Xiao Li worked as a cloth inspector speculated that her so-called heart condition had been caused by sexual promiscuity before marriage. On one occasion when Xiao Li showed a piece of flawed cloth to another worker, the worker turned to her and said, "What's the big deal about inferior cloth when there are inferior people? A hen can lay eggs when it is the right time. A woman who can't give birth after she gets married is not even as good as a chicken. A person with no sons or grandsons—what has she got to be so proud about?" [60]

In yet another case, a husband and wife who decided to postpone having children found themselves severely harassed by the leadership at the husband's work unit. The husband was a Party member, and at a meeting of his Party "small group," one of the leaders declared, "Zhou Ling's not having a child indicates his desire for material comfort and his aversion to enduring hardship. This shows that he has been influenced by Western bourgeois thinking. Not having a child is avoiding the duty of a citizen and is a manifestation of liberalism." The leader wanted Zhou to admit his mistake. A good-hearted woman colleague present at the meeting advised him to hurry up and have a child, explaining a popular theory: "If you don't have any children you are guilty of bourgeois thinking; if you have too many children you are guilty of feudal thinking; only by having one child can you demonstrate true proletarian thinking." [61]

While the family planning campaign apparently did little to undermine the social expectation that newlyweds should bear children, it created new pressures on parents—particularly on mothers—to give birth to a son. The pressure was felt most strongly in the countryside, where powerful economic incentives encouraged the production of male offspring. The economic reforms implemented in the early 1980's decreased the size of the production unit, frequently down to the level of the individual household. Households contracted land from the state under the "responsibility system." Since a household was entitled to keep what it earned (after selling a certain amount of grain or other crops to the state at fixed prices), the larger the household, the more money it could earn. The benefit of increased labor power seemed to outweigh the cost of feeding additional family members.[62]

In addition, both urban and rural dwellers showed a preference for sons that dated back to pre-Liberation China. Traditionally, only a son could carry on the family name. Furthermore, in the Chinese countryside, women married out of the village, into the husband's family. Their natal family lost control of whatever income the woman originally earned. This same pattern was reproduced in the cities, although there seemed to be more flexibility and variation in who lived with whom and where the woman's salary went. As long as the son continued to live with his family, taking primary responsibility for the care of the parents in their old age, then sons would continue to be the preferred offspring, and couples who gave birth to daughters would feel compelled to try again.

This preference for sons, combined with the new pressures generated by the birth limitation campaign, resulted in a revival of traditional methods of influencing the sex of a fetus. Some couples used a "sex prediction table" that purported to indicate which sex the child would be on the basis of the day in a woman's menstrual cycle she actually conceived. Others relied on herbal medicines to guarantee a son.[63] A more serious consequence of the child limitation program was the resurgence of some ugly practices common before Liberation. A summary of articles in the official Chinese press in 1981–82 noted that "drowning baby girls, once common in the Chinese countryside, is still widely practiced." The mothers of unwanted girl children were also abused psychologically and sometimes physically, being beaten and tortured by their husbands and other relatives.[64] An article in *China Youth News*, for example, described a man in Shenyang, a large city in northeast China, who before his wife gave birth told her that if she had a son, he would not allow her to continue to work but would want her to stay home and take care of the child full time. If she had a girl, on the other hand, he threatened to abandon her. When she gave birth to a girl, he and his brother beat the wife repeatedly. His mother stood to one side and encouraged him to seek a divorce, while informing her daughter-in-law that drinking insecticide was an efficacious way to commit suicide. When her appeals to various law enforcement authorities were of no avail, the wife did indeed kill herself. The husband and his brother were arrested.[65]

Stories such as this were published by the Chinese media with increasing frequency throughout the early 1980's. This not only indicated that the problem of abusing women who gave birth to daughters had intensified, but in addition attested to the government's critical attitude toward these practices.

As part of this effort to publicize the problem and change popular attitudes, the press simultaneously reported stories of "model" families, in which the birth of a baby daughter was taken in stride. A woman named Zhao Shuying, who had retired from her job in a bicycle factory in Anshan, had three daughters-in-law, all of whom gave birth to girls. It was the elder Zhao who had to comfort the daughters-in-law, as they despaired at having failed to deliver sons. Instructing one of the daughters-in-law, named Tian Youfen, who had just borne a second girl, to stop crying, Zhao said, "It doesn't matter whether you have a boy or a girl—I am happy either way. If you have high aspirations, you will make sure that your daughter gets a good education so that she can perhaps become a female engineer someday." In the meantime, Zhao gave her son money and told him to buy the highest quality medicines to care for his wife. Several years later Tian Youfen became pregnant once again. Planning to adhere to the family planning program and supported by her mother-in-law, she decided to have an abortion. Tian's own mother disapproved and tried to convince Tian of the importance of persisting in her efforts to bear a son. Zhao intervened and patiently scolded Tian's mother. "We are living in a society that is very different from the old one," she said. "Look, your daughter is working at the Anshan Iron and Steel Factory. She has even become a cadre and a Party member. She is even better than my own son!" Hearing this, Tian's mother acquiesced in her daughter's abortion.[66]

In some cases, individual men took the initiative in opposing abuse of women who gave birth to girls. A man from Heilongjiang, for instance, wrote to the editors of *China Youth News*, expressing his horror at the stories of abuse he had read and declaring his determination to "break with the traditional concept that girls cannot carry on the family line." He planned to instruct his parents that "the sex of the fetus is purely accidental; neither the father nor the mother should be blamed."[67] Another similarly determined young man added his opinion that the father, not the mother, should be held responsible for the sex of the child, since only male sperm carry the Y chromosome that produces a son.[68]

Although exposure to the problem apparently swayed some individuals, as long as this publicity was not combined with social and economic changes making daughters truly as valuable as sons, attitudes and practices remained unlikely to change. Infanticide of baby girls as well as psychological and physical abuse of women who gave birth to daughters could be expected to continue. Urban women, and to an even greater extent their rural counterparts, would continue to fear the prospect of giving birth to a daughter.

As the problems surrounding the population control program suggest, women's role in the family, perhaps more than any other aspect of their lives, was shaped by the intersection of traditional values with the modernization drive of the 1980's. Seemingly contradictory trends emerged simultaneously. On the one hand, the traditional value of being a virtuous wife and good mother was resurrected and reinforced to inspire women to take their responsibilities within the home seriously. This complemented the decreased value accorded women's role in the paid labor force that resulted from the 1980's urban economic reforms (see Chapter 7). On the other hand, the emphasis on science and modernity at the center of the reforms was extended to women's role as arbiter of family relations: they were enjoined to become modern, scientific virtuous wives and good mothers. No longer was women's job of preserving harmonious family relations to be accomplished through ignorance and blind obedience; instead women were to acquire the sophisticated skills of emotional management. Yet the upgrading of women's roles as wives and mothers in China took place in the context of a family planning program that brought people's preference for male offspring into relief and jeopardized the physical safety of mothers and their daughters.

Translations

Once married, a woman had to juggle three new roles: daughter-in-law, wife, and mother. Each of these was redefined in post-Mao China. The 1950's attack on the cruel treatment of daughters-in-law by their mothers-in-law was reversed in the 1980's. "Mother-In-Law/Daughter-In-Law" and "What Should I Do When My Wife and Mother Don't Get Along?" both target daughters-in-law for criticism; they are blamed for disharmonious relationships between generations in a household.

In traditional China, a wife was expected to be dependent on and subservient to her husband. In the 1980's, however, she had to worry about preserving her husband's love for her as well. She was advised to acquire a range of skills to avoid the possibility that he might seek companionship elsewhere. The skills of emotional management a wife was expected to master are outlined in the stories "After My Husband Had a New Lover," "The Influence of a Wife," and "What You Must Understand for Your Husband's Sake." Although a wife was expected to assume responsibility for preserving a stable marital relationship, she was not supposed to become more powerful than her husband in the home, as illustrated by "My Husband Hoards Our Savings—What Should I Do?" and "After Transferring My Economic Power."

In the context of the family planning program, a number of books were published in the 1980's to advise young couples on how to handle their sexual relationship. However, very little of the discussion revealed the nature of women's sexual experience. "The Wedding Night," excerpted from Yu Luojin's semifictionalized story "A Winter's Fairy Tale," is one of the few texts that sheds light on a woman's feelings about sex. The one-child-per-family policy adopted by the Chinese government in the late 1970's resulted in new pressures on women to produce a son. Failure to do so, as the story "I Mistakenly Blamed Her" indicates, could destroy an otherwise stable marriage.

Mother-in-Law/Daughter-in-Law

On March 6, 1982, the civil affairs bureau of the Shanghai People's Court in District XX of Shanghai mediated a dispute concerning support of parents. The plaintiff is a woman over seventy years old, named Old Lady Han.

Old Lady Han and her husband, Sun Daming, have two sons. Because neither of the two elderly people has work, they must be supported by their sons. Both the sons have already married. Based on discussion, they decided that each son should support one of the parents. The elder son and daughter-in-law figured it out: they thought the mother-in-law could take care of the housework and help care for the children, and they even wanted her to live with them. The younger son was not so bright—he had to rely on his wife to do all the housework, and she had to assume responsibility for supporting his father, who did not know how to do housework.

Old Lady Han is a very diligent, thrifty, and honest woman. Although she is old and weak, nonetheless in the home of the older daughter-in-law she still helps to take care of the children, do the laundry, buy food, and cook. The elder son and daughter-in-law have relatively high incomes— close to 200 yuan per month. The elder son gives his mother pocket money every month, but she cannot stand to spend it all. She always puts 2 yuan in her savings account, planning eventually to give it to her grandson. The elder daughter-in-law works the night shift, so she sleeps during the day. The mother-in-law tiptoes around the house as she does chores. When she is finished she sits in the hallway, trying to avoid waking up her daughter-in-law. At meals she often waits until her grandsons and daughter-in-law have finished eating, and only then does she eat.

The unfortunate thing is that the elder daughter-in-law is paranoid. She'll say that her mother-in-law stole rice to give to her younger son; she'll say that her mother-in-law stole candy or matches. Each time they cook rice the daughter-in-law measures it first, then gives it to the mother-in-law. Sometimes she uses the pretext of cursing her children to indirectly attack her mother-in-law. If the mother-in-law even snores too loudly, she gets mad. What makes Old Lady Han even more upset is that she cannot speak with her son alone—the daughter-in-law is afraid that she will say bad things about her to her son. Once the daughter-in-law had returned from work and found her mother-in-law talking to her son while doing something else. She shoved the door open and yelled, "Bite your tongue! Now what are you talking about!" Old Lady Han had to quickly close her mouth. Another time the son bought some pork buns on the way home from work. His mother had just taken one to eat when she was seen by the daughter-in-law, who yelled, "Eat your own food! If you want more, use your own money!" Old Lady Han could not tolerate the abuse from her daughter-in-law. Several times she left and went to stay with her younger son.

The younger son's family had much harder conditions than the elder brother's. All the housework fell on the shoulders of his wife. She would work from dawn to dark. She not only had to do the housework for a family with several members, she also had to serve her husband and father-in-law without speaking an angry word. Later, her father-in-law had a stroke and was dependent on her to take care of him. The elder daughter-in-law never said a word. The younger daughter-in-law and her husband earned only about 100 yuan a month, and they had to support three adults and one child on that. So their life was rather difficult. Often they just bought three cents worth of vegetables and ate that for a whole day. When the old man was sick they had to spend money to see the doctor, and this made their life even more constrained. But the elder daughter-in-law never took an interest. Once the younger daughter-in-law wanted to take the old man to the doctor but didn't have any money, so she went and asked the elder daughter-in-law to lend her 15 yuan. The elder daughter-in-law did not appreciate the nature of the emergency, and the younger daughter-in-law had to return home empty-handed. Not long thereafter the old man died, and the elder daughter-in-law was not even willing to pay a cent for his burial. She said, "Each of us is supposed to support one of them, and that means supporting them to the end."

Even so, the younger daughter-in-law never invoked the notion "each supports one" to kick out her mother-in-law. She often said, "Mother-in-law is really my mother; the younger generation must support the older generation. This is the morality of being a daughter-in-law." Whenever the mother-in-law came from the home of the elder daughter-in-law, the younger daughter-in-law always welcomed her warmly. When movie tickets were distributed in the lane, she thought that since she was young she would always have more opportunities to see movies in the future, so she always let her mother-in-law take the ticket instead. In winter, when her mother-in-law forgot to wear her hat when she went to a meeting of the neighborhood committee, the daughter-in-law ran after her to take her the hat. The daughter-in-law had not eaten eggs for many years, but she often bought eggs for the old parents to eat. The mother-in-law's teeth were not good, and it was hard for her to eat pickled vegetables. So the daughter-in-law bought peanut butter especially for her. Every morning she bought her soybean milk. . . .

The elder son and his wife, however, not only did not feel guilty in comparison to the moral behavior of the younger daughter-in-law, but viewed her kindness and virtue as a weakness. The elder son even dared to trick his own blood brother. The house where the younger son lived was a private house bought by his parents, and not very luxurious. The elder son claimed that he had the right of inheritance and wanted to share his brother's house. In view of the fact that the younger son had more people in his family and also that she herself wanted to stay there sometimes, Old Lady Han did not agree. So the elder son finally used the deadly weapon of terminating financial support for his mother. Fortunately Old Lady Han had her younger son and daughter-in-law, so her life was not in any danger.

No one expected, however, that she would file a complaint at the District XX People's Court, demanding that her older son and daughter-in-law give her 25 yuan a month for support. When the masses heard about this, they all supported Old Lady Han's act. They blamed the elder daughter-in-law for her unfiliality and praised the younger daughter-in-law for her virtues. Supporting parents is the responsibility of children. Respecting parents is also a moral duty. No matter whether old people have an income or not, or whether their income is high or low, they must all receive respect. And to be a daughter-in-law, you must help and support your husband in fulfilling his responsibility to take care of his parents, and also take care of them yourself.

In the end, as a result of help and education from the court and leadership of the work units, the level of understanding of the elder son and daughter-in-law was raised. They not only agreed to give the mother-in-law 25 yuan a month, but the son confessed to his mother that he had made a mistake, and said, "Mother, please do not view us on the basis of the past; from now on we will improve." The elder daughter-in-law also said, "Younger brother's wife is really much better than I. I will learn from her!"

SOURCE: Yuan Fuliang, "Gai qianzede he gai zanyangde" (What must be condemned and what must be praised). In Wang Fuchu, ed., *Daode fating* (The court of morality) (Shanghai: Shanghai wenhua chubanshe, 1983), 42–45.

What Should I Do When My Wife and Mother Don't Get Along?

Dear Editors:

Since my father passed away in 1960, my mother has raised me. We supported each other until I got married. Then she retired from her job and has helped me raise my child and prepare meals every day. My family life should be very happy. But recently I have dreaded going home. Each time I enter the door my wife looks at me with a long face and asks: "Who do you want, your mother or me? If you want me, you had better find a separate home for us soon." My mother then tells me how her daughter-in-law avoids doing housework and offends her. She complains that I have forgotten her ever since I got married. I am being attacked by both sides. What should I do?

Huang Chun, Xinyang, Henan

Dear Huang Chun:

I was asked by the editors to write to you about my own experiences and to tell you my opinions about how to handle conflicts between a mother-in-law and daughter-in-law. I will tell you frankly what I know.

My family is very similar to yours. My wife is a textile worker and my mother is retired. The conflict within my family worried me, too. After a little thinking I realized that the conflict had several causes. First, the daughter-in-law was annoyed by the mother-in-law's lack of understanding of the hardships she had to deal with; she was annoyed by the mother-in-law's pampering of the grandson, and by her habit of talking too much. The mother-in-law complained about the daughter-in-law's failure to take the initiative in doing housework, her habit of spending money freely, and her lack of respect for the aged.

What was the main cause of this conflict? In the old society, the mother-in-law ruled the family. People believed that "the daughter-in-law is like a purchased horse: you can ride or beat her as you please." But things are different now. The daughter-in-law has an independent income; she is literate and articulate. When there is conflict, the daughter-in-law is the main cause of it. Take my home, for example. My wife is a high-level worker in her workshop. Naturally she thought that after walking sixty *li* back and forth during the day she deserved a break. Therefore she did less housework. Of course she also believed that since she earned her own money, she should be able to spend it however she liked. Thus she seldom consulted her mother-in-law.

To solve this conflict I patiently tried to make my wife realize that she should see more of the positive aspects of the old woman, and appreciate the hardships she had to go through in doing the housework and raising our child. I also told her how difficult it had been for my mother to raise me all by herself after my father died. Even if my mother could not do anything useful, it was still our responsibility to take care of her in her old age. My mother had been thrifty her whole life, and that was a virtue we lacked. As for her habit of talking too much, I said it was common among old people. We would probably talk even more when we were old. My wife laughed at my joke. Later, each time we received our pay, we gave it to my mother to keep. After work I would take care of our child while my wife would help my mother do the cooking. Actually we did not help all that much. But when my mother saw that the younger generation could understand and respect her, she was so happy that she would finish the cooking very early every day. As for spending money—my wife and I actually always had our way. The more the younger generation respects the old, the more love they will give us.

Certainly we should not give in to certain old ideas, such as pampering the grandson. Our experience is that usually it is better for the son to talk to his mother than for the daughter-in-law to talk to her. It is even better if when some gifts such as tonics or clothes are bought for the mother-in-law, the daughter-in-law gives them to her. By the same token, it would be better for me to send gifts to my mother-in-law. When I am with my mother, I often tell her how tiring my wife's work in the factory is. On holidays or weekends we try to share more of the housework so that my mother can go to the theater or visit relatives. Now my mother praises my wife in front of everyone. To sum up, when there is a conflict between the mother-in-law and the daughter-in-law, the husband should be the mediator.

Liu Tao, Wuxi

SOURCE: "Poxi buhe, wo zenme ban?" (What should I do when my wife and mother don't get along?), *Zhongguo qingnian bao*, January 1, 1980.

After My Husband Had a New Lover

The love between my husband, Xiao Shi, and me was based on free choice. After we were married on New Year's Day in 1977, we had mutual respect and love for each other. Our life was very harmonious and everyone believed that we were a fortunate family.

At the end of last year a beautiful young woman named Zhang came to work at my husband's unit. Because of their work she and my husband had quite a lot of contact, and they found each other's company congenial. As time passed she began to love Xiao Shi. What about Xiao Shi? He shared her feelings. The affection between them was unbounded.

In early June of this year I discovered that my husband was engaged in improper behavior, and I got very angry. I argued with him and watched him all the time. If he was five minutes late coming home from work, I would interrogate him. As this went on our love for each other diminished, and we both suffered. It was in the midst of misery that I had a sobering thought. I realized that if my husband had taken a wrong turn in life, it was partly my fault. I had always just gone along with whatever he said, and never expressed my own ideas. Now that there is a problem I should not just get angry, but should reach out and grab him.

Every evening I therefore started to take the opportunity to chat with him, and gradually overcame the tense atmosphere that had developed between us. Then I purposefully took my husband for a walk at the place where we had first fallen in love, and with him recalled our happiness from that time through the first seven years of our marriage. I spoke freely with him about my hopes for the future of our harmonious family. When my husband was moved, I directly raised the issue of his problem. I told him that if he were an upright person with a strong sense of morality, then a "third party" would have no way to crawl in. I also helped my husband analyze the reasons that his thinking and feelings for me had changed, and discussed the danger of his allowing the relationship with the "third party" to continue.

He gradually came to understand, and I tried to be more caring and trusting toward him. When he would go by himself to see a movie or visit friends, I would not try to obstruct him. He was moved by my behavior and admitted his mistake. I forgave him. At the same time I went to have several heart-to-heart talks with Xiao Zhang. In the middle of August, exhausted from work, Xiao Zhang collapsed. Her family lived somewhere else, so I took charge of going to the hospital and preparing her food and medicines. I took care of her for three days. She was very ashamed, and said to me, "Elder sister, will you forgive me?" I answered, "Where is there an elder sister who will not forgive her younger sister?" When she heard this she began to cry. On the eve of National Day I heard that she had found the man of her dreams.

SOURCE: "Zhangfu youle 'waiyu' zhi hou" (After my husband had a new lover), *Jiefang ribao*, November 23, 1985.

The Influence of a Wife

How does a young wife make use of the influence she has over her husband? A husband may feel uneasy soon after marriage. What should the wife do?

When the young husband feels that being with the guys is more interesting, when he feels that it is much more fun and that the beauty of life can be experienced more fully when he is out amusing himself than when he is home keeping his wife company, then how should you, as his wife, handle this new challenge? A wife must not overlook this potential crisis and must handle this problem calmly and with reason. If the wife shows any sign of anger in her speech or treats her husband stiffly, then he will feel that his outside life is freer, more casual, and less restricted. He may even feel that this companion at home has become an obstacle in his path. Gradually an emotional rift will develop.

Generally speaking, a husband is sentimentally attached to the newlywed life. But one must not forget that the content of a person's life is varied and colorful, especially that of a young person whose interests are also very broad. The husband's friends may come to visit him often, and he may also visit them often. As the wife, you must actively inquire about your husband's friends, find out about their past and present. You must realize that they play an important role in your husband's growth and development. Because he knows them well, they may be more interesting to him than you are in some respects, such as card-playing, car-driving, horseback-riding, and maybe even other not-so-healthy activities. You must pay close attention to all these activities, and whenever necessary must also take decisive steps to protect your family's happiness.

Whenever your husband plans to go out, it does not hurt to ask him where he wants to go, and you may even suggest that you are willing to accompany him. You and your husband should "cherish the same ideals and follow the same path," and make an effort to cultivate common interests. This way, as you come more and more to speak the same language, your two hearts will naturally draw closer together. But if you restrict his speech and activities too much and are too demanding, then while he may listen to you and do what you want in front of you, when you are not around he may just decide to do things he did not intend to do in the first place.

As a wife you must not have a bad temper or change your mood frequently or for no apparent reason. Otherwise your husband is likely to get tired of married life very quickly and will try to break away from it. On the other hand, if you are gentle and civil, considerate and dignified, and always radiant with smiles, then your husband will feel that he is respected. He will be anxious to see you every day, and he will walk faster than usual to get home when he thinks of you.

SOURCE: Jie Zhuanguang, "Qizi de yingxiangli" (The influence of a wife), *Qingnian yidai*, 5 (October 1982), 22–23.

What You Must Understand for Your Husband's Sake

Some people say that the term "mate" is outdated, but this is completely wrong. To be a wife you must simultaneously be a friend, lover, mother, and nutrition expert.

Your husband's longevity depends primarily on him, but also, to a great extent, it depends on you.

Thirty-six percent more men than women die at an abnormally early age. Why is this?

In general, when women face anxiety or a setback they can, by crying or expressing their feelings in some other way, overcome their bad mood. But men cannot do this. From the time they were children they were taught the following: men do not cry, men must be brave and strong. As a result of this they show their masculinity, but many also develop gastric ulcers and high blood pressure. Perhaps your husband is among them. As a wife you must help your husband release his worries and troubles.

When a husband has come home from a very tense day of work to be greeted by a quarrelsome wife, then not only can he not rest, but he will become even more tense. This will be harmful to his health. Being afraid of one's wife is a major cause of gastric ulcers and high blood pressure. You wives who are wildly ambitious, wives who like to complain a lot, wives who like to chatter a lot—is it possible that at the time you got married you really did not hope to make your husband's life better?

"Ah, of course not!" You would perhaps say: "I hoped that our lives would get better every day, but it turns out that my husband has some unsatisfactory characteristics."

Young wife, do you really understand your husband? Do you ever realize that in order to meet your ever-expanding list of demands, he gets up very early every day and hurries off to work? He works at least until 6:00 P.M., and then rushes home. He gulps down dinner, and then there are visits, housework, plus your incessant chatter. When can he relax? Of course he cannot relax at lunchtime, because he is still thinking about work while he eats. The higher he climbs on the ladder of success, the more pressured his time will be. Therefore, he needs rest time more than you do; he needs a peaceful, happy, and harmonious family life. And he can only have these things if he has a wife whose heart is one with his, who sees eye-to-eye with him, and who has common goals with him.

Perhaps you truly love your husband, and make him delicious foods every day. Gradually you begin to notice that his stomach is protruding. "He is clearly bigger and stronger, and we are more prosperous," you say. But if you are a careful and thoughtful wife you must realize that as a man gets fat, he may begin to have difficulty breathing, he will tire more easily, and he may even have trouble tying his shoelaces. Being overweight may shorten his life. Therefore you must be careful. A smart wife will not make greasy, difficult-to-digest foods for an overtired husband. She should understand that fat turns into cholesterol, and too much cholesterol will cause hardening of the arteries.

Everyone knows that one must eat to live. Yet how many wives understand what kinds of foods are appropriate for their families and what kinds are inappropriate? Most women only understand "modern life"; they lack knowledge of the kind of nutrition needed by their hard-working husbands. In general, your husband needs to eat high-protein, low-fat, low-caloric foods. This must be combined with plenty of sleep, exercise, and regular physical examinations.

You must expand your knowledge of nutrition. Nutritious eating habits can make someone who is weak become strong. Only if you have a strong and healthy husband are you assured of a happy life. Therefore you should learn to love your husband scientifically, and how not to harm him. Women who work during the day often like to prepare a big dinner for their husbands when they get off work. Actually this is not scientific. The correct way is to eat a big breakfast, a filling lunch, and a small dinner. Therefore, smart wives will make more delicious breakfasts and lunches for their husbands.

SOURCE: "Weile zhangfu ni yinggai dongde" (What you must understand for your husband's sake). In Funü zhiyou zazhishe, ed., *Funü baike quanshu* (Women's encyclopedia) (Jilin: Beifang funü ertong chubanshe, 1985), v. 2, 299.

My Husband Hoards Our Savings—What Should I Do?

Comrade Editor:

The couple that lives next door to me is really interesting. The wife manages her husband very strictly and totally controls their finances. One time the wife said to me, "Only by strictly controlling your husband can you be sure he won't have a change of heart." I thought this made sense, so I laid down the rule that my husband must turn over his monthly salary and bonus to me. On the surface my husband complied, but secretly he is still hoarding our wealth. What should I do?

Ge Lin

Comrade Ge Lin:

Excuse my frankness, but the reason for your husband's hoarding falls on your shoulders. Under the socialist system, relations between people are to be equal and comradely; relations between a husband and wife are also to be equal. They should have mutual love and respect.

A wife who wants a henpecked husband is no different from a husband who dominates his wife. The reason the movie "The Model Husband" received so much criticism is that either consciously or unconsciously, it promoted the disgusting idea of "voluntarily fearing one's wife." A husband and wife are partners in a shared life, oarsmen on the same boat. How can you make the relationship between a husband and wife into an oppressive one? Your husband's hoarding money clearly shows at least two things:

First, there is still not equality between husband and wife. After the husband lost his economic status in the family, even his spending money came under control. Hoarding his savings is a secret means of resistance. Second, there is still not mutual trust between husband and wife. Love between a husband and wife is not built on the word "control," but rather on trust. By trying to use the forceful method of control to make her husband loyal, the wife is accomplishing just the opposite. Being controlled from head to foot is likely to make a husband feel that he lacks family warmth. Sooner or later he is likely to feel cold toward his wife, and eventually have a change of heart.

How can this situation be changed? I believe in the following:

1. Implement economic democracy in the home. The husband and wife should jointly control the family income and jointly plan expenditures.

2. Based on the premise of guaranteeing equality of spending, the wife should let her husband have some spending money for himself. This will contribute to his having "normal" social activities.

3. Once you discover that your husband is hoarding money, you should not start a big argument. If your husband is saving money to buy books, magazines, or stamps, and not to engage in some "irregular" activities, then you should ignore it. But if he wants to have money to leave you for a new woman, then that is, of course, another matter.

SOURCE: *Xinmin wanbao*, August 9, 1985.

After Transferring My Economic Power

My husband is ten years older than I. He does marketing for a factory. He smokes and drinks, and therefore spends a lot of money. For the first two months after we married, I controlled the family purse. We often

quarreled over financial matters. Later I discovered that his job often required him to run from one place to another to buy goods that were both
good and cheap, and that he was careful in how he spent his own money. I
thought, why not let him control the family purse? This would give him a
sense of pride and responsibility.

Therefore, on payday of the third month, I gave him my entire salary
plus the money I had left over from the month before, and said, "From
now on, you take care of the family purse and handle our budget. Other
people do not trust their husbands, but I trust you and believe you can do
a good job taking care of our finances. You might even be able to do it
better than I because you are not a spender by nature." But I also reminded him, "From now on it will be entirely up to you to act properly."

My turning over the family purse to him gave him a lot of "face." He
often bragged to his friends, "My wife trusts me and gives me all of her
money." To preserve "face" he spent a lot of time considering the most
economical way to spend the money. He did a very good job of handling
food purchases. When it came to repaying favors that others did for us, he
was very considerate. At the end of the month when he would add up our
expenses, the money left over was always more than I expected. From
then on I never asked him about his expenses. He feared I would worry,
and so whenever he bought something he would always tell me the reason. There were some things I did not think we needed at the time, but he
had already bought them. I would then calmly say to him, "This is something we don't need this year and we could wait until next year to buy. But
since you've already bought it, don't worry. However, this is called over-
stocking, and it will hurt our budget." After I said this two or three times,
he rarely bought things we did not need.

Because I completely trusted him, he felt very fortunate. Although
taking care of the family budget took a lot of work, it made him very
happy. We lived very comfortably, and our love became deeper and deeper.
He became more and more careful in handling the family purse, and
though it might seem strange, the amount he spent on cigarettes and wine
gradually decreased.

SOURCE: Zhang Ping, "Xiafang jingjiquan yihou" (After transferring my economic power),
Jiefang ribao, December 7, 1985.

The Wedding Night

[This is an excerpt from "A Winter's Fairy Tale," a semi-fictionalized
autobiographical account by Yu Luojin. In this part of the story she re-
calls the night of her wedding to a man she eventually divorced.]

That night I had a dream. I dreamt about something I did not even want to remember—my wedding night. . . .

"Let's hurry up and go to bed!" It was not even nine o'clock and Zhiguo was urging me. There was something that made me uneasy in his embarrassed look. . . . Up until that time we had not spoken one word of love. We had not even held hands! This really was the Chinese custom of "first get married and then fall in love." I am Chinese and am not opposed to Chinese customs. But I cannot say that I felt happy. I basically did not love him.

That night I attended my first class in marriage. My mind was like a blank sheet of paper. I had never read any medical books, my parents had never talked about this, and in school no one had told us anything. . . . Every young woman must pass through this gate. Was it possible that it was now my turn? . . .

I spread out our quilts on the bed so that they were separate. . . . "Put our two quilts together," Zhiguo commanded just as I had finished fixing the bed. I obediently changed them and felt even more uneasy. Zhiguo was in the other room washing his feet. I took off my outer jacket and lay down.

Was I happy? . . . No. Embarrassed? . . . No. Fortunate? . . . No. Satisfied? . . . No. Afraid? Yes. Worried? Yes. Bitter? Yes. Did I have fantasies? . . . I turned my face, for I did not want to see Zhiguo's look when he entered the room. It was so disgusting! I closed my eyes, and peacefully dreamed. . . .

[I dreamed that] we were lying in our quilt-nest, and were holding hands as if we were good friends—this was our first contact. He embraced me very gently, stroked my hair, and tenderly looked at me as if I were a pitiful child. . . . In this unspoken love and exchange of feelings I felt deeply satisfied, sweet, and fortunate. All the unhappiness and bitterness in my heart disappeared. The pleasant sound of his breathing had a cleansing effect on me, washing away all my humiliation and bitterness. . . . In this peaceful bliss I fell asleep. . . .

Suddenly a huge foot came under the quilt, right next to me. I opened my eyes, and my fantasy came to an end. It was a foot that wore a size 12 shoe—so huge it would have scared anyone. . . . I could not help shutting my eyes and stiffening my neck, pulling the blanket tightly around myself. My body was as cold and stiff as a sheet of iron. All I felt was him using his big hand to bore into the quilt-nest. . . . I lay there like a slaughtered fish. . . .

Was it possible that this was marriage? From now on I was just to suffer like this? I would rather die! All the blood in my body rushed to my head. . . . I quickly opened up my box and took out a pair of sewing shears. The silver blades glistened in the moonlight. I leapt back onto the *kang*, grasping the scissors in my right hand, and glaring at him said: "I'm telling you, Zhiguo, if you ever so much as touch me again, I will not spare your life! . . ." I put the scissors under my pillow. From now on my scissors would forever accompany me to bed. . . . I would never admit that he was my husband, and I never wanted to be his wife.

SOURCE: Yu Luojin, "Yige dongtiande tonghua" (A winter's fairy tale), *Xinhua yuekan*, 9 (1980), 116–17.

I Mistakenly Blamed Her

Comrade Editor:

My name is Wu Jinbo. I am a bricklayer for the Steel and Mining Construction Company in the city of Benxi. My wife, Jing Lijie, works at the Water Company. Because I had the feudal notion of "respecting men and looking down on women," and furthermore did not understand basic biological facts, I believed it was my wife's fault that she gave birth to a daughter. I cursed her and beat her, and I even proposed divorce. Fortunately the leadership and comrades in the pertinent agencies educated me and forced me to recognize my mistake, and now I have made up with my wife.

Originally my wife and I played together as children, and as we grew older, fell in love. We cared for each other a great deal and lived very happily together. We hoped that we could have a son as soon as possible.

Because of my desire to have a son, when my wife became pregnant last February, I asked someone to consult a "sex prediction chart." In addition a child who had just learned to talk wished me luck, and I engaged in several other superstitious activities. All of these indicated that my wife would bear a son. My wife even dreamed that she gave birth to a son. So I believed that it was almost certain that we would have a son, and I was extremely happy. Every day I made her special food, and I did not let her do any work. I even went to Shenyang especially to buy 700 eggs for her to eat during the first month after delivery.

The day my wife was to give birth I waited at the hospital, and did not eat a thing, looking forward to the good news. Finally a nurse came and told me, "It's a girl." At that moment my head throbbed, and I almost fainted. Finally I reeled out of the hospital.

From the time my wife gave birth to a daughter, I felt increasingly disgusted with her. I didn't like to return home after work. Either I would stay at my unit and play poker or checkers, or I would hang out on the street. I really did not want to see mother or daughter. I was even prepared to take the eggs I had bought for my wife and sell them. As soon as the baby was a month old I made my wife do heavy tasks, and even kicked her out sometimes. Once I swore at her and she talked back. I was so furious that I took a water ladle and beat her on the head until her nose started bleeding. She couldn't stand it and went to stay at her work unit. The baby was starving and wouldn't stop crying. I grabbed a belt, went to her unit, and whipped her with the belt. She was so angry that she went to court and filed a complaint against me.

Those days were terrible. When I'd get home from work the baby would be crying, the fire in the stove would be dead, and we didn't have much to eat. Plus, every other day the court would subpoena me. I resolved to get a divorce.

I never would have imagined that the leaders of my work unit would brave a snowstorm to come visit me. They talked to me and pointed out that a husband and wife are not only partners in daily life, but also comrades in revolution. They must love each other, help each other, study together, and encourage each other to work well. They also brought a copy of the Constitution and the Marriage Law for me to study. The Constitution stipulates: "With respect to their economic, social, cultural, and family position, women are equal to men and have the same rights." "Marriage, the family, mothers, and children will receive the protection of the government." Through their education and criticism, I finally understood the true meaning of being husband and wife. In the past I had treated my wife as inferior to me. I regarded her as simply a tool to produce a son for me. When she failed to do that I hated her and beat her. This was not only immoral but also illegal.

After listening to the head of the family planning office, Mr. Ma, talk about the scientific aspects of childbirth, and seeing the educational film strips "Produce a Better Child," "Cultivating Intelligence," and "Children's Family Education," I came to realize that whether a baby is male or female actually depends largely on the father's sperm. Now I understand how ignorant it was of me to blame my wife.

To restore our relationship, I admitted my mistake to her. Every day after work I help her with housework, and share with her the job of taking care of our child. I am also willing to publicize my experience in order to help others who discriminate against daughters, and who curse and beat their wives for having borne a daughter, to come to a better understanding of the issue.

Wu Jinbo

SOURCE: Wu Jinbo, "Wo cuoguaile ta" (I mistakenly blamed her), *Zhongguo funü*, 10 (October 1982), 43.

6
Divorce

CHINESE WOMEN, until the early twentieth century, could not initiate divorce. Their husbands, on the other hand, could divorce their wives by invoking any one of the "Seven Outs": barrenness, wanton conduct, neglect of parents-in-law, garrulousness, theft, jealousy and ill will, and incurable disease. Divorced, a woman had nowhere to go but back to her parents' home (if they would accept her); any children she had borne remained with her husband. According to one anthropologist, social stigmatization of a divorcée was so great that she would have little choice but to become a beggar, a prostitute, or a nun.[1]

Divorce was very rare in imperial China. But because the divorce law was such a clear expression of women's inferior status, changing it was a priority of almost every family reform program of twentieth-century revolutionary parties. The Guomindang government abolished the old law during the 1930's. Although a new law was entered in the books, it was never widely implemented outside the cities.[2] The Chinese Communist Party was more successful in implementing a new law before 1949, but it was enforced only in the Communist-controlled base areas.[3] Thus, women throughout China obtained the right to request a divorce for the first time when the CCP promulgated the new Marriage Law in 1950.

Taking advantage of this new law, large numbers of women sought to extricate themselves from arranged marriages, making divorce an explosive social issue in the early years of the PRC.[4] As Kay Ann Johnson points out, women's newfound freedom to initiate divorce "threatened to disrupt the exchange of women upon which patrilineal families and rural communities were based."[5] Precisely because of this threat to the traditional family structure, she convincingly argues, the campaign to implement the new Marriage Law was terminated. After 1953, although a marriage (and divorce) law remained on the books, divorce was almost nonexistent in rural areas, and in cities an extensive mediation process made divorce extremely difficult to obtain, except for political reasons. Not only did the incidence of divorce dwindle; after 1953 so, too, did public discussion of the issue.

More than two decades passed before divorce, like love and courtship, once again commanded popular attention. Beginning in the late 1970's, as divorce became more readily available, the media published articles exploring many aspects of divorce. In addition to a prolific reporting of divorce cases, magazines such as *Chinese Women* and *Democracy and the Legal System* sponsored ongoing discussions of the criteria for divorce, the ethics of divorce, and the problem of divorce caused by extramarital affairs. Moreover, the issue of divorce became one of the major concerns of the newly re-established sociological profession. New journals began to publish the results of investigations of the divorce problem undertaken by sociology students and scholars.

Divorce and the Law

This renewed discussion of divorce was closely linked to the passage of a new Marriage Law in 1980—a law that changed the criteria for divorce in a radical way. The old law had simply stated that in cases in which either the husband or the wife requested a divorce, the courts should conduct a mediation; if the mediation failed, divorce could be granted. The courts insisted on "legitimate" reasons for divorce, and particularly from the Anti-Rightist Campaign through the Cultural Revolution (1957–76), "legitimate" usually meant that the couple had to have serious political differences.[6] In *Son of the Revolution*, Liang Heng relates the story of his parents' divorce, typical of many that took place during this period. In 1957, his mother was labeled a "rightist." "Father's traditional Confucian sense of family obligation told him to support Mother," Liang recalled, "while his political allegiance told him to condemn her. In the end, his commitment to the Party won out, and he denounced her." Hoping to disassociate himself from her, and thereby protect his own political future, Liang's father divorced his mother.[7]

In contrast, the new Marriage Law of 1980 made absence of love a primary criterion in the consideration of divorce cases. "If love and affection (*ganqing*) have truly been destroyed," the new law stated, "and if mediation is ineffective, then a divorce should be granted." Furthermore, as Elizabeth Croll points out, while the 1950 law stated that divorce *might* be granted when mediation failed, the 1980 law decreed that it *should* be granted.[8]

It is not entirely clear why the requirements for divorce were changed from those of the 1950 law. According to one official explanation, the 1980 law made the absence of love and affection a criterion for divorce "because marriage is based on love. As the saying goes, 'tying a man and a woman together cannot make husband and wife out of them.' If we forcibly maintain a marriage in which the woman and the man are just nominally married, then we not only make them both suffer, but such a marriage will also interfere with learning and work. . . . This is harmful to their children, the family, and society as a whole."[9] This recognition of "love" as a basis for marriage (and hence the absence of love as a criterion for divorce) was a reaction to the exclusive emphasis placed on political criteria for marriage during the Cultural Revolution, and was part of a more general attempt to dismantle the ideology of the Cultural Revolution. In addition, the backlog of politically safe but unhappy marriages made during the Cultural Revolution may have created a popular impetus for the changed law. Finally, the new law could be understood as part of an effort begun in the late 1970's to strengthen the legal system. Providing people the protection of the law rather than subjecting them to the dictates of a feudal family system was regarded as a major step toward the creation of a modern society, and "modernity," in the 1980's, was a positive value.

The 1980 law divided divorce cases into two general types: those in which both husband and wife desired divorce, and those in which only one partner sought to dissolve the marriage. The procedures for divorce in the first category were simple and straightforward: the couple went to the local marriage registration office and completed an application for divorce. After the office staff investigated to make sure that neither person was being coerced, a divorce certificate was issued. When only one of the marriage partners desired divorce, the procedures were slightly more complex. He or she could begin by going to the marriage registration office to apply for divorce; the office would conduct a mediation to try to bring about a reconciliation. If that failed, the case was then passed on to the People's Court, where plaintiffs had to pay a fee ranging from 10 to 50 yuan.[10] It was also possible to go directly to the court to apply for divorce. Once the case was in the hands of court officials, they began the mediation process. At best this process resulted in a reconciliation between husband and wife; at a minimum, though, it determined whether their love and affection for each other had truly been destroyed. If so, a divorce would be granted.[11]

A report on the 1982 divorce of a man named Zhang and a woman named Wang illustrates the process of court mediation. A crisis in their already less-than-happy marriage was provoked by Zhang's involvement with another woman, beginning in 1979. Three years later he filed for divorce, but Wang contested it. The court's mediation was described as follows:

The court and Zhang's lawyer first tried to reason with the husband. During mediation, they tactfully pointed out his shortcomings and mistakes, and stated the possibilities for reconciliation should he decide to change his mind. They suggested he consider his son and daughter, who were not yet adults, and the feelings of his wife, who had been with him for nearly twenty years. The judge and the lawyer even took time to visit Zhang personally.

The court and Wang's lawyer also talked to [Wang], encouraging her to take the initiative to be on good terms with her husband.[12]

As it became apparent to the court and lawyers that little hope remained of establishing harmonious relations between the two, they persuaded Wang to agree to the divorce. "She finally came to understand that by opposing the divorce she was only prolonging her suffering," the report concluded.[13]

Once the wife agreed to her husband's request for divorce, the remainder of the mediation process focused on dividing their property and custody of the children. According to the 1980 law, if the mother was still nursing, the child would automatically stay with her. In all other cases, court officials were to make decisions about child custody based on the preferences of the parents and child, the character of the parents, and their respective financial situations.[14] In the case of Wang and Zhang, both children stayed with their mother. Zhang was required to give Wang money for child support; in addition, he bought her a television set.

Not all court mediations were as clear-cut as that of Zhang and Wang. Determining whether "love has been destroyed" frequently involved complicated and debatable judgments. Moreover, the courts sometimes concluded that a couple should stay together despite their unhappiness. In a case tried by the courts in 1985, for instance, the judge rejected a husband's request for divorce despite the obvious estrangement between him and his wife. "Although the relationship between the plaintiff and defendant has been marred, the defendant remains very clear in her hopes," wrote the judge in his final decision. "The plaintiff must treasure the feelings between husband and wife, and consider the interests of the children. Both must respect and forgive each other. Their marital relationship will be restored."[15]

The Increasing Divorce Rate and Its Causes

One immediate result of the passage of the new law was that divorce became an increasing possibility, and more frequently a part of the experience of urban women.[16] No comprehensive statistics about divorce rates in urban China are available; nonetheless, the surveys conducted by sociologists in several cities all confirm a steady increase in the number of divorce cases since 1980. In Shanghai, for example, the number of divorce cases filed at the People's Court in 1981 represented a 53 percent increase over the number filed in 1980, a 78 percent increase over 1979, and a 100 percent increase over 1978.[17] These high rates of increase may obscure the relatively small number of divorce cases. For example, in Shanghai, where the population is approximately 12 million, only 1,304 divorces were granted in 1981.[18] It was thus the rate of increase, and not the actual number of divorces, that caused public concern. Moreover, despite the seemingly small number of divorce cases, they represented some one-third of *all* cases handled by Chinese courts in 1986.[19]

Noting the increase in divorce cases since the passage of the 1980 Marriage Law, some observers cited the law itself as a major reason for divorce. In some cases the relationship was indeed very clear. For example, one woman had married a man nine years her senior to help relieve her own family's financial difficulties. The couple never got along very well, and from 1970 on, they lived separately. She wanted a divorce, but since her husband did not agree, she assumed that she was not entitled to file the request with the courts. After the publicity accompanying the new law, however, she realized that it was not necessary for both partners to want to divorce; she had the right to apply for one herself. Apparently a sizable number of divorce cases heard right after the passage of the new law involved similar situations: many people who had tolerated unhappy marriages for long periods suddenly learned that they could apply for divorce.[20]

The Breakdown of Cultural Revolution Marriages

Although the increased divorce rate might be attributed partly to implementation of the new law, it must be understood in a broader historical context. A large number of divorce cases, particularly those involving young women, were the product of marriages contracted under circumstances specific to the Cultural Revolution and its aftermath. Urban educated youth who had been sent to the countryside frequently married for reasons that had little, if anything, to do with personal attachment. For some educated youth who anticipated permanent residence in the countryside, marriage to another sent-down urban youth was a way to survive psychologically. For others, particularly sent-down urban women, marriage to a peasant who was a Youth League or Party member and reputed to be a hard worker was a means of obtaining as secure a future as possible in the countryside. For those determined not to spend the rest of their lives in the countryside, marriage to an urban resident became one of the only means of moving back to the city.[21] By the early 1980's, with the goal of their marriage long since fulfilled, many of these couples hoped to obtain a divorce.

A man from Shanghai named Sun, for example, had been sent to a rural area in the northeast, and desperately hoped to move back to Shanghai, or at least to an urban area. On his way to Shanghai for a vacation in 1974, he met a twenty-eight-year-old waitress working in the city of Changchun. It happened that she had her heart set on finding a mate from Shanghai. Learning that Sun was from Shanghai and hoping to impress him, she told him that her father was a senior official, although in reality he was a dispatcher. Thinking that a senior official would be able to engineer his move from the countryside, Sun was "attracted" to Wang. Thus, the report of their divorce case remarks, "for different purposes they began dating, and in 1975, when Sun went to call on Wang's family, they had sexual intercourse for the first time." (The article does not say why Sun, having seen the Wang family's house, failed to realize that her father was not a senior official.)

In 1978 Sun was able to move to a small town near Shanghai and therefore lost interest in Wang. He wrote and asked her to end their engagement. Hoping to persuade him to change his mind, Wang immediately went to Sun's home in Shanghai, bringing fifty kilograms of local farm goods from Jilin as a gift. She discovered that Sun was already engaged to another woman. Furious, and having no one in Shanghai to turn to for help, Wang attempted to commit suicide by drinking insecticide. She was saved, however, and when the local police heard what had happened they pressured Sun to marry Wang. Several promises and broken promises later, in 1979, they married. "But lacking mutual understanding and real love, the couple failed to be kind to each other and often fell into quarrels," the report observed. In spite of reconciliatory efforts from the court, they were divorced in August 1980.[22]

Marriages made for the sake of returning to the city from the countryside were only one cause of divorce common among sent-down youth. Many young people who were sent to the countryside found a local sweetheart and married, intending to remain in the countryside for the rest of their lives. When new policies were enacted in the late 1970's, making it possible for educated youth to return to the cities, the basis of many of these marriages was called into question. Suddenly the prospect of returning to the city depended on obtaining a divorce.

The most notorious case of a Cultural Revolution marriage ending in divorce—and the one around which most discussion of this issue revolved—involved a woman named Yu Luojin.[23] When the Cultural Revolution began, both her parents—intellectuals who had been labeled rightists in 1957—lost their jobs; her elder brother was arrested and eventually executed for his political activities. Yu herself was accused of being a reactionary and was eventually sent to work on a production team in the Lin Xi district of Hebei province. There she came under increasing pressure from her parents to marry. They had calculated that their only hope of avoiding transfer from Beijing to a poor, remote village rested on Yu's marriage. If she could marry someone in a richer area, then the official residence of her parents and brothers could be transferred there. Her parents therefore located a potential husband for her in the northeast, and for the sake of her family's survival, Yu married him. "I never would have dreamed that I, who was so full of lofty ideals, would make such a casual decision to get married," Yu later wrote of her marriage. "Even if it had been to a brothel, I would have been willing to go. All I cared about was that my family could live well. . . . I had become completely numb to everything else." [24]

Yu never loved her husband, and in fact refused to sleep with him after their wedding night, but she remained married to him for several years. Then she met another educated youth from Beijing who also lived in the northeast, and fell in love with him. Hoping to marry him, Yu requested, and was granted, a divorce.[25] She did not, however, succeed in marrying the man she loved, for his parents refused to allow their son to marry a woman who was not only an alleged counter-revolutionary, but a divorcée as well.

After the divorce, Yu was transferred from one production team to another and, as a divorced woman, found herself treated as an outcast wherever she went. She resolved to return to Beijing, where the rest of her family then lived, having found a means of returning from their temporary residence in the northeast. Once again, marriage was the only way in which Yu could transfer her official residence from the countryside to the city. Someone introduced her to Cai Zhongpei, a worker in Beijing who also had been recently divorced, and Yu married him in 1977. Unable to obtain a job, she was completely dependent on Cai for financial support.

One year later, Yu once again fell in love—this time with a newspaper editor, a married man more than twenty years her senior. Once her label as a counter-revolutionary was removed, she was able to return to work and earn an income of her own. Yu then informed her husband that she was in love with someone else. She moved out of their home, and in 1980 filed for, and was granted, a second divorce. Her husband appealed, but after a great deal of discussion, the court upheld its original decision.

Yu Luojin described and publicized these experiences in two short stories, "A Winter's Fairy Tale" (an excerpt from which is given in Chapter 5) and its sequel, "A Spring Fairy Tale." The former created an immediate sensation, and for several weeks after its publication, heated arguments about Yu Luojin's divorce case dominated conversations at universities throughout China. These debates were fueled by the publication of scores of articles pertinent to her second divorce trial. Articles by

Yu defending her request for a second divorce prompted articles by her second husband accusing her of being ungrateful; articles by Yu's legal representatives were answered by her husband's legal representatives; essays were even contributed by the judges involved in the case.[26] Almost everyone took sides: some sympathized with her as a social victim; some heralded her as a "liberated woman"; some denounced her as a morally bankrupt opportunist.

For the courts, Yu's case was one of the first major tests of how to interpret the "alienation of affection" clause in the 1980 Marriage Law. The case pitted legal officials who believed that love's meaning was derived from politics and class struggle against those who insisted that love was a matter of emotions and feelings between two people. Yu Luojin summarized these two positions in her fictional treatment of the case when she had two judges engage in an angry exchange:

[Guo Jie]: The words of our revolutionary teachers are forever inscribed in the heavens—love has a class character! It does not matter whether or not the two people are close. The question is one of class. There is no such thing as abstract love, nor is there abstract hatred. When we judge divorce cases we must use the criterion of class struggle to observe, analyze, and manage everything.

[Da Ji]: Engels has said, "Marriages without love are the most immoral of marriages." When we judge divorce cases we always neglect to examine whether or not there is love in the relationship. . . . Some people even turn the corrupt ideas and values of feudalism into a weapon of Marxism-Leninism. By treating the question of love or feelings as a capitalist element, they make their decision, and the result is that feudalism penetrates our thinking even more deeply.[27]

Guo Jie's view represented the one that had prevailed in most divorce cases during the Cultural Revolution. It appears that a group of judges, and perhaps the government as well, hoped to use Yu Luojin's case to discredit what they considered an ultra-leftist definition of love, one based strictly on shared politics and revolutionary commitment.[28]

Even among those who rejected the ultra-leftist definition of love, Yu's case raised troubling issues about how to define "mutual affection" in divorce cases. Was a marriage that was voluntary inherently based on love? Was love automatically present after two people had shared their lives for a number of years? To many people, the desperate circumstances under which Yu Luojin had married both times, and the fact that she had had no alternatives, made the question of love almost irrelevant. Yu herself argued that she had not loved Cai when she married him, but had hoped that their marriage could demonstrate the maxim "first get married, then fall in love."

Many observers found substantial evidence to show that love had indeed developed during the marriage of Yu and Cai. "In fact, after marriage they took care of each other, lived in harmony, and democratically shared their earnings," one person wrote in a letter to *Democracy and the Legal System*. "They not only established the sentiments of 'husband and wife,' but also implemented the principle of 'equality of men and women.'"[29] Their marriage, this writer implied, could be cited as exemplary.

To many, the fact that Yu's husband had spent his own money and a great deal of effort to transfer Yu's residence from the northeast to Beijing, sought "back doors" through which to arrange temporary work for Yu, persistently badgered the Public Security Bureau to expedite the clearing of her elder brother's name, and bought her birthday presents all proved that Yu and Cai "spoke a common language." That Yu took care of Cai when he was in the hospital was seen as additional evidence of the love that had developed between them. In other words, if a husband and wife could get along and help each other meet the needs and demands of their daily lives, their marriage satisfied the requirements of "love" specified by the Marriage Law.

Yu, however, advocated a more radical definition of love. To her, love required an intellectual and spiritual bond between two people, and she concluded that her marriage to Cai held no potential for the development of such a bond. Cai did not appreciate literature, nor did he like the movies she liked. When they went to the Fragrant Hills outside Beijing, instead of expressing appreciation of the autumn foliage, he could only talk about where one could buy the cheapest fish in Beijing. "I cooked for him every day, and we very democratically pooled our wages," Yu admitted to her opponents. "But there was no love! There was no content to our relationship other than eating and sleeping together. . . . Unfortunately it seemed that I was surrounded by couples who could 'make do.' Of course I could not say they were wrong if they wanted just to 'make do,' but why did they have to be so accusing of those who did not want simply to 'get along'?"[30]

The concept of love articulated by Yu's critics—a mutual affection that develops between a husband and wife who help each other meet the needs of their daily lives—had a long historical tradition in China and was still widely held at the time of her divorce case. However, as observed in Chapter 3, notions of love among young urban people were changing rapidly in the early 1980's, and moving in the direction of Yu Luojin's views.

Although the court ultimately granted Yu Luojin her second divorce in May 1981, the decision skirted the issue of how to define "mutual affection," or love. At a minimum, Yu's case set a precedent for those who married during the Cultural Revolution and now wanted to secure a divorce. It also left open the possibility for any person who felt his or her marriage lacked love to apply for divorce.

Changing Status, Changing Mates

In the case of Yu Luojin, it was a woman who declared that her marriage lacked love and requested a divorce. However, women did not always benefit from the law that "alienation of affection" was grounds for divorce. Frequently women were victimized by the law, particularly in the context of a problem the Chinese referred to as "disliking the old and loving the new" (*xixin yanjiu*), a problem that might also be called one of "changing status, changing mates." Most often this involved rural couples who had courted when their work and social status were similar. Then one of the partners—almost always the husband—moved up in the occupational hierarchy, and subsequently had little in common with his wife. In such cases women became casualties of the new demand for companionate marriage. The predicament of these couples was one illustration of the cultural and social gulf between city and countryside, worker and peasant.

The usual approach to this problem, in both reportage and fiction, was to vilify the disloyal man, praise his hard-working wife, and contrast her steadfastness to his infidelity. The story of a couple who lived near the city of Zhangjiakou, Hebei, typified this approach. After Li became engaged to marry a peasant woman named Zhao in the mid-1970's, he was recommended for admission to Tianjin University. While he studied, Zhao was especially thrifty so that she could give him some money. After graduation in 1978 Li was assigned to be a teacher at a technical school in Tianjin, and in 1980 he and Zhao married, but she continued to live in the countryside. From then on Zhao took care of both his parents and her own, often sent Li the special local products of her home village, and went to visit him whenever she had a vacation. "But," writes the author, "as Li changed from being a peasant to a university student and then to a teacher, his thinking changed too, and he no longer thought a peasant wife glamorous enough for him." He fell in love with a woman who was also a college graduate and teacher and had sexual relations with her; she became pregnant. At just that time, he learned that his wife was also pregnant. He declared he wanted to divorce her and forced her to have an abortion; she barely survived an attempt at suicide. After recounting the subsequent cruelty and brutality to which Li subjected Zhao, the story concluded by observing that Li and the woman with whom he had an affair were rightfully punished, and "the masses applauded."[31] The disapproval and condemnation of Li for "changing status, changing mates" was unequivocal.

One public discussion of the issue, however, which ran in *China Youth News* throughout the summer of 1982, revealed the problem in more of its complexity. A letter from a young man named Li Jianxin provoked the discussion by asking, "If the goal of a struggle changes, should love also be renewed?" Li was a native of a mountain village who had married a fellow villager at the age of twenty-two. It was a love match. Two years after his marriage, he was sent to work in the county waterworks. No longer a farmer, he had studied hard at his new job and was preparing to write an article on irrigation mapping. "I have been working and studying with other young people from the same bureau, and we talk very congenially," he reported. "But each time I return home and stay with my wife, I have a strange feeling. She spent only two years in a primary school and reads neither books nor newspapers. She cannot understand me when I talk about my research. We have less and less of a common language. . . . I am thinking of divorcing her, but cannot make up my mind. . . . Comrade Editor, what should I do?"[32]

Li's query brought an unprecedented 5,000 letters in response. Most people agreed with Li that "love needs to be renewed from time to time," but chided him for interpreting this need as a license to change his spouse. One person asked, "If you are supposed to change your spouse every time your status changes, suppose Li Jianxin continues to add to his knowledge, to raise his aspirations, wouldn't he then have to change wives three or five times? If everybody behaves that way, what will our society look like!"[33]

There was less consensus, however, on just what the proper basis of marriage was supposed to be. Some readers encouraged Li to help his wife read and study more, to enlarge their common language. Many wrote of their own marriages, in which partners did different work but shared a common concern for each other. And still others reminded him that loyalty was as important as love: "You should not steer the boat of your happiness on the tears of pain of other people."[34]

When the editors summed up the discussion several months after it began, they concluded that 98 percent of those who wrote in had criticized Li for his attitude. Nevertheless, they added, he had exposed an important social problem. That is, when one's status changes, the change does introduce new contradictions into a marriage. The question is how one deals with those contradictions.[35] To many people, such as Li, divorce seemed to be the only solution.[36]

Failure to Deliver the Marital Goods

Many cases of divorce had little to do with emotional incompatibility or changing social status. They were products of one partner's dissatisfaction when the other failed to perform as hoped. As observed in Chapter 3, the promise of material goods was often a primary criterion in the selection of a mate. In some cases, failure to provide the goods resulted in divorce. For example, a young woman worker named Wang, impressed by the boasts of her suitor Zhou that his family could provide a sofa, television set, and sewing machine, married him. Not long after they were married, however, the furniture and appliances in the house started to disappear. As they were moved out one by one, Wang asked Zhou what was going on. Zhou was evasive at first but finally confessed: to achieve his goal of marrying Wang, he had borrowed all the furniture and appliances, and now he had to return them to the owners. Wang, realizing that she had been duped, was enraged, and began to quarrel with Zhou. She left his home and afterward submitted a request for divorce to the court.[37] In this case, the divorce was granted. In another case, after the couple had completed the marriage registration procedures but had not yet begun to live together, the wife discovered a crack in the mahogany furniture purchased by her husband for the new household. Immediately dissatisfied with her husband, she fell in love with someone else and filed for divorce. This story came to a tragic end when the man she was in love with discovered she was divorced and refused to marry her. She then committed suicide.[38] In this case, it seems plausible that serious personal differences preceded the discovery that the mahogany furniture was not satisfactory. The case was presented in the press, however, as a straightforward instance of "marital materialism."

In deciding divorce cases like these, the critical issue, as defined by the courts, seemed to be the absence of a "foundation of love" before the couple married. Young couples were chided for having rushed into marriage before taking time to really get to know their partners. This problem of "hasty marriages" was particularly pronounced in the early 1980's. Some analyses treated this as a legacy of the Cultural Revolution: by the time many educated youth returned from the countryside, they were already in their late twenties or early thirties and felt it imperative to marry as soon as possible. They married the first prospect introduced to them; in some cases the couple was able to develop a sense of mutual affection after marriage, but for others, living together simply revealed their incompatibility.[39]

In some divorce cases, dissatisfaction with the "goods" did not refer to material possessions, but to a spouse's sexual performance. In some of these cases the court was sympathetic, for the Marriage Law stipulated that impotence was grounds for divorce. (In theory, the premarital physical examination was supposed to discover such problems, so that the couple could change their minds about marriage.) The case of Pang and Shi illustrates the problem:

Pang is an only daughter. One year after she fell in love with Shi they registered to marry. Based on their mutual agreement, the husband became a member of the wife's family. After they got married, the wife discovered that her husband was not able to engage in sexual activity. But she was shy and did not understand, and did not dare say anything about it. Later she discovered that her husband's medical record from before their marriage said he was impotent. Then she told her mother. Her parents really wanted to be grandparents. After they found out, they were extremely upset. They went everywhere to try to find someone who could cure their son-in-law. After one year of treatment there was still no apparent result. Because of this they had many arguments. At this time the husband said his wife's sexual demands were too high. This made the wife furious, and she moved to her parents' room to sleep. The husband decided he had no interest in staying, so he moved away too. From then on their relationship changed, and the wife went to the court, requesting a divorce.

During the process of hearing the case, the husband said that the wife had made him take a great quantity of aphrodisiacs, and they had destroyed his health. When she heard this she was outraged, and to prove that she was telling the truth, she went to the gynecological section of the hospital for an examination. The report was that "the woman's hymen is fully intact," proving that although they had nominally been married for two years, the woman had remained a virgin. At the same time this proved that the man did have a physical defect. The court granted a divorce. The Marriage Law stipulates: Anyone who has a disease that, from a medical point of view, makes marriage inappropriate is prohibited from getting married. Therefore, to conceal physical problems, and deceive someone into marriage, is violating the stipulations of the Marriage Law, and is also immoral behavior.[40]

One cannot help but suspect that Pang's dissatisfaction with her husband was partially prompted by her parents. They had arranged for him to join their household presumably because they desperately hoped that their only daughter would provide them a grandchild to continue the family line. In this case dissatisfaction with a spouse's sexual performance overlapped with a more prevalent concern, the production of offspring.

Many divorce cases brought before the courts involved husbands who were disappointed by their wives' failure to produce children, specifically sons. We have already observed that the one-child policy placed enormous pressure on women to give birth to a son, and that failure to do so often resulted in physical abuse by their husbands (see Chapter 5). Some men whose wives gave birth to daughters petitioned the courts for divorce, perhaps hoping that they could remarry and subsequently try again for a son. The courts, however, were unequivocal in refusing to grant divorces under these circumstances. The refusal to grant divorces when women were abused for having borne a girl did not necessarily help women a great deal. At best it offered them economic protection; at worst it trapped them in marriages to husbands who, hoping to coerce their wives into agreeing to a divorce, abused them.

The case of a woman named Qu Hua from Qiqihaer, Heilongjiang, illustrates this possibility. She married a worker named Xu Baocheng in 1980, and they got along very well until she gave birth to a girl. Then Xu immediately began to beat Qu, and forced her and the baby to live in a small shack. As soon as the baby was one month old, Xu illegally filed for divorce. (The Marriage Law prohibits a husband from applying for a divorce during the first year after his wife gives birth.) Qu did not agree to the divorce, for she feared she would have no place to live afterward. Eventually, after she was hospitalized for injuries caused by her husband's beatings, Qu went to the courts herself and accused Xu of beating her. He was found guilty and sentenced to two years in prison. After three months, though, he was released and returned home, where he continued to beat Qu for having borne him a daughter. At the time Qu wrote a letter to the editor of the *Workers' Daily* (Gongren ribao) in 1983, pleading for help, she was still married to Xu, for the courts had not agreed to his request for a divorce.[41] For someone like Qu Hua, the law, intended to protect women, actually created a no-win situation.

Divorce Caused by Extramarital Affairs

Most individuals or couples requesting divorce claimed that their marriages lacked "love and affection." In a large percentage of cases, this charge resulted from the presence of a "third party" (*disanzhe*). In other words, the person requesting the divorce had fallen in love with someone else, or was involved in an extramarital affair.[42]

Before the passage of the 1980 Marriage Law, individuals were extremely reluctant to request divorce on the grounds that they had fallen in love with someone else. They feared that the courts would brand their behavior immoral, refuse to grant the divorce, and punish them as well.[43] In a case reported in the mid-1950's, a man from Beijing named Le Baoyi, hoping to divorce his wife, confessed that he was engaged in an extramarital relationship. After criticism by officials at his work unit failed to change his behavior, he was removed from his administrative duties and his Party membership was made probationary. As a last resort, he did everything imaginable to make his wife miserable, hoping that eventually she would initiate the divorce.[44] Most people caught in a similar predicament never admitted to their extramarital affairs; instead they simply tried, as Le ultimately did, to destroy their marriages so that the desire for divorce would be a mutual one.[45]

The 1980 law's provision making "alienation of affection" cause for divorce changed this situation. After the law took effect, extramarital relations became one of the major causes of divorce. According to a survey of divorce rates in the Xuhui district of Shanghai from 1978 to 1980, some

41 percent of the cases involved extramarital affairs; in Canton the figure rose to 80 percent in 1984.[46] Although colleagues, relatives, and friends might frown upon a person's having an extramarital affair, the courts considered it legitimate evidence of a breakdown of mutual affection, and in many cases granted the divorce.[47] This often placed the courts in an awkward conflict between the mandates of justice and those of morality. As one legal official observed, in cases involving extramarital relations, "from the perspective of the law, since love has been destroyed, the person should be granted a divorce; however, from the perspective of morality, since the reason is not 'proper,' the person should be condemned."[48] Often in such cases the law prevailed, but the conflict between morality and the law generated widespread public discussion of divorce caused by extramarital affairs.

Analyzing the causes of the apparent upsurge of extramarital affairs, numerous sociologists cited unhappy marriages as the major culprit. Optimistic observers perceived the prevalence of unsatisfactory marriages as a historical legacy that would eventually disappear. A survey of divorces caused by extramarital affairs in Zhengzhou (Henan) revealed that the majority of cases involved couples in their thirties who had married during the Cultural Revolution—proof to one author that these affairs were indeed "due to problems of the past." He was careful to explain that the 1980's economic reforms were not to blame for the soaring divorce rate, and that in fact they would eventually help to bring it down:

[T]he increase in cases of extramarital affairs is not due to the development of productive forces in recent years. The result of the increased standard of living is that previous contradictions are coming to light. . . . Solving the problem of third-party interference, as with other problems, depends primarily on the development of productive forces, raising the standard of living, and raising the cultural level of the people.[49]

Other writers suggested, however, that it was precisely those recent policies raising the standard of material and cultural life that led people to engage in extramarital affairs. They implied that many Chinese people mistakenly associated "modernization" with sexual liberation. "They think one's sex life should not be restricted to the legal relationship of husband and wife," one writer complained. He cited the case of a man, guilty of having an affair, who chastised his wife for "feudal thinking." "You should be more liberated," he told her. "We are now in the 1980's. You can find a man and I won't mind."[50]

Some Chinese observers also blamed extramarital affairs on the increased exposure to the West that accompanied the Four Modernizations. One writer cited the case of a man who, yearning for a Western life-style, began to dislike his wife "for never taking the initiative to hug or kiss him when they met or said goodbye. He happened to meet a girl whose way of thinking was the same as his. They hit it off perfectly and engaged in adultery many times." Rather than troubling with divorce proceedings, the man attempted to flee across the Chinese border with his paramour, declaring that their love "could not be satisfied in a socialist country."[51]

Whatever the reasons for extramarital affairs, the major concern of government officials and magazine editors was controlling the problem. Many writers appealed to people's sense of morality, warning them that it was immoral to build their happiness at the expense of others. In at least one city, Shanghai, engaging in extramarital affairs was branded semicriminal. In 1985 the local regulations to protect the legal rights of women and children made third-party intervention in a marriage illegal; those found guilty would be "instructed to correct themselves."[52] Some people advocated that the national legal code make adultery a crime.[53]

More positively, stories of "model couples" who successfully weathered extramarital affairs were reported to inspire others. One man related his experience of having to leave his beloved wife to work in another town. "Later," he wrote, "because my work necessitated it, I made frequent contact with a young woman. We talked about everything and kept no secrets from each other. Gradually an inexplicable kind of sentiment developed between the two of us. Whenever I went home I found that nothing pleased me, and I would fight with my wife for no good reason." His plan to divorce his wife was thwarted when his colleagues at work intervened, chiding him for his behavior and warning him that he would be censured by public opinion if he proceeded with the divorce. "When that happens, how are you going to talk about being happy?" they asked him. He decided his colleagues had a point, terminated his "dishonorable love affair," and abandoned his plans for divorce. The story concluded with a happy, and hopefully instructional, ending:

When I saw my wife again and noticed her thin cheeks, pale from overwork, my heart was filled with regret and self-reproach. I decided to love my wife and children twice as much so as to atone for what I had done. And the happiness of the old days returned to our family again. In the meantime the young woman, through the introduction of comrades, found and married someone else and now she, too, has a happy family.[54]

Stories with tragic endings were published to warn readers of the perils awaiting those who engaged in extramarital affairs. One such story, based on a real event, involved two people from Shanghai—a factory manager named Zou, and Tian, a doctor at a factory clinic with whom he fell in love. Tian had been a classmate of Zou's wife, and frequently went to their house to visit. (Although the article alluded to Tian's two children, her husband's whereabouts were never mentioned.) On these occasions

Zou's wife would go to the kitchen to cook, leaving Zou to eat and drink with Tian, creating, according to the author, "just that kind of environment in which relations between people of the opposite sex can develop." Zou's sister apparently noticed the "dubious relationship" that developed and cautioned Zou, but to no avail.

One day in November 1984, Zou phoned Tian and arranged to meet her at a local entertainment hall (*yule chang*) that evening. "Who would have guessed that when they were standing together in a dark corner they would be discovered by a plainclothes public security officer?" They were taken to the police station, but released because of their relatively high social status. However, both were reprimanded at their work units; neither could imagine how to regain their "lost face." In early December, they boarded a train from Shanghai to Wuxi, where they both committed suicide.[55] The author omitted details that would make the story more plausible (why did the plainclothes policeman arrest the couple?), and offered no commentary on this case. Presumably the tragic ending spoke for itself.

Although most accounts criticized both parties involved in extramarital affairs, the "third party" was often portrayed as particularly villainous. In almost all cases, this villainous third party was a woman. Only rarely did press reports describe cases in which a married woman had fallen in love with another man. And one survey conducted in Shanghai indicated that most of the people who became third parties were young, unmarried women. The author believed they were prone to become third parties because "young women lack social experience, have rich emotions, and do not have the kind of family restrictions that married women have."[56] Another writer argued that "old maids" (see Chapter 3) were partly responsible for the problem. According to some research materials, the article stated, "the number of old maids who are third parties cannot be overlooked." This was allegedly because they had become very picky about whom they would marry, and as soon as they met an ideal person, were so overcome with emotion that they unwittingly disrupted the relationship between that person and his wife.[57]

The extent to which young women were held responsible for the prevalence of extramarital affairs was indicated by a poem published in a Beijing women's magazine. Entitled "Butt Out!," it was directed at "third parties who interfered with other people's families." In a harsh and impatient tone, the poem demanded that young women "who have naively woven a dream of love" look at the pain and suffering they caused. "Your feet are trampling notes of a harmonious melody," the poet exclaimed, "crushing clusters of beautiful flowers, toppling nests of happiness. . . . Interloper, please butt out! . . . You should never create your happiness at the expense of someone else's bitterness!"[58]

Wives of married men who engaged in extramarital affairs were thus treated as the "bitter" victims. They were not considered completely innocent, however, for as we saw in Chapter 5, it was incumbent on married women to make themselves "attractive" and "interesting" so that their husbands would not feel the need or desire to replace them with others. Moreover, while their husbands' extramarital activities never received society's approbation, women were told with increasing frequency to agree to divorce a husband wishing to marry someone else. By late 1983, the emphasis on reconciling marriage through mediation, which had dominated articles published immediately after the passage of the new Marriage Law, was replaced by a spate of articles advising women to "liberate themselves" through divorce.

The story related by a thirty-eight-year-old woman named Ma Ying was typical. She had married a middle school teacher in 1974. "The first few months of marriage were fine," she recalled, "but after a year, thanks to the intrusion of a third party, he became distant toward me and requested a divorce."

At that time society was not so liberated in its thinking as it is today. Many people believed that getting divorced was a bad thing. I myself believed that divorced women were inferior to other women. So I thought we should just stick it out. Although we did not fight, his silence was worse than cursing, and I could not stand this spiritual pain. Finally I agreed to the divorce. After getting divorced I felt much more relaxed. There was no reason to let myself be oppressed by someone who did not love me. Later, through the introduction of colleagues, I met an engineer, and in 1981 we married. Now we care for each other, trust each other, help each other with work, encourage each other, and live very happily.[59]

Editors of some women's magazines as well as some officials in the Women's Federation concurred with Ma Ying. One writer, after presenting a lengthy denunciation of divorce, concluded her article by criticizing women who refused to divorce in order to take revenge on husbands who had fallen in love with someone else. "Some female comrades do not pay any attention to their own spiritual or even physical misery," she said, pointing out that many were subject to physical abuse by their husbands. "This kind of desire for revenge among women who have been victimized is understandable, but it is not a method of solving any problems."[60] The head of the legal consultative committee of the Beijing Women's Federation, Wu Changzhen, not only criticized women who "tried to safeguard their rights by rejecting divorce," but encouraged them to "try to break out of the tragedy and look for new love."[61] Others, such as Shang Shaohua, editor of *Chinese Women*, instructed women to bravely face the challenge of divorce. "Women should not give themselves up completely and place all their hopes on their husbands and children, for this in itself is a kind of surrender." She believed that by overcoming their sense of inferiority and weakness, turning their energies to their careers, and regaining their independence, women could make up for the misfortune of divorce.[62]

The Divorced Woman

Those advocating that wives agree to a husband's request for divorce assumed that women would ultimately benefit. They would escape a situation that was emotionally, if not physically, damaging; in addition, they might find a new mate and establish a more satisfying family life. In some cases, such as that of Ma Ying, this proved to be true. Frequently, however, divorced women found it difficult to find a new mate. As one divorced woman complained, "Since I have refused potential mates several times, many people gossip about me. Some say, 'An ordinary worker who is divorced—how can she set conditions. She should just find someone and settle for that.' There are also some who say, 'Any man who meets your requirements is not going to pay attention to a divorcée like you.' This kind of discussion has added to the bitterness I already feel."[63] In other words, rather than creating a range of enticing new opportunities, being a divorcée often rendered a woman vulnerable in a variety of new ways.

One of the most poignant discussions of the predicament faced by divorcées is a story entitled "The Ark," written in 1982 by Zhang Jie, a woman writer whose stories were particularly popular among Chinese youth.[64] The story focused on three women who lived together—two were divorced and one was separated from her husband. That the three lived together made them most atypical; many of the problems they encountered, however, were ones commonly faced by divorced women. Their experiences, though fictitious, attested to the difficulties of being a divorced woman in China.

"The Ark" offered many reminders of the stigmatization faced by divorced women. One of the characters, Liangqin, was pressured by her father's friends to refrain from divorce because having a divorced daughter would damage his reputation. The father of another character, Liuquan, had all but severed relations with his daughter when she married a man he considered too "businesslike." When Liuquan mentioned divorce, though, he was violently opposed; he preferred a detestable son-in-law to a divorced daughter. In other words, in considering divorce a woman not only had to consider what friends, colleagues, relatives, and neighbors would think of her; she also had to contemplate the social disgrace she would cause her family. No wonder that Jinghua, the third character in "The Ark," concluded that "anyone who wants a divorce must be a very courageous person."

They will have to throw away all their pride and reveal their secret and embarrassing reasons—they will even have to reveal things like how they have suddenly lost certain biological capacities, or how married life has become full of terror and suffering. They will have to tell these things to all kinds of strangers who have the right to interfere with their marriage. They will have to retell the reason and appeal to these people more than a hundred times, hoping they will be merciful and understanding. The reasons may seem ridiculous to others, but to the people involved they may be a matter of life and death. It's like having to take off all one's clothing and stand naked before hundreds and thousands of people.

"Has anyone's divorce not brought disgrace and ruin upon them?" she finally asked.[65]

One of the most troubling aspects of being a divorcée for the women in Zhang Jie's story was the constant reminder that others regarded them as sexually available. At one point in the story, for instance, the woman who lived in the apartment next door to the three women knocked on their door. When Jinghua answered, the woman asked,

"Has our cat come over to your place?"
"No. Why would your cat want to come here?"
"Oh my! Comrade Zao (Jinghua), don't you know that your female cat has really stirred up the six male cats in this building? Hahahaha." Jia (the woman next door) kept laughing, clearly implying something else.[66]

Having tolerated a number of similar incidents, Liuquan thought to herself:

Why did she have to be born a woman? To be a woman is bad enough, but why did she also have to be an attractive woman? Most people know that to be ugly is unfortunate. But they don't realize that it can be just as unfortunate to be attractive. On top of everything else, why did she have to be a divorced woman, who no longer belonged to somebody? To not belong to somebody, it's as though you belong to everybody![67]

A woman, in other words, was a person only in the context of a family; as an outsider she was completely unprotected.

These problems of being regarded as "indecent" and promiscuous by other women, and as sexually available by men, were exacerbated by other, more concrete forms of discrimination faced by divorced women. This discrimination was most clear when divorced women looked for housing. We have already seen that in some cases, women endured physical abuse by their husbands rather than face the prospect of having nowhere to live. In "The Ark," Liuquan related her attempts to secure housing after her divorce. The person in charge of housing looked at her incredulously when she submitted her request.

"What do you want housing for?"
"Don't you know that I am divorced?"

"That won't do you any good. We have married people here who don't have housing yet. You're divorced and you want housing—if we did that, then everybody would fake divorce just to get housing!"

Unable to secure housing, Liuquan had to give up custody of her child.[68]

It must be remembered that a divorced man would not have found himself in this predicament. Given housing allocation practices (see Chapter 4), most couples lived in housing assigned by the husband's work unit. When a married couple divorced, it was therefore often the woman who had to leave the home and find somewhere else to live. As one divorced woman complained in a letter to *Chinese Women*, "At the time of divorce the man can very rationally and coolly state, 'The apartment belongs to my work unit. I want to give it to my wife, but my work unit does not agree.' And just like that, the court gives the apartment to the husband."[69] If a divorced woman could not obtain housing through her work unit, she had little choice but to return to her natal home. And if she had brothers who had settled their families in the parents' home, she often was not able to count on this possibility. Thus, as in the case of Liuquan, women's difficulties in obtaining housing—coupled with their lower incomes—sometimes made it impossible for them to win child custody. Under these circumstances, the law guaranteeing women equal consideration for child custody was little more than a statement of good will.

The right to initiate divorce and the ability to terminate a "loveless" marriage was welcomed by some women. Perhaps the extensive public discussion of divorce eventually will reduce the stigma faced by divorcées. Ironically, though, in the short run the law denied women some security. It was no longer enough for a wife to be loyal and hardworking. She could now be rejected and divorced for not having mobility opportunities, or interests that developed in the same direction as those of her husband. It was usually men who moved up in the world, and presented their wives with new, "modern" demands for intellectual and emotional companionship. The question of "love" remained entangled in a gender hierarchy in which men had more freedom to make such demands. Thus, as long as the increased freedom to divorce took place within the context of basic social and economic inequality, women remained unequal beneficiaries.

Translations

The number of people filing for divorce increased dramatically after the passage of the 1980 Marriage Law. As "The Flowers of Reconciliation Bloomed

Again" suggests, judges were often loathe to grant a divorce if they believed the marriage had been based on love. Some divorce petitioners argued that the basis for love no longer existed. Whether or not divorce should be granted in these situations became a subject of debate, as in "When the Object of Struggle Changes, Must Love Also Be Renewed?"

The new divorce law was sometimes used by men whose wives had borne daughters and who hoped to remarry and try again for a son. "The Accusation of an Abused Woman Worker" illustrates the hardships such a situation imposed on women.

Extramarital affairs were frequently cited as a major contributor to the increased divorce rate in the 1980's. As the poem "Butt Out!" suggests, single women were considered the primary culprits in extramarital affairs. At the same time, wives of men who sought divorce in order to marry someone else were increasingly advised to consent to divorce rather than seeking revenge by maintaining a miserable marriage, as exemplified by "Gather Your Courage, Become Aware of Your Own Strength."

Many women resisted divorce for fear of the difficulties associated with being a divorced woman. As the articles "Do Not Discriminate against Divorced Women" and "The Worries of a Divorced Woman" make clear, a divorcée in China was stigmatized. And as "I Want a Divorce" shows, even if a young woman was not afraid of the stigma, her parents' fears led them to do everything in their power to prevent their daughter from seeking divorce.

The Flowers of Reconciliation Bloomed Again

My husband's name is Chen Yulin. He is a worker at the Changzhou Bunker Installation Plant. We fell in love with each other in 1966. I liked literary and artistic activities very much then, and spent many evenings rehearsing at the unit where I worked or at the cultural center. My husband and I got married in October 1967.

I did not expect that he would dislike my going to rehearsals in the evening. But he thought that a wife should be submissive and do what the husband says, that she should stay home where she belongs, managing household affairs, taking care of the children, and attending to the husband's needs. Also he felt that she should not be going out and showing her face everywhere. He considered my going to social activities such as rehearsals to be disrespectful of him.

I certainly could not let myself give in to these feudal ideas of his. In 1975 he laid down some restrictive rules: I must not go out at night, must not speak to men, must not go to the movies alone, must not participate in cultural activities, etc. We quarreled very often, since I refused to be restricted.

One day in March 1978 I invited a neighboring female comrade to go to a play. But because she suddenly was called to work the night shift, she told her husband to go with me instead. When we got back from the movie my husband, Lao Chen, saw that I had been with a man. He slapped me on both cheeks, and then pushed me onto the bed and started to beat me. He also cut off part of my hair and forced me to give him all the keys to the house. I ran to my parents' house and took thirty sleeping pills. Fortunately it was discovered in time, and I was saved. After that I moved into a dormitory at my work unit. In August 1979 I officially asked to divorce Chen Yulin.

After the separation I was often in a daze, especially at night because that is when I missed my child terribly. One day I brought some bread and candies and went to see my child at school. It was between classes when I got there. The other children were all playing except my son, who remained seated on his chair. A strange feeling suddenly rushed to my heart. With tears in my eyes I called him, but he only stared at me with fear. I handed him the things I had bought, but he said, "I don't want your things. Father says you're not a good mother. You don't love us."

His teacher told me that my husband was having a hard time coping with both the household work and his job. Not only was the house a mess, but the quality of his work had also fallen off. In addition the child's grades had dropped because he lacked supervision at home. He had even failed some courses. The teacher finally said, "If the affection and love between you and Lao Chen hasn't reached a hopeless point, I urge you to make up for the child's sake!"

At that time I was still determined to get a divorce. After I had appealed to the court for a divorce, the comrades at the court analyzed the whole story and concluded that my husband and I still loved each other. They believed that the reason things had gotten so bad was that Lao Chen had been deeply influenced by the idea that the husband should rule the family. They decided to try to persuade us to make up.

The comrades of the court talked to Lao Chen several times to persuade him that he should not be suspicious of his wife and make groundless accusations. They also educated him in socialist morality—making him understand that in a socialist society, husbands and wives must respect and love each other and treat each other equally. When a disagreement arises between a couple, they must talk it over calmly, instead of the husband beating and scolding the wife. With the help of the comrades from the court, Lao Chen began to feel regretful for what he had done, and subsequently began to consider the idea of making up.

It was New Year's Day 1980 when Lao Chen came to see me with our child, and he even brought me my favorite dumplings, New Year's cake, etc. He was all choked up when he said, "I was wrong to interfere with your life. I especially should not have beaten you. I am making a self-criticism for what I have done to you. For our child's sake please forgive me." At this time the child also threw himself on me and said, "Mother, please come home, please come home!" At this I shed tears.

Lao Chen told me later that it was his own idea to come and visit me, but it was the comrades at the court who reminded him to bring along my favorite goodies. These comrades also asked my mother to bring my child to visit me during the Spring Festival, and to urge me not to refuse to yield just because I was right. . . .

And that is how my husband and I finally made up. One day in March 1980 the comrades from the court even threw a reunion party especially for us. With tears in our eyes we thanked the comrades of the People's Court again and again.

Ever since then Lao Chen no longer has had to be busy rushing around doing all the household chores himself. He became happy and his work also improved. Not long ago he was even chosen as a model of individual skill and became a team leader. Our child's personality has become more lively. The warmth of family life has finally enabled us to taste happiness.

I still actively participate in cultural activities. Lao Chen has never again tried to stop me. Once Lao Chen even accompanied me to the cultural center for my rehearsal. Before we parted he smiled and said, "If you like I will take you to your rehearsals all the time. But you must take good care of your health!"

SOURCE: Wu Fengying, "Hehuanhua you kaile" (The flowers of reconciliation bloomed again), *Funü*, 1 (1984), 10.

When the Object of Struggle Changes, Must Love Also Be Renewed?

Dear Editor:

I am twenty-five years old and an employee in my county's Hydraulic Agency. Before I started working here, I worked in a commune in the mountains. Three years ago, I fell in love with a girl in my village and later married her. She is industrious and capable. We worked our land well, cooperated in running our home, and loved each other a great deal. Our life was more than happy.

The year following our marriage, I was hired to work in the county seat. During the last two years, the world around me has changed a lot. My goals are no longer to have a few acres of land and a house with several rooms. With the help of some old technicians, I have read a lot and participated in field surveys. I am preparing an essay on hydraulic measuring in rural areas. I am working toward a successful career.

When I work with some of the young people in our office, I feel at home. But when I return home and stay with my wife, I have a strange feeling. She spent only two years in a primary school and now reads neither books nor newspapers. She cannot understand me when I talk about my research. We have less and less of a common language. Now I even regret that I got married to her at such an early age.

Several times I have tried to say to her, "If I leave you and you find another young man in the countryside, life will be happier for you." But I don't have the heart to say it. All this has escaped her notice and she loves me just as she used to. This tortures me even more.

I am thinking of divorcing her, but cannot make up my mind. Love, to me, should be the only foundation for marriage. As Engels said, "The only moral marriage is one based on love." Why should I maintain this marriage in form when I no longer love her? In Lu Xun's story "Sadness," Juansheng said, "Love must be renewed all the time." Why can't my love be renewed along with the new goals in my life? Nevertheless, I am worried that people will condemn me as immoral. People all curse "Chen Shimei." But they do not know that Chen Shimei had his difficulties, too.

Comrade editor, what should I do?

Li Jianxin

[Chen Shimei, a Song dynasty scholar from a poor family, married a woman who was also from a poor family. When he received the top score on the civil service examination, the Emperor wanted Chen to marry his own daughter. Determined to take advantage of this rare chance, Chen pretended he was not married. When the truth emerged several years later, however, the Emperor ordered Chen killed.—EDS.]

"Love should be renewed when the goals of one's life are altered." This view expressed in Li's letter is common among young people whose profession and social position have changed (such as those who have moved to the city, been promoted, or entered a school). We hope our readers will express their opinions on the issues raised by his letter, such as how to interpret the notions that "the only moral marriage is one based on love," or that "love must be renewed from time to time." What is "a common language"? How should one regard the rights and responsibilities of love? Please express your views.

Editor

SOURCE: *Zhongguo qingnian bao*, July 10, 1982, 1.

Readers' Responses

After giving up a luxurious life, Jenny . . . ran the house diligently so that Marx was able to throw himself completely into the revolutionary cause. Recalling the days when he wrote *Capital*, Marx said: "I will never forget that Jenny did a great deal to help me finish the book."

The progress Li has made in his career, I think, is largely due to his wife's "diligence and capability in running the home." It is not only selfish, but shameful, too, for Li to attribute all his achievements to his own effort and to abandon his wife, who has actually done much to make this achievement possible. I wish Li could remember: your spouse's help has been indispensable to your success!

Wang Hongzhou

SOURCE: *Zhongguo qingnian bao*, July 20, 1982.

Li's view, "with the alteration of my goals in life, why can't I renew my love?" seems immoral. But actually it is marriage no longer based on love that is immoral.

While Li works hard toward his goals, he needs someone who can understand him, work with him, and do research with him. But his wife cannot read, nor does she know anything about his work. It is the loss of a common language between them that has taken away his love for her. Their relationship is no longer one between two people who can learn from each other and share each other's ideals and goals in life.

Marriage is based on love, and love is based on mutual feelings. If one side has no more feeling toward the other, . . . what is marriage but a cold corpse? It is not fair that Li has to live in this dead marriage while he no longer has any feeling for his wife. Under such circumstances, it is reasonable for him to consider divorcing her. But he fears that people will think he is immoral. However, let us consider the case once again. If divorce is immoral, then what shall we call marriage without love? If it is moral for Li to maintain his marriage with a wife he no longer loves, then what shall we say about his wife, who allows her husband to sacrifice his future and happiness for her interests?

It is the law of nature for the new to replace the old. Marriage is an organic part of the world, and therefore it will grow and disappear too. Likewise, if Li's love for his old wife has disappeared and he needs someone new to love, what is wrong with that?

Shen Jianhua

SOURCE: *Zhongguo qingnian bao*, July 20, 1982.

A common language is one of the standards set by many people when they seek a lifelong companion. How should we define the term? Should it mean a common expertise, professional jargon, or world view? In my opinion, the key is whether this common language is based on mutual understanding, mutual help, mutual support, and mutual respect.

I am a graduate of the Harbin Teachers College. But my husband is an ordinary worker. We have been married for four years and still have a very good relationship. He knows very little about my profession, but he understands the importance of my work. He often says to me: "A teacher must be serious about teaching, otherwise the students will be led astray." He has given me a great deal of support in my teaching. At home he always tries to do more housework so that I can have enough time to prepare for my classes. Often I ask him to play the role of student so that I can test the effectiveness of my lectures. In this way I become more familiar with the content of my lectures and he can also learn something. He has given me advice about teaching methods. For the past few years, he has always encouraged me whenever I take part in a proficiency-training program or some academic activity. I have never had to worry about things at home. For my part, I have always encouraged him to raise his level of literacy and I have tried to create a better environment for him to study. As the result of our efforts, he has succeeded in enrolling at a workers' school.

Life has taught me that in spite of the differences in our social positions and degree of literacy, we have something in common: our pure thought and feeling. This is the source and foundation of our common language.

Wang Min

SOURCE: *Zhongguo qingnian bao*, July 27, 1982.

The Accusation of an Abused Woman Worker

The Constitution of our country stipulates that maltreatment of women is prohibited. Yet currently the phenomenon of maltreating women who give birth to girls still exists in society. This cannot be tolerated. Hopefully the plea of the woman worker Qu Hua from Qiqihaer, that [her husband] Xu Baocheng be punished, will receive the attention of the departments concerned.

Editor

My name is Qu Hua. I am a young woman worker at the Number Two Machine Tool Factory in the city of Qiqihaer in Heilongjiang province. In 1980 I married Xu Baocheng, a worker at the main railroad material factory in Qiqihaer. We got along quite well after the marriage.

However, after I gave birth to a baby girl in March 1981, I was subjected to beating, scolding, and maltreatment by Xu Baocheng's entire family. My mother-in-law despised me, and yelled at me, "There is land, yet the grass does not grow; you have given birth to a girl and snuffed out the Xu family's incense burner."

During the time I was in the hospital after giving birth, my mother made a special trip from Inner Mongolia to take care of me. But nobody from the Xu family came to see me. When I returned home, Xu Baocheng kicked me out of the house and sent me to live in a dark, sunless little hut. During the winter, when it was freezing cold, I was not allowed to burn coal to keep warm, even though we had it. The family made me sleep on a cold *kang* and wash with cold water. Once, because she wanted to grab a diaper, my mother-in-law actually threw the baby onto the ground. They not only did not try to provide nourishment for me, but in addition scolded me, saying, "What do you think you're doing eating eggs?" They even ate the nutritious food my parents and relatives had sent for me. . . .

Xu Baocheng made up excuses to scold me and beat me almost every other day. Sometimes he even stripped off all of my clothes to beat me. Once he beat me until my mouth was full of blood. He stripped off my clothes and shoes and stabbed me with a pair of scissors. I ran barefoot to his work unit, so cold I could not speak. The leader of his unit saw that I was in such a pitiful state that he borrowed some clothes and shoes for me.

On the day the baby completed her first month of life, Xu Baocheng stole an official seal and wrote an illegal letter of introduction from his work unit requesting a divorce. He tried to force me to agree to divorce him, but I refused. He beat me, and then threw me and our daughter out of the hut, telling me to go live in the chicken coop. He refused to give me any daily necessities except for bedding. I lived through the next four months in an inhuman state. . . .

On New Year's Day in 1982 my mother-in-law invented an excuse to beat my face swollen with a slipper. At noon on the following day Xu wanted me to take my mother-in-law some pancakes (*yang you bing*). But since she had beaten me up the day before, I didn't want to go and I said, "Why don't you go yourself?" Xu exploded when he heard this. He said, "Fuck you! You don't want to get along with me any more!" He then picked up the kitchen cleaver and was about to strike me with it. Fortunately my sister-in-law grabbed him. I ran to the landlord's house. Xu ran after me there with the cleaver in his hand. He grabbed me by the collar and started to chop. He chopped and wounded four of my fingers; my pants were also cut and torn. Fortunately the landlady and others did all they could and seized the cleaver. That is how I managed to escape death.

Once I discovered that Xu and a female illustrator of a certain work unit were involved in a relationship. I proceeded to give him some well-meaning advice. But Xu said to me, "Let's get a divorce. I will remarry and have a son, and you can find another man and have a son. We can still maintain our married relationship secretly. Then if you have any problems I will do my best to help you." I strongly disagreed and for this he beat me up. He said, "Then you'll just have to put up with me!" One day, after I had been beaten, some kind comrades from the railroad station took me to the hospital. The diagnosis was recurrent traumatic bleeding under the skin (*pi xia chu xue*), head injury, cerebral concussion, and broken ribs on the right side of the chest.

With the support and sympathy of the work units of both parties, I filed a suit at the People's Court of District Tie XX of Qiqihaer against Xu Baocheng. After an investigation, the court arrested Xu Baocheng on April 18, 1982, and sentenced him to two years in prison and three years of probation. Xu Baocheng repeatedly begged for my mercy when he was in jail. He wrote a "blood letter" [a letter written in one's own blood to express one's sincerity], pledging that he would be kind to me. He eventually succeeded in tricking me into forgiving him. He was released from jail three months later.

Who could have known that the first time we met after he had been released he would publicly announce that he would not live with me anymore? At present Xu Baocheng is still swollen with arrogance and continues to cruelly injure me, leaving me to wander about destitute and without a home. I have wanted to commit suicide several times, yet I couldn't bear to abandon my young daughter. I beg the department concerned to protect the legal rights and interests of women and children in accordance with the law and to punish Xu Baocheng, who has maltreated and cruelly injured a woman.

SOURCE: *Gongren ribao*, December 20, 1983, 3.

Butt Out!

For "Third Parties" Who Have Interfered with Other People's Families

Have you seen the lonely child
With teardrops on its face?
Have you heard the child who has lost tender care
Cry its heart out?
Have you heard the curses
Stabbing your spine from behind?
Have you seen the eyes
Burning with hatred in front of your face?

Ah! It seems that you have not seen anything,
And you have not heard anything.
Otherwise why does the misery continue,
Why does the tragedy still take place?!

Originally you had your own wonderful family
And yet you were unwilling because of this to tend your own garden.

With your fingertips you pluck flowers that do not belong to you,
And do not hesitate to bring to ruin yourself and others.
Perhaps you are really a young girl
Whose feelings have just begun to emerge,
And have naively woven a dream of love.
If only someone sends you a rose of love,
What does it matter if he has a wife and home, and is much older.

Perhaps you see yourself as a contemporary pioneer,
Selling your soul under the tattered banner of "sexual freedom."
It is clearly a piece of rubbish picked from a garbage heap.
Yet it is marked with a tag that says "human progress" or "civilized
    society."

Perhaps . . .
Perhaps you still have thousands of excuses and pretexts.
But you still have not even an iota of morality and humanity.

Your feet are trampling notes of a harmonious melody,
Crushing clusters of beautiful flowers,
Toppling down nests of happiness,
And even pulverizing the lives of those who are unfortunate.

Whenever a husband and wife separate or a family is destroyed,
In the spirits of the next generation
It is worse than an earthquake that hits 9 on the Richter scale or a
    12th-degree typhoon.
Their hopes for the future are mercilessly destroyed;
Their yearning for happiness is snatched from them.

All hearts are made of flesh,
Blood flows through the veins.
Why is it that your heart is hard like a rock?
Why is it that your blood is already frozen like ice?
Interloper, please butt out!
Do not dig a bitter well so deep that the bottom cannot be found.
Do not engage in another race of misery;
Do not create and spread even greater misfortune.

Let your feet run along the path of the Four Modernizations;
Let your feet find a firm footing in the torrent of life!
You must rely on your own struggle to have a happy life,
And you should never create your happiness at the expense of someone
    else's bitterness!

SOURCE: Xiaoming, "Shouhui nide jiao ba!" (Butt out!), *Beijing funü*, 3 (September 1983),
27.

Gather Your Courage, Become Aware of Your Own Strength

I work in the County Women's Federation. I come into contact with many women who visit us because of divorce. I sympathize with them, and do everything I can to save their families on the verge of collapse. This work has given me a new attitude toward the issue of divorce.

Once I ran into a young woman on the street. She was wearing a light green polyester blouse with silver threads, and had two short braids. Her eyes were full of life, her cheeks red, and she wore a happy smile. When she saw me she stopped, and greeted me as if I were a relative. I paused, wondering who it was. Then I realized that a young man was walking with her. She could tell that I was confused, and quickly said, "Don't you recognize me? I am Qiu'e!" "Ah, Qiu'e!" As soon as I heard that familiar name I was stunned. In my memory Qiu'e was a woman whose eyes were always full of tears, whose face was always full of anger, pale, who dressed in ragged clothes. She bore absolutely no resemblance to the young woman standing in front of me. I finally realized that it really was she, a person who had formerly been cast off by someone else. She proudly pointed to the man beside her and said, "This is my husband." I then realized that the two of them were carrying a bag of vegetables. She told me that her life was now full of happiness. After she left I could not calm down.

When Qiu'e was sixteen she and a man named Liu from the same village decided to get married. Everyone in the village had praise for her character and work. Later, after twelve years, her husband became a teacher for a state-run school. But she continued to work on the production brigade. Before they had married she had sought the opinion of her husband—if he did not really want to get married, then he could forget it. But he had insisted that he wanted to get married. Not long after they married, he began to dislike her, and conflicts developed between them. She felt hurt and cried all day. When she saw that there was no way to consolidate their relationship, she made up her mind to divorce him. Not very long after that she established a new, happy family. I kept contemplating the situation and concluded that it was right for her to get divorced. To keep living with someone who has no feeling for you will only cause misery and tragedy. Leaving him means leaving misery, bitterness, and unhappiness. From this I realized: for families in which love has truly been destroyed, the sooner they divorce, the sooner there will be happiness.

Recently another woman came to our office. Her hair was dirty and tangled; her eyes were blank. In an instant we recognized her: she was Chen XX, who often came to our office. She would not say a word or answer any questions. Previously she had had a mental problem. Chen

XX was both diligent and capable and had a very good character. Then the man she had been married to for ten years fell in love with someone else. For the past few years he has constantly argued and fought with Chen, and despite a great deal of "education," he has shown no willingness to change. Chen XX was obsessively determined not to divorce him. Her nerves were tormented, her life was tormented, and she frequently was subjected to cursing and beating by her husband. Originally, brightness had shown through her sad eyes; a certain grace had emerged from her frail body. But now she had become mentally deranged. How could this not upset people? Although we did our best to help her find a cure for her illness and take care of her financial problems, her husband still refused to change his ways.

From this we became aware of a certain principle: although we do not advocate that married couples casually seek divorce, when it is clearly time to get divorced, it is best to do so. This is because in the family women and children are the weak ones, and if there is not a divorce, then the ones who will suffer the most will be the women and children. Freedom of divorce is the legal right of women. Why can't we destroy the feudal idea of "following one to the end"—that set of spiritual shackles that lies on our shoulders. We can't we use the law as a weapon to get rid of our misery?

Of course, those who "like the new and detest the old" must be given an education in communist morality, and should be punished. We absolutely cannot allow this poison of extreme selfishness to spread in our socialist country. We must promote those things that are good and punish those that are evil, and at the same time we must appropriately solve these marriage and family problems. We who work for the Women's Federation have the responsibility of educating ourselves and our sisters. We must be aware of our strength; we must gather our courage. We must get rid of those despicable, shameless, and fickle husbands, and steer our ship of fate toward the harbor of happiness.

SOURCE: Long Zhongmei, Women's Federation of Bu county, Hebei, "Guzu shenghuode yongqi, kandao zijide liliang" (Gather your courage, become aware of your own strength), *Zhongguo funü*, 11 (November 1983), 32–33.

Do Not Discriminate Against Divorced Women

In the past I was a relatively happy person. I believed that if the love between a husband and wife had diminished, they should separate. However, ever since I got divorced last year I have encountered many problems and difficulties. I finally have really come to understand that things are not so simple.

We are a socialist country, and from a political point of view, women have "turned over" (*fanshen*). The Constitution also clearly stipulates that men and women are equal. However, in reality there are many ways in which men and women are not equal. Take housing, for example: many work units assign housing to men; at the time of divorce, the man can very rationally and coolly state, "The house belongs to my work unit. I want to give it to my wife, but my work unit does not agree." And just like that, the court gives the house to the husband.

When I divorced, I experienced that exact situation. I had my mother to take care of and had no house to which I could return. I had no choice but to sleep in the office. In winter my mother and I slept on the cold, hard desk and chair—how our backs ached! In the summer it was hot and humid, and mosquitos bit us. It was impossible to sleep.

There are still some people who think in old ways. They believe that a divorced woman is "ruined" (*diu ren*). They don't care what the reason was—they always blame the woman. After I divorced, some people would look at me in peculiar ways, stare at me, and gossip about me. If I had any contact with a man, people would start gossiping: "She's getting herself another mate!" "They're engaging in 'irregular' activities." Because of this some people who used to be good friends of mine have now become quite distant.

All this has made me very bitter, and my personality has changed. I implore people to attack old beliefs. Do not look down on or discriminate against a divorced woman!

Qu Le, Changchun City Automobile Factory

SOURCE: Qu Le, "Buyao qishi lilehunde funü" (Do not discriminate against divorced women), *Zhongguo funü*, 11 (November 1983), 35.

The Worries of a Divorced Woman

Comrade Editor:

After experiencing bitter struggle, deeply wounded in my heart, I finally realized that a dead love could not be revived. After breaking up, relief from the pressure made me feel a bitter kind of happiness. I hoped so much that I would be able to live in a peaceful environment. Raising my daughter, diligently studying, and working would bring me happiness.

However, shortly after I received my divorce certificate, a person who is a woman's husband and the father of a son came here and treated me in an "irregular" way. My strong sense of self-confidence was wounded. I was furious and resolutely refused him. I am opposed to bourgeois sexual freedom. Moreover, I was not going to be a shameless "third party." Just like that I was again "fitted into a smaller shoe" [put in an awkward situation]. At work I faced a great deal of trouble and bitterness.

Getting divorced was not my fault or desire, but happened mainly because I gave birth to a daughter. Bad luck trapped me and my newborn girl. Mother and daughter—it was suddenly as if we were criminals. We were treated in brutal and insulting ways. It was very hard to survive. My husband had no choice but to divorce me because his family wanted him to marry again and have a son. Just because of this there were people who said behind my back that a person who gets a divorce is no good, and that a good person does not get divorced. How unfairly life treated me!

I struggled to study and devoted myself to my work. I still had to put up with people making fun of me. I studied tailoring and knitting, and people made fun of me for that. It seemed that a divorced woman loses all her rights.

Many well-intentioned people advised me to quickly find another good husband to get revenge on my first husband. People also came to introduce me to potential mates. I cannot carelessly get married for the sake of revenge, risking my fate and my daughter's. I opposed the introductions of some well-meaning people; I don't like such an unnatural way of getting to know someone. Furthermore, I have already lost interest and faith in life. Although I love life and have hope for the future, people do not understand my feelings.

I am certain that there is no such person in the world—a good husband who shares my goals, who understands and supports me, and who is also able to love someone else's child. Not to mention that I must take care of my parents. Such a person exists only in fiction, and I cannot dare hope to meet one. . . .

Comrade editor: I do not want my daughter to be hurt. What shall I tell her when she is old enough to understand things and asks about her father? I also would like my daughter to change her surname to mine. Can this be done? . . .

Your faithful reader,
Li Li

SOURCE: Li Li, "Yige lihun nüren de fannao" (The worries of a divorced woman), *Xiandai jiating*, 5 (May 1985), 22–23.

I Want a Divorce

Comrade Editor:
No matter what, I want a divorce. There is no way that I can continue

to live like this. But I cannot get my parents' forgiveness and understanding. To win your sympathy and support, I will do my best to explain my situation carefully.

That evening, as I stormed out the door in a state of exasperation, I made my decision. I was desperate. I ran back to my parents' house to announce my decision to them.

When they heard what I said they were stunned. After a while, my mother wiped the tears from her eyes, and my father turned off the television. He said, "Don't you two get along quite well? Xiao Ma is very honest and has a good reputation at work."

How could he say we got along well? My father only knows how to be a bureaucrat, and can't even begin to understand the emotions of younger people.

"He beat me! We don't have any love for each other. After two years of marriage, he is still himself and I am still myself. We will never be able to love each other."

"What do you mean, you don't love each other? I never heard you quarrel. What happened today? Marriage and divorce are serious affairs, and cannot be treated casually. You must realize that if you get divorced it will be very difficult for our family to handle relations with his family. Moreover, it is not easy to find a family like that of Xiao Ma."

My father was acting just like a father. . . . All he could think about was getting along with them, whether this would damage his relations with his superiors. But what about his daughter—*her* feelings, thoughts, and value? If it hadn't been for those two old men scheming about me in the beginning, I would never have fallen into this mess. Once I think about it, I become furious and can't stop crying.

My mother rushed to my side and hugged me. The two of us wept. My father sternly said, "What are you crying about? You're the one who wants a divorce."

The thirty-two years separating my father and me created too great a gap in our thinking.

My mother cried, "I knew it from the beginning. I knew there was no real happiness when you married him. I suspected that long ago. But now, having reached this point—getting divorced doesn't sound good. You know what people will say about you if you are divorced. And it will be very difficult to remarry."

I am well aware of how society treats divorced women. People look at you as if you are strange, gossip about you, and say all kinds of things about you. There are three women in my work unit who are divorced, and they are constantly the object of people's gossip. People talk about the details of their private lives all the time. I am truly scared of that. This is the truth.

But, do I have to put up with [my husband]? How long am I supposed to tolerate him? Is it possible that I have to wait until one of us dies? From now on, how much cruelty will I have to accept? Look how I have lived these last two years. I've had enough! I've already suffered enough, and I don't want to take any more!

I never want to enter their door again. I never want to sleep on their fancy, high-class bed with its soft mattress. What do I owe him? What has he ever given me? Whenever I think about those crude "love words" he'd say every day, I can't stand it!

The problem was that my father and his father were comrades in the army. . . . Under pressure from my father, I figured that eventually he would love me, so I decided to marry him. But I put forward three conditions:

1. He could not be a male chauvinist. If he had criticisms of me we would discuss them, and he was never to hit me.

2. He must let me control my earnings. We would share the household expenses equally.

3. All major decisions had to be made jointly. No one could decide something unilaterally.

He agreed to these three conditions, so there was nothing I could say. We married. . . .

He has absolutely no desire to advance. He does not want to read books or do any research. His job is easy, he's got a wife, so he just wants to enjoy himself. He drinks, smokes, and goes to movies. He never asks me about my work, nor does he support my studies. When I receive an award for my work, he pays no attention. I study Japanese at an evening college, but he doesn't even notice. When I get together with male friends, I am subjected to his suspicion. Yet when we walk on the street he is always looking at pretty women, talking about how this one has a beautiful face, that one has a sexy bottom—it's disgusting! As a woman, I have deep emotions, but he never cares for me; when I am upset, he does nothing to console me; when I am sad, he does nothing to brighten my mood. When I am successful and proud, he is oblivious. . . .

This is not all. Recently, a department store was sponsoring a lottery. When he saw that the prizes included a motorcycle and a trip to Hong Kong, he got very excited. There was nothing that we lacked at home, but he decided to buy everything he could to get more lottery tickets. He bought ten tubes of toothpaste, ten bottles of shampoo, two pairs of high-class leather shoes for himself (at home he already had three or four pairs of leather shoes!), and two pairs of shoes for me—but they were not a style that I liked at all. I asked him why he wanted to buy all these things we would never use. He said that once he won the prizes, he would get back one hundred times the original cost. Who would have guessed that he would buy a radio that cost 700 or 800 yuan?! And we already had a perfectly decent radio at home. He said this would make it more convenient to invite people to our house to dance. All of a sudden he had three or four hundred lottery tickets, each worth one or two yuan. He was so pleased with himself. I was furious that he had never discussed this matter with me in advance. I cursed him, and then he hit me in the mouth. He had violated my conditions of marriage.

I cannot stand men who beat their wives. He won't understand a thing, but now he had better understand, because I have reached the end with him.

No matter what, I want a divorce from him. Tomorrow I will go to the court. I don't care if my father curses me, I don't care if people gossip about me. I simply cannot continue to live with him.

SOURCE: Song Xiaoying, "Wo yao lihun" (I want a divorce), *Jiating*, 5 (1985), 17–18.

✾ 7
Women and Work

FROM THE TIME the Chinese Communist Party took power in 1949, its leaders firmly believed that paid employment outside the home was the key to liberating women and building a society based on genuine gender equality. In the cities of post-Liberation China, then, it was the rule, not the exception, for women to work. In fact, the percentage of urban women employed outside the home was substantially higher than that in most Western capitalist countries, as well as other developing Asian states.[1] As a number of recent studies of Chinese women have demonstrated, however, women's participation in the workforce was not the harbinger of liberation that Marxist theory (or Mao's interpretation of Marxist theory) predicted.[2] This was partly because in the decades after 1949, urban women frequently entered the workforce on a clearly unequal basis: they were most often assigned the least-skilled, lowest-paying jobs, frequently in neighborhood-run enterprises that offered fewer welfare benefits than the state-owned sector. Furthermore, the Chinese government was not unequivocal in its commitment to women's participation in the paid labor force. When the reality of urban unemployment conflicted with the goals of full female employment, as was the case in the mid-1950's and early 1960's, women were encouraged to leave their jobs and contribute to socialist construction by engaging in housework.[3] A final reason that women's participation in the labor force failed to ensure gender equality is that, as Jean Robinson points out, "in Chinese policy there is an implicit assumption that women have two major roles to fulfill: that of mother and of worker." So long as women were perceived as bearing primary responsibility for childcare and housework, employers considered them incapable of devoting themselves to jobs as fully as men did.[4]

All these phenomena were visible as themes in the public discussion of the role of women in the workforce that developed in the late 1970's. The problems faced by urban women workers in the 1980's, however, were not simply extensions of previous trends; they were also the product of changes brought about by the economic reforms implemented since 1978. During the previous decades, all work assignments had been centralized, individual work units had no say in the hiring or firing of workers (indeed, firing workers was unheard of), prospective employees had only a minor say in the kind of job they were given, and most job assignments were permanent. Private enterprise was illegal. After 1978 much of this system was dismantled: work units were given expanding rights to select new employees, and the establishment of private enterprises was encouraged.

These policies created a range of new job opportunities for young urban residents, including women. The rapidly increasing cost of living in Chinese cities made women's contribution to family income even more imperative than in the past, and the number of women working increased.[5] Yet at the same time, as the following discussion shows, work units used their newly acquired powers to discriminate against women. Finding it increasingly difficult to secure jobs in the state sector, women were disproportionately tracked into small, individually run enterprises, particularly those that engaged in work such as cooking, sewing, and childcare, traditionally considered the purview of women.

Entering the Workforce

The first problem women faced was securing a job, which most women sought to do after graduation from middle school. Graduates did not commonly apply for jobs directly, though they could indicate their general preferences. Instead, in most urban areas the labor bureau assigned jobs to young people, based on lists of available positions. Starting in the mid-1970's, particularly as large numbers of "educated youth" who had been sent to the countryside during the Cultural Revolution returned to the cities, it became increasingly difficult for the labor market to absorb all the available young people. Thus, many middle school graduates had to wait several years before being assigned a job. Although technically unemployed, they were referred to as "youth waiting for employment" (*daiye qingnian*).

The labor surplus enabled work units to be selective, and they showed a clear tendency to select men. In some cases work units, or even entire cities, established lopsided ratios of men to women for new employees. In one district in Jiangsu province, the labor bureau posted a notice in 1984 announcing that a total of 351 new workers would be recruited for several enterprises, including the Chemical Fiber Industry and the Postal and Telegraph Bureau. The notice further specified that 269 of the recruits would be male and eighty-two female, even though almost twice as many women as men had taken the job examination.[6] One of the most extreme cases occurred in Tianjin, where at the end of 1984 it was stipulated that

97 percent of the total number of new workers recruited would be men. The Women's Federation protested, and after a prolonged series of arguments with the city's labor bureau, succeeded in getting the percentage of women recruited raised to 20 percent.[7] In other cases work units did not announce precise ratios, but simply refused to hire many women, even for jobs that clearly did not require physical strength. According to one survey, the ratio of men to women hired by the Post Office and Telegraph Bureau in some districts in Shanghai in 1984 was 20:1.[8]

Various reasons were given to justify this preference. Some units pointed to the fact that women were not as strong as men and therefore not physically suited to their jobs. Others claimed that once women married they would be burdened with housework and childrearing and would therefore be unable to concentrate on their tasks.[9] Even the thirty-year-old female head of the crew department of China's national airline CAAC lamented that these "disadvantages" would force her to employ more men in the future, despite her sympathy for women who faced discrimination in the job market. "As a manager," she said, "I am in favor of employing more men. Male employees have higher attendance rates than women because women are always asking for leave for a variety of reasons. Many of the stewardesses never fly their full eighty hours a month, which is a headache for me. Besides, men are more capable of doing the chores on large aircraft such as the Boeing 707 and 747." [10] Or, as one factory head less apologetically declared, "When I look for new workers I am not looking for trouble. Not long after a woman enters the factory she will get married, have children, and take maternity leave. What good is she?" [11] One final reason officials gave for preferring to hire young men was the fear that if too many of their employees were female, they would be obliged to provide costly services such as nurseries and kindergartens.[12] Because parenting and childcare were presumed to be a woman's responsibility, it was frequently assumed that facilities such as nurseries should be provided by the mother's work unit, not the father's.

In most cases where middle school graduates were being recruited, work units did not explicitly declare their preference for men. Rather, they required prospective employees to take an examination and insisted that women score substantially higher than men to qualify for a job. A young woman from Longyou county in Zhejiang protested to *China Women's News* (Zhongguo funü bao) that in her county, men needed sixty points on the test to be recruited, women 120. The result was that of the 192 workers recruited by nine units in 1984, only fifty were women, and some 600 of the 800 "youth waiting for employment" were women. (The jobs for which workers were being recruited were not specified.) "Ours is a socialist country," she declared, "where the principle of equality between men and women is supposed to be in effect. If this current method of recruiting workers does not change, and if work units can freely decide the ratio of men to women workers, then when will we ever have genuine equality?"[13]

Complaints such as this occasionally prompted change. For example, the labor bureau in Fengyang county, Anhui, boasted in early 1985 that it would henceforth recruit workers strictly according to their examination scores. The result was that twice as many women as men met eligibility requirements.[14] Unfortunately, though, even when city or county labor bureaus had the best of intentions, they could not always force the units under their supervision to comply. This happened in Shanghai when the Number One Machine Bureau issued a regulation insisting that male and female workers be recruited on the basis of examination scores. Individual units subordinate to that bureau simply sent home the women workers they had been assigned.[15] No law or enforcement agency existed to prohibit these practices. Moreover, despite the opposition of many government officials to discrimination against women, anti-discrimination measures were left to local, not national, initiative. Government intervention in the hiring process may even have been perceived as a violation of the spirit of the economic reforms that granted work units more independence.

The preference for hiring men was reflected in the disproportionate number of young women "waiting for employment." No systematic nationwide statistics are available, but local reports consistently confirm that close to two-thirds of the youth waiting for employment were women. In Shanghai, for example, 70 to 80 percent of those not assigned jobs in 1984 were women.[16]

The difficulties faced by young women securing jobs after graduation from middle school attracted the attention of authorities, who began to publish advice to young women. None suggested that women resign themselves to becoming full-time housewives; instead they encouraged women to take advantage of their "special strengths" to solve their employment problem. Women's first strength, according to these authors, was their manual dexterity, which qualified them to engage in a variety of handicraft industries, often organized as household production.[17] As the author of one article observed, "The tools required are very simple and the technique is very easy to learn. Furthermore, most young women already know how to crochet or knit, and based on our experience, after just a few days of instruction most women are ready to engage in production."[18] Another writer pointed to the long history—particularly before 1949—of female handicraft production in cities such as Shanghai, noting that through this work women made major contributions to family income and therefore enjoyed a great deal of respect. This same author chided young women who were unenthusiastic about handicrafts, feeling that such work lacked prestige and envying "other people who go to and from work every day while they just stay at home."[19]

A second "special strength" that women were advised to draw on was their training in household chores. "Most girls, while they are going to middle school, help their mothers do housework. They have learned how to wash clothes, cook, and sew." Therefore, the articles argued, it would be most appropriate for them to take advantage of the new economic policies that encouraged semi-private enterprises, and open food stalls or laundry and sewing service centers near their homes.[20] This would be preferable to a factory job, women were told, because by working so close to home they could avoid having to take crowded buses to and from work every day.[21]

The third "special strength" on which unemployed women could draw was their "civil and careful" nature—a basic requirement for childcare work. Some writers saw childcare as one of the greatest opportunities for women, for there was simultaneously an oversupply of capable young women and a severe shortage of childcare personnel. (According to 1983 statistics, less than half the preschool children in Chinese cities could be accommodated by available childcare facilities.)[22] "Perhaps some young women will say," one writer noted, "'Having gone to school for so many years, isn't it a waste of our talents to look after children?'" He addressed this concern as follows:

I know an old comrade who has been in charge of a nursery for many years. She once said to me, "Now if you want to find a decent middle school teacher it is relatively easy. But if you want to find a decent nursery teacher it is very difficult." One can thus see that to become a good nursery teacher is difficult. Because the number of only children has increased in recent years, parents pay even more attention to their children's education. Although it is difficult to get children into nurseries, parents have very high demands on the quality of education their children will receive there.[23]

If they could not find jobs by drawing on these female "special strengths," unemployed women could also try to enroll in training classes or technical schools to enhance their marketability. In many cases, however, the only technical schools in which young women could enroll were ones established exclusively for women. Yet these schools explicitly tracked women into the same kinds of traditionally female occupations described above. For example, in 1984 the Women's Federation in Dalian established the Vocational School for Girls when it learned of the need for trained nurses, daycare and kindergarten teachers, and secretaries. An article praising the school in the English-language publication *Women of*

China boasted: "Students from the school are trained in a variety of skills within their field. For example, a graduate of the travel and tourism department will be equally competent as a tour guide or as a hotel staff person or waitress. With this flexibility it will be easier for the young women to adapt to the job market and find work suited to their skills."[24] Unstated was the author's assumption that women's best, if not only, chances for a job were in the traditionally female occupations described above.

In theory, at least, a woman could try to qualify for other types of jobs by applying to vocational schools not designed specifically for women. However, admission to most of these coeducational schools was based on examination, and as with the tests for jobs cited above, women had to obtain substantially higher scores than men in order to enroll. For example, at the technical school of the Shenyang Number Six Pharmaceutical Factory, men needed 173 points for admission in 1983, women 317;[25] at a technical school in Fujian where men who had scored 194 points were admitted in 1984, women had to have more than 300.[26] Some schools justified this discrimination by claiming they lacked adequate dormitory facilities for women.[27] As in job recruitment, the technical schools that refused to discriminate by gender were exceptional, although they were sometimes cited as models for others to emulate. For instance, the editors of *China Women's News* lavished praise on the Capital Steel Mill in Beijing for admitting more women than men to a two-year training class in computers and technical design—basing admission strictly on achievement, rather than sex.[28]

Although the hope and promise of better job opportunities impelled many women to take exams for admission to technical schools, it is difficult to determine what actually happened to those women who were admitted and completed the courses. Did they in fact secure the jobs for which they were trained? Or were they, like ordinary middle school graduates, considered more trouble than they were worth by prospective employers? The answer is perhaps suggested by the predicament faced by college and university graduates.

The Special Problem of Women College Graduates

Access to higher education was extremely limited; in 1980, only about 8 percent of those who took the college entrance exams were admitted.[29] Women made up only slightly over one-fourth of this tiny elite.[30] And while their male classmates could look forward to a prestigious career after graduation, increasing discrimination in hiring denied women the same guarantee.

Starting with the graduation in early 1982 of the first class of students admitted to college on the basis of national competitive examinations, many women found their sex a serious handicap in securing a job. For example, *China Women's News* reported the case of a woman who had graduated from the Northeast Industrial College in 1983. She had achieved outstanding grades, had been elected a "three-good" student (good in studies, physical fitness, and moral character) throughout her years at the college, and had received honors for her graduation thesis. Members of a laser research institute, after reading her thesis, declared that "this kind of talent is truly rare," and did everything in their power to have her assigned to their institute. When they learned that the student in question was female, however, they changed their minds and refused to hire her.[31] In a similar case, a woman who had graduated from the Gardening Institute in Beijing in 1984 was assigned to work at the Diaoyutai Hotel, a guest house where visiting heads of state frequently stayed. This assignment had been approved by the Ministry of Foreign Affairs, and the hotel had issued her an official work document. Yet when she reported for work and the leadership realized they had hired a woman, they insisted that because of the "special nature" of the job, she was not qualified. She persisted in going to work every day, but her employers refused to acknowledge her presence, and she finally had to be assigned a job elsewhere.[32]

Many work units explicitly instructed colleges and technical institutes *not* to assign them female graduates. According to an investigation conducted by one reporter, an equal number of men and women graduated from the Beijing Foreign Languages Institute in 1983. (Foreign languages was considered a field of study especially suitable for women.) Yet almost all the units requesting graduates of that institute specified that they wanted only men.[33] The same year, approximately one-third of the units requesting graduates from Fudan University (the most prestigious liberal arts university in Shanghai) declared that they did not want women. This included units such as the reading materials department of the Shanghai Municipal Library, which would be hard put to sustain an argument that the work was "unsuitable" for women.[34] The leaders of Fudan University complained to municipal authorities about the situation; the following year, however, it was apparently no better.[35] Even in the Foreign Languages Department at Fudan itself, although more than half the students were women, all the 1985 graduates assigned to the coveted positions as members of the Fudan faculty were men.[36]

The blatant discrimination against women university graduates provoked a public expression of anger, particularly by the parents of these women. One commented, "I hope work units that reject female university students will consider the following: in today's attempt to build the Chinese economy and to implement the Four Modernizations, do we or don't we need knowledge? Do we or don't we need talent? If the answer is yes, then female university graduates should be respected and utilized."[37]

Partly in response to the influx of angry parental letters, reporters from *China Women's News* interviewed the Minister of Education, He Dong-chang, about this issue. He appeared to share their concern, declaring that in the fall of 1984 the student department of his Ministry had published an article in *China Youth News* imploring work units to "appreciate female university graduates." He complained that the article did not receive adequate attention, and expressed his worry at the emergence of what appeared to be a vicious cycle: since university authorities were having such a difficult time securing jobs for female graduates, some had already decided to reduce the number of women admitted. When asked by the reporters what could be done to solve this problem, he lamented that the phenomenon of work units refusing to hire women was part of a much larger social problem of discrimination against women, and thus could not be solved in isolation. "People's thinking has to change first," he stated. He therefore encouraged the reporters to write articles praising women graduates who made contributions to society and criticizing those units that refused to hire women. In the meantime he hoped that women university students would develop self-confidence and struggle against the old idea that women are inferior to men.[38] He did not suggest that his Ministry should issue regulations or play a more active, interventionist role in confronting the problem.

The Problem of Keeping Jobs

Once assigned to a work unit in China, a person could usually count on having that job for the remainder of his or her working life. This security, referred to by Chinese people as "eating from an iron rice bowl," became less and less dependable for urban women in the early 1980's. The new economic reforms made enterprises responsible for their own efficiency and profit, and many factories responded by trying to limit female participation. At the same time, acute urban unemployment made female labor more expendable than ever.

During the early 1980's, women's work was redefined in Chinese factories. The rejection of the Cultural Revolution notion that "women can do anything men can do" prompted officials to move women out of jobs that required physical strength. In Beijing an ordinance passed in 1984 prohibited work units from hiring women for jobs "that were especially heavy or might be harmful to a woman's health." (The ordinance also specified that "protecting women" could not be used as an excuse to refuse to hire women for other types of jobs.)[39] Some units shifted women to different jobs within the same enterprise. For example, some women who had previously engaged in construction jobs at the Tianjin Number Six Building Company were switched to jobs as assistants, errand runners, or security guards.[40] To absorb the remaining women workers, the company took advantage of the economic reforms and established its own shoe factory, garment factory, print shop, hotel, store, and restaurant—innovations praised by the Tianjin Women's Federation.[41] More commonly, though, work units could no longer employ women who had formerly engaged in tasks requiring physical strength. Some units successfully assisted these women in transferring to jobs in work units deemed more suitable to women's "special characteristics." For example, "to show concern for women's health," sixty young women whose work had involved transporting cement, bricks, and tiles at the Xi'an Municipal Transport Company were transferred to a local textile mill "to become 'weaving girls.'"[42] "Everyone knows that men and women are different," the author of another news article explained, praising the Tianjin Transport Bureau for transferring women formerly engaged in heavy loading work to units where the work drew on women's strengths: thriftiness, cleverness, deftness, patience, and meticulousness. "We absolutely must not ignore women's biological nature and the limitations of their physical strength and blindly persist in the principle that 'whatever men can do, women comrades can certainly do too.'"[43] In many cases, though, no "appropriate" work unit was found for the women transferred out of physically taxing jobs, and they were left unemployed. Some of these women eventually took advantage of the new economic policies by opening businesses of their own.[44]

It is difficult to ascertain whether women themselves appreciated the concern for their health and welcomed the change in jobs. Those who moved into the private sector, while giving up the job security and welfare benefits granted workers in state-run enterprises, in some cases were able to earn more money. One former transport worker in Hunan, for example, opened a shop selling various homemade rice brews, and was able to earn 200 yuan a month.[45] Information about the wages of women who were transferred to other jobs in the state sector is not available. However, their transfer out of transport work almost certainly involved a decrease in salary, since transport was one of the best-paid occupations. Furthermore, as Jean Robinson points out, this "helps make rigid the *zhongnan qingnü* (regarding men as superior and women as inferior) mentality by creating a situation in which women workers cluster in the lower-paying sectors of the economy."[46]

A second trend, more alarming to women workers, was the proposition that they were the cause of urban unemployment and should therefore be removed from the workforce. In 1980, several prominent economists in Shanghai issued a report proposing the withdrawal of women from the workforce as a solution to the problem of unemployment. This marked a radical reversal of the Cultural Revolution emphasis on women's active participation in the workforce, and echoed proposals made during previous periods of high unemployment, such as the mid-1950's. The Shanghai Women's Federation immediately called a meeting and denounced the proposal.[47] The suggestion that women leave their jobs and devote themselves to housework, thereby creating more jobs for men, was never implemented. Nevertheless, its proponents were not completely silenced, and after 1980 they made several further attempts to persuade the public of their wisdom. But the Women's Federation continued to successfully oppose them. "The superiority of socialism must be manifested in creating opportunities for women to gain employment, not in restricting their employment or in asking those who are employed to go home," representatives of the Women's Federation in Nanchang declared in early 1985. "This notion of ordering women to go home is a reflection of feudal thinking that is thousands of years old in our country."[48]

The Women's Federation conducted several surveys to demonstrate that the overwhelming majority of women workers were not willing to give up their jobs and return home. When 200 women working in nine different occupations in Beijing, Shanghai, and Tianjin were asked whether they would want to return home if their family's financial situation did not require their income, 76 percent said that they would still want to work. Many concurred with a woman who declared, "We women are first and foremost people with careers; being a woman comes second."[49] Another woman, a factory switchboard operator whose husband was a taxi driver, explained her desire to work as follows: "We could easily live very comfortably on my husband's income of 300 yuan a month. My 90 yuan a month is not at all necessary for our family's livelihood. But I believe that contributing to society through my work is the most important thing; the household comes second."[50] More surprisingly, the surveys indicated that few men were interested in having their wives devote full time to managing the household. Six out of fifty men interviewed said they were willing to have their wives return home only if their own wages were increased to compensate for the loss; the remaining forty-four men said that "no matter how much they increased their wages, they were not willing to have their wives go home to become housewives."[51]

The Women's Federation was not alone in its denunciation of the proposal that women return to their homes in order to create more jobs for men. "[Men's] employment should not be achieved at the expense of women workers," the editors of the English-language *China Daily* declared. "If all wives stay at home, they will lose their economic independence, and the basis of equal rights will be removed. This is contrary to the Constitution, which says that men and women have equal rights."[52] One writer even published an article pointing out that the "crooked theory of 'sending women back to the home'" was originated by none other than the "fascist Adolf Hitler," an association that presumably would deter proponents of the idea.[53]

A number of factory officials developed two methods of reducing female employment that had a much larger impact than the radical proposal of professional economists. One was to encourage women, particularly nursing mothers and those who were considered elderly, to voluntarily leave their jobs in return for 60–70 percent of their salary.[54] A second method, begun in 1980, was to encourage female employees to take "prolonged maternity leave." Although this measure was rationalized in terms of "protecting women's health," a number of Chinese observers—particularly officials from the Women's Federation—perceived it as no more than a thinly disguised plan to move women out of the workforce.

In most work units using the system, "prolonged maternity leave" was available to women who were either more than six months pregnant or nursing. Instead of the ordinary fifty-six days of maternity leave, this option granted women three years at home, during which time they were issued 75 percent of their basic monthly salary.[55] Despite the seemingly advantageous conditions, few women eligible for the prolonged maternity leave expressed interest. For example, an investigation conducted by the Federation of Labor and the Women's Federation at the Dalian Shipbuilding Factory revealed that of 400 women workers qualified for the leave in 1980, only twenty volunteered to take it; at the Dalian Port, only twenty-six of the 500 qualified women took the leave. This unenthusiastic response prompted the leadership of these units to push more aggressively for women to take the leave. They held meetings with workshop heads, instructing them to actively encourage the eligible women in their workshops to return home. Ultimately, 48 percent of the women eligible for prolonged maternity leave at the Dalian Shipbuilding Factory took it—some, according to the authors of the survey, "because they had little choice." For instance, the leadership refused to transfer recalcitrant pregnant women to lighter jobs; they denied mothers time to nurse their infants and eliminated the nursing room—all in an effort to force women to take prolonged leaves.[56]

In some cases, a desire to save money by eliminating the welfare facilities required by pregnant or nursing women underlay the insistence of factory managers that women take prolonged maternity leave. By eliminating a nursery a factory could not only save operational costs, but could actually increase income by transforming the nursery into a profit-making venture. According to a 1985 report in *China Women's News*, a number of work units in Beijing disbanded nurseries and created hotels in the newly available space. Many of these factories subsequently offered women employees prolonged maternity leave. When a news reporter asked some of the women if they were willing to stay home, they replied, "It would not do us any good to be unwilling; we must be willing, for this is the factory's policy." [57]

Those conducting the investigations found a number of reasons why the majority of women workers were so reluctant to take prolonged leave. First, many feared that being away from their jobs for that long would hinder their careers. One woman worker at the Dalian Shipbuilding Factory, who had a seven-month-old child and was enrolled in one of the technical classes offered by the factory, angrily declared, "When I heard they wanted to give us prolonged maternity leave, I was really upset. The 'ten years of chaos' [i.e., the Cultural Revolution] destroyed our chance to study, and after the fall of the Gang of Four, we hoped we could begin studying both culture and technique. Although I have a small child and it is a bit hard to handle work and study, I can manage and overcome the hardships. I really do not need prolonged maternity leave." Another pregnant woman worker told the investigators, "I have made up my mind— once I have finished [regular] maternity leave, I will return to work. I am still young, and if I stay at home for a year or two I will fall behind at work. How will I be able to contribute to the Four Modernizations?" [58]

A second concern of women workers was that the reduced income during the prolonged leave would make it difficult for their families to make ends meet. When the factory leadership tried to persuade one woman to take a prolonged maternity leave, she replied,

It is good that the leadership is concerned about us. But I am a second-level worker and I support three or four people. Usually it is rather tough to meet our expenses. If I take prolonged maternity leave and lose 30 yuan a month, how will I be able to support my family? Furthermore, if wages are increased in the future, will the time we were on prolonged maternity leave be counted in the calculations? It seems that if we take the leave, our living standard will decline. [59]

The main concern of many women was that even though they would still earn 75 percent of their regular salary while on leave, they would not be entitled to the bonuses or special subsidies issued by their units, which often represented a sizeable portion of a worker's income. For example, a woman driver at the Shenyang Electric Tram Company earned a basic salary of 54 yuan a month, but her bonuses and subsidies brought her an additional 100 yuan a month. [60] For someone like her, the reduction in salary would have been substantial. To compensate for this loss of income, some women who reluctantly took the leave had to seek temporary jobs such as house-cleaning.[61] In addition to their fears of lost time or lost income, some women felt that once they agreed to take a two- or three-year leave they would never be given their jobs back, and that without a regular job they would be looked down on by society.[62]

Investigators also explored the circumstances of those women who were willing to take advantage of the prolonged maternity leave. They found that almost all were in one of the following situations: (1) their families were relatively affluent; (2) the husband and wife worked in different cities and the prolonged leave would therefore afford them the opportunity to live together; or (3) the mother or infant was sick, so continuing to work was especially difficult.[63]

Although the Women's Federation did not oppose allowing those women who desired the prolonged leave to take it, it did object to using women's withdrawal from the workforce as a means of contending with unemployment. "We think units that have too little work and too many workers should not make women workers shoulder the problem," representatives of the Liaoning Women's Federation declared. "It may sometimes be appropriate to give women longer maternity leave, but it must be voluntary, not forced or mandatory."[64]

The opposition expressed by many women workers to the proposition that they leave their jobs should not be interpreted as an unambivalent attitude toward work. On the one hand, as indicated above, many women feared the reduction in income and the possible loss of status that leaving their jobs would bring. On the other hand, though, most had jobs that were boring, repetitive, and low-paying, making the opportunity to leave in some respects appealing.[65] Moreover, many recognized that even without a job outside the home, their time would be fully occupied by the demands of housework.

Housework

In addition to their jobs outside the home, urban Chinese women—like their counterparts in most countries—were responsible for managing their households. Unaided by the modern conveniences to which many Western women were accustomed—from vacuum cleaners and washing machines to food processors—they found the tasks of shopping, cooking, and cleaning much more labor-intensive and time-consuming.

The American supermarket had no counterpart in Chinese cities. The food items needed by a family were scattered among several types of shops: rice, noodles, and flour at the grain store; soy sauce, oil, chili sauce, hot bean paste, and pickled vegetables at a "sauce" shop; vegetables, fish, meat, and bean curd products at either state-owned stores or free markets. Until the appearance of free markets in the late 1970's, shopping at the state stores required that people stand in line as early as 4:00 A.M. to purchase fresh vegetables. Prices at the free markets were usually higher than at the state stores, but most people preferred the shorter lines and greater availability of goods. Although refrigerators became increasingly common in urban homes in the early 1980's, most people continued to shop on a daily basis.

Cooking was equally laborious. In large cities such as Shanghai and Tianjin, the quality of cooking facilities was a crucial feature of the family's standard of living. Ideally, a family had its own small kitchen, with a sink and a double gas burner. More commonly, four or five families who lived in the same building shared a kitchen in which each family had its own double gas burner and bamboo cupboard for storing utensils. Many families lived in districts where no gas was available. In Shanghai and Tianjin this was particularly true of the working class districts that were located beyond the boundaries of the pre-1949 foreign concessions. Families in these neighborhoods had to cook outside on portable charcoal-burning stoves. Firing up these stoves added to the time that cooking otherwise demanded; it was even more time-consuming to fashion homemade coal briquettes to burn in the stoves, as many families did.

Prior to 1980, privately owned washing machines were virtually unheard of in Chinese cities, and doing laundry was an arduous manual chore. The increasing availability of washing machines in the early 1980's substantially reduced the amount of time devoted to laundry, although erratic or inadequate supplies of electricity often hindered the use of washers; lack of running water in some homes made their use altogether impossible.

For families who did not have plumbing in their homes, fetching water was added to the list of daily chores that had to be performed. "It's really a pain not to have plumbing," a woman in Harbin complained.

Every day we need about four or five buckets of water. To get from the house to the water station takes about three minutes. But then each time I fill a bucket I have to stand in line for a long time. Every day it takes more than an hour just to get the water, and then once we've used it I have to get rid of it! By the time I go to work in the morning I'm already exhausted, and by the time I get home at night I'm not interested in reading or studying or anything.[66]

For women, and to varying extents men as well, running a household claimed large amounts of what otherwise would have been free time. On work days, men and women might spend from three to five hours doing household chores; Sundays were frequently devoted entirely to these tasks. As the authors of one survey of housework in Chinese cities observed:

The original idea behind Sundays, of course, was that they should be mainly for rest and recreational activities. But in some Chinese cities, Sunday has become "housework day," with men spending six to eight hours and women as many as eight to nine hours. For many workers, Sunday housework is an all-day affair— washing the week's laundry, cleaning out storage spaces and vegetable cellars, lining up at the grain store to stock up for the week, running around town to line up to buy those hard-to-get items or take care of other chores which have been put off for too long. The common saying "uptight Saturdays, fighting Sundays, exhausted Mondays" gives a pretty clear picture of the situation.[67]

Perhaps more important than the amount of time taken by housework or the availability of modern conveniences was the fact that it was considered women's responsibility. Although most men performed some housework—indeed, one could not help but be struck by the number of men buying vegetables at the free markets or carrying an infant to the nursery—it was commonly assumed, by both men and women, that housework was primarily women's responsibility. Shanghai men, who had the reputation of participating more extensively in housework than their counterparts elsewhere in China, were jokingly said to suffer from *qiguan-yan*. The term literally means tracheitis, or inflammation of the windpipe, but the word is a homonym for "strict management by one's wife"— the Chinese equivalent of "henpecked husbands." It became popular in the late years of the Cultural Revolution and continued to be featured in many jokes about family relations in the 1980's.

The assumption that housework was women's responsibility was most dramatically presented in a short story by Shen Rong, "At Middle Age." The story is about a woman eye surgeon, Lu Wenting, who suffers a heart attack in her mid-forties because of the extraordinary pressures of her work. In the story we learn that during the Cultural Revolution, when the laboratory where Lu's husband worked was closed, he did most of the housework while Lu concentrated on her job. Once his lab reopened after the fall of the Gang of Four, though, this "abnormal" arrangement ended and "most of the housework was shouldered once more by Lu."[68] The day before her heart attack she not only prepares for three operations, but during her lunch hour first picks up her sick daughter at school, then dashes home to prepare lunch for her son. "Every day at noon she went home to cook. It was an effort to stoke up the fire, prepare the vegetables, and be ready to serve the meal in fifty minutes so that Yuanyuan, Fu, and she herself could return to school or work on time."[69] Despite these pressures, Lu feels guilty that family responsibilities keep her husband from accomplishing as much as possible. The night before the heart attack she confesses to her husband, "I'm a selfish woman, who thinks only about her work. . . . I have a home but I've paid it little attention. Even when I'm not working, my mind is preoccupied with my patients. I haven't been a good wife or mother." [70] She then proposes that her husband move into his institute so that he can fully devote himself to his work, and leave the housework and children to her. He reluctantly agrees; however, her illness develops before the arrangement can be implemented.

This story provoked widespread public discussion when it was published in 1979. It was perceived as a poignant depiction of the excessive and unrewarded burdens imposed on middle-aged intellectuals. Despite the explicit descriptions of housework in the story, women's double burden of work and housework was never an issue in the public discussion. Even the author herself seemed to accept the premise that housework was women's responsibility.

In a similar but nonfictional account, entitled "The Two of Us Chose Happiness," a woman named Ming Wen described her good fortune in having a "model husband." Even after eight years of marriage, they loved each other as deeply and passionately as when they first met; they never ran out of things to talk about. She boasted that he shouldered far more of the burden of housework than most husbands. Each morning, over breakfast, they conferred about how they could most efficiently and equitably divide the daily household chores. Yet her belief that housework should be shared had clearly defined limits. Ming Wen castigated herself for feeling frustrated when her husband's commitment to his job conflicted with their home life. "Often, when everyone else had already gotten off from work, I still did not see even his shadow at home," she complained.

At first I was very angry, and as soon as he came home I would blow up at him. He would silently wait until I had finished, and then patiently explain to me the reasons he was late. After several instances like that I began to understand him, and I never again got angry with him for coming home late. Instead, I thought about how busy he was at work and how tired he must be, and so I would make a few extra dishes that he was especially fond of. Sometimes I would even clean up our room so that as soon as he opened the door and came in, he would feel relaxed and comfortable. [71]

The limitations to her sense that housework should be shared became even clearer as the demands of her husband's job increased. During the eight years of their marriage, he had moved up from ordinary electrician to assistant factory manager. "As his responsibilities at work became heavier, I took on more and more of the burden of housework," she wrote. Her sense that a woman had to sacrifice herself for her husband's career was epitomized by her behavior when he had to go away on business. Immediately after he left she developed a serious intestinal illness, which caused her to vomit constantly and run an extremely high fever. Eventually she had to be hospitalized. When her neighbors decided to phone Ming Wen's husband to tell him to return home, she forbade them to call. Instead, she wrote him a letter herself, telling him that "everything at home is fine" and wishing him success at his work.[72]

Statistics confirm this portrait of housework as primarily a woman's responsibility. A 1984 survey in Beijing showed that while women spent an average of three hours and forty-five minutes a day on housework, men devoted only two and a quarter hours to it.[73] A 1980–81 survey of housework in the northeastern cities of Harbin and Qiqihaer revealed that women spent 5.2 hours a day on housework, men 3.9 hours. The authors of the study pointed out that this meant women spent approximately 470 more hours on housework per year than men.[74] Household practices varied by profession and class. The same study showed, for example, that male workers spent the least time on housework, male intellectuals the most.[75]

Perhaps because men—albeit to a lesser extent than women—were also burdened by household chores, the issue of housework became a subject of public discussion. Social science journals published studies, accompanied by readers' responses, concerning the nature of housework, comparisons between the amount of time spent on housework in China and that spent in other countries, and proposals for alleviating the burdens imposed by housework. Initially these studies assumed that housework was primarily women's responsibility, and that provisions should be made to enable women to more effectively engage in these tasks. One article concluded:

Some people think the only way to raise women's status is for all women to return to the home; others think women should become exactly like men. Both these views are mistaken. First, the time for maternity and childcare leave must be lengthened. Raising good children is also a contribution to society. Second, we must begin with the actual state of social production in China and provide more time for women to engage in housework. For example, we could move up the retirement age for women in certain occupations to let younger labor power participate in production. Work schedules could be changed to offer part-time employment, half days, or three-day work weeks, and so on. Some trades could let women work in spurts as the job demands, such as the morning and evening markets, which could employ women for two or three hours a day. Some businesses that have only a few rush hours each day could employ more people during the busy hours and retain only a few people for the rest of the day. In this way, not only could women participate in social labor and add a certain amount to the family income, but the tension on the home front in terms of housework and childcare would also be relieved. This system would enable women to combine their work capacity with their capacity as mothers, so they could do a better job of raising and educating the children.[76]

When the sociology journal *Shehui* ran a discussion in 1983–84 of whether or not one person should take care of the home so the other could be devoted entirely to work, a woman named Wang Yiling systematically outlined the reasons that even in intellectual homes, women should do all the housework. She noted that the major household chores were cooking, shopping, laundry, sewing, and childcare. "Wives are much more skilled at these tasks than their husbands," she proclaimed, leaving the reader to conclude that therefore women should do this work. She cited a survey of 138 women working at the Shanghai Academy of Sciences, which showed that the majority spent four to five hours a day on housework. "This proves that women already do most of the housework," Wang observed—evidence, presumably, that they should continue to do so.[77]

Another reason Wang believed that women should do housework was that men were usually "a notch above women at work," and furthermore, since men retired later than women, they had greater potential for development. (The retirement age was sixty for men, fifty-five for intellectual women, and fifty for ordinary women workers.) "More is expected of men, and so they are under greater pressure at work," Wang explained. And therefore, the reader was left to assume, men must be freed from the burdens of housework. In case the reader was not yet convinced, Wang concluded her list of reasons by noting that for a wife to take care of housework for her husband manifested women's traditional virtue (*meide*). Finally, the reader was reminded that had Jenny Marx not done all the housework, Karl Marx would never have been able to make such substantial contributions. Wang concluded her article by suggesting that she was not proposing inequality for women. "In the homes of intellectuals," she wrote, "this arrangement of the wife taking care of her husband is absolutely equal."[78]

Ideas similar to Wang's were expressed in a variety of places. The author of an article recounting the death of a scientist from exhaustion and poor nutrition concluded his comments by implicitly blaming the scientist's career-minded wife. If a husband and wife were equally dedicated to their careers, he suggested that the wife sacrifice her work outside the home "because women are more skilled than men at doing housework." If she was determined not to allow the burden of housework to hinder her progress at work, then a career-minded woman would be well served by selecting a mate who was unambitious and mediocre at his job, presumably so that he could carry the burden of housework.[79]

As described in Chapter 5, women were offered advice on how to become expert in their capacity as housewives. In at least one city, Dalian, a special course was established to teach women housekeeping skills, such as cooking and entertaining guests. The course also aimed to "encourage women, while they are engaged in working hard at production, to widen their horizons and actively support their husbands' work." This was accomplished by taking the students to visit local factories and explaining to them local plans for economic development. One of the students, a woman who had previously been frustrated by the seemingly excessive time her husband had to spend at work and the little time he had to help at home, exclaimed after the factory visits, "He really does work hard and from now on I must support him!"[80]

Articles such as these communicated several messages to women. First, women had two jobs: one outside the home and one inside. Second, their job outside the home was less important than their husband's job, and perhaps even less important than their function as housewife. Third, for their husbands to be successful at work, women had to acquire the scientific knowledge required for good housekeeping.

These views, however, were not completely unopposed. Wang Yiling's initial article in *Shehui* was described by one writer as "conservative," "reactionary," and discriminatory toward women. This writer believed that housework should ideally be shared equally by husband and wife. It was conceivable, she said, that the burden of housework might severely hamper one person's career and the other should assume primary responsibility for the housework. However, she insisted, this did not mean it had to be the woman.[81] Another female reader responded to Wang's argument by contending that it was precisely because women were burdened by housework that they had not been able to achieve as much as their husbands at work, and therefore, if true equality was to be achieved, housework would have to be shared more equitably.[82] The concluding essay in the *Shehui* discussion was written by Tan Fuyun, the head of the Shanghai Women's Federation. Under no circumstances, she insisted, should it be assumed that wives had to do all the housework. Instead they should share the work equally, until the time in the future when housework was sufficiently socialized that neither would have to be burdened by it.[83]

In the early 1980's, some preliminary efforts were made toward the socialization of housework. In several cities, housework service companies (originally formed during the Great Leap Forward, when urban women were mobilized to work outside the home) were established.[84] In December 1984, *China Daily* reported that the northeastern industrial city of Shenyang had organized thirty such teams. They not only alleviated the housework burden of some working couples, but simultaneously provided employment for young women who had graduated from school but had not yet been assigned a permanent job. In addition to helping with the tasks of shopping, cooking, laundry, and sewing, these teams provided such services as house renovation and decoration, furniture building, and electrical appliance repairs.[85] Similar service teams were established in Beijing and Shanghai. In addition, some neighborhoods in Shanghai had housework service introduction agencies, which assisted families seeking help to contact people who were available to do housework.[86]

Among wealthier urban families, it also became common to hire a live-in maid (*baomu*) to assist with childcare, cooking, and shopping.[87] Most of those seeking jobs as maids were from rural areas. Some were married, middle-aged women, who hoped to earn more money than they could in the countryside. Others were young peasant women, in some cases fleeing to the city to escape arranged marriages. A number of young unemployed urban women, unable to secure other work, took jobs as maids.[88] In addition to room and board, a maid could usually earn 25 to 30 yuan a month.[89] The demand for maids far surpassed the supply. One newspaper report described the frantic scene enacted each morning in front of the Women's Federation building in Harbin:

Early in the morning people from all over the city who hope to get a maid gather in front of the city's Women's Federation office. At 9:00, when ten or twelve girls from the countryside appear, everyone waiting immediately tries to grab one of them. One woman who had brought her daughter-in-law along was trying to persuade a maid to go with her by saying, "We live in an apartment building; there is heat, color television, a washing machine. . . . We just need someone to look after our children." It was not long before all the girls had been snatched up by someone.[90]

Because the demand for maids was so great and because the use of maids was seen as a means of relieving some women of their household tasks, a training class was begun at the Shanghai Girls' School (Shanghai nüzi xuexiao) in 1985. After a month of training in cooking, household chores, childcare, and care of the elderly, the students received a certificate.[91]

Aside from supply, cost was probably the major obstacle preventing maids or the household service teams from becoming a viable solution to the problem of housework. According to one study, most urban families could not afford even to purchase prepared foods instead of shopping and cooking themselves.[92] It is therefore doubtful that they could have paid for the services of a maid or household service team. Although described in the Chinese press as progress toward the socialization of housework, the availability of maids and service teams did not create a situation in which all working women had access to household help. In fact, the majority of women continued to shoulder the dual burden of housework and a job outside the home.

Even if the household service teams or maids were to become affordable by a greater number of families, the household division of labor would remain an issue. In the 1980's there was no indication that the tasks associated with childcare, food preparation, and home maintenance were becoming gender-free. Instead, members of the household service teams and maids were virtually all female and, as observed above, unemployed young women—not men—were being channeled into this work. Their provision of services meant that some women were paid for housework while others were at least partly relieved of the household tasks they had to perform while working outside the home. But this would not necessarily challenge women's subordinate status in the workforce. As long as housework and childcare were perceived as primarily (if not exclusively) women's work, and as long as women's biological functions (such as menstruation, pregnancy, childbirth, and nursing) were seen as obstacles to women's full participation in labor outside the home, women's status in the workforce would remain both precarious and unequal.

Translations

In contrast to the period of the Cultural Revolution, when women were told they could do "anything men can do," the 1980's witnessed the development of a more rigid sexual division of labor. As the report "Men and Women Are Different: Cultivate the Strengths and Avoid the Weaknesses" shows, women were increasingly channeled into jobs that did not require physical strength. Urban unemployment, combined with the preference of employers for hiring men, resulted in job discrimination against women. Some people protested the unfair treatment of women, as did the man who asked, "Is It Right to Refuse Someone a Job Just Because She Is Female?"

Almost all urban women had to contend with a "double day." "How to Handle the Conflict Between Housework and a Career" reflects the belief that even in two-career families, women should assume primary responsibility for housework. "Do a Good Job of Holding Down the Home Front" relates the experience of a woman who had initially resented the fact that her husband took frequent business trips, leaving her to do most of the housework. Some women, such as the author of "Helping a Lazy Husband Change," managed to convince their husbands to do more of the housework. Yet a husband who did too much housework risked being called "henpecked," as "I Cured the Henpecked Disease" illustrates.

As China embarked on a modernization program in the 1980's, housework, too, was increasingly presented as a modern, scientific activity. The new skills a woman was expected to acquire are suggested by the quiz "Are You a Good Housewife?"

Men and Women Are Different: Cultivate the Strengths and Avoid the Weaknesses

Everyone knows that men and women are different. From ancient times a division of labor has existed: men plant, women weave. During the last few years, under the influence of the ultra-leftism of the Gang of Four, there has been a one-sided emphasis on the idea that men and women are exactly alike. To mobilize women to "hold up half the sky," people insisted that things men could do, women could do even better. All of a sudden women were being sent to do work at high temperatures, in high altitudes, in cold storage, diving, and mining. It was as if not to arrange things this way would be to discriminate against women. The result was that certain tasks were not completed and women's health was impaired.

It has been reported that the Tianjin Transportation Bureau, taking a realistic attitude, has transferred 70 percent of the women from units where they were doing heavy loading work to places where they can do work more appropriate to women's special characteristics. This not only is beneficial to the health of these women, but also better enables them to contribute to the Four Modernizations. Their method of "cultivating women's strong points and avoiding their weaknesses" should be studied.

Women represent half the population. How to mobilize them to "hold up half the sky" in the Four Modernizations is an important question. People often say it is necessary to cultivate the strengths and avoid the weaknesses in order to fully use women's abilities. Thus, we must cultivate women's strengths of industriousness and thriftiness, their cleverness and deftness, patience and meticulousness. The female weaknesses that we must avoid are the "three periods": the menstrual period, pregnancy period, and nursing period. We should, as much as possible, allow women to engage in textiles, handicrafts, crafts, service, finance, culture, and education. We absolutely must not ignore women's biological character and the limitations of their physical strength and blindly persist in the principle of "whatever men can do, women comrades can certainly do, too."

SOURCE: *Tianjin ribao*, October 15, 1980.

Is It Right to Refuse Someone a Job Just Because She Is Female?

I am a staff officer in the People's Military Equipment Department of Xiangpiao county in Hunan. My wife is a statistical worker at the Xiangpiao Steel Factory. The fact that our workplaces are far apart causes great hardship for our work, study, and life. Going through my work unit, the county Party committee, and the personnel bureau, we reached an agreement to transfer my wife to the county's statistical bureau. There was apparently a shortage of statistical workers in the county bureau. However, the leadership of the bureau then said, "We will not accept this person because she is a woman."

My wife is twenty-eight years old and is a member of the Chinese Communist Party. She graduated from the Hangzhou Metallurgical Statistical School and therefore has a certain level of skill. She is considered a statistician. I ask you: is this manner of ignoring a person's ability and performance, and rejecting her simply because she is female, correct?

SOURCE: Wang Junhe, "Yinwei shi nüde jiu bu anpai gongzuo, dui ma?" (Is it right to refuse someone a job just because she is female?), *Zhongguo funübao*, January 9, 1985, 2.

How to Handle the Conflict Between Housework and a Career

I have been married for twenty-four years. My husband is a middle-aged professor. In addition to training graduate students he also shoulders the responsibility of leadership in his department. I teach college extension classes. I often have to travel to various places around the country to give briefings and instruction. Our elder daughter, after graduating from college, went to do research work at the Chinese Academy of Sciences; our younger daughter is preparing to take the graduate school entrance exam. Everyone in our family is busy with their own career, and no one, it seems, has the time to really take care of the housework. So, how do we handle the relationship between career and housework?

I personally believe it is critical for the housewife to manage this contradiction; female comrades must take the lead in shouldering the burden of housework. When I was thirty years old one of my children was three years old, the other just two. There was a lot of housework to be done, we did not have much income, and our responsibilities at work were very heavy. . . . At that time I did not do a very good job of managing the contradiction. I argued a lot, lost my temper, hit the children, and got angry with my husband. Frequently while I was cooking I would yell, "I'm always waiting on you people. Who is going to wait on me?" Sometimes I would have prepared a sumptuous feast, but because I had been cursing at everyone, no one had any appetite left. Eventually I realized that my husband was working day and night and that his health was getting worse. The Party and organization had entrusted him with important work. Whether his health was good or bad, whether or not he was able to complete the tasks given him—all this depended on me. Although I too wanted to work at my career, relatively speaking his work was more important and more urgent than mine. To be a wife one must do a good job of taking care of the housework, so that when the husband returns home he can be comfortable, eat well, and rest. A good living environment should be created for him so that he can increase his productivity at work. Once I realized this I made a plan to do housework, and gave some thought to how I could do it more efficiently. It did not affect my work, and I still managed to go on business trips and publish teaching materials. . . .

In recent years we have rarely argued. My husband is a cultured person and has a certain status in society. But in our home he treats everyone as an equal. He never asks anyone else to take care of him. For example, he always washes his own clothes and sews his own missing buttons; at home he washes dishes, fetches milk, cleans the toilet, and does repairs. When I have to teach, my husband makes breakfast for me, gets my materials ready, and pumps air into the bicycle tires. Although these are all small things, they all demonstrate his concern, love, and support. He also is very concerned with our children's studies and work. The energy he puts into housework is, in his own words, an opportunity to get some physical exercise, to shift the focus of his intellect a bit, and to strengthen the unity of the family. It also increases his work efficiency.

We have always paid a great deal of attention to our children's training and education. This is not only because of our duty as parents, but also because it is very advantageous to our careers. From the time they were very young, our children got in the habit of liking work. When they started school we let them wash their simpler clothes and help their parents with minor tasks around the house. After they graduated from primary school they were able to really take care of themselves, and the amount of time we had to spend taking care of them was very little—so we could spend more time reading and working on our research. At that time I often had to travel on business and my husband was very busy at work, so most of the housework fell on them. They know how to buy food, cook, clean the toilet, and mend clothes. . . .

Whenever I think about my family I feel very content. I often look at the strong, healthy evergreen tree in front of our house and say: this evergreen tree is so beautiful! It symbolizes our family—if a husband and wife love each other and the family is happy, then one's career can advance.

SOURCE: Jing Ying, "Fuqi en'ai shiye fazhan" (If a husband and wife love each other their careers can develop), *Jiating*, 4 (1985), 14.

Do a Good Job of Holding Down the Home Front

Because his work necessitates it, my husband is often away on official business and therefore many heavy household duties inevitably fall on my shoulders. How can I manage to act like a "woman who holds down the home front" (*yazhai furen*) while my husband is away on official business? I had an experience that started in a very troublesome way but ended happily.

My husband is a newspaper reporter. He works very hard and spends two-thirds of every year away from home. Home has become a temporary hotel for him while hotels have become his regular home. As soon as he leaves home I have to take care of my old, sick mother-in-law and our young, mischievous daughter all by myself. I am a worker at a textile mill. Because we want to surpass our production target, the sisters and I work very hard, and I am usually thoroughly exhausted after work. When I get home I still have to line up to buy food, cook dinner, do the laundry, help my child with her homework. . . . There is not even time to take a breath. When my husband finally comes home, he is usually totally absorbed with his articles and often works until late at night. I have become increasingly perturbed by this.

One time after he left, our child suddenly developed a high fever in the middle of the night. It was raining hard. I held the child in my arms and stared out the window at the rain pouring down in the dark night. I was so panicky that I cried. Fortunately my mother-in-law called a neighbor and the child was taken to the hospital. This incident only made me angrier than ever. I tried everything, from making sarcastic comments to making a big scene to locking up his luggage, to stop him from going away. All this almost destroyed our affection for each other.

When the leaders of our work units found out about our problem they came to mediate several times. Once the secretary of the Party committee of my factory talked with me about his own wife. He told me that in the third year of their marriage he had to go to the front to fight the Japanese. He was away for fifteen years. When he left home his wife was still a young and beautiful woman, but when they reunited in 1952, she already had some white hair. During those fifteen years she had stayed at home and labored to raise the children. She had even spent some time in a Guomindang prison. Her health was seriously damaged. Yet she never complained. "And what did she get out of all this?" asked the Party Secretary. "She did it because she firmly believed in our careers and supported my work. Because she believed that I was working for the well-being of the people, she was able to overcome her own difficulties."

What I found surprising was that even my quiet mother-in-law once talked about her past. Her husband had volunteered to fight in another country when she was three months pregnant with my husband. Her husband died on the battlefield in Korea. . . .

These two stories moved me deeply. During wartime and the early period of our country's construction, many wives had to see their husbands go off to battle. They were willing to suffer the pain, to be separated from their husbands for years, for the cause of liberating the people. The temporary peacetime separations between my husband and me mean only that I must take care of more of the household duties. This is nothing compared to what the earlier generations of women experienced. Amid all those fights I had only been able to see my "little home" instead of our homeland's "big home." My husband is a reporter and it is his job to go out to gather the news. His concentration on his work is all for the sake of the Four Modernizations of our homeland. As his wife, I really should not reproach him!

I am in a much happier mood now that I have thought through this whole thing. Ever since that time, whenever my husband is out on official business, I always try to take good care of the house so he does not have to worry and my mother-in-law is happy. When he comes home, I try my best to let him write in peace. When he is tired I quietly get him a cup of tea. . . . He has felt very moved, and now he also does some housework whenever he finds the time. We have lived in harmony ever since.

SOURCE: Hu Rong, "Dang hao 'yazhai furen'" (Do a good job of holding down the home front), *Qingnian yidai*, 5 (October 1982), 22.

Helping a Lazy Husband Change

My husband is a welder at the shipyard and I am a weaver at the woolen mill. In principle we match perfectly and should enjoy the good things and go through the hard times together. But things are not as they should be. In the first three years of our marriage he never washed a bowl or a pair of socks. He was so lazy that his body almost rotted [lit., "maggots were crawling out of his body"].

The summer before last the factory gave me a week to rest in Wuxi. Before I left I reminded my husband time and time again, "The weather is hot, so you must change and wash your clothes every day." When I got home a week later, I found a pile of dirty shirts and socks on the sofa, and the smell really irritated my nose. I endured it and took the clothes to wash.

Our child, Little Rongrong, was born in August of last year. After my maternity leave ended I had to get up at four every morning to light the fire and cook breakfast. After that I would take the basket and go to the market. At 5:30 I would grab the child and rush to the factory. When I got home in the evening, as soon as I put the child down on the bed, I would have to busy myself picking over the vegetables and cooking dinner. Even if the child cried until she drowned in tears, I would still have to "have a heart of stone" so that when my husband came home he could have a hot meal. I lost more and more weight every day and yet my husband still would move only his mouth and not his hands. I thought about picking a big fight with him but decided not to, since fights could damage our affection.

One night after dinner I simply could not take it any longer and I said to him, "Because of Little Rongrong I have already lost more than ten *jin*, yet you never even bother to say something nice to me. . . ." As I talked on I began to cry. At first he was scared stiff for a moment, but then he took out his handkerchief to wipe off my tears. The next day he got up an hour earlier than usual, took the basket, and went to the market. When he got off work he also spent half an hour doing housework.

Then something fortuitous happened. A couple of days later, because he wanted to sleep a little longer in the morning, he rushed to work without any breakfast, forgetting to take along his house key. He called me at noon and said he would come by my factory after work so we could go home together. I decided to take this opportunity to show him around the workshop and let him see with his own eyes how hard the weavers had to work. This actually worked! He held the child on the way home so I could walk home briskly. Ever since that day he has begun to make contact with pots and bowls and ladles.

My mother came to see us one Sunday, and it just so happened that we had the makings of a meal at home. My husband wanted to be the big chef. It was like a person who has not been a vegetarian for even three days and yet wants to go to heaven—he wanted to show off in front of his mother-in-law. He put on the apron in a very serious manner and said that he wanted to cook a few good dishes for her. My mother already knew what the "real him" had always been like and was surprised by this "magnificent act" of his. Of course she was very happy. But he was disappointed: a two-*jin* carp was supposed to be made into a sweet-and-sour fish, but it turned into a bitter-and-sour fish. We did not utter a word of criticism; on the contrary, we praised him for having mastered the art of cooking. After that, whenever he was interested in cooking, I would, with Rongrong in my arms, stand on the side and assist him, telling him when to add the salt and sugar. After a period of technical training he actually enjoyed cooking more and more.

Recently, following the "Home Economics Education" and the "To the Young Fathers and Mothers" columns of some magazines, we have divided up our household chores appropriately. For example, he does more of the heavy chores while I do more of the light chores; when our child is sleeping I do more of the work and when the child is crying he does more of the work. I draw on his strength and he learns from my skillfulness. We learn from and help each other. Housework is no longer my responsibility, but rather *our* responsibility. Now I am happy that my lazy husband has become diligent.

SOURCE: Hai Gui, "Ganhuale lan zhangfu" (Helping a lazy husband change), *Qingnian yidai*, 5 (October 1982), 24.

I Cured the Henpecked Disease

My neighbors all used to say that I suffered from being henpecked, and this really bothered me. Once my neighbors were playing poker and needed a fourth person. One young man said, "Zhang Shifu, why don't you come and play a few rounds with us?" Another guy yelled, "Zhang Shifu is afraid of his wife. Forget it!" Those words triggered anger that had been building in me for several days. I said, "Who says I'm scared of my wife? I'm definitely going to play a few rounds!" Just as we had settled into playing, my wife, Xiao Yang, came angrily stomping by. "I see that you're having a great time playing cards, while no one is at home to take care of our child. And I have to run around washing clothes and cooking." Ordinarily I would have just silently left the card game and obeyed her. But that day I was going to resist. When she saw that yelling did no good she snatched up the cards on the table. I was furious that she made me lose face in front of the neighbors, so I gave her a push. Seeing me go so far as to become fierce, she snatched the cards from my hand, pulled my clothes, and grabbed my face. Having my manhood challenged in public like that, I couldn't help but box her ears. That stirred up a hornets' nest, and she kept hitting me. I did not realize what I had done, and fortunately the neighbors pulled us apart.

That evening we ignored each other. I could hardly sleep, and I deeply regretted what I had done. It is often said that now both husbands and wives work, so housework, too, must be shared by both husband and wife. I think that for me not to do any housework but to go play cards was really being too much of a male chauvinist and was wrong. The next day I admitted I was wrong to my wife, and also promised that from then on I would share housework with her. Ever since then, when I return from work I take care of the children while she does household chores and cooks. She never gets angry. In the evening, after she has put the children to sleep, she smiles and says to me, "Go ahead and play cards. Just don't stay up too late playing or it will affect your work tomorrow." I can then go play poker with my neighbors. Seeing that my wife does not come to find me, they no longer say I suffer from the henpecked disease.

SOURCE: Zhang Shuyi, "Wo zhihaole qiguanyan bing" (I cured the henpecked disease), *Zhongguo qingnian bao*, November 30, 1985.

Are You a Good Housewife?

1. If your household was lacking a number of items, but you could only choose one, which would you choose?
   —A refrigerator (30 points)
   —A television (5 points)
   —A washing machine (20 points)
   —An overcoat (10 points)

2. Do you frequently organize your clothing cabinet?
   —Yes (20 points)
   —No (5 points)

3. Do you have a set time each week to sweep your home?
   —Yes (20 points)
   —No (5 points)

4. Do you have all the cooking preparation done by the time guests arrive?
   —Yes (20 points)
   —No (5 points)

5. Have you ever served burned food to guests?
   —Yes (10 points)
   —No (15 points)

6. Does it make you happy to entertain guests?
   —Yes (15 points)
   —No (6 points)

7. Do you make a list of what you need to buy before going to the store?
   —Yes (20 points)
   —No (3 points)

8. Is there a dish you make that is your "specialty"?
   —Yes (12 points)
   —No (6 points)

9. Do you have cookbooks?
   —Yes (12 points)
   —No (6 points)

10. Does your husband help you with housework?
    —Yes (12 points)
    —No (6 points)

11. Are your cooking utensils always arranged neatly?
    —Yes (25 points)
    —No (5 points)

12. Do you believe that an electric refrigerator is something your home should have?

—Yes (16 points)

—No (4 points)

Now you must add up your total number of points. If you have less than 155 points, then unfortunately you are not a very good housewife—because this shows that you do not know how to allocate your time. If you have 156–95 points, then you are a diligent housewife. You know how to arrange things. . . . If you have over 195 points, then your home is really too ideal!

We wish you all good luck in becoming good housewives!

SOURCE: *Shehui bao*, June 13, 1985.

❈ 8
Violence Against Women

Violence against women in 1980's China was a deeply disturbing fact of life. At every stage of her life, a Chinese woman was vulnerable to violence precisely because she was a woman. She could be killed at birth by parents who wanted a son; raped by assailants who were strangers, suitors, neighbors, or relatives; abused by her parents for asserting her right to marry a man of her own choosing; kidnapped and sold into marriage far from her native place; or battered by her husband and members of his family for a variety of offenses, real or imagined.

Violence against women elicited a great deal of attention in the 1980's press in China. Many authorities felt it had been on the rise since the breakdown of social and political order during the Cultural Revolution. Though the statistical evidence that might support this argument was not made available, it seems plausible that certain types of violence, such as female infanticide, rape, and kidnapping, were in fact increasing. Others, such as wife-battering, were taken for granted in many quarters as part of normal marital behavior. This widely shared social assumption was just beginning to be called into question.

In many areas discussed in this book, such as adornment or marital choice, the boundaries between the public and private realms shifted in the 1980's in such a way that the private sphere grew larger and the intervention of the state receded. Domestic violence, and violence against women in general, was an exception. Here the state began to assert itself to regulate activity previously regarded as people's own private affair. This was not the first attempt of the communist government to eliminate domestic violence. As early as the 1930's, CCP revolutionaries in the base areas began to regulate family relations when they forbade husbands to beat their wives. But enforcement of such measures waned after the early 1950's and was further attenuated with the weakening of the legal system during the Cultural Revolution. In the 1980's, in the name of reasserting the rule of law—though not always specifically in the name of women's rights—state authorities began once again to push back the boundaries of private domestic behavior. In the process, a rejuvenated Women's Federation and an emerging women's press began to focus public attention on the varieties of violence against women. Gender violence was decried as a form of lawlessness and explained as a product of Cultural Revolution chaos or, alternatively, of the rapid influx of Western ideas into China in the 1980's. Except in the case of infanticide, violence against women was usually not linked in a systematic way to the subordinate position of women in society.

Infanticide

A female in China was perhaps most vulnerable because of her gender at the moment of her birth. As Chapter 5 explained, sons were still preferred to daughters in many Chinese families, particularly in rural areas. This preference was partly the result of a tenacious tradition dating back thousands of years, buttressed by Confucianism and thoroughly entrenched in the patterns of Chinese family life. Only a son could carry on the family name, whereas a daughter left home at marriage and joined another man's family as a reproducer of *his* family line. The communist government challenged the explicit Confucian dictum that men are superior to women, but did little to alter the patrilineal and patrilocal traditions that gave it force in daily life. Nor did women gain equal status by participation in paid labor, as Marxist theory promised. Under the commune system in effect in most areas until the early 1980's, rural women earned workpoints in collective labor and contributed to the family income. But discrimination in the workpoint system meant they usually earned less than men, even men doing the same work. Moreover, workpoints earned by a woman were paid out to the head of her household, usually her father or husband. For married rural women, the double burden of running a household further reduced their participation in the collective sector; a household that had to depend exclusively on the wage-earning labor of its female members was a household in trouble. Even in the best of times after 1949, rural girls were regarded as temporary members of their natal families and inferior contributors to the family income. They were last in line for family resources and access to education.[1]

Under the new responsibility system in agriculture, widely implemented in the early 1980's, sons became more desirable than ever. A household with more members could generally earn more income, and increasing rural prosperity meant that many families could hope to support more children until the children were old enough to contribute to the family wealth. At the same time, some of the meager social welfare measures available in the Chinese countryside were dismantled with the demise of the commune system. Peasants needed their children more than ever: to work the land and participate in sideline industries, and to serve as a social security system for the older generation. The opportunities for women to add to the family income increased under the agricultural reforms, but the money-making options available to men were still greater. Perhaps even more important, in the main girls still married out of their parents' households.

At the same time, the state campaign to reduce the birth rate meant that peasant families were under pressure to limit the number of children they bore. Although the one-child policy was found to be unenforceable in many rural areas, peasants with two or more children were subject to political pressure and economic penalties. Particularly in 1982 and 1983, disturbing reports indicated that forced abortions and sterilization were common in some rural areas, as badly trained and inflexible local cadres raced to meet strict birth-limitation quotas handed down by the central government. Peasants frequently responded to these tactics by fleeing, illegally removing IUD's, and attacking birth control cadres.[2]

One of the unintended consequences of the post-Mao reforms, in combination with the family limitation program, was to increase this preference for sons to the point where it began to threaten the lives of girl babies. Caught between the family and the state, many women became the objects of domestic abuse for their failure to bear sons. And female infanticide, a common practice in poor families before 1949, was once again on the rise in rural areas. The Chinese government published no statistics on infanticide (and much infanticide doubtless escaped the attention of the authorities), but Western demographers analyzing census data collected in 1982 estimated that in 1981 alone, as many as 232,000 baby girls may have been drowned, smothered, or abandoned by families desperate for sons.[3] Infanticide was not always the result of direct family pressure and was not invariably performed by men. In one case that was reported in the Shanghai suburbs, a woman threw her nine-day-old baby girl out the hospital window. She told police that her husband's family had not said anything about a particular preference for a son. But she had been convinced by a fortune-teller that she was going to have a boy and had suffered greatly from the whispers of other people on the ward, where she was the only one to bear a girl. She had not known, she said, that killing an infant was against the law. An analysis of this case in a Chinese sociology journal blamed the murder on an "ideological social trend that is tinted with heavy feudal superstition and regards men as superior to women."[4]

Families who did not kill their girl babies outright might later try to rid themselves of the unwanted burden in other ways. A 1984 letter to a legal journal from Zhejiang villagers reported that a couple in their village was denying medical care to their seriously ill two-year-old daughter, in hopes that she would die and they could try again for a boy. The legal consulting group of the journal advised them that the parents could be prosecuted for maltreating a family member if the girl died, and that the village leadership should force them to get medical attention.[5] But such cases must have far outnumbered the capacity or desire of local authorities to interfere. In August 1985, two Reuters reporters of Asian descent were approached in a market in Shenzhen (Guangdong's Special Economic Zone) by a peasant woman who offered to sell them her baby girl for the equivalent of 154 U.S. dollars.[6] And a 1986 article in the Chinese press reported that a one-year-old baby girl had been left in the hospital by her family, who insisted that the mother had given birth to a son and that the baby must have been stolen and replaced by a girl.[7]

In 1982, the Chinese government began to show belated but vigorous concern about female infanticide in the countryside. Official commentary blamed the problem on feudal ideas, now given new life by the state birth control policy. The government publicized the harm caused by feudal attitudes, encouraged media attention to cases of wife abuse and infanticide, promoted legal sanctions (sentences ranging from three years in prison to death for those convicted of homicide), and strengthened the education and advocacy role of the Women's Federation. Local authorities in many rural areas were lenient in enforcing the family limitation policy, and national regulations permitted many exceptions to the one-child rule. Some commentators proposed that men move in with the families of their brides, so that daughters would no longer be regarded as temporary family members. Others recommended improvement of social welfare for aged persons with no children, so that having a son would no longer be so crucial to survival in old age.[8] Most of the measures adopted by the government relied on a combination of ideological work and legal regulation. Whether they could be effectively carried out by the same local authorities who were pressed to enforce the birth-limitation program is unclear. Whether they were sufficient to actually alter the economic pressures that made sons in peasant families more valuable than daughters is even more dubious. Ironically, state policies intended to raise the living standard of the entire population—the agricultural reforms and the family-limitation program—had the unintended consequence of putting the female half of that population at an increased risk of fatal violence.

Rape

In August 1983, the government named rape as one of the most serious criminal offenses, along with murder, arson, and robbery. Chinese courts in 1984 sentenced more than half a million people for these four offenses, as part of a national crackdown on violent crime.[9] Press commentaries made it clear that officials were worried about what they regarded as a rise in violent crime in general and rape in particular. Whether the national incidence of rape was actually increasing or was only perceived as increasing is not completely clear, because the government did not publish the relevant statistics. A 1985 study stated that in one coastal city, the incidence of rape had begun to rise 25 percent a year after 1979, and in 1983 had shown a 73.2 percent increase over the previous year. The same study asserted that the rural incidence of rape was also rising, and had surpassed the urban rate in the early 1980's. But the study gave no figures on the actual numbers of cases involved.[10] Rape cases became more common in the courts partly because a strengthened legal system encouraged better reporting and more vigorous prosecution. Nevertheless, it is probable that the incidence of rape did increase, fueled by many factors: the general breakdown in public order during and after the Cultural Revolution; discontinuities in rural law enforcement caused by changes in local government; the return of "sent-down" youth to the cities; and the increased geographic mobility of many sectors of the population under the economic reforms. And it is almost certain that, as in other countries, the actual incidence of rape far exceeded the number of cases reported or successfully prosecuted. Even if the incidence of rape was rising, however, it certainly had not reached the epidemic proportions found in U.S. society. The streets of Chinese cities at night remained relatively safe places for women alone. Yet public awareness of rape and official concern with the problem certainly increased in the early 1980's.

Article 139 of the criminal code defined rape as "going against a woman's will, using violence, coercion, or other means to force a woman to have sexual relations."[11] In discussing the law, a 1981 article in a legal journal illuminated some of the forms of sexual violence against women in China. The article explained that "violence" referred to beating, tying up, gagging, strangling, or pushing a woman down, whereas "coercion" meant threatening her with anything from murder to the ruin of her reputation. "Other means" included exploiting the fact that a woman was asleep, sick, or mentally incompetent, or getting her drunk or drugged so that she was incapable of resistance. Rape, the article continued, had to be distinguished from adultery and willing sexual relations between hooligans, both of which were voluntary on the part of the woman. But the article carefully pointed out that even a woman whose sexual behavior was less than reputable (*zuofeng buhao*) was protected by the rape law, if she was forced to engaged in sexual relations against her will.[12]

Wives, on the other hand, were not so well protected, at least from their husbands. In cases of "stealing the bride" (*qiangqin*), where a man used force to take his fiancée, wife, or ex-wife to his home and have sexual relations with her, the key point in establishing rape was whether the two were legally married. A divorced woman or one who had broken off an engagement was protected from being "stolen." But a woman who had legally registered her marriage and then changed her mind about the match before cohabitation took place could be "stolen" and forced to have sexual relations, since the perpetrator was, after all, her legal husband.[13] Marital rape did not exist as a legal category; if a woman was married, the question of whether the sexual act was "against her will" did not arise.

The law further defined rape under "especially serious circumstances" to include multiple rapes by one man, gang rape, rape in which the victim sustained physical or mental injury (including her subsequent suicide), rape in broad daylight or in a public place that created an "evil political influence," and a series of rapes in a single district that disrupted the social order. Causing "severe injury or death" in the course of a rape was a charge distinct from these, as was deliberately murdering a woman after raping her. The rape law dealt separately with sexual assaults on children under the age of fourteen; these were defined as rape whether or not the child consented to sexual relations. Genital contact rather than actual penetration was sufficient to constitute rape in such cases.[14] Rape was punishable by a sentence of three to ten years, with heavier sentences, including death, meted out for rapes involving "especially serious circumstances," injury, or death.[15]

Most of the public discussion of rape took the form of reports in the press on individual cases, rather than general analyses of the causes and characteristics of sexual assaults. Women were sexually assaulted both by strangers and by those they knew, though no public statistics were available on the relative frequency of each type. In cases where the woman knew her attacker, press commentary not only condemned the rapist but often criticized the victim for not taking sufficient precautions. A survey of several cases of "acquaintance rape" illuminates the vulnerability of women to attack in a wide variety of situations, as well as the degree of responsibility they were expected to assume for their own safety.

Women were often forced into sexual relations with their superiors at work, as in a 1984 case that the press dubbed "three heads taking liberties with a woman." The "three heads" were one local government official and two leading cadres from a wine factory near Loyang. While attending meetings in Beijing, the three convinced a female employee of the wine factory to join them in drinking games, using a combination of persuasion (When will you have the chance to drink with the deputy county

Woman harassed by three officials. Wu Mu,
"'Sanzhang' xinü" ("Three heads" taking liberties
with a woman), *Minzhu yu fazhi* (Democracy and
the legal system), 7 (July 1985), 20.

head again?) and implicit threats that made her fear offending her immediate superiors in the factory. When the "three heads" and the woman
were all thoroughly inebriated, the men attempted to rape her, desisting
only when public security officers, alerted by her shouts, used a passkey
to open the door of their hotel room. The three men were remanded to
their home county and eventually sentenced to prison. In addition to cas-

tigating the would-be rapists for their sexual misconduct, an editorial comment at the end of the article rebuked the woman for letting the men get her to drink and for being afraid to offend them. The commentary encouraged women to use the law and their self-respect to defend themselves against such incidents. Yet power relations in the workplace would certainly have made resistance difficult.[16]

Other men in authority also took advantage of their position to assault women sexually. A doctor in a Shanghai hospital was convicted in 1984 of assaulting a young married peasant woman as she lay on the X-ray table. Using his prestige and her awe of the hospital, he convinced the naive patient that his sexual advances were a "work requirement." When, after a second incident, she finally summoned the courage to complain to the authorities, it was discovered that the doctor had assaulted others as well. He received a fifteen-year prison sentence.[17]

Women were also raped by their boyfriends and ex-boyfriends. One 1980 incident involved a woman who was beaten by an ex-boyfriend, who then pushed her into a river and threatened to drown her if she did not resume the relationship with him. She consented, then fainted; he dragged her to his dormitory and raped her.[18] Another case where thwarted seduction led to rape involved an unhappily married woman whose husband had ignored her and their child for years. Frustrated, she began to go to movies, parks, and restaurants with a young man from her factory. Eventually, she reported, he raped her and then threatened her (presumably with exposure of her conduct) if she refused to continue the relationship. She was advised by a legal consultant that the man's persistence made him a rapist, even if she too must share some blame for wrongdoing in the early stages of the relationship. She was encouraged to bring charges against him and to seek the forgiveness of her husband and child.[19] In both these cases, romantic involvement with a man made the woman vulnerable to violent assault.

Rape within a woman's natal family was a topic very seldom treated in the Chinese press,[20] but in some cases male relatives of a woman's husband or boyfriend forced her to have sexual relations with them. A young woman factory worker from a city in Guangdong province, for instance, complained to the local Women's Federation about the conduct of her boyfriend. After the couple began sleeping together, she had moved in with his family, but when he got a job in Guangzhou he left her there and became involved with another woman. While she was still living in his house, his father, a factory doctor, raped her.[21] Reports of other cases, particularly those set in rural China, suggested that sexual assault by the father or brothers of one's husband might not be uncommon.

One type of rape case that received a great deal of attention in the Chinese press was sexual assault by the sons of the politically powerful. The victims of these rapes were seldom criticized for contributing to their own downfall through imprudent or improper behavior. Coverage focused on the arrogance with which sons of cadre families forced themselves on young women, confident that the status of their parents would protect them. High-ranking parents who upheld the law were praised; those who shielded their criminal sons were criticized. In a 1982 Chengdu case, for instance, a man named He Deming and two of his accomplices were given long prison sentences for raping a woman. He Deming's father, an army officer, expressed his support for the sentences.[22] The parents of Xu Jianhua, a Jiangxi man, chose another course. Xu was a petty criminal who had been arrested for offenses ranging from car theft to pickpocketing. His father, a high cadre, used his influence with the Nanchang city government to have the prison sentences reduced. Eventually Xu set up a gang headquarters, forced women to go there by threatening them with a foot-long pig-slaughtering knife, and raped them. His parents ignored complaints from the neighbors about the screams emanating from the gang's lair. Xu was arrested in April 1983 and executed, despite his parents' efforts to protect him. A report on this case asked pointedly who had pushed Xu toward the "criminal abyss," blamed the parents for permitting Xu's activities, and criticized their friends in the bureaucracy for allowing Xu special treatment.[23] The point of these stories was to direct attention to the abuse of power by some Party members and their children, as well as to contribute to public understanding and awareness of rape. In these cases, violence against women was brought to public attention in the service of a "larger" political goal: the purification of corrupt elements in the Party.

In response to the problem of rape, magazine editors began to proffer advice on how to contend with sexual assault. A 1985 article called "How Women Can Defend Themselves Against the Crime of Rape" warned women to avoid deserted places at night and to keep their distance from men they suspected of following them. If they thought an assault was imminent, they should run and call for help. The article explained that rapists were fearful when committing sexual assaults, and that screams or physical resistance were a psychological weapon that could be used to increase their fear. Women were instructed how to use their fists, elbows, and feet against a rapist. They were told to attack the face and groin to disable their attackers, and to use anything that came to hand (e. g., stones from a construction site) as weapons. If attacked inside a building, they were advised to break a window or throw things out of a room to attract attention. Above all, the article said, women should not give in to fear. To reinforce this point, the author described two situations: in one, a woman struggled and screamed when attacked, attracting the attention of passers-by and preventing the rape; in the other, a woman assaulted by the same man was too frightened to resist and was raped. A woman who was psychologically prepared to deal with a rapist, said the article, would be able to avoid becoming a rape victim. An accompanying commentary noted that self-defense was legal in the case of criminal assault, and that citizens had a social and moral duty to defend themselves and struggle with criminals.[24]

This message was strengthened by frequent stories in the press of women who had successfully foiled violent sexual attacks. Woman worker Zuo Lijun, for example, was assaulted on her way to work one morning. She fell off her bicycle when her assailant threw sand in her eyes. When he grabbed her, she talked him into letting her go. Then she stood up, scratched his face, and yelled for help. He was later apprehended and identified by the fingernail marks on his face.[25] Even armed attackers, press coverage implied, could be fought off by determined women. Two women students at Xiamen University were praised for using their bare hands and an umbrella to defend themselves against a man with a knife who broke into their dormitory one afternoon.[26] In Tianjin, an older woman worker rushed to the defense of a younger woman who was being sexually assaulted in the shower room of the factory dormitory. The older woman sustained serious stab wounds as she wrestled the man to the ground and took away his knife.[27] In several other cases, women successfully turned the weapons of their assailants against them. A seventeen-year-old woman disarmed and fatally stabbed a man who assaulted her on a deserted rural road near Jilin; she was honored at a public meeting attended by one thousand people.[28] A substitute primary school teacher in rural Heilongjiang was attacked by a man with a knife as she slept with her six-month-old infant. She grabbed the knife, stabbed the assailant, picked up her baby, and fled through a window; the man bled to death before he could get out of her house. Praised for ridding society of a menace, the woman was promoted to a regular teaching position and received a raise and a bonus from the county government.[29]

Nowhere in these tales of heroic resistance was it ever suggested that fighting with an armed attacker might lead to worse consequences than rape. Rape was regarded as a sex crime, not a brutal assertion of power that could be accompanied by homicidal violence. The debate over how best to resist sexual assault, so prominent in recent literature on rape in the United States,[30] was not part of the public discussion in China. Yet some accounts of rape cases suggested indirectly that physical resistance was not always successful. In one murder case, a man tricked a woman who had just arrived at the Beijing train station into a car, drove her to the suburbs, and raped her. She bit his lip in the course of the struggle. Fearful that the mark would be used as evidence against him, he strangled her and hit her on the head with a hammer more than thirty times. This story was told to make a legal distinction between rape leading to death and outright murder (this case illustrating the latter).[31] The author drew no conclusions about the dangers of physically resisting an armed assailant. On the contrary, women reading the press coverage of rape in the early 1980's would have had to draw the conclusion that physical resistance was the only honorable course open to them, and that failure to successfully deflect an attack should be taken as a personal disgrace.

Women had other pressing reasons to do all they could to resist rape. In putting up a struggle, they risked losing their lives; in becoming rape victims, they faced almost certain lifelong stigma. Though official commentary on rape made it clear that victims deserved sympathy and support from those they knew, a far more common response was gossip, disgust, and shame. Shunned by her family, judged by her neighbors, a rape victim frequently saw no course open to her other than suicide. This was true in urban settings, where cases were often reported of women who drowned themselves after their husbands reviled them for being raped.[32] It was undoubtedly even more true in the countryside, where traditional concepts of chastity had great staying power. In one 1985 case, a thirteen-year-old village girl was raped. Her attacker was arrested, but her father felt that he had been disgraced in the eyes of the village. He slapped her, accused her of running around like a "wild chicken" (a euphemism for prostitute), pulled her out of school, moved her into a separate room, and decided to marry her off to a twenty-five-year-old relative. When she protested, he told her this was the only way to combat village gossip. But after she overheard him telling her mother that the gossip really would only abate with her death, she drowned herself.[33] The report concluded by asking rhetorically who was responsible for her death; other press coverage of such cases stated clearly that family members who helped drive rape victims to suicide were themselves guilty of a crime.[34] Yet attitudes showed little sign of change. Legal advisers in the press repeatedly advised rape victims that they had the right and duty to press charges against their assailants. But these writers did not address the question of the social prejudice a victim might face if her experience became known.[35] Fear of public humiliation and family wrath undoubtedly led to underreporting of all types of sexual assaults, just as it did in the United States.

Rape victims internalized these attitudes of condemnation and shame. Regarding herself as damaged goods, an unmarried woman raped by a suitor might well choose to stay with him rather than file charges. A woman graduate of a Beijing normal school wrote to a magazine in 1985 describing such a situation. As a sophomore she had been raped by a classmate, who gagged her and sprained her wrist in the process. Afterward he professed his undying love for her, and she felt that she now had no choice but to pursue a relationship with him. After a year, during which she had an abortion, he abandoned her in spite of her pleas. When she pursued him, he and members of his family beat her and tried to give her an overdose of sedatives. She attempted suicide twice, fainted repeatedly in the street, and lost a great deal of weight. After a brief rapprochement he left her for good, telling her that no one could prove he originally had raped her. At the time she wrote to the magazine, asking how she should deal with him, she still seemed to be half-hoping for a reconciliation. She was willing to stay in an abusive situation because she felt tied to him by their sexual relationship, although she had entered into it unwillingly. She probably also assumed, correctly, that with such a history no other man would marry her.[36]

Government insensitivity often added to the psychological burden of rape victims. A number of articles in 1980 castigated local government officials for indifference or downright obstructionism in the prosecution of rape cases. In a well-publicized Tianjin case, a young woman factory worker was raped in 1978 as she returned from work. When she found she was pregnant, she attempted suicide but was discovered and saved. The factory leadership intimated that perhaps her pregnancy was the result of improper sexual conduct on her part. A zealous neighborhood cadre treated the pregnancy as a violation of the family planning policy, under which permission was required to have a child. He called a series of meetings to force her to admit that her pregnancy was the outcome of an illicit relationship, telling her that it was not possible to become pregnant from "one shot." Finally the young woman and her mother drowned themselves in the city's largest park, leaving a note that said their suicide was intended as a protest of the way the leadership had handled the situation. Press commentary and letters to the editor blamed the "ultra-left" workstyle of the factory and neighborhood cadres for the double suicide. The local officials were particularly criticized for using study group meetings to pressure the young woman; this method was characterized as an unwelcome remnant of the Cultural Revolution. The neighborhood cadre who had organized the meetings was arrested in connection with the deaths.[37] In other cases, officials were called to task for being lackadaisical or reluctant to interfere in cases where a woman was assaulted by someone she knew.[38]

Public discussion of rape in 1980's China did not devote much attention to a social analysis of rapists, although fragmentary statistics suggested that many of them were under eighteen.[39] Rapists were sometimes characterized as men who had not learned to control their sexual impulses. When the elder sister of a rapist wrote to a legal journal asking how her brother could have committed such a crime, his lawyer replied that the young man had "an unhealthy consciousness of sex," and had progressed from curiosity to reading and watching pornographic material to masturbation and then to rape. (A similar continuum of disaster, and its allure for young people, are discussed in Chapter 2.) He allegedly became so stimulated at the sight of a woman wearing flimsy clothes that he raped her. The lawyer felt that improved sex education, better knowledge of the law, and a life of study, work, and athletics could help prevent rape.[40] Another explanation was that rapists were men whose parents had neglected to bring them up properly. In a 1985 Fujian case, two brothers were executed for rape and other crimes. Their father was depicted in the press as a hard-drinking man who beat his wife and children, taught the boys to drink, and led them in attacks on the neighborhood government office. The mother was portrayed as a greedy woman who encouraged the boys to keep valuables they found on the street. Both sons were involved in burglary, robbery, and extortion, as well as sexual assault. The article concluded that the shadow of the parents could be seen behind the corpses of the sons.[41] If rape was the result of inadequate self-control and improper education, then rapists presumably could be reformed if they penitently submitted themselves to re-education. Like other criminals, they were expected to rehabilitate themselves through labor. The press occasionally published stories of model prisoners who renounced their rapist ways and earned awards for hard work at labor camp.[42]

Many of the issues that have dominated the discourse on rape in the West in the late twentieth century were not part of the public discussion in China: the role of patriarchy, the social and psychological sources of male hostility toward women and their expression in sexual assault, the function of rape in controlling women's behavior and constricting their freedom, the question of whether rape should be seen as a dysfunctional expression of sexual desire or an act of violence. What interested Chinese commentators, rather, was the way in which the social strains of the 1980's gave rise to a climate that permitted rape. Their analyses focused on the breakdown of social order during the Cultural Revolution, the spread of pornography and Western notions of sexual liberation, insufficient education at home and at school, ignorance of the law, and the tendency of male adolescents to form gangs and dare one another into illegal behavior.[43] Perhaps because they saw these factors as products of a specific period of social disruption, Chinese writers did not explicitly link rape to the continuing problem of female subordination in Chinese society. In spite of the limited nature of the discussion, though, the public spotlight on violent sexual crimes against women—a topic that until the 1980's had been shrouded in silence—raised the possibility that women might one day move in a landscape where the rape victim was not blamed so unilaterally, and where men's violent sexual access to women was not taken for granted.

Forced Marriage

The Marriage Laws of 1950 and 1980 guaranteed freedom of marriage, forbade arranged or mercenary marriages, and prohibited interference in marital choice by any third party. In spite of campaigns to publicize and enforce the law, however, young women in the 1980's who tried to exercise these legal rights sometimes encountered violence. A woman might meet resistance from her own family, the family of the groom, the larger lineages on either side, or the groom himself. In addition, her right to choose could be crudely violated by groups of kidnappers who roamed some areas of the Chinese countryside, abducting women for sale as brides.

Parents who did not approve of their daughter's choice of sweetheart could exert considerable psychological pressure and even invoke a parental veto (see Chapter 3). When these were unsuccessful, some parents turned to economic threats and physical violence. A 1982 case of violent parental interference that gained considerable attention was that of a young Anhui couple, Chen Yuansheng and Wu Xianyun. Wu, the daughter of a cadre, was willing to marry Chen even though he lived in a run-down house with his father (a retired worker), his mother (an unemployed mute), and his eighty-five-year-old grandmother. As the only child, Chen would be responsible for supporting all three of them. Wu's father, a Party member and cadre, opposed the marriage because the backgrounds of the two families were so divergent. "I'm not asking you to marry up," he told his daughter, "but at least you must find someone who matches you in social and economic status. His father is a worker; how can he match me? His mother is a mute; what about your mother? We have a TV and bicycles; what can his family offer?"

When Wu persisted in her determination to marry Chen, her father beat her repeatedly, threatened to break her legs, and led a group of people to trash Chen's house. Wu first attempted suicide, then sought protection from the local police, who refused to intervene in a domestic dispute. The young couple eloped to Xinjiang, but were sent back by officials since free migration was not permitted. Back in Anhui, Wu was denied the grain coupons and clothing that would normally be provided by her family. Her father told her that if she did not return home, she would have to pay her family a lump sum of 15 yuan for each month of the eighteen years she had lived with them, an amount well beyond the means of most Chinese.

Unable to find legal recourse, the couple turned to the press, which played a crucial role as muckraker and advocate in many such cases.[44] Once their story was published, local Youth League and Party authorities investigated their case and promised a quick solution. The father was publicly criticized for his feudal attitude, and the local authorities for their reluctance to become involved. Sympathetic readers of *China Youth News* showered the couple with money, grain coupons, and clothing.[45] Yet although Wu's father had violated the Marriage Law and employed physical force against the couple, no charges were brought against him. The authorities remained unwilling and unable to take an extensive role in guaranteeing either freedom of marriage or freedom from physical coercion, particularly when the victim was a dependent daughter.[46]

In rural China, marriages were often arranged by parents, sometimes years before their children came of age. Betrothal agreements typically involved substantial payments of cash and goods to the bride's family. Once a betrothal was arranged, breaking it off could involve substantial losses of money and face for them. When young women tried to challenge such an arrangement by choosing their own partners, they threatened not only parental authority, but their parents' financial and social status. In this situation, mothers as well as fathers sometimes used violence to force their daughters' compliance with an arranged marriage, even in cases where the mothers themselves had suffered from the choice made for them by their own parents.

In 1982, the mother and cousin of Wen Qiaohua were sentenced to short jail terms for violating the Marriage Law. Wen, a rural Gansu woman, had refused to marry the man her parents had picked out when she was still a child, and asserted her right to marry Lei Guisheng. Her parents beat her brutally and sped up their marriage preparations. She fled to Lei's family, but her mother tricked her into returning by agreeing to break off the original engagement. Once Wen was home, her mother had male relatives beat her with icy ropes, pour urine down her throat, and lock her in the house. The mother then forced her to go through with the traditional wedding ceremony, although the marriage was not formally registered with the local government. Eventually Wen filed a legal complaint with support from Lei's family. The court declared her forced marriage null and void. Without the support of her fiancé's family, it is extremely unlikely that she would have been able successfully to resist her family's plans for her.[47]

Rural women who violated their parents' wishes sometimes found that the authority of the lineage, as well as the family unit, was invoked against them. In a 1983 Hubei case, Huang Fengying sought refuge in her boyfriend's house when her family insisted that she marry another man. Her father and uncle decided that she had broken the rules of the lineage. Declaring their intention to bury her alive, they gathered thirty relatives armed with ropes, sickles, and other weapons. The mob tied up the boyfriend's family and dragged Huang homeward. They were stopped by local people (described only as "the masses" in the press). The father and uncle eventually received jail sentences, and Huang married the man of her choice.[48]

If the family of the bride was concerned to protect its familial authority and financial standing, the family of the groom was determined to ensure that he got the woman his family had paid for. In rural areas, the custom of "stealing the bride" (*qiangqin*) persisted into the post-Mao period (see above, "Rape"). In 1979, for instance, a Fujian woman discovered that the man her parents had chosen for her was a chronic gambler who was often involved in local brawls. She convinced her family to break off the engagement, returning 600 yuan and a wristwatch to the man's family. Her erstwhile fiancé, with the aid of male relatives and the local Party Secretary, tricked her into going to his house, tied her down, drugged her, and raped her.[49] In the Shanghai suburbs, a bride-stealing was given a modern twist when the family of the man borrowed a car and mobilized ten relatives to abduct a recalcitrant fiancée. When she insisted that she would not marry him, his family threatened to detain her until she paid back some 740 yuan they had spent to secure the betrothal. They released her only when ordered to do so by the local court.[50]

The lineage authority of the groom's family, as well as the bride's, could be used to pressure an unwilling woman into marriage. In a Zhejiang village dominated by the Wu lineage, the Wu's forced the only village family surnamed Liu to promise a daughter in marriage. Discovering that the intended groom was retarded, the Liu family resisted, but could draw on no lineage support of their own. The Wu lineage threatened them with expulsion from the village. The young woman took the only escape route that seemed open to her: she killed herself. Undaunted, the Wu's then expressed an interest in her younger sister. At this point the father of the two girls committed suicide as well. Writers for a national legal journal advised the Liu family that the head of the Wu lineage could be prosecuted under Section 2, Article 179 of the criminal code, for "causing the death of another by interfering with freedom of marriage."[51] This crime, which made a person criminally liable for contributing to the suicide of another, carried a sentence of two to seven years.[52] The difficulty lay in finding a court independent enough of local lineage authority to hear the case impartially.

When young women were caught in conflicts between their own families and their suitors, either party could turn violent. A young woman who tried to extricate herself from a love affair might risk inciting her rejected suitor to murderous wrath. In one 1985 case, a young woman factory statistician actively sought a relationship with a temporary worker a head shorter than herself. Both families opposed the match because of the discrepancies in their physical and social stature. The young woman's mother trailed her to and from work, making it virtually impossible for her to see her sweetheart. When she finally obeyed her parents and broke off the relationship, he asked to see her one more time, then stabbed both her and her mother, who had secretly followed her to the rendezvous.[53] In press coverage, the pernicious custom of parental interference was held partly responsible for the crimes of the young men.

Virtually everyone a young rural woman knew, from her suitor to both sets of parents and their extended lineages, was a potential roadblock to her freedom of choice in marriage. Pressure from any of these sources, interwoven as it was with close personal ties and family authority, was almost impossible to resist. But far more impersonal, and therefore probably more terrifying, was the threat of kidnapping and sale as an unwilling bride far from home. In the early 1980's, the press began to report on a series of well-organized abductions throughout the country. In Wuqing county near the city of Tianjin, for instance, a county policeman noticed two teenaged girls buy rat poison and head toward the outskirts of a small rural town one night in 1980. Hearing them speak with an accent foreign to the region, he followed and questioned them. He discovered they were members of the Zhuang minority from rural Guangxi, far to the south. A month earlier they had left their homes to buy clothing in the county seat. At the train station, two men approached them and offered to obtain train tickets for them. The inexperienced girls agreed, only to find too late that the tickets were for a distant city. Still pretending to protect and escort them, the two men brought them first to Beijing, then to Wuqing county. There a relative of one of the men met them and sold them as wives to two local peasants for 600 and 700 yuan respectively. These sums, while considerable, were less than the cost of obtaining a local bride. The two young women repeatedly tried to escape, but were always caught. Finally they decided to take rat poison and commit suicide. When they were taken under police protection and their case was publicized, four other girls aged fourteen to eighteen fled to the police with similar stories.[54]

The practice of selling women from the south to villagers in the north was apparently widespread. Although coverage of kidnapping cases did not explain the reasons for a south-north marriage axis, most cases seemed to involve women from poor, remote regions of the south being transported to northern villages that were too poor to attract local brides. A 1981 investigation in Ninghe county, Hebei, found that more than 600 women from Guangxi had married into the county from 1976 to 1980. An unspecified number of them had been kidnapped; one human trafficker alone was responsible for the sale of ten women. The county government reported that one swindler, promising to find brides in the south, had tricked seven or eight local peasants out of more than 3,000 yuan, then gone south and disappeared. Another peasant unwittingly bought and married a woman from Guangxi who was already married. The county government responded to these cases by tightening up its marriage registration procedures.[55] Local governments in the south also expressed their concern about the outflow of women from their region. A report in the *Yunnan Daily* stated that every day in 1982, five or six cases of women leaving the area were reported to the Dayao county court. From January to March, the report continued, "some 750 married and unmarried women have left the county for Shandong and Henan provinces, of which 60 percent are not old enough to marry and about 10 percent are married women. More than 95 percent of these women have gotten married without the proper registration."[56] Some cases did not involve south-to-north migration: abductions were also reported from Sichuan and Hubei to Henan, from one part of Zhejiang to another, and from Hubei to Guangxi.[57]

Not all these cases involved physical coercion. Some women or their families were offered large sums of money; other women were only too willing to escape unhappy marriages and start over.[58] Often the bride traffickers tempted young women from poor and remote rural areas with promises of better material conditions elsewhere. By the time the women realized they had been tricked, they were far from home, penniless, and dependent upon their escorts.[59] Sometimes, though, kidnappers raped the women before selling them.[60] And in at least one case, a woman who demanded to be taken home and threatened to report her abductors to the police was strangled and her body thrown into a ditch.[61]

The press encouraged local law-enforcement officials to ferret out cases of kidnapping, prosecute the offenders, and return the women to their home counties. Local authorities who did so were singled out for praise in women's magazines.[62] The trials and sentencing of kidnappers were also highly publicized. Sichuan courts in 1982 sentenced 83 people for abducting and selling women and children; five members of a kidnapping ring in Guangdong received sentences ranging from five to fifteen years; a gang in Jiangxi was given similar treatment; kidnappers who raped or murdered women in the course of abductions in Anhui and Hubei were executed.[63]

Coverage of this problem in the Chinese press tapered off after 1983, when a major campaign to crack down on violent crime was concluded. It is unlikely, however, that the subsequent lack of publicity reflected a complete disappearance of the problem. The abduction of women, though certainly not common everywhere in rural China, was one end of a continuum along which women were pushed, cajoled, or forced into marriages not of their choosing. Abductions of the "stealing the bride" variety showed the continuing importance of powerful lineages in regulating rural marriage. Other, more impersonal kidnappings reflected the changing conditions of a market for women in the countryside. Most rural marriages in the 1980's involved substantial exchanges of cash and goods for wives. As the countryside became more prosperous under the economic reforms, and as the income that women could bring into the household increased, the value of women—and the brideprice they could command—increased. Although boys were more valued at birth, leading to the practice of female infanticide, women who reached marriageable age not only became a desirable economic asset, they became expensive as well.

The difficulty experienced by many rural men in finding brides, discussed in Chapter 3, exacerbated the problem. Nationally, the 1982 census showed 106.3 men for every 100 women. For certain regions and age groups, however, the ratio was much more lopsided. In Hebei, for instance, the ratio of twenty-two-year-old men to twenty-year-old women was 135 to 100.[64] In a marriage market where women were relatively scarce and expensive, powerful forces in the family and in society at large wrestled for control of this precious resource. Thus parents arranged the most advantageous marriages possible for their rural daughters, and bride traffickers and kidnappers roamed the landscape hoping to profit on the sale of cut-rate brides. The increased mobility permitted the rural population under the reforms made it easier for kidnappers to operate. But it was the rising value of women on the marriage market, combined with their continuing subordinate position within the family, that prevented them from making their own marriage choices. Their value increased, but their autonomy did not keep pace. Forced marriage, whether arranged by kin or connived at by predatory strangers, was the result.

Wife-Battering

Wife-battering in China, as elsewhere in the world, was underreported and infrequently prosecuted. The criminal code forbade maltreatment and injury, but a man was charged with such crimes only if they led to grave physical injury or death, or if they were discovered in the course of a campaign against special privilege or some other offense of concern to the state. For many local authorities, and certainly for batterers and their wives, a certain amount of physical violence was taken for granted as normal marital behavior. Press coverage reported only the most notorious cases, those considered newsworthy and of most interest to the reading public. These cases involved unusually sadistic or murderous husbands, or men who invoked politically powerful relatives to cover up evidence of wife abuse. Everyday abuse was not recorded. Yet even though these batterers cannot be taken as representative of all men who beat their wives, an examination of their motivations, their treatment by the government, and their portrayal in the press reveals a growing awareness of wife-battering as a serious and unacceptable phenomenon.

Some wife abusers appeared in the press when they went beyond battering to murder, usually because the men wanted to divorce and their wives refused. This type of case was common in the countryside, where divorce was difficult to obtain. Hebei peasant woman Li Da'an, for instance, died suddenly after childbirth in 1982 when she drank "holy water" provided by her husband. Before her death she had warned her son that her husband might try to kill her so he could marry a neighbor. When the marriage took place as she had predicted, the brother and sister of the deceased brought charges against him. A four-month investigation and an autopsy revealed that the "holy water" contained arsenic, and that Li had known of her husband's affair with the neighbor but had maintained the marriage so as not to disgrace the family. The husband was executed. Editorial commentary accompanying the story criticized Li for not struggling openly with her husband when she suspected him of trying to poison her.[65] In another Hebei case, a peasant man went off to school in Beijing in the 1950's, leaving his wife Song Xiufen in the countryside to care for his mother and their child. After almost thirty years, during which she maintained the family home while he worked in Beijing, Song found that he was having an affair with a young woman in the city. Knowing that village opinion would never tolerate his divorce from such a model wife, he tried various means to poison her (including feeding her moldy peanuts, which were thought to contain a powerful carcinogen). Finally he obtained some poison from Beijing, killed her, and remarried. He was arrested and executed; his new wife received a fifteen-year sentence as an accomplice.[66] In each of these cases, the focus of the article was on the painstaking work of the public security organs, the sterling character and naïveté of the murdered wives, and the perfidy of the husbands, rather than on the theme of wife abuse.

In a variation on this theme of violence as a substitute for divorce, some men deliberately abused their wives to the point of suicide as a way of freeing themselves from unwanted marriages. A Liaoning man reported in 1982 that his wife had committed suicide after he caught her committing adultery with a neighbor. The following year, a letter from "the masses" sent to the procurator's office in Dalian city hinted that the truth was not so simple; it reported that the husband had beat his wife and neighbor until they admitted to adultery, and that the wife had then killed herself. Further investigation showed that the husband had for six years been having an affair with a married Dalian woman. His wife knew of this and his other sexual adventures, but put up with them for the sake of the family and their children. The husband trumped up the adultery charge, hoping to force her to suicide, then left DDT lying around the house to provide her with a convenient means of ending her life. In 1984 he was sentenced to death for his role in his wife's suicide and for seducing a number of other women. An editorial pointed out that attacking a woman's reputation for ulterior motives, as he had done, was a common practice, and that protecting a woman's character and reputation should be part of the campaign to protect the legal rights of women. As in many other cases, the fact that this man had battered his wife was mentioned only in passing, since it was the murder and his seduction of other women that brought the case to light.[67]

Unusually imaginative batterers, and those who murdered their wives or directly contributed to their deaths, were thus among the wife abusers most likely to come to public attention. A third type of offender who drew the attention of the official press in the 1980's was the batterer who used official connections to avoid prosecution for his crimes. Like rapists from well-placed backgrounds, these men were criticized in the press in the course of a campaign against the abuse of power. Zhao Guoxuan, a municipal official of the Communist Youth League in a Henan city, was the target of such a campaign. Zhao repeatedly abused his wife, Ding Yanfang, using the fact that she had lost her virginity before marriage as an excuse to beat and torture her. He burned her with cigarettes, tied and beat her, forced her to kneel on a board full of splinters, stuck needles into her fingers, and even used a rack and gave her electric shocks. He demanded that she cut his nails, wash his clothes, and empty his commode, punishing minor infractions with further beatings. When she wrote to the provincial and national levels of the Women's Federation in 1983, he was arrested and charged with maltreatment. But his father, a former vice-mayor who continued to hold a number of official posts, protected his son, with help from many of his cronies in local government. The national media and the Women's Federation took an interest in exposing the cover-up, and both Zhao's parents were roundly criticized in the press. Zhao was eventually convicted of intentional injury, as well as the rape of several other women, and sentenced to death. His case was publicized during a national campaign to assure everyone equal treatment under the law.[68]

Very little attention was devoted in press commentary to the root causes of wife abuse; when reasons were given, they were usually superficial. The lack of exploration into this subject was striking in the more bizarre cases of wife-battering. Zhao Guoxuan, who put his wife on a rack and administered electric shocks to her, was described only as dissatisfied that his wife was unable to "tease him and satisfy him" like "bad women in the movies."[69]

Sometimes wife-battering was explained in passing as the result of incorrect conduct on the part of both batterer and victim. Li Jin, an army officer, was executed in 1985 for shooting his wife as she slept in her eighth month of pregnancy. The account of their unhappy marriage stressed their short courtship, her strong personality and shrewish behavior, and his expectation that he could command at home as he did in the army. Their fatal conflict occurred over a pork chop that he expected her to prepare for his dinner; instead she deliberately left it lying around until it spoiled. In explaining why he killed her, the commentary in the press put equal stress on his lack of understanding of her and her harsh verbal abuse of him. The purpose of the coverage was to propound the moral that home affairs must be properly handled, not to explore the individual or social reasons why marital conflict erupted into wife murder.[70]

Another explanation given for wife abuse was sexual jealousy on the part of the husband. In a 1983 Beijing case, an attractive woman factory worker in Beijing married an ordinary-looking construction worker. Because he felt his family background, job, and physical appearance were inferior to those of his wife, he became convinced that she must be seeing other men. At various points he attacked her with his fists, scissors, an awl, and a belt. Eventually she was granted a divorce and he was given a short jail sentence. In this and similar cases, an important point in proving wrongdoing on the part of the husband was to establish that the wife had not, in fact, been involved with other men.[71]

A final explanation offered for wife-battering was the failure of a woman to bear male offspring (see Chapters 5 and 6). Women who gave birth to girls, or who were suspected of being pregnant with girls because of their food cravings or the shape of their abdomen, were often beaten and sometimes driven to suicide. Such cases occurred not only in the countryside, where sons were a real necessity for the economic survival of the family, but also in urban areas, where sons were valued because they carried on the family name.[72] In 1982, the Women's Federation of Shenyang city reported that local cases of maltreatment of women who gave birth to girls were on the rise: twenty cases had been reported in the first half of the year, in contrast to almost none a year before. Some commentators recognized this phemomenon as an unintended result of the one-child policy.[73]

The public discussions of wife-battering, then, offered reasons why men beat their wives, but did little to provide explanations of why women should be the targets of such abuse. Neither the individual pathology of the batterer, nor the acceptability of that pathology in a society that devalued women, was subjected to critical scrutiny. On the few occasions when commentators attempted broad social explanations for wife-battering, they focused on either the distant or the recent past. Husbands beat their wives, some said, because of "the feudal consciousness that men are superior to women," or because of the "influence of the ten years of internal chaos, remnants of feudal thinking, and decadent capitalist thinking."[74]

If public discussion of wife-battering gave little clue to the individual makeup and social tolerance of the wife-abuser, it also offered only scattered insights into the psychology of the battered. The woman whose jealous husband repeatedly attacked her said at his trial that she did not resist because resistance only made his abuse worse.[75] In many marriages, wives remained with their husbands out of economic necessity. Many urban women drew salaries that provided some insurance against economic disaster if they left their husbands, though obtaining housing was difficult for a woman (see Chapter 6). But rural women, unless they returned to their parents' homes, had literally no place to go. For instance, Zhang Binghong, a rural Hebei woman, in 1982 married a Tianjin man who had been sent to the countryside during the Cultural Revolution. Shortly thereafter, he succeeded in transferring back to the city and sought to rid himself of his peasant wife. He beat Zhang, tried to force an overdose of medicine into her mouth, and one night suddenly stuffed a handful of salt in her vagina during intercourse, apparently hoping to terminate her pregnancy. He abandoned her after she gave birth to the child (who died), and people from her home village wrote to a women's magazine urging that the authorities help her, since she had no home to which she could return.[76] After the land was decollectivized under the 1980's reforms, one husband who wanted a divorce first beat his wife, then cut off her food supplies and gave away the right to farm the land the family had contracted from the state. His wife and their two children were forced to go out begging.[77] Social factors kept women entrapped as well. In both city and countryside, taking legal action against one's husband entailed a loss of face and exposure to public gossip that many women found unendurable. Although the press and other official voices admonished battered women to respect themselves and use the law as a weapon,[78] little was done to analyze, publicize, and ameliorate the circumstances that prevented many victims from doing so.

In addition to the psychological, economic, and social dependence of women on those who battered them, another factor discouraging women from bringing legal action against abusive spouses was the unresponsiveness of many local authorities. A woman who risked revenge from her spouse and social ostracism from her community to bring a complaint often heard her plight dismissed as a "domestic dispute" with no legal significance.[79] In one 1984 Shanxi case, a woman won the attention of authorities only after she committed suicide by throwing herself on the train tracks in the city of Taiyuan, after carefully placing her baby out of harm's way. She and her husband, both municipal employees, had been married for almost two years. In that time she had sustained more than twenty serious beatings and several death threats. He beat her four times during her pregnancy: once because he suspected the baby would be a girl, once because he found a trace of dust on the table, once because he caught her sleeping after he had forbidden her to sit down in the house without his permission, and a fourth time over housework. Though her work supervisors were sympathetic and found dormitory housing for her, the legal authorities refused to consider her complaint. Only after her death and the attendant publicity did the authorities move to arrest her husband.[80]

In 1985 a rare case was reported where a woman met violence with violence. Her husband lost interest in her after she gave birth to a daughter. He tried to prevent her from treating the baby when it fell ill, then got involved with another woman. When his wife refused to divorce him, he beat her and threatened her friends and relatives when they took her in. He dragged her around the house by the hair and tried to force her head into the stove. Finally she filed for divorce. At that point he stomped on her, beat her with an ax handle, and threatened her whole family with death. As he slumped on the bed in a drunken daze, she decided that she had no reason to kill herself, and that if she went through with divorce proceedings he might take revenge on her family. She grabbed the ax from him and killed him. Given a three-year suspended sentence, she was nonetheless criticized by her own defense lawyer both for putting up with the abuse for so many years and for killing her husband rather than relying on the law.[81]

In some cases, battered wives found that the legal authorities actively obstructed investigation of their complaints. This was especially true when the husband was from a powerful family,[82] but it also happened in cases where the wife failed to accommodate the authorities. One Shanxi woman, for instance, was approached sexually by a legal official when she went to court to complain about her abusive husband. When she refused to sleep with the official, he helped her husband file for divorce, granted the divorce, and awarded her inadequate child support. Two years of appeals proved fruitless, and only when a nationally known woman legal official intervened was the husband brought to trial for maltreatment and abandonment.[83]

Redress

In spite of the uneven response of local authorities, battered women who tried to free themselves from abusive situations could draw upon several sources of support. First and probably most important, particularly for rural women, were their natal families. In case after case, the family of a battered woman provided her with physical refuge, financial support, psychological relief, aid in seeking legal redress, and in some cases extralegal revenge. If a woman died under suspicious circumstances, it was most often her family who insisted upon an investigation.[84] The role of the natal family in protecting its sisters and daughters was not new; it had been one of the few places a woman could turn to in pre-Liberation China as well. What is striking is that almost forty years after the revolution, the natal family was still the most reliable, if not the only, source of relief for battered women in the countryside. Victims of abuse who could not turn to their families were among the most vulnerable.

Given the role of the natal family, it is not surprising that when the Women's Federation took up the issue of protecting the legal rights of women in 1983, it explicitly called itself *niangjia*, the term for a married woman's natal family, to show that it was as devoted to women as their own families were.[85] In April 1983, the Secretariat of the Central Committee of the Chinese Communist Party decided to make "protecting the legal rights of women and children" a major component of women's work.[86] Local branches of the Women's Federation responded with a number of innovative institutional measures. They set up open-air legal consultation services for women in urban parks, and trained and appointed women to act as courtroom advocates in cases of wife abuse.[87] In one Shanxi county, the Women's Federation and other local organizations in 1985 set up a "letter and visit network for women's problems" (*funü wenti xinfangwang*) with branches in every village, to take complaints from women about parental interference in marriage choice and maltreatment. Village women no longer had to leave their home communities to air grievances. The purpose of the network was to resolve problems through mediation before legal action became necessary.[88]

The heart of the Women's Federation work, however, was intervention by dedicated local women cadres who wanted to see justice done. In the course of the campaign to protect women's legal rights, such cadres were singled out for praise. In one rural Liaoning case, Women's Federation cadres learned of a woman who had been maltreated by her husband for six years. When she demanded a divorce in June 1983, he cut out her tongue. The Women's Federation conducted an investigation, provided information to the Party and government organs, and saw that the case was publicized in the press. Their efforts resulted in the man's trial and execution for causing grievous injury to his wife.[89] In another 1983 case, a rural Yunnan woman hanged herself because she could no longer endure maltreatment from her husband and stepson. After her death, her natal family decided not to bring charges because they could not spare the labor power to visit government agencies, and because they felt a lawsuit would not bring her back to life. The Women's Federation, playing the role her family had declined to take on, decided to bring charges instead, and saw that the stepson was convicted and the husband publicly criticized.[90]

The renewed attention to a strong legal system and the training of active advocates for women were two important steps in the move to control gender violence. Certainly they gave millions of women access to protection from abusive male authority. The campaign to protect the legal rights of women and children also generated a great deal of publicity and discussion about the attitudes that permitted violence to continue. But the assumption that a combination of legal sanctions and moral exhortations would eliminate violence against women bears examining. In a society where infant girls were killed, women raped and forced into marriage, and wives routinely battered, legal and moral measures might help to contain the problem, but they seemed unlikely to solve it. Violence against women in China was rooted not only in the patriarchal attitudes of the past and present, but in a set of government policies that, sometimes inadvertently, permitted unequal gender relationships to be continuously reproduced. At a minimum, state policies such as the one-child family and the tolerance of discrimination in hiring were in need of reevaluation with respect to their effect on gender relations. Yet it is doubtful that even a thoroughly gender-conscious government with a capacity for massive intervention could have done away with violence against women. Women were killed, raped, and battered in their capacities as daughters, sexual beings, wives, and mothers. The reasons why these intimate relationships are so often suffused with violence, the nature of the connections between private aggression and public inequality, have not been featured in the public discussion of gender violence in China. When Chinese analysts and activists begin to raise them, it will be an important step toward the understanding and elimination of violence against women in China.

Translations

In the 1980's rape, formerly not much discussed in the Chinese press, was dealt with extensively as a legal, social, and psychological issue. "A Denunciation in Blood and Tears" is a first-person account by a rape victim who demands legal redress. "After Your Daughter Is Raped" warns parents against blaming the victim, and explores the lasting psychological damage sustained by rape victims. "Is This a 'Domestic Dispute' or a Violation of the Law?" illustrates several important aspects of wife-battering, including the vulnerability of women who give birth to daughters and the difficulty of obtaining legal protection from one's husband. "We Should Poke Our Noses into Other People's Business" describes the work of the Women's Federation in aiding battered women.

A Denunciation in Blood and Tears

I am a twenty-one-year-old woman. I want to denounce a brute who abused me.

On April 10 of this year, a Sunday, at about 1:20 in the afternoon, I went to a roadside public toilet. I saw a man hanging around near the bathroom and thought he was waiting for someone. After I went into the bathroom and squatted, I heard someone coming. But I would never have imagined that it was a man! I quickly pulled up my pants, and saw that it was the man who had been hanging around outside. He rushed at me and pinned me in his embrace. I shouted, "Help! Help!" He said, "If you shout I'll strangle you." I tried desperately to struggle free. Then he hit me on the nose and the eyes. In a flash I was beaten bloody. How could I, a thin, weak girl, successfully fend him off? Even though I kept shouting and struggled desperately, he still pulled off my clothes by force. He attacked me brutally. My breasts, face, stomach, and thighs were all covered with bites and scratches. Even more disgusting, and what causes me the most grief, is that he tore my private parts. (Blood soaked through my underpants and pants.) He attempted to rape me, and once again I desperately shouted and cried. He said, "You're really something. I'm going to have to strangle you." Saying this, he got my neck in a lock and choked me until I could not breathe. At that moment, a middle-aged woman came into the bathroom. He said to her, "This is none of your business. Get the hell out of here quickly or I'll rape you too." The woman tried to pull him off me. She couldn't budge him and she left. Meanwhile he also took my wristwatch and turned all my pockets inside out. The middle-aged woman ran home, called her mother and a crowd of others, and only then was the criminal caught. I came out of the bathroom covered with injuries, drenched with blood. I was a complete mess. Passersby who saw me all turned their eyes away, cursing this brute.

I was taken to the hospital with quite a few serious injuries. My breasts were bitten, my nose was badly swollen, my eyes were black and blue, and handfuls of my hair had been pulled out. I had a bump on the back of my head as big as a goose egg, and I had to have stitches in my private parts. The doctors who heard I had been abused by a hoodlum were all sympathetic. . . . At present, I am still almost legally blind, my nose is broken, I have dizzy spells, and my back aches.

I am only twenty-one. Having suffered such a catastrophe and received injuries that will leave permanent damage, what will my life be like from now on? I hope the government will uphold justice and put this brute, this representative of the dregs of society, to death. Otherwise, we women will have no guarantee of life and limb. Every family has a wife and daughters—how will they dare leave the house after this? If this brute is not put to death, I will go to my death and bring him to justice in the netherworld. I ask the government to back me up. Execute this criminal and rid the nation and womanhood of this scourge!

A young woman victim

[An editor's note adds that the rapist, Chen Yanjun, was tried and convicted. He was executed on August 23, 1983.]

SOURCE: "Xueleide kongsu" (A denunciation in blood and tears), *Beijing funü*, 3 (September 1983), 4.

After Your Daughter Is Raped

Comrade Editor:

I am a faithful reader of *Family Doctor*, and I know that you will be able to help me solve my problem.

Lately my daughter, who is in the third year of junior middle school, seemed as though she was in a trance. In class she didn't concentrate and was scolded by her teachers several times. At home she went off and cried by herself. When I saw her like this, unable to eat or sit still, not herself at all, I was really worried. When I questioned her closely, she told me, "On the fourth of last month, when I was coming home at night after studying with some classmates, I was raped. I haven't gotten my period this month." This was really a bolt from the blue! Since she was small our family has treated her like a precious treasure. We have sent her to school, hoping that in the future she would accomplish something great. I scolded her. How can we hold our heads up after something like this? I had her take sick leave from school and have been taking care of her at home. But aside from saying, "It would be better to die," she doesn't open her mouth. She is usually very sensible—how can she think of taking her own life? What is she thinking and feeling? What should I do? Comrade Editor, please help me out! Thank you.

Mei

Comrade Mei:

The editorial department passed your letter on to me. I understand your anxiety. You didn't enclose your address, so I can only answer you by borrowing a corner of the magazine.

You should accompany your daughter to report this incident to the local government agencies as soon as possible. You must not suffer in silence, afraid to report it because you are worried about "face," and thus let the offender remain beyond the reach of the law. To tolerate this kind of evil is to abet it. It often helps the criminal to commit another offense, or gives him an opening to threaten or blackmail you. Your daughter is an innocent victim who has done nothing shameful. The relevant agencies will look out for her interests and preserve confidentiality, as well as helping you deal with the aftermath of the incident. I hope that you will rely on the local government agencies, take appropriate measures, and limit the damage to your daughter as much as possible.

Of course, the psychological wound suffered by your daughter cannot be healed by mere administrative measures or by an abortion, no matter how skillfully and deftly performed. Making it possible for her to live, study, and work normally is a real problem. I am happy to help you out. It's too bad that you did not provide many details, so I can only briefly guess at the psychological changes your daughter went through after she was attacked.

Generally speaking, rapists leave a strong impression on their victims, one that is hard to erase. First is the complex web of fear, shame, and loathing caused by injury to the body and spirit. The fright suffered by the spirit, the abuse suffered by the body, and in addition the pressure of having "lost her chastity" in the traditional view, may cause her to lose her emotional equilibrium and in serious cases may induce mental illness. After suffering a very bad scare, a person's morale is sapped. She may not be able to eat or sleep, may become uncommunicative, cry in secret, or suddenly tremble with fear. She may exhibit such symptoms as heart palpitations, shortness of breath, or nausea. Because she is worried about "face" or fears being scolded or even beaten, she may pretend that nothing is wrong, but a careful observer can still see that her mood is unstable, she loses her temper easily, has trouble concentrating, and shows other signs of abnormality. If the victim is emotionally unstable to start with and does not get effective help from relatives and friends after the assault, or even encounters more problems from them (like being scolded by family members or avoided by friends), then her fear and shame are quite likely to produce a sense of inferiority, despair, and loss of hope, leading her to consider suicide. From your letter one can see that your daughter may at present be in such a state.

In dealing with these "immediate" and "short-term" psychological reactions, the rape victim and those around her must understand very clearly that she is not at fault in the slightest. It is just like a person who, while walking along the street obeying all the traffic regulations, is suddenly hit by a vehicle that careens onto the sidewalk. The blame is not at all with the pedestrian. A person who blames the pedestrian in this kind of traffic accident for "not reacting quickly enough" or "not dodging" would be generally regarded as guilty of fallacious reasoning. Yet in dealing with rape victims, some people consciously or unconsciously blame the victim. Statements like "What was a girl doing out alone at night?" or "She was asking for trouble by dressing like that"—when people around the victim don't distinguish right from wrong and speak or act accordingly, it rubs salt in the victim's wounds. I am not opposed to the idea that on the road of life one must be both full of faith and vigilant. At present, after all, evil people still exist in society, and it is important to defend oneself against them. Women, who are comparatively small and weak, should pay special attention to their personal safety. But this is a matter of propaganda and education before something goes wrong, not of blame after the fact. When a rape has been committed, the view that "the evildoer is criminally liable and the victim handled things inappropriately" just compounds the injury. Some people, arguing from the feudal standpoint, believe that a woman who is raped has lost her "chastity," that "a flower has become damaged goods." Actually, "chastity" refers to a woman's having unblemished moral principles. If a woman herself preserves lofty moral sentiments, then the small anatomical change that is caused by external violence does not constitute a blemish at all. I hope you will stop scolding your daughter, patiently try to understand her psychological state, help her, treat her with warmth, and put an end to her being upset by the kind of "groundless talk" described above. Only in this way can bad long-term consequences be avoided.

Speaking of bad long-term consequences, the main one is the victim's sense of inferiority. This kind of inferiority complex may in future lead to her developing an unsociable and eccentric disposition. Especially in regard to marriage, she may decide to remain celibate, or casually take up with anyone who seeks her out. This kind of compensatory psychological state may also take the form of deliberately setting standards so high that they thwart any man who is interested in her. Aside from this, because of the suppression of her former fear and shame, in her sex life after marriage that abhorrent scene may often flash before her eyes, to the point where it makes her feel cold toward or even averse to sexual activity.

In contrast to the situation described above, there are also those who give up on themselves because they were raped when young. Feeling that "since the bottle's cracked, might as well break it," these people sleep around and degenerate into a life of crime.

You can see that understanding your daughter's psychological changes, helping her through this stage of emotional upheaval, and eliminating the influence of this setback she has suffered on the road of life are important for the present and in the long run. I hope that you and those around you who understand the situation will not look at her any differently. Your "scolding" her and "having her take sick leave from school" are not good methods. You must give her reason to have faith in you, feel the warmth of her family, deal correctly with life, understand its rich connotations, and not lose her belief in life because of a setback. You must help her be able to study and live as usual. Speaking from a psychological point of view, you must help her turn her attention to other matters, such as an extra-curricular activity she is fond of, or encourage her to take up a new field of study on her own, to "sublimate" in order to compensate for the setback.

I hope you and your daughter can deal with this correctly. I hope your daughter will soon return to a normal life of study.

Lin Le

SOURCE: "Nüer zaoshou baoxing zhihou" (After your daughter is raped), *Jiating yisheng*, 6 (June 1986), 21–22.

Is This a "Domestic Dispute" or a Violation of the Law?

Comrade Editor:

Enclosed is a letter from a woman who was looked down upon, mal-treated, and abused by her husband.

We believe that this case goes beyond the scope of an ordinary domestic dispute. We are forwarding it to you to call attention to the injustice suffered by this abused woman. She is Deng Xiaoming, a twenty-eight-year-old woman who works as a doctor of traditional medicine in Yuechi county, Sichuan. In 1981 she married Lü Yongxin, a policeman in the Chengguan township station. He was a twenty-nine-year-old ex-service-man and a member of the Communist Party. After their marriage, because Lü was an extreme male chauvinist, he looked down on and mal-treated his wife. In spite of remonstrations by local officials, he did not change his behavior. Recently, he seriously injured Deng Xiaoming. An investigation showed that Deng was telling the truth about the situation. Deng, a quiet, hard-working young woman of impeccable character, is an outstanding student of the Correspondence School of Traditional Chinese Medicine. Her husband was not only unsupportive of her studies, but also abused her whenever he pleased. Deng Xiaoming repeatedly re-ported her situation to the relevant authorities, but they felt it was a "do-mestic dispute" and refused to intervene. It has been more than a month since she was seriously injured, but the relevant authorities have not yet taken it seriously or intervened. Deng Xiaoming cannot return home. We believe that Lü Yongxin's treatment of his wife goes beyond the scope of an ordinary domestic dispute. His behavior is an example of feudal habits rising from the ashes, a deliberate violation of the law. He should be pun-ished according to the law. . . .

Chen Ying and Zhang Xiaoli

[What follows is Deng Xiaoming's letter.]

My Accusation

With tears in my eyes I write of the unfortunate treatment I have suffered, and accuse my husband Lü Yongxin of discrimination, mal-treatment, and abuse. I beg you to back me up.

In 1978, I was introduced to Lü Yongxin, and we registered our mar-riage two years later. He said we couldn't have a wedding ceremony yet because "children born in the fifth month of the lunar calendar are the smartest." So we had to postpone the ceremony until the Spring Festival of 1981, which he considered an appropriate time. Just before the wed-ding, when we were hanging up mosquito nets in the bridal chamber, I accidently stepped on his hat, which he had left on the bench. He thought this would bring him bad luck. He cursed me out and whipped me with a rope.

After the wedding, Lü's male chauvinism and feudal thinking about women became more apparent. He set up three rules for me: 1. I could not touch him on the head or face. 2. I could not touch his clothes, shoes, or hat with any part of my body below the waist. 3. Our clothes were not to be washed in the same pan, and even our clean clothes were not to be put away together. He made me guarantee that I would not break these rules. In the first three years of marriage, he played completely by the rules. If there was a minor infraction, he would curse or beat me. I walked around with my heart in my mouth, afraid of his abuse.

In March 1981 I became pregnant. Because the expected date of birth was not in the fifth lunar month, as he wanted, he forced me to get an abortion. After the abortion he not only neglected me, he also changed the lock and barred me from his bedroom, saying, "It is inauspicious for a woman who has just given birth to enter the room." At the same time, he would not let me tell other people the real reason for the abortion. In the fifth lunar month of 1982, I gave birth to a girl. Lü was furious with this. In the first month he cursed me, but this was still not enough to vent his feelings. Less than fifty days after I gave birth, he kicked my leg and injured it. His dog was more important to him than me or our daughter.

He was the "master of the house," and I had to obey him in everything. I have my own salary, but I had no say about our family finances. He spent money as he pleased and never discussed it with me. As for housework, he felt that "washing and cooking have been the natural occupation of women since ancient times." I had to serve him at every meal.

Aside from going to work and doing all the housework, I tried to keep up with my studies at night after the child went to sleep. I wanted to learn a little more while I was still young, so that I could do a better job. And I also wanted to win his respect and support with my industriousness and achievements at work. But reality proved that I was too naive. Lü's deep-rooted feudal thinking, and his ignorance and brutal nature, proved difficult to change. He didn't study himself, and he was opposed to my studying. He often blamed me irrationally and made things difficult for me. He tried every means to keep me from studying, ripping my books and throwing my pens around, cutting off the electricity, or dousing the stove to cut off the heat.

Lü was a tyrant at home, beating and cursing me as he pleased. Once he asked me something and I didn't hear him clearly. He said I was deliberately ignoring him. He pulled my hands behind my back, sat on me, twisted my head, and choked me. He only stopped when I admitted I was in the wrong. In the first three years of marriage, he beat me seriously on at least ten occasions and hit me countless times. He beat me for small things, like accidentally spilling water on the floor or handing him something too slowly. If he was in a bad mood he would threaten me, saying, "These days I feel my eyelids jumping. Watch out or you'll get a beating." I was terrified all the time. Even more frightening, sometimes he beat me for no reason. One day in July of this year, he had just finished dinner when someone came over to ask him to process a household registration [part of his duty as a policeman]. He didn't want to go, but since it was someone he knew, he couldn't refuse. He stood up and with no warning slapped me across the face several times.

Usually I didn't dare fight back when he beat me. Once I showed my injuries to his superiors, who took him to task. Afterward he beat me even more severely, but only in places on my lower body that I could not show people. He shamelessly said to me, "Go to my supervisor and complain about me now! Let him see your private parts!" Because of his heartlessness I thought of divorce, but I was afraid that people would laugh at me if I got divorced so soon after getting married, so I bottled it up and watched my step. I thought to myself, he is an ex-serviceman and a Communist Party member, maybe he will change one day. But time after time, reality taught me that his personality was difficult to change. He mistook my tolerance for weakness, and his mistreatment of me got worse. At around 10 o'clock at night on September 8 this year, because I hadn't killed all the mosquitoes in the house, Lü pulled me out of bed and out the door and dragged me around, hitting and kicking me. He said that he was beating me for people to see, and that he was going to pull off my clothes and throw them on the street. That evening he beat me for more than an hour. None of the neighbors could stop him. He beat me until I was covered with injuries. My right ring finger was broken, and I had a cut on my head an inch long. He beat me silly, then said viciously, "In the past I beat you too lightly, and you weren't afraid. This time you will remember!" "Go and file charges! What can the authorities do about me? I'm still a Party member and a cadre!" I wasn't his wife; he was the master and I was the slave, a prisoner in his hands.

To assert the basic personal freedom of a citizen, and the basic rights of a woman, I appealed many times to the relevant authorities. They always made the excuse that they were too busy, even saying that "right now our main job is to bring criminals to justice. Yours is a domestic dispute. We'll deal with it later." My case was passed like a football from agency to agency, but they all closed their eyes to it. How serious does a "domestic dispute" have to get before it is regarded as a violation of criminal law? How can criminal elements be brought to justice while vicious wife abusers are permitted to remain outside the law?

At present I have nowhere to take my complaint, and a home I cannot return to. I am staying with relatives, nursing my wounds, bitter beyond words. I beg you to help me find a way out and break free of this grim fate!

Deng Xiaoming
County Hospital of Chinese Medicine, Yuechi, Sichuan

SOURCE: "Zheshi 'jiating jiufen' haishi chufan xingfa?" (Is this a domestic dispute or a violation of the law?), *Zhongguo funü*, 12 (December 1983), 37–38.

We Should Poke Our Noses into Other People's Business

Last April 15, a cadre of the Women's Federation of Nantong county, Jiangsu province, off on a business trip, heard of an outrageous incident.

Chen Shumei, a commune member from the Number 15 Brigade of the Chen Bridge Commune, had a husband who was working away from home. Her father-in-law and brother-in-law suspected her of improper sexual conduct and beat her badly. They broke three of her ribs and punctured a lung. They would not let Chen Shumei go to the hospital for treatment. They also colluded with a brigade cadre to threaten her not to tell anyone, and they kept her school-age child locked up at home. Only on the third day, when someone from Shumei's natal family arrived, did they send her to the hospital.

When the Woman's Federation cadre heard of this incident, she hurried to the hospital, comforted Chen Shumei, and said to her, "The Women's Federation will back you up." This cadre, along with the Party Committee and the Women's Federation of the commune, investigated the incident and made arrangements for Shumei's medical treatment and a place to live. The cadre immediately reported the incident to the county Party Committee. The county Women's Federation and the police conducted a joint investigation, and the assailants were punished in accordance with the law. At the court session where judgment was pronounced, the cadre from the county Women's Federation said, "The Women's Federation speaks up for battered and abused women, and protects their legal rights and interests."

. . . Some say the cadres of the Nantong county Women's Federation like to poke their noses into other people's business. True, they are nosy. But they do a good job of poking their noses into other people's business, and their actions are appreciated by the people.

SOURCE: "Zhezhong 'xianshi' jiu gaiguan" (We should poke our noses into other people's business), *Zhongguo funü*, 1 (January 1981), 44.

❋ 9
Feminist Voices

OVER THE seven-year period covered in this book, the status of women increasingly came to be recognized as a social issue. Most of the problems faced by women in 1985 existed in 1979, yet in the late 1970's, few women thought about gender discrimination. The female Chinese friends we made in 1979–81 usually insisted that "men and women are equal." When we talked to them about inequalities we saw, they not only rejected our observations, but often added, "You sound just like those Cultural Revolution radicals!" To them, an emphasis on women's equality was associated with a period of extreme political repression and brutality.[1] Instead, they focused on the damage wrought by the Cultural Revolution, opportunities in the new educational system, the economic reforms, and the increasing availability of consumer goods. Those who thought about gender discrimination at all usually denied its relevance to their lives. By 1985, however, many of these same women were speaking angrily about the multiple forms of discrimination they faced.

This new visibility of women's status as a social issue was not confined to private conversations, but extended to the press as well. In the late 1970's and early 1980's, little overt discussion of gender discrimination found its way into the press. Only in the context of reports of rape and marriage arrangements did it come up at all, and even then the term "discrimination" was never employed. And there was almost no discussion of unequal treatment in the workforce. By the mid-1980's, though, the plethora of newly founded women's magazines explicitly discussed women's problems at work and in the family. The pages of *China Women's News* were filled with exposés and denunciations of discrimination faced by women. "Feminist outcries" began to appear with some regularity in print. This recognition of gender inequality also found expression in the emergence of separate women's organizations—schools, professional societies, and women's studies groups.

The increased attention to gender discrimination, the appearance of "feminist outcries," and the emergence of women's organizations can be explained in several ways. Though gender discrimination was by no means a new phenomenon in post-Liberation China, urban women in the mid-1980's had reason to be more conscious of their unequal status than ever before. Discrimination became increasingly explicit and overt in the decade after the end of the Cultural Revolution, particularly in the context of the economic reforms. The principle of the reforms that "the more one works, the more one earns" (*duolao duode*) made it clearer than ever before that women's opportunities were not equal to those of men. No matter how hard they worked, women often found that their jobs were considered "less important," and therefore paid less, than those performed by male workers.[2] The gap between the rhetoric of women's liberation and the reality of gender discrimination perhaps had become too wide to be ignored.

The political liberalization of the post–Cultural Revolution decade made it possible for women to publicly discuss these dissatisfactions. The status of women was only one of a wide variety of social and political issues, taboo during the Cultural Revolution, that became subjects of public discussion. The increased freedom to debate the issues of sexuality, courtship, marriage, family life, divorce, and violence also fueled the public discussion of gender discrimination. The increasing availability of information about Western countries that accompanied political liberalization also contributed to the emerging consciousness of women's issues. Newspapers and magazines frequently contained reports about the lives and problems of women in the United States and Europe, about feminism and the women's movement in the West. A number of Chinese women who had the opportunity to study in the West applied what they learned of Western feminist ideas to an understanding of their own predicament. The development of an active women's movement in the West and its effect on China made the discussion of women's issues in the 1980's profoundly different from previous discussions, such as those that took place in the mid-1950's.

Finally, the increasing consciousness and legitimacy of women's issues may be attributed to renewed state interest in gender discrimination. The Chinese Communist Party, almost from its inception, endorsed women's equality. After the 1950 Constitution guaranteed equality between men and women, and after sweeping attacks were made in the 1950's on the abuses and injustices suffered by women in the "old society," Chinese government publications generally asserted that the task of liberating women had been accomplished. Only when the reality of women's continued subordinate status conflicted with the goals of major political campaigns did the government promote discussion of gender inequality. One such juncture was the Great Leap Forward of 1957–58, when the state sought to socialize housework so more women could work in industry and agriculture. In the 1980's, the family planning campaign—essential to China's attempt to modernize—created a similar situation. Acceptance of the one-child family required that many parents be content with a daughter, and this in turn mandated government interest in raising the status of women. The problems of female infanticide and abuse of women that the family planning policy fostered made it even more urgent that the government directly confront the reality of gender inequality. Under these circumstances, discussion of persistent inequalities between men and women was not only tolerated, but actively encouraged in the official press.

Feminist Outcries

In the early 1980's, public voices that Western observers could describe as feminist were few and far between. In this context, a woman student at Beijing University who ran for election to the National People's Congress in 1980 attracted a great deal of attention when she put up a poster entitled, "Women Are Human Beings Too." "Are courage and the spirit of self-sacrifice the prerogative of the male sex?" she asked.

Women are human beings too. Why should their specific attributes, their interests, their development as a sex, and many other aspects of their womanhood not be important questions? Don't the interests of women mingle with the ocean of the interests of the people? Shouldn't women's rights form part of democratic rights? Why do people just find fault with me when the question of women is raised? . . . Women are not baby-making machines. They are human beings, and as such they must fight for their rights, their interests, and their fulfillment.[3]

Although the text of her poster included ideas that Western feminists would find puzzling (the theme of her campaign was "Oriental Beauty"), her bold call for "women's rights" won her recognition as a lone "feminist" in China.

Only in fiction were other feminist voices publicly heard. Zhang Jie's 1982 short story about three divorced women, "The Ark" (discussed in Chapter 6), was heralded by one Western writer as China's first feminist work of fiction.[4] Perhaps even bolder than the story itself was its epigraph. Drawing on a phrase commonly used to introduce female characters in traditional Chinese literature, the epigraph warned, "You will be especially unfortunate because you are a woman." This phrase would have been deemed appropriate to describe the inferior status of women in old China, but the suggestion that it applied to new China was a radical one.

Daring as they may have been, these voices were isolated and tentative. Only in 1983 did it become common to find such statements in a variety of newspapers and periodicals. The statements did not represent a unified view. Some were the angry outcries of women who simply hoped to call attention to the social injustice they believed women suffered. Others suggested solutions: calling on women to change themselves, insisting that only if men's thinking changed could women's liberation be achieved, appealing to the government to take more active steps to guarantee equality. The statements shared only an assumption that in the 1980's, Chinese women were treated as inferior to men.

One of the first public statements denouncing discrimination toward women was a poem entitled "Four Questions," published in March 1983 in *People's Daily*. Each stanza began with a phrase of Chairman Mao's that had been used by the Communist Party to proclaim its success in liberating women after 1949: "Times have changed; men and women are equal." Why then, author Wang Fuhua sarcastically asked, are men and women not equal? The poem criticized discrimination toward women in almost every sector of society: in pay for agricultural work, factory hiring, college admissions, and treatment in the family.[5] Although Wang was not exposing previously unknown facts, she was one of the first to publicly describe these phenomena as gender inequality. "Four Questions" was not remarkable for what it described, but rather for being one of the first public proclamations made in the post–Cultural Revolution era that Chinese women were *not* equal to men.

A 1983 article discussing the increasing popularity of the term *qiguanyan* is significant for similar reasons. As explained in Chapter 7, *qiguanyan* was a term used to describe henpecked husbands. The proliferation of jokes about henpecked husbands did not, according to the author, reflect a social reality in which the majority of Chinese women had become "dictator in their home." Pointing out that "the things that people laugh at are those that go against common practice," she argued that people made fun of men allegedly suffering from *qiguanyan* precisely because it violated the social norm of *fuguanyan*—literally, a wife being managed strictly by her husband.

In China's feudal society women were the ones who suffered from the worst oppression, and yet many stories of men fearing their wives have been passed down. This does not mean that in feudal society many men were afraid of their wives and that it was common for women to oppress men. It is precisely the opposite: it only proves that the idea that a wife must be loyal to her husband was sacrosanct or, from another angle, that women's position was low.[6]

The author was saying in effect that the growing popularity of jokes about henpecked husbands really indicated an increasing assertion of male dominance. The jokes also may have been an attempt to trivialize women's growing assertiveness, an assertiveness that challenged the still-dominant mode of male superiority. Like the poem "Four Questions," this article was not the first discussion of the topic, but rather one of the first to criticize contemporary Chinese society for being male-dominated.

The greatest number of "feminist outcries" were provoked by assertions that women's intelligence was inferior to men's, that women should strive to be meek, weak, and sweet, and that women's work outside the home was less important than their husbands'. For example, in a letter written to *Fujian Youth* (Fujian qingnian) in early 1985, a man named Si Ji had expressed the bitterness he felt because his wife was "more capable than he," causing him to "lose his masculinity." His complaint that she lacked the female qualities of tenderness, meekness, and sweetness triggered a three-month discussion in *Fujian Youth* about whether or not women should be strong and powerful.[7] Many men wrote letters—and in some cases were even interviewed by the magazine's editors—about their views of women. More significant here, though, was the number of women who wrote indignant letters to the magazine, challenging prevailing assumptions that women were inherently meek, weak, and sweet. "Meekness is not a quality Chinese women are born with," one woman angrily responded to Si Ji. "In general, the degree of meekness is directly related to the degree of oppression. . . . Meekness is not only *not* a virtue of Chinese women, it is really a shackle placed on Chinese women by feudal oppression. No clear-minded Chinese husbands should demand that their wives be meek. The more intelligent and capable your wives are, the more dignified you should feel."[8] Eventually the heated nature of the correspondence prompted the magazine's editorial board to invite a group of women to its office to discuss their views. Almost all the participants agreed that women's main problem was that they were too weak, and if anything, needed to become more powerful. "If a woman who has complete political and economic independence and is diligent and capable is considered 'too powerful,' then imagine the fate of women who do not have political or economic independence," one woman said.[9]

Not all the assertions that women should be powerful presented a challenge to the status quo. Several women, in the process of refuting the belief that women should be frail and meek, unwittingly called for the reinforcement of traditional female virtues. One woman, after declaring that women should be powerful, warned that they must avoid the kind of "boastful power" prevalent during the Cultural Revolution, when "women wore men's clothing, marched like men, and did battle against men every day."

Instead, women should establish their credit. They need to receive a more complete education than men—to cultivate refinement, become knowledgeable, develop poise, be civilized and generous—so that they can become the mistresses of society. They must be outstanding workers at their jobs and outstanding wives in their homes. They will get used to "feeling ashamed of being crude and rude," and the "glory of respecting other people." This is where women's power lies. When people see women, including their own wives, being polite, well-behaved, and well-dressed, they will say, "This is such a civilized society, and those are such respectable women." [10]

Despite this author's qualified definition of "female power," she shared with most women participants in the *Fujian Youth* forum a belief that women should not succumb to men's desire for submissive and unaccomplished wives.

Si Ji's letter to *Fujian Youth* was not the only statement that provoked women to declare their refusal to aspire only to the fulfillment of domestic duties. The increasing currency of the "virtuous wife and good mother" notion provoked a similar cry of outrage. "I wonder whether men should also have to uphold traditional morality by striving to become 'virtuous husbands and good fathers,'" one woman wrote after seeing the film "Country Couple" (discussed in Chapter 5).

Why is it that if a woman sacrifices everything it is considered a virtue, whereas if a man makes even the tiniest sacrifice people say that he's a "good-for-nothing" and afraid of his wife, and laugh at him. I cannot help but suspect that this kind of "virtue" is nothing more than a spiritual shackle imposed by men in order to control women. Sometimes it is necessary for one spouse to compromise, but it cannot always be the woman who must make the sacrifice. [11]

Perhaps one of the most radical critiques of the prevailing wisdom that women should sacrifice their careers to become virtuous wives and good mothers (even the modern, scientific variety) was a play entitled "The Return of an Old Acquaintance on a Rainy Night" (*Fengxue guren lai*). The author, Bai Fengxi, wrote the play partly to express her anger at the unequal treatment still being accorded women. "In my years as an actress," she told reporters for *Women of China*, "I saw all the discrimination, prejudice, and persecution of women. Perhaps that's what helped me create believable characters for this play." [12]

The main protagonists are a mother and daughter, both strongly career-minded. The mother, Xia Zhixian, is a well-known obstetrician, whose husband had divorced her for "neglecting her family duties" when she accepted an opportunity to study abroad. The play begins on the wedding day of her daughter, Yinge. Having just graduated from the university with a brilliant record in mathematics, she has been selected to study abroad for a doctoral degree. Her husband's mother, a woman who gave up her career as a doctor to become a housewife, adamantly opposes the idea of Yinge's going abroad. She warns her son, "Has it ever occurred to you that in four years, when she returns—a doctor of mathematics—and people meet you, you'll be introduced as Dr. Peng Yinge's husband? Where will your pride be then!?"[13] She takes it upon herself to persuade officials that her son should go in Yinge's place. Even Yinge's mother worries about the risks to her marriage that Yinge's going abroad might entail, and she, too, tries to persuade Yinge to stay home. Feeling betrayed, Yinge shouts at her mother, "What are you suggesting I do—give up my future career and the chance to study abroad so I can be a virtuous wife and good mother?"[14] Yinge adamantly refuses to be pacified by the argument that her husband's success would win her sufficient glory. "Woman is not the moon," Yinge declares. "She needn't depend on the light of others to shine."[15]

The conflict is eventually resolved by the unexpected return of an old acquaintance on a rainy night. The acquaintance is Yinge's father, who has come to confess that he had been wrong to divorce his wife for persevering in her career. "I'm a paleontologist," he says. "Every day I study ancient animal fossils to decide how old they are. But how old are the ideas in our minds?" He criticizes Yinge's mother, mother-in-law, and husband for the "old ideas" underlying their belief that a wife should not be more successful in her career than her husband. "I don't see why there has to be a problem if it's Yinge that goes," he concludes.[16]

The play was received as a sympathetic portrayal of the difficulties endured by career-minded women, and as a criticism of the notion that a woman's success was to be achieved in her role as wife and mother. The play not only provoked widespread discussion, but also inspired other "feminist outcries." For example, an essay entitled "Woman Is Not the Moon" was published on the front page of a new women's magazine, endorsing the sentiment expressed in the play that women are not, and must not be, mere reflections of male splendor.

The problem is that many people are oppressed by old ideas and old consciousness. They believe that as women, we do not need to be strong. They believe that as long as one finds a good husband to depend on and lives out one's life, that will do. Old ideas such as "Woman is made from one of man's ribs," and "If a woman does not have a husband her body does not have an owner," etc., still influence some people. . . . History and present circumstances oppress and constrain many women comrades. This makes it impossible for us to display our talents, intelligence, and creativity. We just become men's servants or their burden.

Woman is not the moon. She must rely on herself to shine. These are words that many pioneers of the women's liberation movement, masculine women, and heroines have inscribed with their own actions, tears, and blood. Let us treasure these words, remember them, and implement them. Hopefully each person can find her own path in life and develop her own brilliance.[17]

Although "Woman Is Not the Moon" was primarily a critique of women's dependence on men, it also suggested a tentative solution in female self-reliance. Other "feminist outcries" were more explicit in their suggestion that the first step toward achieving gender equality had to be taken by women themselves. For example, on the occasion of Women's Day in 1984, a female student at Beijing University named Wang Youqin called for the development of "a new women's viewpoint." After criticizing the unequal opportunities for women in higher education, Wang proclaimed that "'Spiritual footbinding' has deformed our souls. . . . It is not high mountains and wide rivers that hinder our footsteps, but rather our own spirit." [18] Although Wang's essay dealt with an important question, women's internalized sense of inferiority, it verged on blaming the victim. Like "Woman Is Not the Moon," it placed primary responsibility on women themselves for achieving a more equal status.

One woman extended this argument even further, declaring that if women were to overcome the demeaning popular belief that the female sex had "long hair but short sight," they must "have ideals, careers, self-confidence, and strength." So long as they submitted themselves to "constraint by their husbands, children, and the small circle of the family," they deserved their reputation of being "short-sighted." As a solution, she advocated that "a woman should be successful both in her profession and in managing her home. Women need to work twice as hard as men. . . . Women's determination is the crucial thing." [19] The problem, according to this author, was that women had been too limited by their domestic duties. She did not suggest that women relinquish those responsibilities, nor did she propose that they be shared with men. Instead, she insisted that women must become stronger and more determined to succeed in their careers.

Rather than place full responsibility for overturning "feudal" views on women themselves, another critic of female subordination advocated that parents dedicate themselves to the cultivation of "a strong personality in girls." They should "eliminate feudal ideas from their own minds and firmly implant the concept of equality between men and women [in their children]." [20] In other words, if the younger generation could be educated to believe in equality, perhaps changes would eventually occur.

Some critics of women's inferior social status challenged the assumption that women's liberation depended upon women themselves. They believed that men, imbued with feudal male chauvinist ideology, were the major obstacle to the achievement of gender equality. Specifically, they believed that if men assumed more responsibility for housework, women would become more equal not only within their families, but in society as well. "We should strongly oppose outmoded male-chauvinist ideas that men who do laundry, cook, or take care of children have lost their masculinity," declared one woman.[21] And another woman, determined to discuss the issue of women's liberation with her husband, complained that he utterly failed to translate his intellectual belief in gender equality into his personal life.

You, being a husband, often get done with work earlier than I, yet you are not willing to enter the kitchen. If you are hungry, you just wait for your wife to come home and cook for you. After dinner you just get up and leave, as if you were in a restaurant. You never think of touching the dirty clothes in the basket; instead you often complain "I don't have any clean clothes to wear!" You simply assume that these are all things for a wife to take care of. . . .

Comrade husband, do not overlook the attitude of men toward housework. . . . Since you know that the liberation of women is a yardstick of the general liberation of a society, then get moving and do some housework; at least reduce your dependence [on your wife]. The family is the cell of society. If only equality between men and women can be achieved within each cell, then the day when women will be liberated will soon follow.[22]

The suggestions that women recognize their own strengths, that parents try to socialize their daughters to have more self-confidence, and that men overcome the idea that a wife should be fully responsible for maintaining a household were the farthest that most "feminist outcries" went in suggesting remedies for the social inequality they criticized. They all stressed changes that had to take place in self-perceptions and social attitudes. In this context, "Some Ideas on How to Develop the Abilities of Women Intellectuals," by Zhou Guangyu and Cai Queyi, is noteworthy as one of the rare proposals that the government adopt concrete measures to raise the status of women.

In what was originally a speech prepared for a meeting of the National People's Political Consultative Council, Zhou and Cai began by declaring: "As women we have a constitutional guarantee of the right to equality with men. However, the Constitution and the concern of the Central Committee of the Communist Party are still not equivalent to an absolute guarantee of women's rights." They pointed out that women did not have equal political representation, that publications often stressed the superiority of "male intelligence," and that women were discriminated against in employment. Zhou and Cai believed that government commitment to gender equality required more than a general constitutional guarantee. They proposed that the government implement specific laws to prevent discrimination against women in job recruitment and admission to educational institutions. They also requested that the retirement age for women intellectuals be made the same as for their male counterparts.

The majority of women intellectuals who must, by present regulations, retire at age fifty-five, are still healthy and have accumulated a great deal of expertise. Also, by that age their household responsibilities are lighter. To make all women retire at that age is very destructive of women's initiative, of the manifestation of women's talents, and of the cultivation of women who can become high-level specialists.[23]

Finally, Zhou and Cai proposed that in order to be able to make informed policies regarding women, the All-China Women's Federation should implement a women's studies program to conduct research on women's gender-specific experience.

Those who pleaded for a recognition of women's strengths and capabilities, as well as those who called assertively for the adoption of measures to eliminate gender discrimination, shared an assumption that in China of the early 1980's, men and women were not equal. In the late 1970's, such statements would have been unimaginable. These feminist outcries were significant because they expressed the awareness that the status of women was a social issue that remained unresolved.

Separate Spheres: Women's Institutions

Statements calling attention to the status of women were only one indication of an emerging feminist consciousness. This consciousness was also evidenced in women's institutions—in the changing nature of the Women's Federation and the appearance of new women's organizations.

From the time the Communist Party assumed power in 1949, the All-China Women's Federation and its local branches became the official and exclusive organization representing women. As long as the Women's Federation existed, ran the assumption of government policy-makers, women's interests were protected and there was no need to form other organizations within or independent of the government. Like many other mass organizations, the Women's Federation was inactive during the Cultural Revolution, and reorganized only in 1979. During the early 1980's, the primary function of the Women's Federation was to mobilize women to participate in government-sponsored political campaigns, rather than to represent the interests of women to the government. Moreover, many urban people considered work for the Women's Federation worthy of little, if any, respect. The suggestion that a woman should be assigned to do Women's Federation work was synonymous with saying she was incompetent.[24] Few urban women perceived the Women's Federation as relevant to their lives. One of our female classmates, when asked about the Women's Federation, replied, "Don't ask me about that. The Women's Federation has nothing to do with me. Maybe my mother knows more about it." Her mother was similarly unenthusiastic. In fact, no one with whom we spoke in 1979–81 could recall a situation in which the Women's Federation might have assisted her.

As urban dwellers began, in the liberalized atmosphere of the early

1980's, to express more frustration at the concrete problems they faced in their daily lives, at least some women became angry at the failure of the Women's Federation to defend their interests. A letter from a woman worker in the city of Baoji (Shaanxi province), written in 1980, was the first to make public this criticism of the Women's Federation. The previous year she had written a letter to *Chinese Women* complaining about the difficulties faced by women workers in her city. Disappointed at the lack of response, she decided in 1980 to write directly to Deng Yingchao, Deputy Chairman of the Women's Federation. "I am an ordinary young woman worker," wrote Shi Xingrong.

I know that you are occupied with important matters and that every minute is extremely valuable to you. Still, after thinking it over, I have decided to tell you the ideas and suggestions about women's work that have been buried in my heart for a long time.

When the Fourth National Women's Congress was held, we laboring women congratulated ourselves that after the ten years of chaos [the Cultural Revolution], we had at last found our "mother." . . . Reports and decisions made at the Congress were very encouraging indeed. But three years have passed since then and the record of work among women is very disappointing. Some Women's Federation cadres have not taken the implementation of the spirit of the Congress as their own responsibility. They have remained ignorant of the problems facing women workers and, even when they have been aware of our grievances, have shown little response. We do not even know who is the chairwoman of the city or district Women's Federation, nor do we know how the representatives to the various levels of the Women's Federation are elected, or whose interests they represent. I have heard that some are appointed by the leadership. Why don't women have the right to elect their own representatives? How can we expect representatives appointed by the leadership to communicate to the higher levels of government the problems we working women face? . . . A few statistics show how little they have done to help women publicize and solve their problems.

Violations of women's rights have been frequently reported by the press. But I don't know whether the Women's Federation has conducted any investigations or done anything to solve these problems. After each incident the Women's Federation and women's magazines express their indignation. But it is really a pity that so many of these "Zhuge Liang's" [clever strategists] are never around when the incidents take place.[25]

Shi's letter to Deng Yingchao documented many of the problems she and other women workers faced: discrimination against women in the calculation of wage increases, priority given to male workers in housing, and the lack of adequate childcare facilities. She concluded by calling upon the Women's Federation to stop relying on phone calls, reports, and meetings to solve these problems, but instead to send its cadres to the factories, homes, and dormitories of women workers to learn about their daily lives. "What we need is not lofty, empty words, but action!"[26]

Shi Xingrong's letter did provoke some action: she received letters from Deng Yingchao as well as from the editors of *Chinese Women* (which eventually asked Shi for permission to publish the entire exchange). The national Women's Federation instructed the officials from the Shaanxi Province Women's Federation and from the Baoji Municipal Women's Federation immediately to investigate Shi's complaints, and in one of her letters Shi described the delight of the women workers at her factory when Women's Federation cadres came to interview them both at work and in their homes (although in Shi's own case her 2.3-square-meter room was so small that the leaders had to meet with her in the hallway). "Although the problems faced by me and by other women cannot possibly be solved overnight," Shi wrote in her final letter, "the serious attitude of the All-China Women's Federation toward the demands and proposals of an ordinary woman worker has shown me that they have not forgotten us or confined themselves to empty words." [27]

The response of the Women's Federation to Shi Xingrong's letter was perhaps indicative of an increasing tendency for the Federation to concern itself with the concrete problems faced by both urban and rural women. In some cases it even began to act as an advocate for women. In previous chapters of this book we have seen that some local branches of the Women's Federation were aggressive in investigating cases of infanticide and abuse of women; in other cases the Women's Federation played an active role in opposing factories' attempts to impose "prolonged maternity leave." When economists proposed the withdrawal of women from the workforce to solve the problem of urban unemployment, the Women's Federation denounced and eventually scuttled the proposal.

Beginning in 1982, in response to increasing wife abuse and infanticide resulting from the one-child-family policy, the Women's Federation undertook a government-initiated campaign to protect the rights of women and children. In the context of this campaign the activities of the Women's Federation became increasingly varied. It opened legal counseling offices to help women "cope with such problems as ill-treatment by husbands and parents-in-law, infidelity, and worries about property and child support after a divorce." [28] Women who were physically abused by their husbands and girls whose parents intervened in arranging their marriages could seek legal advice from the Women's Federation. The response to this service was so enormous that the Federation had to set up classes to train more women to serve as legal advisers. [29]

Some cities adopted local regulations for the protection of women's and children's rights, making it possible for the Women's Federation to punish individuals found guilty of violating women's rights—either by imposing a fine or, in serious cases, sending them to labor reform. In one case at a weaving factory in Shanghai, for instance, a male worker had gotten his girlfriend pregnant and then forced her to go to the country-side for an abortion three times in one year. His work unit tried to punish him for what it considered irresponsible behavior, but until the local regulations to protect the rights of women and children were adopted in 1985, there was no legal basis for charges against him. Once the regulations were passed, the Women's Federation worked with factory officials to impose a hefty fine on the man.[30]

In addition to these activities to protect women's legal rights, the Women's Federation expressed concern about other aspects of women's lives. In Shanghai, for example, the Women's Federation set aside three days every week when women could come to its office to discuss any problems they had either at home or at work. Furthermore, the Federation established a research section (staffed at least partly by women who had studied sociology at a university) that regularly visited factories, schools, and other work units employing women, to conduct surveys and interviews and identify the major problems facing women.[31]

Although it is difficult to determine how far-reaching these efforts of the Women's Federation were, it is possible that the Federation gradually became an organization perceived by women as more relevant to their daily lives. No matter how far the Women's Federation moved in the direction of representing and defending women's interests, however, it remained a top-down, government-sponsored organization, rather than one independently formed by women. Moreover, most of its efforts on behalf of women were still undertaken in conjunction with state policy.

Independently organized, grass-roots women's organizations were not allowed in the decades after 1949; the existence of the Women's Federation was presumed to obviate the need for any other women's organizations. Yet in the mid-1980's, several women's associations emerged—some formed with the encouragement of the government, some formed spontaneously by women themselves. These were indicative of an increasing belief that women needed a "separate sphere." As one young woman wrote when proposing the establishment of a "women's palace" (*funü gong*): "Now almost everywhere there are 'youth palaces,' 'workers' cultural palaces,' and 'recreation centers for old cadres.' The only people who do not have their own center are women. 'Women hold up half the sky' should not be an empty slogan. . . . Why don't women have their own 'women's palace?'"[32]

A number of professional and intellectual women joined mutual-aid organizations known as "friendly societies" (*lianyihui*). It is difficult to determine exactly how many of these societies existed; a Women Engineers' Friendly Society in Shanghai, a Women Journalists' Friendly Society in Shenyang, and a Shenyang Women Intellectuals' Friendly Society were all reported in the press. In addition, an All-China Women Entrepreneurs' Association was formed for women managers.[33] Although confronting issues of discrimination against women in the professions did not appear to be an explicit goal of the friendly societies, they were concerned with the failure of professional women to advance as rapidly as their male colleagues. Surveys revealed that few women participated in the already existing mixed-gender professional societies. In Shanghai, for example, whereas close to 40 percent of technical workers were women, only 10 percent of the membership of the more than one hundred societies for technicians were female. This meant women missed "many opportunities for study and exchanging ideas."[34] The major goal of the friendly societies, then, was to provide women a forum where they could establish contact with one another and exchange information. The Shanghai Women Engineers' Society also offered technical classes for women, and planned to establish programs for communication between Chinese and foreign women engineers.[35] Ultimately, the friendly societies were intended to establish an "old-girls'" network in a society based on "connections" (*guanxi*).

The women involved in forming the friendly societies might not have thought they were doing anything radical, but some men found the establishment of women's organizations threatening and criticized their existence. Commenting on the proliferation of women's friendly societies, for example, a man named Zong Weizi wrote an article declaring that even though the societies were "advantageous for raising the voice of women . . . from the perspective of society as a whole the number of women's professional societies should not be allowed to increase." He argued, first, that the formation of gender-based associations was historically regressive. "The establishment of social contact between men and women was one of the achievements of the May Fourth Movement. If too many women's friendly societies are established today, that is equivalent to letting women have separate activities." This, he believed, would be found undesirable by the majority of women. To prove this he proposed that two meetings be held on the same day: one for young news reporters, the other for female news reporters. "Then see which one more of the women attend." (Presumably he expected them to prefer the first.)

Furthermore, he argued, if women were to have their own activities, the number of unmarried men and women would increase because they would have fewer occasions to meet. Social get-togethers between male steel workers and female textile workers in the 1950's had been organized precisely to help people find mates, he recalled. Since the majority of women joining the friendly societies were established professional women who most likely were already married, the relevance of this concern is not clear, but it underlines the threat this author felt at the withdrawal of women to a separate sphere. Zong's final reason for opposing the friendly societies was that he perceived no rationale for their existence. "If women's friendly societies are going to be established, they should be in professions in which women are discriminated against, so they can struggle for women's rights. But there is absolutely no need to set up such an organization for women news reporters—how many people are there who look down on women reporters?" Zong concluded by criticizing what he perceived as separatist organizing as a means of achieving gender equality. "If people really want to advocate equality between men and women, then they should organize groups in which men and women will work together to study women's problems." [36]

The idea of forming separate organizations for women extended beyond professionals. In 1985, trade unions in many cities organized special women's committees, charged to "fight sexual discrimination and protect women's rights." They were also supposed to encourage women to play an active role in management and in political affairs. [37] We have no information indicating how many of these committees were actually formed, or how effectively they functioned.

Another type of women's institution that began to emerge in the mid-1980's was women's schools. These were not an entirely new phenomenon in socialist China; coeducation had not become the norm until the Cultural Revolution. In some cases, all-girls' schools were reinstituted in the 1980's in order to give women greater opportunities to develop intellectually. As the president of Fudan University, Xie Xide (herself a graduate of Smith College in the 1940's) said, praising the opening of a senior middle school for girls in Shanghai, "Separate schools for girls are very important; they give girls more self-confidence because they have no boys to compare themselves to." [38]

More commonly, however, the newly founded women's schools were not designed to help women eventually compete with their male counterparts. Instead, as observed in Chapter 7, they aimed to track women into traditionally female professions. In at least some cases their establishment was part of the rejection of the radical ideology of the Cultural Revolution which insisted that women could do anything men could do. As the female vice-governor of Gansu province said, commenting on the opening of a women's vocational school in her province:

In the past in our country, educational institutions did not consider the biological differences between men and women. A few years ago, they had those "March 8th Women's Drilling Teams," classes for women electricians, etc. . . . Having women do work that men can do better is not suitable or scientific. Now reforms are taking place in the cities, and women have become "surplus people." Moreover, there are many jobs that should be done by women that women do not know how to do.

The Gansu Province Women's Vocational School thus offered classes in education, psychology, ethics, aesthetics, and family relations, as well as clothing design, cooking, cosmetics, nursing, and typing, to girls between the ages of fifteen and twenty.[39] The Dalian Women's Vocational School and the Shanghai Women's Vocational School offered almost identical curricula.[40] The idea was to combine basic education with vocational training in areas deemed suitable for women.

Of all the women's institutions that emerged in the mid-1980's, only the women's studies groups formed at several universities appear to have been genuine, spontaneously formed organizations concerned with analyzing and eliminating gender discrimination. A first, tentative effort to form a women's studies group was made at Beijing University in the aftermath of the 1980 elections for representatives to the National People's Congress. The woman who had run on the slogan that "women are human beings too" apparently decided, after losing the election, to organize a group to study women's problems; its goals would be to improve "Chinese women's awareness of themselves and women's personal development, put an end to women's self-censorship, and call on society as a whole to alter the context of women's lives."[41]

In 1984 a women's studies group was formed at Fudan University in Shanghai by members of the Foreign Languages Department.[42] It was initiated by two faculty members who had spent the 1983–84 academic year studying at Smith College, where they were exposed to women's studies courses. Initially, they did not intend to apply what they had seen of women's studies programs in the United States to China. But when they returned to Fudan, both found that many of the older women in their department were angry and bitter about their unequal status. In essence, faculty women had been penalized for their superior language skills: since their ability to speak foreign languages surpassed that of their male colleagues, the women were consistently assigned to teach the time-consuming basic language classes, while men taught the more interesting literature classes. Whereas most women had to teach eight hours a week, many men in the department taught just two hours a week. This meant that the women had much less time than men to conduct their own research, and as promotions were based on publications, they were at a severe disadvantage.

Discrimination against women seemed evident in almost every aspect of the Foreign Languages Department. Although the majority of students in the department were women, only male students were assigned to remain in the department as teachers. Almost all the highly coveted opportunities for faculty members to earn advanced degrees abroad were given to men. Anger and frustration thus made women in the department receptive to the idea of forming a women's studies group. Yet forming such a group without official sponsorship was a radical step. Although the political climate in the mid-1980's was relatively relaxed, no precedents existed for such an organization. As one of the members remarked, "This is the first time that any of us have done something on our own initiative. We're used to being told what to do by the leaders. This is the first time we feel really free to say whatever we want." Moreover, women's studies was utterly nonexistent in China, and women had reason to believe that officials would discourage rather than approve its establishment as an area of inquiry. But at Fudan the group obtained official approval from the president of the university, Xie Xide, perhaps because she was a woman who had studied and traveled extensively in the United States and Western Europe.

Although the group was formed largely in response to women's dissatisfaction with their unequal treatment in the department, most of the group's activities had an academic bent. The group's avowed long-range goal was to develop an interest in women's studies in universities throughout China by conducting research and writing about achievements of women, the changing roles of women, and comparisons of Chinese and foreign women. The group also hoped to offer courses in women's studies and to develop its own library.[43]

Elsewhere in China, women's studies groups began to appear in a variety of contexts. For example, convinced that women did not have equal status, some women members of population research institutes in several cities agreed to form a women's studies group.[44] Yet another type of women's studies group was formed by female historians in 1984. At the annual meeting of the Association for Research on American History (Meiguo lishi yanjiu hui), a historian from Beijing University, Qi Wenying, proposed to develop a program in women's history. She received the support of many women members of the association. The group agreed to collaborate in editing an abridged translation of *Notable American Women*, and to prepare an introductory textbook in American women's history. They hoped that eventually their writings would provide a methodology that could be applied to research on Chinese women.[45]

Perhaps responding to this spontaneous emergence of women's studies groups, the Women's Federation in several cities began to integrate them into Federation-sponsored women's studies programs. The Shanghai Women's Federation, for instance, established a women's studies section in

1985, and a city-wide women's studies association in mid-1986. To celebrate the occasion, the Federation held a conference on theories of women's studies, the first of its kind to take place in China.[46] Papers were presented on topics such as "Women's Studies and Theories of Women's Liberation," "China Must Have Its Own Women's Studies," "The Relationship Between the Economic Reforms and Women's Liberation," and "The Development and Current Status of Women's History Abroad."[47] The Canton Women's Federation subsequently held a conference to establish a women's studies society in fall 1986, and the All-China Women's Federation planned a national women's studies conference to be held in spring 1987. The newness of these women's studies organizations in 1986 made it impossible to assess their impact. On one hand, the independently formed groups would most likely be absorbed into the Women's Federation, changing their agendas and their grass-roots nature in the process. On the other hand, though, government involvement in women's studies granted it unprecedented legitimacy as an area of inquiry.[48]

The authors of feminist outcries, and the women involved in the establishment of women's schools, professional associations, and women's studies groups, shared neither an analysis of women's problems nor a vision of solutions. They did not constitute an organized women's movement. Indeed, little if any dialogue took place among these critics of women's unequal social status. In some cases they did not even know of one another's existence. Nonetheless, they represented an emerging feminist consciousness.

From the May Fourth Movement of 1919 on, feminism in twentieth-century China was primarily an urban intellectual phenomenon. The feminist consciousness that emerged in the mid-1980's was no exception. Only urban women enjoyed the material conditions that made it possible to think critically about their status: most had jobs that gave them an income of their own, access to housing apart from family, and the possibility of divorce. As avid readers of the press and popular magazines, urban women were more likely to be aware of the commonality of their problems than their rural sisters. Finally, exposure (and in some cases travel) to the West was a factor in the emergence of a feminist consciousness, affecting urban women far more than their rural sisters. The latter, constituting the vast majority of Chinese women, most likely knew nothing about women's and feminist movements in Western countries. As one of our friends commented, "If peasant women accepted Western feminist ideas, then the whole country would really be turned upside down!"

Translations

By the mid-1980's, women such as the authors of "To Discriminate Against Women Is to Discriminate Against Your Own Mother" and "Four Questions" began to publish statements protesting the multiple forms of discrimination they faced. Other writers were quite specific in their critiques. For example, the woman who wrote "A Reply to 'Women Are Too Powerful'" objects to the increasingly popular notion that meek and submissive women were the most desirable wives, while "strong" women who were committed to their careers were to be avoided. The author of "Woman Is Not the Moon" eloquently argues that women should not depend on their husbands to make them feel successful, but should strive for their own achievements. In "An Analysis of 'Long-Haired, Short-Sighted,'" a writer encourages women to overcome the narrowness of their lives, so that they can achieve greater equality. Sometimes a woman's major obstacle to equality was within her own home, and convincing a husband to respect her career was a necessary first step, as described by the author of "Discussing Women's Liberation with My Husband."

To Discriminate Against Women Is to Discriminate Against Your Own Mother

"Baby boys and baby girls are both born of their mother's flesh to be loved dearly." Then why are baby girls being killed and abandoned? One very important reason is that the bad habit of looking down on women, held over from the old days, has not yet been eliminated.

In recruiting workers and admitting students, some places have required that women get a much higher exam score than men. In the better work units, admission of children to nurseries and permission to have a child are granted to women. But allocation of housing, fuel, etc., are granted to men. There is even an instance at the Lanzhou Petroleum Machinery Factory where male employees who live in factory housing pay no rent; those who live outside are given a rent subsidy of 1.5 yuan each month. But female employees must pay full rent, and those who live outside receive no subsidy at all. In the Electricity Bureau of a certain city, male employees pay 5.5 cents per unit while female employees pay the standard price of 21 cents. At the Zhangyu County Knitting Factory, women workers make up 65.4 percent of the workforce. Once, when wages were being adjusted, the leadership used the excuse that they had to show special concern for the difficulty male workers had finding mates to justify raising their salaries one grade (except for one man, whose work was unsatisfactory). But only a few "particularly outstanding" women received promotions.

This phenomenon of discrimination against women happens every-

where. The examples are too numerous to mention. In 1948, at a conference on women's work held at Pingshan county in the Xibaipo Liberated
District, I had the opportunity to hear with my own ears Comrade Zhou
Enlai say something like this: How can one discriminate against women?
Our mothers are women. From now on, if someone looks down on
women you can say to him: To discriminate against women is to discriminate against your own mother!

Those who want to achieve women's liberation—and that includes
everyone who wants human liberation—should remember Comrade
Zhou Enlai's teaching.

SOURCE: Liu Heng, "Qishi funü jiushi qishi ni ziji de muqin" (To discriminate against
women is to discriminate against your own mother), *Renmin ribao*, January 19, 1984, 4.

Four Questions

Times have changed,
Men and women are equal.
Then why, in a certain production brigade,
Are men and women not treated equally?
They get different pay for the same work.
So men and women are different.

Times have changed,
Men and women are equal.
Then why in a certain factory
That is recruiting workers are they not treated equally?
If a man is hired the terms are flexible,
If a woman is hired the terms are strict.

Times have changed,
Men and women are equal.
Then why in a certain family
Do they respect boys and look down on girls?
If a baby boy is born the mother is happy,
If a baby girl is born she does not like it.

Times have changed,
Men and women are equal.
Then why is it that when a certain school
Admits students they are not treated equally?
To admit women they look at the score,
To admit men the score can go down.

Times have changed,
Men and women are equal.

It is natural to have both men and women.
The old feudal thinking
Must be eliminated to the core!

SOURCE: Wang Fuhua, "Si wen" (Four questions), *Renmin ribao manhua zengkan*, March 5, 1983.

A Reply to "Women Are Too Powerful"

I have heard it said that at present Chinese men admire weak women who are "meek, submissive, sweet, and neat," and that they are wary of strong women who have personality, vibrancy, and talent. They are afraid to marry strong women, fearing damage to their self-respect and prestige.

Therefore some "old maids" . . . must hide their loneliness and search for happiness in their profession. Therefore those heroic husbands who cannot stand the virtue of "being on an equal footing" first quarrel with, and then leave, their wives. Therefore, "real men" (*nanzihan*) cry out, "Women must not be too powerful!" "Return to the stove!" "Men plant, women weave, this is an unalterable principle!" "You must stand behind your husband's success!"

Women's liberation is so difficult; being a woman is difficult, and being a strong woman is even more difficult! How many women, in order to launch a career, have had to worry about all kinds of things, face all kinds of competition, struggle day and night, and still bear the pressure that comes from society, home, and even relatives? Imagine if women returned to the stoves and depended on their husbands—all day following their husbands, waiting on them. Men would still sigh, "Ah, those women, those women."

Of course, I do not agree with the notion of a kind of "manlike woman" or "womanlike man." Strong women are not crude shrews. The feelings of Eastern women are very introverted and deep. The traditional virtue of gentleness must still be cultivated. It is not necessary to pit women against men in an antagonistic relationship. In society, women and men should receive the same pay for the same work; in the family, the couple should respect and love each other. The duty of being a wife and mother is also important.

SOURCE: Chen Bin (female), "Wei 'nüren taiwei' dabian" (A reply to "Women are too powerful"), *Fujian qingnian*, 5 (May 1985), 18.

Woman Is Not the Moon

The play "The Return of an Old Acquaintance on a Rainy Night" (*Fengxue guren lai*) contains the following words: "Woman is not the moon. She cannot depend on the brightness of someone else to make herself shine." This is a verse that comes from real-life experience. It is a general philosophy that expresses what a large number of women feel in their hearts. Many people know this truth, but there is no better way to express it than these words. It is a pure truth.

Woman is not the moon. It is true, a woman is not an appendage of a man. As a member of society she has independent qualities; she has all the behavior, morality, intelligence, and ability of a human being. She can work and be creative. Isn't that true? Take Madame Curie—everyone has heard of this famous scientist—her contribution to society is certainly no less than that of her husband, Pierre Curie. In the scientific sky full of so many shining stars, hers is one shining all by itself, beautifully and brilliantly. Nothing can compare to it, and it will shine eternally.

Didn't our own country's contemporary woman writer Ding Ling (*The Sun Shines Over the Sanggan River*) win the Stalin Prize for Literature? The famous scientists Ling Lanying and Xiu Ruijian, the gynecologist Lin Qiaozhi, the singer Zhu Mingying—aren't they all women? Who among them did not depend on her own hard struggle and self-sacrifice to contribute to society and thus make herself shine?

These are things that many of us women understand. The problem is that many people are oppressed by old ideas and the old consciousness. They believe that as women, we don't have to be strong. They think that as long as one finds a good husband to depend on, it will be enough to just live out one's days. Old ideas such as "Woman is one of man's ribs," "If a woman does not have a husband, her body does not have an owner," etc., still influence some people. [Many believe that] man is the supporter of the family; the only thing that a woman can do is help him at home as a virtuous wife and good mother; getting ahead is something for men to do. History and present circumstances make many of us women comrades oppressed and constrained. This makes it impossible for us to display our talents, intelligence, and creativity. We just become men's servants or their burden.

Woman is not the moon. She must rely on herself to shine. These are words that many pioneers of the women's liberation movement, valiant women, and heroines have inscribed with their own actions, tears, and blood. Let us treasure these words, remember them, and act on them. Hopefully each person can find her own path in life and develop her own brilliance.

SOURCE: Ting Lan, "Nüren bushi yueliang" (Woman is not the moon), *Nüzi shijie*, 6 (June 1985), 1.

An Analysis of "Long-Haired, Short-Sighted"

Perhaps some women will be angry when they read the title of this article. "Long-haired, short-sighted" is obviously a phrase making fun of women. What is there to analyze about it? Actually the fact that it is a sarcastic phrase does not prevent our dissecting it. From this we may learn something.

What is "sight" (*jianshi*)? People usually say that "sight" means having foresight and sagacity, broad vision, and the ability to tell truth from falsehood. Where does sight come from? "Seeing a lot and having broad knowledge"—this phrase suggests its origins. It comes directly from life experience and social intercourse, and indirectly from reading and education. Yet women go through life burdened by feudal teachings such as "A woman without knowledge is virtuous" or "Men are the masters of external affairs, women the mistresses of domestic affairs." Their companions are pots, bowls, ladles, plates, needles and thread, and brooms. Women are thus imprisoned in the home, eliminated from the world of social activity. Given this, is it fair to mock women for being "long-haired and short-sighted"?

And yet even in such restricted societies, there are still some heroic women, with literary or artistic talents, who have bold visions. Since the May Fourth Movement, among the pioneers of the revolution and among the Communist soldiers, some great women have made their mark on history. This is an effective response to "long-haired, short-sighted."

Since Liberation, the status of most women has undergone a fundamental change. There are notable women in almost every social field, women who work hard. However, among couples in which both husband and wife work, most of the housework and childrearing is the responsibility of the wife. Some real inequality still exists between men and women. Because of the weight of thousands of years of tradition, the idea of "respecting men and looking down on women" still often flashes before the eyes of some female comrades. Some women are not very open-minded and their vision is not very broad. They submit themselves to constraint by their husbands, children, and the small circle of the family. Pardon my saying this so directly, but they really are a little "short-sighted."

Women who are angry at the phrase "long-haired, short-sighted" should do everything they can to oppose it. They should have ideals, careers, self-confidence, and strength. They should use this reality to overturn the sarcastic phrase "long-haired, short-sighted." Each woman should embody the three roles of pioneer, mother, and wife. A woman should be successful both in her profession and in managing her home. Women need to work twice as hard as men. The new women of China are truly great. They are cautious and conscientious, work as hard as oxen, endure humiliation in order to fulfill their responsibilities, and are able to overcome every hurdle. Women's determination is the crucial thing.

At this point I must say a few words to our male comrades. You should not think that you are the only ones who should have careers, that you are the only ones who possess talent, and go looking for a tender "servant" for a mate. Can't women have careers? Is the formula true that "One career-minded person plus another career-minded person equals a chaotic and messy household?" If two people encourage each other, support each other, and share the housework, then the results will be better than if each acted independently.

In addition I would like to plead that society speedily develop "the third industry" (service work), to solve the problems of housework, childcare, and transportation. Women's household responsibilities need to be lightened by socializing housework. This will give women more time to study, enhance their abilities, participate more broadly in social activities, and "lengthen their sight."

SOURCE: Ouyang Man, "Xi 'toufa chang jianshi duan'" (An analysis of "long-haired, shortsighted"), *Zhongwai funü*, 5 (May 1985), 9.

Discussing Women's Liberation with My Husband

Perhaps when faced with this subject you will mockingly laugh and ask, "How much more do you want to liberate women?" It is true, in terms of employment, wages, and education I have not suffered any discrimination; nor have I endured the misfortune of an arranged marriage. So why did I insist on discussing women's liberation with my husband?

We need not dwell on the significance of women's liberation because you well know that in any society, the extent to which women have been liberated is a measure of the degree to which the entire society is liberated. However, whether or not a person's viewpoint is old or new is not measured by what he thinks, but rather by his actions, feelings, and emotions. An American woman, in an essay about women's liberation, wrote the following: One day she was driving the car by herself, and because of a part that had been on the blink for ages, the engine died. At the time she was furious at her husband—how could a husband allow his wife to drive a car that was not in working order! But then she suddenly reconsidered, and decided her reaction was wrong. Why had she assumed that fixing a car was a husband's responsibility? We should learn from the realization and self-criticism of this American woman. At the same time, we can see from this example that the subtlety of certain ideas not only permeates a person's thinking, but also seeps into a person's subconscious.

There are also an old and a new view on how to handle housework. This is absolutely not just an alarmist statement. You frequently ask, "Where are my socks?" "Where is my shirt?" "What about that pair of pants?" One scholar has described this phenomenon as male dependency on women. This scholar also said that men's dependence on women has become a major obstacle to the achievement of gender equality. Since we were married, shopping, cooking, and doing laundry have naturally fallen on my shoulders. It's as natural as it is for green leaves to grow on a tree in spring, and to fall from the tree in autumn. You, being a husband, often get done with work earlier than I, yet you are not willing to set foot in the kitchen. If you are hungry, you just wait for your wife to get home and cook for you. After dinner you just get up and leave, as if you were in a restaurant. You never think of touching the dirty clothes in the basket; instead you often complain, "I don't have any clean clothes to wear!" You simply assume that these are all things for a wife to take care of. This attitude is deeply embedded in your mind.

Our family, like thousands of young couples, has only a small room. We have space for only one desk. But the amount of time I have to use the tiny amount of space on the desk is too little. The desk is always covered with your books and papers. It never occurs to you that your wife might also need to use the desk.

Like you, I am a public servant with a job, and like you, I must contend with this world—studying, working, struggling, and carrying on. We exert the same amount of spiritual and physical energy. Because we are both human beings, after we married and formed a household we had even more of a struggle over dividing the housework. We both need spare time to study and improve ourselves. But just because I am a wife I must devote most of my spare time to cleaning the house, as if I were a maid. . . .

Perhaps you will say that this is a social problem, that I must wait until the level of production has been raised and the economy further developed so that housework can be fully socialized. Yes, I believe that the day will come when people can use robots as servants, and the concept of housework will completely vanish. But that day is still too far away. We still belong to this historical epoch, and we must acknowledge all that housework involves. Can you analyze this: upon what assumptions and ideas is your letting the housework fall to me based? You are like millions of ardent youth: you are absolutely willing to be an advocate of new ideas, but at home you still act according to old ideas. This is because these ideas are advantageous to you. Apparently the subconscious is very utilitarian in choosing between old and new values.

Comrade husband, do not overlook the attitude of men toward housework, just as that American woman did not overlook her anger at her husband. This is a choice between old and new values. Since you know that the liberation of women is a measure of the general liberation of a society, then get moving and do some housework; at least reduce your dependence [on your wife]. The family is the cell of society. If equality between men and women can just be achieved within each cell, then the day when women will be liberated is not far off.

SOURCE: Xiaoshi (no surname), "Yu zhangfu tan nüxing jiefang" (Discussing women's liberation with my husband), *Zhongguo funü*, 2 (February 1986), 9.

Conclusion

How are the changes of the 1980's affecting the status of Chinese women? No clear-cut answer presents itself; it is impossible simply to say that women's position is either clearly improving or unequivocally deteriorating. The changes are too complex, and too recently begun, to permit such a judgment. Yet the lives of women have been changing more quickly than at any time since the early 1950's, and a preliminary assessment of those changes is in order.

In the 1980's, young women were no longer told, as were women in prerevolutionary China, that they were worthless and a burden to their families. Yet the message that they were inferior was still communicated to them, and given a scientific gloss that made it difficult to dispute. Official advice to young women emphasized that the Constitution guaranteed them legal equality, and that they should take responsibility for overcoming their own weaknesses and achieving real equality. Women of extraordinary achievement in the working world were presented as models for them to emulate. These models looked and behaved somewhat differently from the Iron Girls of the Cultural Revolution, but like the Iron Girls they were praised for making it in a man's world and contributing to the larger economic goals of national construction. Role models did little to prepare young women for the realities of gender discrimination.

Adornment and sexuality, topics that had been off-limits to the generation of the Cultural Revolution, dominated publications for young women in the 1980's. Attention to beauty and fashion was part of a growing concern with the quality of personal life, and clearly captured the public fancy. But the bejeweled, high-heeled, tastefully made-up young woman was no more free to create her own image than the Iron Girls of yore, and the image of the Iron Girls may have presented women with more possibilities for participation in the public realm. It remained to be seen whether codes of female dress and beauty would become less compulsory, or whether the compulsory standard of female appearance was merely becoming more Westernized.

Open discussion of female physiological development and sexuality replaced the silence and ignorance of earlier years. Yet though youthful sexual activity was apparently on the rise, traditional social values still condemned it as morally degenerate. Women were told by their elders that in a world of increasing sexual danger, they should take responsibility not only for their own chastity, but for keeping the sexual desires of men within acceptable social limits.

Love (how to recognize it, what to do about it) and courtship (when to initiate it, how to conduct it) were two of the most popular topics of debate and advice. Matchmaking became "modernized" with the advent of marriage introduction bureaus and personal advertisements. Couples were encouraged to value emotional attachment and compatibility rather than accepting the traditional criteria of family status or the more recent variation of matching political backgrounds. However, economic status remained an important consideration when young people chose a mate, and women attempted to marry men with higher socioeconomic status than their own, just as they had before 1949. Moreover, traditional notions of what made a good wife, although muted, still permeated public discussion. Many men wished to marry women less capable and less educated than they, and women looked for men whose strengths overshadowed their own. Women who were "too assertive" or "too career-minded" or "too old" found themselves at a disadvantage on the marriage market. As parents pulled out of the decision-making and political criteria became less important, new but equally rigid notions of desirability began to govern the process of courtship. And marriage remained virtually compulsory.

Funded by income earned under the economic reforms, weddings became increasingly extravagant. Efforts by the state to pare down wedding celebrations were not effective because the reforms had the overall effect of strengthening the family unit and giving it more money to spend. Still, women and their families were blamed for much of the extravagance. This was partly because women were considered guardians of almost all aspects of the domestic sphere. They very well might have been responsible for the extravagance, however, as weddings were one of the only occasions when a woman's value received public recognition. Insufficient gifts might suggest to the community that a bride was "second-rate."

In urban China, family structure began to change in the years after 1949, and with it patterns of family relationships. When women married, they no longer necessarily moved in with their husband's families. Depending on the availability of housing, young couples often obtained an apartment of their own, and in some cases they took a room in the home of the wife's parents. No matter where they lived, women maintained their ties to their natal families. Furthermore, in the cities at least, they had increasing power in the family because their jobs gave them access to income and social networks that were not directly dependent on the family. By the 1980's, state concern about the breakdown of traditional family relationships led to a renewed emphasis in the official press on how to be a good wife and daughter-in-law. These traditional female roles were dressed in modern garb. Women were told, for instance, to study the science of nutrition, and a host of new magazines instructed them in the fine arts of modern housewifery and motherhood. The assumption remained that it was the woman's responsibility to maintain a peaceful, harmonious family. Yet family harmony was often disrupted by the conflict between the state family planning policy and the desire of many families to have a son. Women bore the psychological and physical costs of this conflict.

Divorce was on the rise in the 1980's. It became increasingly easy to obtain because of the alienation-of-affection clause in the 1980 Marriage Law. Women were no longer necessarily trapped in emotionally dissatisfying marriages. Yet divorce remained economically and socially difficult for women. Their low salaries made it difficult for them to support a household, and divorcées were socially stigmatized. In addition, new mobility opportunities for men, such as attending a university, led some of them to abandon their wives. Women either did not have these advantages or were discouraged by social pressure from using them in this way.

To both Chinese and Western observers, the most disturbing effect of the economic reforms on women was the effect on employment outside the home. The reforms strengthened and in some cases reconstructed the sexual division of labor, keeping urban women in a transient, lower-paid, and subordinate position in the workforce. Female participation in the workforce was a crucial component of the Marxist strategy for women's liberation, and so the voices of women and women's advocates in China were raised in vociferous protest of discrimination against women in hiring. However, this discrimination was never presented as a result of new state policies. Rather, it was portrayed as the result of misguided decisions made by work units when they were allowed to take over the hiring process. Notwithstanding its stated commitment to equality for women, the state did not move to devise legal or administrative means to enforce equality in the workplace. In fact, to do so would have violated the spirit of the economic reforms, designed to grant local work units more independence in managing their own operations.

The economic reforms increased household income, and with it the ability to buy washing machines and other devices that saved female labor. Such devices were increasingly available to urban women. But the burden of housework and the responsibility for childcare remained primarily theirs. As the sexual division of labor in the workforce became more pronounced, it seemed unlikely that women's double burden would become lighter. The assumption that the household responsibilities of women took precedence over their outside jobs helped perpetuate their inferior position at work.

A woman was vulnerable to violence at every stage of life. Its forms ranged from female infanticide to forcing daughters to marry against their will to wife-beating to rape. Press reports indicated that violence had become more widespread because of the breakdown of public order during the Cultural Revolution. The increase may also have reflected better reporting. Government condemnation of violence against women dovetailed with two state interests. The first was the desire to establish the firm rule of law, after a period during the Cultural Revolution when the influence of law on daily life had been minimal. The second was the concern to limit population; continued preference for male offspring threatened the success of that policy, and related crimes like female infanticide and wife-beating were indications of the depth of popular resistance to it. Violence against women was not a new phenomenon in Chinese society, and its causes had not disappeared in the forty years since the revolution. It continued to constrict the lives of women at every point.

Responding to the changes brought about by economic reform and political liberalization, some women in the mid-1980's began to denounce publicly the unequal status of women in Chinese society. They differed, though, on the strategies necessary to improve their situation. Some called upon women to decrease their psychological dependence on men; others targeted male attitudes or state intervention as the crucial factors in women's liberation. This discussion was conducted by urban women; feminist voices were heard primarily in the cities. Despite their limited arena, these voices represented a growing culture of protest.

China in the 1980's was not a society silent about its social problems. Chinese writers attributed the inferior status of women to three main causes. The first was what they called "feudal remnants"—traditional attitudes that caused people to look down on women, and women's internalized notion of themselves as inferior. The press offered an upbeat solution to these problems: women should depend on the law and the Party to chastise discriminators, and never lose faith in their own abilities. Behind this advice was an assumption that it was just a matter of time until these feudal remnants disappeared. This analysis overlooked inequalities that were preserved or actively generated in the new society. It paid little attention to the pervasiveness of discrimination, or the difficulty of believing in oneself while being socialized to think that one was inferior.

The chaos caused by the Cultural Revolution was the second factor blamed for the problems of women. Chinese writing of the post-Mao decade exhaustively described the breakdown in social order and the ensuing damage to fundamental human relationships. It was said that China had lost a decade of economic and social progress, progress that would have raised the status of women. Women's organizations stopped functioning during this period, and serious advocacy for women came to a halt. In public political discussion, gender issues were subordinated to those of class. Yet the Iron Girls and some of the campaigns associated with the Cultural Revolution had had some positive influence on the self-perceptions of young women.[1]

In its effect on women the Cultural Revolution was seen by many American feminists as a positive period from which there was a subsequent retreat, one disastrous for women. Most Chinese writers of the post-Mao decade, in contrast, characterized it as a disastrous period that they were glad to leave behind. Both these viewpoints obscure important historical continuities between the Cultural Revolution and the present. In both periods, gender issues were subordinated to "more important, larger" issues—class struggle during the Cultural Revolution, modernization during the 1980's. In both periods, women were told they could succeed by overcoming their own natural limitations. The Cultural Revolution formula for success challenged the sexual division of labor and put women to work at such tasks as repairing high-voltage lines. In the 1980's, the sexual division of labor was actively supported by state policy, but women were still told that success lay in daring to think and act like men.

The third cause of women's subordination was said to be the new opening to the West. Contact with foreign culture was often presented as positive, but it was also criticized for bringing in "bourgeois influences." Western influence was frequently blamed for the increase in premarital sex, the threat of divorce, the decline of the harmonious Chinese household, and violence against women. Chinese readers were warned to be discriminating about what they took from the West, because some Western values were injurious to women. Chinese authors frequently asserted that China had a higher socialist moral order than the West, yet the socialist values they trumpeted sounded suspiciously like the traditional Chinese values for women—chastity, loyalty, unselfishness, and vigilance.

All three explanations of gender discrimination had something in common: they failed to explain why old problems persisted and new ones appeared. The causes were relegated to the distant past, the recent past, or external influences. But simply referring to a developmental stage such as feudalism, capitalism (as embodied in Western values), or even socialism was not adequate to explain these problems. How did historical forces combine with current social policies and arrangements to generate an inferior status for women?

After 1949, women were called upon by the state to contribute to economic construction. They bore many of the indirect costs of that construction, a trend that continued under the economic reforms of the 1980's. The state continuously expressed its commitment to gender equality after 1949, but that goal was just as continuously subordinated to other revolutionary concerns.[2]

Perhaps the most serious flaw in Chinese discussions of gender was the assumption that since China had had a socialist revolution, time alone would solve all remaining problems. Yet until gender was put at the center of an analytical model, it seemed likely not only that these problems would persist, but that their causes would remain opaque to those who raise criticism from within Chinese society about the situation of women.

State policy was crucial to women's status because in China the state has a virtual monopoly on political activity. Under these circumstances, change could not be expected to come from an autonomous and politically active women's movement. The situation of women could not change without state initiative. Undesirable as this situation might seem to feminists, it defined the possibilities for change in 1980's China. And as long as the state was controlled by people who eschewed gender as an important category of analysis, and made policy accordingly, women's subordination seemed certain to continue, if not by machination then by default.

In most respects, women's lives in 1980's China were radically improved from the situation before 1949. Discussion of "the woman question" in China in the 1980's was more detailed and critical than it had been at any time since Liberation, and it was no longer wholly guided by the assumption that women's liberation was virtually complete. It was acknowledged in China in the 1980's both that women had come a long way and that they had a long way to go. But where they came from and where they were going could not be understood simply by referring to progress from feudalism to socialism, or even from socialism to some version of Western-style industrialization. Important continuities marked the situation of women at all these stages, and not all these continuities could be explained as feudal remnants. The assumption that men were superior to women was not withering away; in fact, in some ways it was being reinforced. As long as this assumption remained intact, Chinese families would continue to prefer sons to daughters. And so long as they did, it would remain impossible for China to achieve balanced and limited population growth. A failure of population policy would in turn imperil the entire modernization effort, and with it the stability of China. Gender hierarchy in China was not "just" a peripheral issue of concern only to women. It was central to the way society was organized, and was perhaps the most important factor determining the quality of China's future.

Reference Matter

Notes

The following abbreviations are used in the Notes and Bibliography. Complete authors' names, titles, and publication data are given in the Bibliography, pp. 363–80.

JPRS	Joint Publications Research Service
MF	*Minzhu yu fazhi*
RMRB	*Renmin ribao*
ZF	*Zhongguo funü*
ZFB	*Zhongguo funü bao*
ZQ	*Zhongguo qingnian*
ZQB	*Zhongguo qingnian bao*

Introduction

1. For a discusson of the May Fourth Movement, see Chow; Spence; and Schwarcz.

2. For an analysis of the Party's attempts to mobilize women in the 1920's, see Gilmartin.

3. See Johnson; Stacey.

4. For an account of this campaign, and the serious resistance it met in many rural areas, see Johnson, 115–53.

5. Stacey, 211–16.

6. For a concise and lucid summary of the political history of the Cultural Revolution, see William Joseph, "Foreword," in Gao Yuan, *Born Red*; for one person's account of his experiences in that movement, see Gao Yuan.

7. This point is developed further in Young, "Chicken Little in China."

8. In addition to the works by Johnson and Stacey mentioned elsewhere in this introduction, the following works have been particularly useful to us: Wolf, *Women and the Family in Rural Taiwan*; Wolf, *Revolution Postponed*; Wolf and Witke; Parish and Whyte; Whyte and Parish; Croll, *Feminism and Socialism in China*; Croll, *Chinese Women Since Mao*; Diamond; Pasternak; Davin; and the essays in Young, *Women in China*.

Chapter 1

1. *Gei shaonü de xin*, i.

2. A typical book of advice, *Gei shaonü de xin* (Letters to Young Women), sketches the lessons that adults want adolescent girls to learn. The book is divided into 26 letters, each supposedly written to a different young woman by an uncle, aunt, teacher, older friend, or cousin. Strong stylistic similarities indicate that the

entire book is the work of a single author, and that the letter format is simply a device that allows the author to lecture his audience.

3. *Gei shaonü de xin,* 116; Zhang Qingyun et al., 72.

4. Zhang Qingyun et al., 72.

5. *Gei shaonü de xin,* 117; Zhang Qingyun et al., 75–78.

6. *Gei shaonü de xin,* 117; Zhang Qingyun et al., 73–74.

7. ZQB, Aug. 1, 1982, p. 3.

8. Research in North America indicates that the variations in brain structure are complex, little understood, and a matter of disagreement among scientists. Although the Chinese literature on the subject does not specify its sources, the theories presented are substantially the same as those developed by Jerre Levy in the United States. The work of Levy and other scientists in the field is meticulously reviewed and devastatingly critiqued by Anne Fausto-Sterling in *Myths of Gender,* 13–60.

9. ZQB, Aug. 1, 1982, p. 3. These assessments of female occupational potential echo the work of Garai and Scheinfeld, reviewed in Fausto-Sterling, 23–24 and *passim.*

10. *Gei shaonü de xin,* 118–19.

11. *Ibid.,* 5.

12. Zhang Qingyun et al., 74.

13. In interviews at six Chinese sites in 1980–81, anthropologist Margery Wolf found that people in both urban and rural areas believed that "once a girl reaches puberty, her intelligence becomes unfocused. . . . Instead of concentrating on her school work, her mind flits about, thinking of clothes and, oddly enough, domestic tasks. She no longer seems to put all of her intellectual energy into her school work, whereas boys are just the opposite." Wolf, *Revolution Postponed,* 131–32.

14. ZQB, Mar. 13, 1982, 4.

15. *Gei shaonü de xin,* 104–5.

16. *Ibid.,* 107.

17. *Ibid.,* 93.

18. Author's visit to a Shanghai day care center, Jan. 1984.

19. "Nan quan, nü wu," ZQB, Aug. 1982, 7.

20. ZQB, Oct. 29, 1981.

21. The percentage of female students to total number of students for 1981–83 are as follows:

	1983	1982	1981
Nationwide	42.5	42.4	42.5
Institutions of higher learning	26.9	26.2	24.4
Secondary specialized schools	35.9	34.6	33.1
Regular secondary schools	39.5	39.2	39.0
Agricultural/vocational middle schools	39.2	38.6	40.1
Primary schools	43.7	43.7	44.0

Data are from State Statistical Bureau, PRC: *Statistical Yearbook of China 1984,* 490; and *Statistical Yearbook of China 1983,* 518. Young people receiving higher education account for less than 2 percent of their age cohort in China. *Nüzi shijie,* 6 (June 1985), 8.

22. ZQB, Feb. 23, 1982; Tan Fuyun, "Funü yao you zhiqi zheng diyi," 31. The analysis of the gender gap in literacy rates is derived from Population Census Office, 316–17.

23. *Gei shaonü de xin,* 19.

24. Zhao Bingren.

25. ZFB, 30 (Apr. 24, 1985), 2.

26. *Nüzi shijie,* 6 (June 1985), 8–9.

27. "China's Report on the Elimination of Discrimination Against Women," supplementary report to *Women of China*, 3 (Mar. 1984), 3.

28. *Gei shaonü de xin*, 20.   29. *Ibid.*, 21.
30. *Ibid.*, 20.   31. *Gei shaonü de xin*, 19–20.
32. *Ibid.*, 121.   33. *Ibid.*, 119.
34. *ZF*, 3 (Mar. 1965), 14.

35. *RMRB*, Mar. 3, 1973, trans. *Beijing Review*, Mar. 16, 1973, in Croll, *Women's Movement*, 27.

36. See, for instance, the account by Ling Qiao in the documentary film "Small Happiness" of how she became a tractor driver. "Small Happiness," directed by Carma Hinton and Richard Gordon, Long Bow Films, 1984.

37. Xin Qin, 24–25.

38. Meng Xiaoyun, Jan. 8, 1986, 2.

39. *ZQB*, 1982: June 29, 2; June 8, 2; May 11, 1; June 12, 2; Aug. 19, 1; Aug. 2, 1; July 3, 2.

40. *ZQB*, 1982: Mar. 18, 4; Mar. 14, 5; He Yaqing, 2–6; Feng Xing, 24–26.

41. *ZQB*, 1982: May 8, 2; June 5, 1; Aug. 17, 2.

42. *ZQB*, 1982: June 17, 2; Aug. 31, 3; Aug. 17, 2.

43. *Gei shaonü de xin*, 10.

44. Zhang Haidi, 26–27. For an update on Zhang's health and outlook on life, see *Baokan wenzhai*, Jan. 16, 1986.

45. *RMRB*, May 19, 1983, 4, translated in *China Report*, June 30, 1983, 66–69.

46. The discussion began in the June 1983 issue of *ZF*; only the November and December installments are cited here. "Bashi niandai de nüqingnian gai zenyang shenghuo?"

47. "Bashi niandai de nüqingnian gai zenyang shenghuo?"

48. *ZF*, 11 (Nov. 1983), 31.   49. *Ibid.*, 30–31.
50. *Ibid.*, 31.   51. Personal interview.

Chapter 2

1. Jin Feng, 5.
2. *Ibid.*, 6.
3. *Ibid.*, 4; *Zhongwai funü*, 1 (Jan. 1985), 4–5.
4. Fan Qingshan, 36.   5. *Gei shaonü de xin*, 47.
6. Zhang Wei, 40–41.   7. *Shizhuang*, 4 (1983), 48.
8. *Ibid.*, *passim* and 13, 22–23.   9. *Ibid.*, *passim* and 20.
10. *Shizhuang*, 4 (1984), 16, 31, 33.   11. *Ibid.*, 5 (1985), 51.
12. "Diyici fuyue."
13. *RMRB*, Dec. 26, 1984; also see *Zhongwai funü*, 2 (Feb. 1985), 38.
14. *ZQB*, July 4, 1982, 8; *Zhongwai funü*, 2 (Feb. 1985), 39.
15. *ZF*, 6 (June 1985), inside cover; Zhang Mingming.
16. Fan Qingshan, 36.   17. *ZF*, 6 (June 1985), 19.
18. *Xinmin wanbao*, Dec. 31, 1984.   19. Zhang Wei, 40–41.
20. Dong Tian'en et al., *passim*.
21. See, for example, *Fujian qingnian*, 5 (May 1985), 46–47.
22. *ZF*, 4 (Apr. 1985), inside front and back covers.
23. *ZF*, 5 (May 1985), inside back cover.
24. *ZQB*, Dec. 19, 1981, 4; *Nüzi shijie*, 6 (June 1985), 39; *Xiandai jiating*, 5 (May 1985), 38; *Zhongwai funü*, 5 (1985), 31; *ZQB*, Apr. 25, 1982, 8; *Gei shaonü de xin*, 52.

25. *ZQB*, Apr. 25, 1982, 8.
26. *Gei shaonü de xin*, 48.
27. *Zhongwai funü*, 1 (Jan. 1985), 5.
28. *ZQB*, Mar. 23, 1982, 3.
29. *Xinmin wanbao*, Oct. 26, 1986.
30. *Gei shaonü de xin*, 3–5.
31. *Ibid.*, 4.   32. *Ibid.*, 99.
33. *Ibid.*, 44–45.   34. *Ibid.*, 56.
35. For a contemporary Western feminist analysis of the role of a feminine aesthetic in perpetuating gender inequality, see Brownmiller, *passim*.
36. Lei Wenxian, Part 3, 30; "Yindao chuzhong nüsheng."
37. Xu Jin, 56.
38. See, for instance, "Xiao meimei mo jinghuang," and Xie Hua.
39. Xu Jin, 56; "Zhengque bawo qingchunqi"; Lei Wenxian, Part 1, 20; Tang Shaoyun.
40. Jiang Yuanming.   41. "Zhengque bawo qingchunqi."
42. Xu Jin, 56.   43. *Ibid.*, 57.
44. Yu Ronghe.   45. See, for instance, Xie Bozhang.
46. *ZQB*, Sept. 11, 1982, 4; *ZF*, 9 (Sept. 1980), 40–41.
47. *ZF*, 8 (Aug. 1982), 47.
48. "Xiao meimei mo jinghuang"; Li Feng.
49. Lei Wenxian, Part 3, 30.   50. *Ibid.*, Part 1, 20–21.
51. *Ibid.*, Part 2, 44.   52. *Ibid.*, Part 3, 30.
53. *ZQB*, Apr. 22, 1982, 3.
54. This public discussion of "premature love" picked up where a 1950's debate on the same subject had left off. "Premature love" and adolescent sexual activity in the 1950's, however, apparently were not as widespread as in the 1980's, or at least were not treated as thoroughly in the press. For examples of the 1950's articles, see "Do Not Start Making Love Too Early," and "Do Not Make Love to Middle School Students Who Are Still Young."
55. Liao Shijie et al., 115.   56. *Ibid.*, 115–18.
57. *Ibid.*, 118–19.   58. Tang Shaoyun.
59. *Jiefang ribao*, Aug. 8, 1985.   60. "Zhengque bawo qingqunqi."
61. "Yindao chuzhong nüsheng."   62. Tang Shaoyun.
63. "Yindao chuzhong nüsheng."   64. *Ibid.*
65. Zhang Zhiguang and Wu Jing.
66. See, for example, "Jieda yige nüzhongxuesheng de nanti."
67. Ke Cunjie.   68. *Gei shaonü de xin*, 38–40.
69. *ZQB*, Mar. 28, 1982, 1.   70. "Xiaomie zhe pohuai."
71. *Ibid.*
72. *ZQB*, Mar. 21, 1982, 1. On other arrests, see *ZQB*, 1982: Mar. 7, 1; Apr. 4, 1; Apr. 18, 8.
73. "Qingchu wuran"; *ZQB*, Apr. 22, 1982, 1.
74. He Xiuping.   75. *ZQB*, May 18, 1982, 3.
76. Chen Xuliang.   77. *Gei shaonü de xin*, 31–32.
78. On the spiritual pollution campaign, see Thomas B. Gold, "'Just in time!,'" *passim*.
79. *ZQB*, Apr. 20, 1985.
80. Xin Zheng.   81. Wang Yanming.
82. "'Xianggang xiaojie' de beiju."   83. Ma Xiaojun.
84. Gong Peide.   85. Wang Qiuliang and Zhu Wenjie.

86. Li Zengliang and An Huijun.
87. Dong Ye, 25.
88. *Ibid.*, 24.
89. Zhang Qingyun et al., 57.
90. *Gei shaonü de xin*, 126.
91. Zhang Qingyun et al., 60.

Chapter 3

1. *Jiefang ribao*, Aug. 10, 1985.
2. *Women of China*, 11 (Nov. 1983), 10. A survey of 739 Shanghai women found that 62.5 percent of those who married between 1977 and 1982 had been introduced by relatives, neighbors, or friends. From 1937 to 1982, the percentage of couples introduced by these matchmakers increased as the percentage of marriages arranged by the parents dropped from 57 percent to zero. Xue Suzhen, 17.
3. Christopher Wren.
4. *Yuelao bao*, 7 (July 1985), 1, 7.
5. *ZQB*, Dec. 6, 1981, 8.
6. See, for instance, *Tianjin ribao*, Feb. 16, 1981.
7. *ZF*, 11 (Nov. 1984), 46; also see *Shanghai qingnian bao*, Oct. 10, 1980.
8. *ZQB*, May 8, 1980; *Tianjin ribao*, Oct. 20, 1980.
9. Shan Guangnai; *ZQB*, Oct. 6, 1981; Aug. 15, 1982, 5; *Tianjin ribao*, cited in *China Daily*, Feb. 6, 1984.
10. Hong Qin, 15.
11. The Tianjin incident was reported in the *Tianjin ribao*. On Guilin, see *ZQB*, Aug. 15, 1982, 5.
12. *ZQB*, Jan. 3, 1982, 1.
13. Wang Ping.
14. Xu Youhua.
15. *ZFB*, June 5, 1985, 2.
16. *Ibid*; Yan An.
17. *ZQB*, Oct. 29, 1981.
18. Shan Guangnai; Hong Qin, 17, reported a success rate of 10 percent in Beijing, 12 percent in Shenyang, and 14 percent in Guangzhou.
19. Cai Xiaofeng and Xu Haimei, 32.
20. Shan Guangnai; Cai Xiaofeng and Xu Haimei, *passim*; Yan An.
21. Cai Xiaofeng and Xu Haimei, *passim*.
22. Yan An.
23. *ZF*, 4 (Apr. 1985), 46.
24. *ZF*, 11 (Nov. 1984), 47.
25. *Ibid*.
26. *Ibid.*, 46.
27. *Funü shenghuo*, 12 (Dec. 1983), 48.
28. Lu Zhenqiu.
29. See, for example, *ZF*, 1 (Jan. 1985), 47, and *ZF*, 4 (Apr. 1985), 46.
30. *ZF*, 11 (Nov. 1984), 47.
31. Ke Fu.
32. *ZQN*, 6 (June 1985), 54.
33. *ZF*, 2 (Feb. 1985), 47; *ZF*, 6 (June 1985), 47.
34. Ding Yuan, 33; *Xiandai jiating*, 1 (Jan. 1985), 34; *Zhongguo laonian bao*, Oct. 18, 1985; Ke Fu.
35. Ke Fu.
36. Ding Yuan, 33; Ke Fu.
37. Lu Zhenqiu.
38. Johnson, 115–53.
39. *The Marriage Law of the People's Republic of China.*
40. *Xinmin wanbao*, Jan. 27, 1986. The forum that released these statistics was sponsored by the Sociology Research Institute of People's University and the editorial committees for two sociological handbooks. The press release gave no information about collection procedures, geographical scope, urban/rural differences, or sample size. Among the Western scholars who have written on parental involvement in marriage choice in post-1949 China are Croll, *Politics of Mar-*

riage, 24–40, and Wolf, *Revolution Postponed*, esp. 169–72. Wolf, 171, found that among sixty young people aged twenty to twenty-nine in four rural sites, 27 percent decided on their own mates, 55 percent had the choice made by the parents, and the remainder made the decision jointly with their parents.

41. Wang Ruowang.

42. *Ibid.*

43. Cases in which physical violence of parents against daughters was the main feature are discussed in Chapter 8.

44. "Sun Jing de zaoyu shuomingle shenma?," *ZF*, 10 (Oct. 1980), 9–10.

45. *Ibid.*, 11.

46. *Ibid.*, 11–12.

47. *Ibid.*, *ZF*, 1980: 11 (Nov.), 4–7; 12 (Dec.), 24–27.

48. *Ibid.*, *ZF*, 1 (Jan. 1981), 39.

49. *ZF*, 8 (Aug. 1981), 27.

50. Sun Yi.

51. *Tianjin ribao*, Jan. 25, 1981.

52. For one such case, see "Meiyou jieju." The case is discussed in Chapter 8.

53. Jiang Yangming.

54. "Dang fumu ganshe."

55. *Xinmin wanbao*, Oct. 15, 1985, 4.

56. "Song Yuexia"; Jiang Yangming.

57. Jiang Yangming.

58. Zhu Jiaxiong.

59. "Qingchu baoban"; "Yige you jieju"; *ZQB*, 1982: Jan. 19, 3, and Mar. 2, 3.

60. *Baokan wenzhai*, Aug. 20, 1985.

61. "Fujian Huian xian."

62. "'Ma Zhuanyuan.'"

63. "Jiujiu qingnian"; "Fujian Huian xian."

64. In rural areas where the amount of land a family could contract was based on family size, some parents used their daughters to increase their allotment of land, then married them off so that their husbands' families could contract for more land as well. This arrangement was presumably worth something in bride-price negotiations. *ZF*, 10 (Oct. 1981), 41. Recent writings in English on the effect of the Chinese economic reforms on the rural family include: Croll, *Chinese Women Since Mao*, 23–42; Davin, "The Single-Child Family Policy in the Countryside," in Croll et al., *China's One-Child Policy*, 37–82; Wolf, *Revolution Postponed*, 268–71; Kallgren.

65. "'Ma Zhuanyuan.'"

66. "Fujian Huian xian"; "Jiujiu qingnian."

67. On this practice in rural Taiwan, see Wolf, *Women and the Family*, 172–85.

68. *ZF*, 6 (June 1983), 43.

69. In the case of "exchanging relatives," it is less clear that the practice is a resurgent rather than a recurrent phenomenon; it may have been constant since 1949 but be more thoroughly reported in the freer press of the 1980's.

70. Two such cases are discussed in *Tianjin ribao*, Jan. 5, 1981, and "Qingchu baoban," 15.

71. "Jiujiu qingnian."

72. "'Ma Zhuanyuan.'"

73. Some cases where official action was taken to oppose parental interference

are found in *ZQB*, 1982: Jan. 19, 3; May 2, 3; *Tianjin ribao*, Jan. 17, 1981; and "Yige you jieju."

74. *ZQB*, May 9, 1982, 8.

75. Li Minghua et al.

76. *Ibid.*

77. Young Chinese in the 1960's were repeatedly admonished that "revolutionary youths in selecting their mates should place political conditions in the first place." *ZQ*, 9 (1965), 26, translated in JPRS 30450, June 7, 1965, 56–57. Although the intention was to emphasize the importance of commitment to Communism, choosing a politically well-situated spouse was also the best way to ensure one's future comfort.

78. Chen Ping, 21.

79. *Xinmin wanbao*, Nov. 13, 1985, 5.

80. Li Minghua et al.

81. *ZQB*, Sept. 23, 1982.

82. *ZQB*, Apr. 4, 1982, 8.

83. *Tianjin ribao*, Feb. 16, 1981; *ZQB*, 1982: Mar. 25, 1, and Apr. 24, 2; Chen Ping, 22; "Xiang chengshi," 10–11. Articles about morticians and pedicurists were printed in *Tianjin ribao* in 1979–80.

84. *ZQB*, Apr. 24, 1982, 2. A 1983 article in the English-language magazine *Women of China* described the marriage of a woman who was a graduate student in economics at Fudan to a worker at a neighborhood-run shoe factory. Although it convincingly described the man's love of study and the couple's common interests, their marriage remained anomalous not only because of the difference in their status, but because she was the more educated of the two. *Women of China*, 9 (Sept. 1983), 20.

85. *ZQB*, Nov. 12, 1981, 1, carried an article about a model woman textile worker who heroically refused introductions to many men of high status. She planned to marry an ordinary worker in the reeling room of her mill. The implication was that she could do "better," that women workers tried to marry up whenever possible, and that her refusal to do so was heroic and unusual enough to merit mention with her other "model" qualities.

86. *Gongren ribao*, Dec. 6, 1983, 3; "Xiang chengshi," 10; Zhen Yi, 22.

87. Meng Xiaoyun, Jan. 8–9, 1986, 2.

88. Huang Yin, 16.

89. Cai Xiaofeng and Xu Haimei, 32. Another Beijing institute reported that 35 percent of women registrants aged twenty-eight to thirty-six had university degrees. The figure at a Xi'an institute was 47 percent, more than three times that for men in the same age group. Meng Xiaoyun, Jan. 8, 1986, 2.

90. *Gongren ribao*, Dec. 6, 1983, 3.

91. Cai Xiaofeng and Xu Haimei, 32–33.

92. *ZF*, 11 (Nov. 1984), 24; Liu Changlin, 32; Zhen Yi, 22–23; Huang Yin, 17.

93. Zhen Yi, 22–23.   94. *Xinmin wanbao*, Jan. 4, 1986.

95. Wen Xianliang.   96. Huang Yin, 17.

97. *Jiefang ribao*, June 15, 1985; personal interviews; also see Chapter 7, "Women and Work."

98. *Jiefang ribao*, Aug. 9, 23, 1985.   99. Meng Xiaoyun, Jan. 9, 1986, 2.

100. *Jiefang ribao*, June 29, 1985.   101. *Jiating*, 5 (May 1985), 24.

102. *Baokan wenzhai*, Nov. 5, 1985; Hu Jiang; Jiang An.

103. Jiang An.
104. *ZQB*, Feb. 12, 1981, 3.
105. *ZQB*, Feb. 26, 1981.
106. *ZQB*, Sept. 5, 1982, 8.
107. *ZQB*, Mar. 23, 1985.
108. "Xiang chengshi," 10.
109. *ZQB*, 1982: May 11, 3, and June 1, 3; "Ding qiaoji"; *Jiefang ribao*, Jan. 17, 1986.
110. According to a 10 percent sample of the 1982 census, 6,060,000 men and 540,000 women aged twenty-eight to thirty-four were unmarried. The same sample showed 106 rural men for every 100 rural women aged twenty-five to thirty-four. The 1983 investigation covered 128 production brigades in nineteen counties and seven provinces. It showed that 2,905 men and 162 women aged twenty-five to thirty-five had trouble finding mates. Zhang Ping, "Qing guanzhu."
111. "Let Them Marry Younger"; Huang Yin; "Xiang chengshi"; a scholarly historical analysis of the practice of men marrying younger women is given in Wang Ge.
112. *ZF*, 7 (July 1984), 14.
113. *Tianjin ribao*, Jan. 10, 1981.
114. Lou Jingbo, 20–21.
115. Huang Yin, 16.
116. Huang Jingyao.
117. Liu Hanhuai, "Zai danshen."
118. Xie Yong; Huang Jingyao; Liu Hanhuai, "Zai danshen."
119. "Nüzi dushen wenti chutan."
120. Xie Yong; Lou Jingbo, 20; Liu Yixian.
121. Liu Yixian.
122. Lou Jingbo, 20.
123. "Mama, bie zeguai."
124. Tang Liqin, 48–49.
125. Huang Yin; Liu Yixian.
126. Su Shan.
127. Liu Hanhuai; Lou Jingbo, 21; "Nüzi dushen wenti chutan"; Yao Guochu.
128. Tang Liqin, 49.
129. Liu Enyu.
130. Huang Jingyao.
131. Ma Xinfang. The distaste for older wives was not universal in China; Margery Wolf notes that they were and are preferred in rural Shandong. Personal communication.
132. Wang Yuxian.
133. Wang Ge, 34.
134. "Lian'ai fangshi taolun," *Jiating*, 7 (July 1985), 27.
135. *ZQB*, Mar. 23, 1982, 4.
136. *ZQB*, May 20, 1980; *Beijing funü*, 2 (Aug. 1983), 9.
137. *ZQB*, Aug. 10, 1982, 4.
138. *ZQB*, Nov. 10, 17, 1981, 3.
139. *ZQB*, Feb. 14, 1982.
140. *ZQB*, Apr. 16, 1981; Wen Jun.
141. "Lian'ai fangshi taolun," *Jiating*, 5 (May 1985), 24.
142. Shasha.
143. "Yao aihu nüqingnian mingyu"; also see *ZQB*, Mar. 6, 1985, 3.
144. "Ta weishenme bianle xin?"
145. *ZQB*, Oct. 22, 1981; "Yiyou hunyue."
146. "Dinghun hou"; "Wo yiding dei yu ta jiehun ma?"
147. Liu Hanhuai, "Lian'ai qinmi judong."
148. "Shi wo wuqing haishi ta budaode?"
149. "Lian'ai fangshi taolun," *Jiating*, 7 (July 1985), 26.
150. *Xinmin wanbao*, Jan. 27, 1986; *Shehui bao*, Oct. 21, 1986.
151. *China Daily*, Dec. 31, 1984, 4.
152. *Baokan wenzhai*, Aug. 27, 1985.
153. Personal interviews; also see "Lian'ai fangshi taolun," *Jiating*, 6 (June 1985), 21.

154. "Lian'ai fangshi taolun," *Jiating*, 5 (May 1985), 25.
155. *Ibid.*
156. Liu Hanhuai, "Lian'ai qinmi judong."
157. "Lian'ai fangshi taolun," *Jiating*, 7 (July 1985), 27.
158. "Meiguo qingnian."   159. *ZQ*, 1 (Jan. 1984), 12.
160. *ZQB*, Mar. 14, 1982, 4.   161. Personal interview.
162. Personal interview.   163. Personal interview.
164. "Xiaye lian'ai xuzhi."   165. *Baokan wenzhai*, Aug. 27, 1985.
166. Bian Ji.   167. "Zhe posuide ai."
168. "Jiaru wo shi Xiao B." The author of the original letter eventually did decide to marry his girlfriend. *ZF*, 10 (Oct. 1985), 12.
169. "Lian'ai fangshi taolun," *Jiating*, 5 (May 1985), 25.
170. "Gei 'shishen' nüqingnian."   171. Liu Chang.
172. Yu Quanyuan.   173. Personal interview.
174. Liu Hanhuai, "Lian'ai qinmi judong"; "Lian'ai fangshi taolun," *Jiating*, 6 (June 1985), 21.
175. "Lian'ai fangshi taolun," *Jiating*, 7 (July 1985), 26–27.
176. "Gei 'shishen' nüqingnian."   177. Wang Youqin, 12.
178. Liu Dalin.   179. Zhou Yan.
180. Liu Hanhuai, "Lian'ai qinmi judong."
181. Wang Youqin.   182. Yang Yong.
183. Liu Dalin.   184. *Ibid.*
185. *Ibid.*; "Lian'ai fangshi taolun," *Jiating*, 7 (July 1985), 26–27.

Chapter 4

1. Croll, *The Politics of Marriage*, 108. Also see Wu chengshi jiating yanjiu xianmu zu, 76.
2. *The Marriage Law of the People's Republic of China.*
3. *Wenhui bao*, Mar. 30, 1981. Some individuals who had reached the legal marriage age were unable to secure the required certificate from work units that were overzealous in their determination to implement the family planning campaign. Others were unable to secure the household registration from parents who opposed their marriage. To deal with these situations, a new set of marriage registration regulations was implemented in 1986, authorizing registration officials to issue a marriage license if investigation indicated that work units or parents were obstructing a marriage. *Jiefang ribao*, Mar. 30, 1986; *Xinmin wanbao*, Mar. 14, 1986.
4. According to a 1984–85 study of a neighborhood in Tianjin, only 13.5 percent of the women surveyed had no wedding ceremony. Wu chengshi jiating yanjiu xianmu zu, 76.
5. Personal interview.
6. According to statistics for one neighborhood in Shanghai in 1983, only sixty-four (7 percent) of the 916 married couples who lived there were living in the home of the wife's family. Cai Hongde, 13.
7. Liu Xinwu.   8. Wang Anyi.
9. Chen Yuexiang, 29.   10. Shenyangshi fulian, 11–12.
11. "Shashi feichu fenfang 'yinan weizhu' louxi" (Shashi eliminates the ugly custom of giving priority to men in assigning housing). As the title of the article suggests, the practice of giving priority to male workers was attacked in 1985. The municipal government issued a document stating that housing should be allo-

cated on the basis of seniority, regardless of a worker's gender. No information is available to indicate whether individual work units complied with this regulation.

12. There were exceptions to this, such as the Foreign Languages Bureau in Beijing, where some women were assigned housing. At least several major universities also assigned housing to women. Personal interview.

13. For a discussion of the persistence of brideprice and dowry in post-1949 rural China, see Parish and Whyte, 182–92; also see Croll, *The Politics of Marriage*, 114; and Wolf, *Revolution Postponed*, 175–80. For an analysis of gift exchange in the cities, see Whyte and Parish, 136–37; Wolf, *ibid.*, 158–60.

14. Xie Wenliang.

15. Anthropologists disagree about the meaning of dowry: some understand it as a "form of pre-mortem inheritance to the bride," while others see it as a "symbol reflecting on the wealth and status of the bride's kin." Croll, *The Politics of Marriage*, 113. For a more extensive discussion of the anthropological debate, see Comaroff.

16. According to a 1984 survey of one neighborhood in Tianjin, the groom's family usually spent between one and two thousand yuan, while the expenditures of the bride's family amounted to several hundred yuan. Wu chengshi jiating yanjiu xianmu zu, 78. Also see Whyte and Parish, 136–37. Whyte and Parish observed that "many marriages occur without any gift demands being made" (*ibid.*, 136). Our own observations suggest that such marriages were the rare exception to the rule. This discrepancy may be due to the different periods being studied: most of Whyte and Parish's data were collected in the late 1970's, when urban consumerism was just beginning. In contrast, most of our data came from the early- and mid-1980's, when the tendency of marriages to involve extensive gift exchange escalated in conjunction with the increasing availability of consumer goods.

17. Chen Huibao, 60. This description of wedding gifts was based primarily on Shanghai customs, where more consumer goods were available than anywhere else in China.

18. Personal interview.   19. Chen Huibao, 60.
20. Xie Wenliang.   21. Personal interview.
22. Honig, *Sisters and Strangers*, 189.
23. Xie Wenliang.
24. *Ibid.*
25. Wu chengshi jiating yanjiu xianmu zu, 78.
26. Personal interview. In rural China in the early 1980's, it was still common for a bride to be required to bow to the relatives of her husband's family, as depicted in the film "Small Happiness."

27. Ning Huaixin.   28. Personal interview.
29. Chen Huibao, 60.   30. *Ibid.*
31. ZQB, Feb. 7, 1982.   32. ZQB, Nov. 21, 1981.
33. ZQB, Oct. 4, 1981.

34. Social discussion of the evils of extravagant weddings also took place before the Cultural Revolution. For example, see ZF, 12 (1964), 19–20, 32, translated in JPRS, no. 239 (JPRS: 28,286), Jan. 14, 1965, 32–38. Also see ZQB, Nov. 19, 1964, 1, translated as "How Did I Break the Outdated Customs in Managing My Wedding?" in JPRS, no. 242 (JPRS 28,337), Jan. 18, 1965, 8–12. Also see *Gongren ribao*, Jan. 6, 1965, translated as "Do Not Bow Before Old Customs," and "Before and After My Wedding Arrangements," in JPRS, no. 247 (JPRS 28,413), Jan. 22, 1965, 36–39.

35. *ZQB*, Jan. 19, 1982, 3.
37. *Wenhui bao*, Mar. 30, 1981.
39. *ZF*, 3 (Mar. 1980), 39.
41. *ZQB*, Feb. 25, 1982, 2.
43. *ZQB*, Jan. 19, 1982, 2.
45. *ZQB*, July 4, 1982, 6.
47. *ZQB*, Jan. 12, 1982.
48. Special advice books for young couples planning travel weddings described the most popular places to go and provided information about all aspects of planning a honeymoon trip. See, for example, Shan Ren.
49. *ZQB*, Dec. 29, 1981.
51. *Ibid.*
53. *ZQB*, Nov. 24, 1981.

36. *Ibid.*
38. Lü Wende.
40. *ZQB*, Dec. 8, 1981, 3.
42. *ZQB*, Dec. 5, 1981, 2.
44. *ZQB*, Dec. 29, 1981.
46. *ZQB*, Dec. 31, 1981.

50. *ZQB*, Nov. 24, 1981.
52. *ZQB*, Jan. 9, 1982.

Chapter 5

1. Wolf, *Women and the Family*, 32–41.
2. It is difficult to determine the percentage of urban couples who lived with parents and the percentage who formed independent households. The few social surveys conducted indicate that an increasing number of couples formed nuclear families. A 1981 survey of the Xuanwu district of Beijing shows that 56.14 percent of the families were nuclear families, while 18.12 percent were extended families in which three generations shared a household. A 1982 study of a neighborhood in Tianjin indicates that 67.21 percent of couples born after 1951 lived in nuclear families, 26.23 percent with the husband's parents. On Beijing see Fei Xiaotong, 36; on Tianjin see Pan Yunkang and Pan Naigu, 58. Further statistics are available in the surveys published in Wu chengshi jiating yanjiu xianmu zu.
3. Ning Qing, 111–18.
4. *China Reconstructs*, 31, 5 (May 1982), 46–47.
5. *ZQB*, Jan. 17, 1982.
6. *ZQB*, Feb. 14, 1982.
7. Jiang Yuanming and Li Tangzhen.
8. "Zheli de xifu dou zheng da hongbian," 46.
9. "Jin Xuerong nüedai popo bei panxing."
10. *Tianjin ribao*, Dec. 28, 1980, 3.
11. *Ibid.*, Jan. 5, 1981.
12. Zhu Guizhen, 38–41.
13. *ZQB*, Jan. 8, 1980.
14. Ke Wei, 2.
15. Feng Bian, 13–14.
16. Zhu Ying, 20.
17. Bai Fengxi, 16.
18. Feng Bian, 13.
19. Sun Honglin, 17.
20. Yang Shanhua, 34.
21. "Xinhun zhihou," 103.
22. *Ibid.*
23. Yang Shanhua, 34.
24. "Xinhun zhihou," 103.
25. Li Shaoqin, 21.
26. Jie Zhuanguang, 22–23.
27. "Dang yige xiandai de 'xianqi liangmu,'" 15–16.
28. Li Shaoqian, 21.
29. "Zhangfu youle 'waiyu' zhihou."
30. Jie Zhuanguang.
31. *Jilin qingnian*, 6 (June 1985), 28.
32. Dai Anmin.
33. Zhang Ping.
34. *Xinmin wanbao*, Aug. 9, 1985.
35. "Dang yige xiandai de 'xianqi liangmu,'" 16.
36. Shi Dezhao, 40–41.
37. Personal interview.
38. Zhang Xinxin and Sang Ye, 23. "Beijing ren" consists of profiles, based on

interviews conducted by the authors, of a variety of individuals who live and work in China.

39. "Moba niaodao dang yindao," 45.
40. Zhou Yuchang, 46.
41. Personal interview.
42. Zhang Xinxin and Sang Ye, 22–23.
43. See, for example, Hu Tingyi. Some of these sex manuals were reprints of books that had been published during the 1950's. For example, *Xingde zhishi* originally had been published in 1956.
44. Zhang Xinxin and Sang Ye, 23.
45. Hu Tingyi, 5.
46. Dr. Ke, in his letter to the young man who asked the whereabouts of the woman's vaginal opening, was slightly more informative on the subject of clitoral stimulation, explaining that "satisfaction for the woman" would be achieved when the clitoris was stimulated during penetration of the vagina. See "Moba niaodao dang yindao," 45.

47. Hu Tingyi, 33–35.
48. *Ibid.*, 43.
49. *Ibid.*, 37–38.
50. Liu Xinwu, 40.
51. Zhou Yuchang, 45.
52. Liu Zheng, 1.
53. For a more extensive discussion of the campaign, see Wolf, *Revolution Postponed*, 238–59. Also see Croll et al., *China's One-Child Policy*; and Kallgren.

54. Kallgren, 147.
55. Hu Tingyi, 54–56.
56. *Ibid.*, 58.
57. *Ibid.*, 56.
58. *Yuelao bao*, 7 (July 1985), 4.
59. Bian Ji and Zhan Lin, 25.
60. *Ibid.*
61. *Ibid.*
62. For a discussion of the ways in which the responsibility system increased the desire of peasant families for sons, see Davin, 57–63.
63. *ZQB*, Aug. 3, 1982. Also see *ZF*, 10 (1982), 46–47. This issue of *ZF* also included an article that pointed out the ineffectiveness of various methods of trying to influence the child's gender.
64. Elisabeth Chang. The articles summarized by Chang originally appeared in the *Liaoning Daily*. Also see *ZF*, 10 (1982), 43.

65. *ZQB*, Apr. 24, 1982.
66. *Funü*, 1 (1984), 12.
67. *ZQB*, Aug. 3, 1982.
68. *Ibid.*

Chapter 6

1. Baker, 46–47.
2. Baker, 180. No systematic research has been done about the implementation or impact of the GMD divorce law. While the law most likely had little effect on rural women, it quite possibly had a greater impact on urban women than has been previously recognized by Western scholars, as women's magazines of the 1920's and 1930's commonly featured divorce as a major topic of discussion.
3. For a discussion of fluctuations in the CCP's divorce law in the pre-1949 base areas, see Johnson, 51–83.
4. No systematic statistics are available on divorce rates during this period. The fragmentary information that exists suggests that divorce rates increased in conjunction with the 1953 campaign to implement the Marriage Law. See Johnson, 147, 261.
5. *Ibid.*, 147.
6. Class of '77, 105–7.

7. Liang and Shapiro, 9–11.

8. Croll, *Chinese Women Since Mao*, 83.

9. Jin Hua and Yan Wen, 72.

10. *China Daily*, Jan. 4, 1985, 3.

11. Jin Hua and Yan Wen, 65–68.

12. *Beijing Review*, 7 (Feb. 1, 1984), 25.

13. *Ibid.*, 25.

14. Jin Hua and Yan Wen, 85–87.

15. ZFB, Apr. 3, 1985, 3.

16. Information about divorce in rural areas is harder to obtain and public discussion less common. We suspect, though, that it continues to be much more difficult for rural women to obtain a divorce, and that divorce is generally less common in the countryside, where traditional attitudes and family structure remain strong. For a discussion of divorce in the countryside in the period following the Cultural Revolution, see Parish and Whyte, 192–98.

17. Su Haobin, 90. According to another set of statistics, the number of divorce cases in the Shanghai courts in November 1980—two months after the new law was implemented—was twice the number filed in November 1979. "An Analysis of Divorce Statistics," 132. In Shenyang, the number of cases in 1981 represented a 61 percent increase over those heard in 1980 before the new law was passed. See Zhao Ziyang et al., 22. In the Dongcheng district of Beijing the number of divorce requests in 1981 was a 39 percent increase over the previous year. See Class of '77, 104–5. An analysis of the rising divorce rate is also presented in Croll, *Chinese Women Since Mao*, 82–85, and Whyte and Parish, 186–89.

18. *Shehui bao*, Oct. 10, 1985.

19. *Xinmin wanbao*, Aug. 25, 1986.

20. Su Haobin, 90.

21. For a more extensive discussion of marriages among sent-down urban youth during the Cultural Revolution, see Croll, *The Politics of Marriage*, 103–5.

22. Minzhu yu fazhi bianjibu, 8–9.

23. For a more extensive analysis of Yu Luojin's case, see Honig, "Private Issues."

24. Yu Luojin, "Yige dongtiande tonghua," 111.

25. Neither Yu's stories nor her essays discuss the problems (if any) she encountered in obtaining her first divorce.

26. For a discussion of these articles see Honig, "Private Issues."

27. Yu Luojin, "Yige chuntiande tonghua," 196. That this dialogue is not completely a fictional reconstruction is suggested by the almost verbatim similarity between Da Ji's statement and an article written by Dang Chunyuan, the judge of the district court that initially granted Yu's second divorce. See Dang Chunyuan, 13–14.

28. That the government hoped to use Yu's case for this purpose is suggested by the nature of the articles and editorial comments published in *Minzhu yu fazhi* (MF), a journal that presumably represents official views. Virtually all the articles about Yu's case written by legal officials concurred with Dang Chunyuan, whereas no articles appeared by those applying the so-called "ultra-leftist" criteria. In many of these articles the specifics of Yu's case were barely mentioned. Instead, her case appears to have provided a pretext for the judges to address larger legal issues.

29. "Ruhe zhengque chuli lihun anjian" (How to correctly handle divorce cases), *MF* (Apr. 1981), 20.

30. Yu Luojin, "Wo weishenme yao lihun," 29.

31. Zhangjiakou shi fulian, 30.

32. *ZQB*, July 10, 1982.   33. *ZQB*, Sept. 7, 1982, 3.

34. *ZQB*, July 20, 1982, 3.   35. *ZQB*, Sept. 7, 1982.

36. A similar discussion took place in *Zhongguo funü* (ZF) from December 1982 through November 1983. The discussion is summarized in *Women of China* (Jan. 1984), 38–41.

37. Minzhu yu fazhi bianjibu, 3–4.   38. Xue Suzhen et al., 91.

39. Class of '77, 109.   40. Minzhu yu fazhi bianjibu, 39–40.

41. *Gongren ribao*, Dec. 20, 1983, 3.

42. The term *disanzhe* or "third party" was not newly coined in the 1980's. It was used in reference to extramarital affairs in the 1950's as well. See "Why Our Marital Relationship Has Broken Down," esp. 51–56.

43. Wu Wenzao, 53.

44. "Why Our Marital Relationship Has Broken Down," *passim*.

45. Wu Wenzao, 53.

46. Xue Suzhen et al., 89; *Xinmin wanbao*, Oct. 30, 1985. These figures may be unusually high. According to another study, about 20 percent of divorce cases were caused by one partner's involvement with someone else. See Liu Tong, 17. Yet another study estimated that in 1985 extramarital affairs caused approximately 25 percent of divorces in all of China. See *Xinmin wanbao*, Aug. 25, 1986.

47. Wu Wenzao, 53.   48. *Ibid.*, 54.

49. Zhou Jinde, 39.   50. Hu Jian, 20.

51. *Ibid.*   52. *Shehui bao*, June 13, 1985, 1.

53. Fang Xiang, 18.   54. Ming De, 15.

55. Xin Huan, 29–31.   56. *Jiefang ribao*, June 8, 1985.

57. Hua Yi, 35.

58. Xiaoming, "Shouhui nide jiao ba," 27.

59. Ma Ying, 3.   60. Tao Kai, 16.

61. *China Daily*, Feb. 3, 1986.   62. *Ibid.*

63. *Gongren ribao*, Dec. 6, 1983.

64. For an extensive discussion of Zhang Jie's story "The Ark," see Yue and Wakeman.

65. Zhang Jie, "Fang zhou," *Shouhuo*, 2 (1982), 9.

66. *Ibid.*, 11.   67. *Ibid.*, 10.

68. *Ibid.*, 24.   69. Qu Le, 35.

Chapter 7

1. Whyte and Parish, 201–2. Based on statistics derived from the *1977 Yearbook of Labor Statistics* compiled by the International Labor Organization, Whyte and Parish calculated that an average of 48 percent of the urban labor force in China was female, compared to 33 percent for sixteen European and American capitalist states, and 28 percent for ten Asian developing nations. The percentage of the Chinese urban labor force comprising women may have decreased since 1977, for reasons detailed in this chapter. According to a 1985 survey, women represented one-third of the urban workforce. *RMRB*, Mar. 8, 1986. For more detailed statistics about women's representation in the workforce in the 1980's, see State Statistical Bureau, 1983, 1984, 1985.

2. See Johnson; Stacey; Andors. 3. Andors, 37.
4. Robinson, 33. 5. *Ibid.*, 36.
6. *RMRB*, Jan. 26, 1984.
7. "Zhongnan qingnü xianxiang youzeng wujian." This article does not mention whether the final agreement specified the kinds of jobs, or the sectors of the workforce, for which women were to be recruited.
8. *Ibid.*
9. Zhao Yanling, 26.
10. *China Daily*, Mar. 7, 1985.
11. "Zhongnan qingnü xianxiang youzeng wujian."
12. Zhao Yanling, 26.
13. Ma Xuehong, 2.
14. "Fengyang zhaogong nügong duo yu nangong yibei," 1.
15. "Zhongnan qingnü xianxiang youzeng wujian."
16. *Ibid.* In the city's Huangpu district, where slightly less than half of the middle school graduates in 1983 were women, some 75 percent of the "youth waiting for employment" that year were women. Zhou Yinjun and Chen Rufeng, 329. In another Shanghai district, 78 percent of the "youth waiting for employment" were women (*ibid.*). In a Beijing district, some 60 percent of the "youth waiting for employment" were women. Zhao Yanling, 26.
17. Duan Yue, 64.
18. *Wenhui bao*, Oct. 5, 1980.
19. Zhou Yinjun and Chen Rufeng, 333.
20. Duan Yue, 65.
21. Zhou and Chen, 332.
22. Jiang Yongping, 92. Also see *ZQB*, Aug. 14, 1982.
23. Duan Yue, 66.
24. Xiao Ming, "Dalian's First Vocational School for Girls," 6–7.
25. "Zhongnan qingnü xianxiang youzeng wujian."
26. Li Guangchun, 2.
27. Personal interview.
28. "Shougang zhuanye peixunban lüqu nüsheng guoban," 1.
29. Pepper, 125.
30. State Statistical Bureau (1984), 490.
31. Chen Benjian, 2. 32. Yang Xingnan, 1.
33. *Ibid.* 34. *Ibid.*
35. *Ibid.* In 1985, some 200 work units refused to hire women graduates from Fudan who had been recommended to them. Tan Manni, 34.
36. Personal interview.
37. Xu Feng.
38. "Quan shehui dou lai guanxin nü daxuesheng de fenpei wenti," 1.
39. *RMRB*, Feb. 20, 1984. 40. Dong Weiling, 15.
41. *Ibid.* 42. *ZQB*, Oct. 6, 1981.
43. *Tianjin ribao*, Oct. 15, 1980.
44. *China Daily*, Feb. 15, 1985. This same article pointed out that in one neighborhood in Xiangtan City, Hunan, two-thirds of self-employed people were women. "Most of these women, who are now running small groceries, restaurants, or snack stands, were retired factory workers or employees laid off by other establishments."
45. *Ibid.*
46. Robinson, 38.

47. Personal interview. The same proposal that women return to the home was also advocated, and rejected, in Wuhan. Xia Bangxin, 16.
48. Bi Bingsheng and Hou Zhihong, 17.
49. "Woguo funü shiyexin qiang."
50. *Ibid.* A more thorough discussion and analysis of why most urban women want to work can be found in Wolf, *Revolution Postponed*, 60–61.
51. Bi and Hou, 18.   52. *China Daily*, Mar. 20, 1985.
53. Liu Guangyun, 3.   54. Dong Weiling, 15.
55. Liaoningsheng Lüdashi zonggonghui, 29–30. Also see Wang Shanling and Lu Shucun, 2.
56. Liaoningsheng Lüdashi zonggonghui, 29–30.
57. ZFB, Jan. 9, 1985. Also see Guo Liwen, 9–10.
58. *Ibid.*
59. *Ibid.*
60. Wang Shanling and Lu Shucun, 2.
61. Liaoningsheng Lüdashi zonggonghui, 29–30.
62. *Ibid.*
63. *Ibid.*
64. *Ibid.*
65. Unfortunately, the surveys of women's opinions about prolonged maternity leave do not specify the exact occupations of the women. It is possible, for example, that opinions varied by status, and that those women who most vociferously opposed the leave were ones with technical jobs. At least one survey, conducted in 1986, suggested that a number of ordinary women workers favored the prolonged maternity leave, while professional women unanimously opposed it, fearing it would impair their chances of career advancement. See Tan Manni, 40.
66. Wang Yalin and Li Jinrong, 154. According to a survey conducted in Harbin and Qiqihaer, only 261 of every 1,000 households had kitchens, toilets, running water, plumbing, and heating. The other 739 lacked some or all of these. *Ibid.*, 155.
67. *Ibid.*, 151.   68. Shen Rong, 23.
69. *Ibid.*, 23.   70. *Ibid.*, 28.
71. Ming Wen, 14.   72. *Ibid.*, 14–15.
73. Sun Zhifeng, 20.   74. Wang and Li, 148–49.
75. *Ibid.*, 150.   76. *Ibid.*, 164.
77. Wang Yiling, 36.   78. *Ibid.*
79. Cai Niansheng.
80. "Dalianshi diyige qizi jiazheng xuexiban chengli."
81. Li Daowei, 36–37.
82. Luo Lu, 21.
83. Tan Fuyun, "Funü yao you zhiqi zheng diyi," 31.
84. For a description of the household service companies in the 1950's, see Croll, *The Women's Movement*, 77–78.
85. *China Daily*, Dec. 8, 1984, 3.
86. Tan Fuyun, "Funü yao you zhiqi zheng diyi," 31.
87. Chen Baoming and Sun Zijin, 34–37.
88. *Ibid.*, 34–35. Also see *Xinmin wanbao*, Jan. 19, 1986; and "Zhengque duidai cong nongcun laide 'xiao baomu,'" 36.
89. *Ibid.*
90. *Xinmin wanbao*, Jan. 19, 1986.

91. "Shanghai youle baomu xuexiao."
92. Wang and Li, 155–56.

Chapter 8

1. For a discussion of the status of women in China since 1949 and its relationship to patrilocality, see Johnson, 93–233.
2. For an extensive report of such practices, based on interviews but unconfirmed in official Chinese sources, see Weisskopf, "Abortion Policy"; also see Aird, 196–99, 204–6, 208–11.
3. 106 males for every 100 females, or a sex ratio of 1.06, is considered an international norm. The 1981 Chinese ratio was 108.5, indicating a "deficiency" of 232,000 girls. Chinese demographers have unofficially estimated that the 1983 ratio was 1.11, meaning that China had 345,000 fewer female births registered than demograhic norms would dictate. Local Women's Federation investigators found baby boys outnumbering baby girls by 5 to 1 in some localities. Weisskopf, "China's Birth Control Policy"; also see Aird, 192–93.
4. Mei Hongjuan, 31 and *passim*.
5. *MF*, 1 (Jan. 1984), 48.
6. *San Francisco Chronicle*, Aug. 15, 1985, 15. Other peasants told the reporters that boys were also available for the higher price of $255, but the reporters did not see any for sale.
7. *Baokan wenzhai*, Jan. 21, 1986.
8. "Protecting Infant Girls"; "Safeguarding Women's Rights."
9. "China Advises Women."
10. Gao Yuan and Zhuang Zi, 212, 218.
11. ZQB, Sept. 26, 1980, 3.
12. Zhou Daoluan, 10.
13. *Ibid.* Before 1949, "stealing the bride" was a common custom that enabled the groom's family to avoid the cost of a wedding.
14. *Ibid.*, 11. It appears that penetration was regarded as the essential characteristic of all other rapes; none of the literature describes how other sexual practices conducted against a woman's will might be classified.
15. "Wo didi," 38.
16. Wu Mu.
17. *Shanghai qingnian bao*, Jan. 6, 1984, 5.
18. ZQB, Sept. 26, 1980.
19. "Wo bei ta."
20. An exception is a detailed but apparently semi-fictional account of father-daughter incest in a 1983 issue of *Jiating* magazine. See Liu Ying.
21. Tan Weiwen.
22. ZQB, Apr. 4, 1982.
23. RMRB, Jan. 15, 1984, 4; for another case, see ZQB, Oct. 28, 1980.
24. Li Lie; also see Sheng Ping et al., 527–37.
25. Qiao Yan.
26. ZQB, Dec. 7, 1981, 3.
27. *Tianjin ribao*, Feb. 15, 1981; a similar case was reported in *Shenghuo zhoukan*, Oct. 26, 1986, 4.
28. ZQB, Mar. 10, 1981, 3.
29. ZQB, May 29, 1980.
30. See, for example, Bart and O'Brien.

31. Zhou Daoluan, 11.
32. Lin Wanxiu; *ZQB*, Mar. 31, 1985.
33. *Baokan wenzhai*, Oct. 22, 1985.
34. Lin Wanxiu.
35. For example, see *Funü*, 1 (1984), 14.
36. "Bei leishui."
37. *Tianjin ribao*, Sept. 22, Oct. 22, 1980; *ZQ*, Oct. 1980.
38. *ZQB*, Sept. 26, 1980, 3.
39. A 1985 survey apparently conducted in the suburbs of Shanghai found that 60 percent of all rapists arrested were under eighteen, and 21 percent of suburban rapists caught in 1983 and 1984 were students. *Baokan wenzhai*, Sept. 3, 1985. Another study found that in an unnamed coastal city, men under twenty-five accounted for 52 percent of all rapists. Gao Yuan and Zhuang Zi, 212.
40. "Wo didi." For a similar analysis, see Gao and Zhuang, 216–18.
41. Zou Nanrong and Cao Yang, "Si xing."
42. *ZQB*, Mar. 22, 1985.
43. Gao Yuan and Zhuang Zi, 215–20.
44. "Meiyou jiejude aiqing gushi."
45. "'Meiyou jiejude aiqing gushi' jiangyou jieju."
46. Sons who refused to accede to the marital choices of their parents sometimes were also pressured and beaten. But far more attention was given in the press to cases of daughter-beating, the implication being that such cases were more common. If this was true, it reflected both the greater physical vulnerability of women and the fact that families stood to lose money if their daughters made an economically disadvantageous match or broke off an engagement after a bride-price had been agreed upon; see discussion below.
47. "Pohun ji."   48. *ZF*, 9 (Sept. 1983), 46–47.
49. *Tianjin ribao*, Jan. 17, 1981.   50. *ZQB*, Jan. 19, 1982, 3.
51. *MF*, 10 (Oct. 1983), 48.   52. "Jinbi ji jingshen zhemo."
53. Chen Ji.   54. *Tianjin ribao*, Nov. 11, 1980.
55. *Tianjin ribao*, Mar. 8, 1981.
56. *Yunnan ribao*, Mar. 21, 1982, translated in *FBIS Daily Report—China*, 1, 068 (Apr. 8, 1982), Q2.
57. *ZF*, 9 (Sept. 1981), 12–13; 9 (Sept. 1983), 31.
58. *Yunnan ribao*, Mar. 21, 1982, translated in *FBIS Daily Report*.
59. *ZF*, 9 (Sept. 1981), 12–13. Most cases seemed to involve movement from a poorer to a richer region, but no systematic data are presented in any of the case accounts. The kidnapping or purchase of young women for sale as brides was reminiscent of pre-1949 practices.
60. *ZF*, 9 (Sept. 1981), 12; *ZQB*, Jan. 30, 1982; *Shijie ribao*, Dec. 31, 1982, 3.
61. *ZF*, 9 (Sept. 1981), 12–13.
62. *Ibid.*; *ZF*, 9 (Sept. 1983), 31.
63. *Shijie ribao*, Dec. 31, 1982, 3; *ZF*, 9 (Sept. 1983), 46; *ZQB*, Jan. 30, 1982; *ZF*, 9 (Sept. 1981), 13.
64. Derived from figures in Population Census Office, 15, 31.
65. Wang Ruichao.
66. Ji Shuhan. This account shows some signs of being semi-fictionalized; it is not replete with the usual wealth of names, dates, and details.
67. Yan Zhijiang.
68. Zhang Gengsheng; "'Yanei' fanfa."
69. Zhang Gengsheng, 32.

70. Zhou Nanrong and Cao Yang, "Yige jiating."
71. Xiao Ming, "Wo wei ni," 4–5.
72. "Ta weihe"; *ZF*, 9 (Sept. 1981), 46; *ZQB*, June 22, 1982, 3.
73. *ZQB*, Aug. 29, 1982, 1.
74. "Zheshi 'jiating jiufen'"; "Tigao zeren."
75. Xiao Ming, "Wo wei ni," 4–5.
76. Zhang Cangniao and Zhan Yuanshui.
77. Jian Shengyuan et al.   78. Zhuang Guangze and Liu Xiaohe.
79. "Zheshi 'jiating jiufen.'"   80. "Ta weihe"; "Huyu jizao."
81. Zhang Hongqiang.   82. Zhang Gengsheng.
83. Jian Shengyuan et al.
84. Zhu Liangyu; Zhuang Guangze and Liu Xiaohe; "Guanyu Wang Feng-xiang"; Zhang Gengsheng; Wang Ruichao; "Ta weihe"; "Huyu jizao."
85. For an example of this terminology, see Tan Weiwen.
86. "Tigao zeren."
87. *Beijing funü*, 2 (Aug. 1983), 30; Xiao Ming, "Wo wei ni"; *ZF*, 9 (Sept. 1983), 46–47.
88. *ZF*, 6 (June 1985), 40.
89. *RMRB*, Jan. 7, 1984, 7.
90. Chen Dawen.

Chapter 9

1. We found this ironic, since political discourse during the Cultural Revolution had concentrated overwhelmingly on class, to the virtual exclusion of gender issues. Our friends were reacting in part to the Iron Girl model of female equality discussed in Chapter 1. They were also showing their revulsion at the violence associated with political struggle during the Cultural Revolution.
2. Rofel.
3. Rind, 197–98.
4. "The Ark" was described as a feminist story by Michael Kahn-Ackermann. See Yue and Wakeman, 883. The story was published in the February 1982 issue of *Shouhuo*.
5. Wang Fuhua.
6. Shi Funan, 20.
7. "Fujian qingnian nannü lunzheng 'nüren buyao taiweile'."
8. Li Yuanzheng, 3.   9. "Nüxing xiuzhen zuotanhui," 32.
10. Tang Min, 19.   11. Xu Dian, 19.
12. "A Play about Chinese Women," 4.
13. *Ibid.*, 5.   14. *Ibid.*, 5.
15. *Ibid.*, 7.   16. *Ibid.*, 7.
17. Ting Lan, 1.   18. Wang Youqin, 1.
19. Ouyang Man, 9.   20. Huang Shuze, 32.
21. Qu Dashen, 27.   22. Xiaoshi, 9.
23. Zhou Guangyu and Cai Queyi, 4–5.
24. Personal interview.
25. Shi Xingrong, "Buyao weida konghua yao shiji xingdong," 2–3. Zhuge Liang was a famous strategist of the Three Kingdoms period (A.D. 221–64), whose deeds were immortalized in the Ming dynasty novel *Romance of the Three Kingdoms*. His name is used to suggest a person who is a master strategist.
26. *Ibid.*, 2–3.
27. Shi Xingrong, "Kandaole guangming de qiantu he xiwang," 3.

28. De Yi, 14.
29. *Ibid.*
30. "Baohu funü ertong hefa quanyi," 1.
31. Personal interview.
32. Gu Shulan, 2.
33. Tan Fuyun, "Funü zuzhi jianshe bixu shiying gaige xingshi," 22–23; "Shenyang zhishi jie nüyou lianyihui zuijin chengli," 2; *Wenhui bao*, June 20, 1985, 2; Zong Weizi, 4; Meng Xiaoyun, 2.
34. Tan Fuyun, *ibid.*, 22. Also see *Nü gongchengshi*, Mar. 4 and July 30, 1985, and "Shenyang zhishijie nüyou lianyihui zuijin chengli," 2.
35. Tan Fuyun, *ibid.*, 23.
36. Zong Weizi, 4.
37. *China Daily*, Oct. 10, 1985.
38. Interview with Xie Xide in Peck, 120.
39. "Liu Shu tongzhi jianyi zhongshi nüzi peiyang," 46.
40. "Dalian chuangban nüzi zhiye gaozhong," 46; personal interview.
41. Rind, 195–201. No information is available about the group's subsequent development.
42. Unless otherwise specified, all information about the Fudan Women's Studies group is based on personal interviews.
43. "Fudan Women's Studies" (mimeo).
44. Personal interview.
45. Interview with Qi Wenying, courtesy of Marilyn Young.
46. Personal interview. Also see *Jiefang ribao*, Aug. 6, 1986.
47. Personal interview.
48. The efforts of the Women's Federation to organize women's studies associations were getting under way just as this book went to press. The comments here are therefore meant to be suggestive, not definitive.

Conclusion

1. For a discussion of the 1974 campaign to criticize Lin Biao and Confucius, which addressed the issue of discrimination against women, see Johnson, 194–207.
2. Stacey, *passim*; for a discussion of the conditional commitment that socialist states make to gender equality, see Molyneaux.

Bibliography

A Mei. "Ruhe anpai nide danshen shenghuo" (How to arrange your single life). *Fujian qingnian,* 7 (1985), 37.

"A Play About Chinese Women." *Women of China,* 7 (July 1984), 4–7.

"Aimeide guniang yao jingti" (Young women who love beauty should be on their guard). *ZQB,* Mar. 2, 1982, 3.

Aiqing hunyin jiating (Love, Marriage, and Family). Wuhan.

Aird, John S. "Coercion in Family Planning: Causes, Methods, and Consequences." *In China's Economy Looks Toward the Year 2000.* Volume 1: The Four Modernizations. Washington, D.C.: U.S. Government Printing Office, 1986, 184–221.

"An Analysis of Divorce Statistics." *In* Chu, 131–37.

Andors, Phyllis. *The Unfinished Liberation of Chinese Women, 1949–1980.* Bloomington: Indiana University Press, 1983.

Bai Fengxi. "Yige gulao you zhanxin de keti" (A topic that is both very old and very new). *ZF,* 7 (July 1984), 16–17.

Baker, Hugh. *Chinese Family and Kinship.* New York: Columbia University Press, 1979.

"Baohu funü ertong hefa quanyi" (Protect the legal rights of women and children). *Shehui bao,* June 13, 1985, 1.

Baokan wenzhai (Periodical Digest). Shanghai.

Bart, Pauline B., and Patricia H. O'Brien. *Stopping Rape: Successful Survival Strategies.* New York: Pergamon, 1985.

"Bashi niandai de nüqingnian gai zenyang shenghuo?" (How should young women live in the 80's?). *ZF,* 1983: 11 (Nov.), 29–31; 12 (Dec.), 29–31.

"Bei leishui dashi de shuxin" (A letter wet by tears). *Qingnian yidai,* 1 (1985), 44–45.

Beijing funü (Women of Beijing). Beijing.

Bi Bingsheng and Hou Zhihong. "Funü jiuyede tujing he qianjing" (The means and prospects for women to obtain employment). *Funü gongzuo,* 3 (1985), 17–18.

Bian Ji. "Qing jujue meiyou aiqingde xing'ai" (Please refuse loveless sexual love). *Qingnian yidai,* 6 (Oct. 1984), 57.

Bian Ji and Zhan Lin. "Wanyu buyu wuke feiyi" (Having children late or not having children is beyond reproach). *Qingnian yidai,* 5 (1984), 25.

Brownmiller, Susan. *Femininity.* New York: Fawcett Columbine, 1984.

"Buxu chouhua funü de xingxiang" (It is not permissible to defame woman's image). *ZF,* 5 (May 1981), 41.

Cai Hongde. "Dui congqijude tantao" (An inquiry regarding matrilocality). *Shehui*, 2 (Apr. 20, 1984), 13–17.

Cai Niansheng. "You yizhong mingzhi zhi ju" (A wise deed). *Jiefang ribao*, Aug. 23, 1985.

Cai Xiaofeng and Xu Haimei. "Zhengque gujia hunyin jieshaosuode zuoyong" (Correctly evaluate the function of the marriage introduction institutes). *Shehui*, 4 (Apr. 1982), 32–34.

"Cases of cohabiting should be handled with care." *China Daily*, Dec. 31, 1984, 4.

Chang, Elisabeth. "China's Unwanted Daughters." *This World* section of *San Francisco Chronicle*, July 4, 1982.

Chang Hanqing. "Chuanjin daiyude nülaomo" (A model woman worker dressed in gold and jade). *ZF*, 2 (Feb. 1985), 18.

Chen Baoming and Sun Zijin. "Baomu de shehui zuoyong" (The social role of maids). *Shehui*, 5 (Oct. 1983), 34–37.

Chen Benjian. "Zhaosheng zhaogong buying qishi funü" (Women should not be discriminated against in recruiting students and workers). *ZFB*, Jan. 9, 1985, 2.

Chen Bin. "Wei 'nüren taiwei' dabian" (A reply to "Women are too powerful"). *Fujian qingnian*, 5 (May 1985), 18.

Chen Dawen. "Women jiushi yuangao" (We are the plaintiffs). *ZF*, 12 (Dec. 1983), 32–33.

Chen Huibao. "Jiehun feiyong xiaoxi" (A small analysis of marriage expenses). *Shehui*, 4 (Aug. 1982), 60–61.

Chen Huoxiang and Lin Jun. "Guniang, mo sangshi jingti!" (Young woman, do not drop your guard!) *Yuelao bao*, 7 (July 1985), 6.

Chen Ji. "Bugai fashengde beiju" (A tragedy that should not have happened). *Zhongwai funü*, 2 (Feb. 1985), 32.

Chen Ping. "Shehui tiaojian dui aiqing hunyinde yingxiang" (The influence of social conditions on love and marriage). *Shehui*, 5 (May 1983), 20–22.

Chen Wendai. "Full Support." *Women of China*, 1 (Jan. 1986), 42.

Chen Xuliang. "Huangse shukan dui wo de fushi" (My corruption by pornographic publications). *ZQB*, Mar. 21, 1982, 1.

Chen Yuexiang. "Nüzhigong ying xiangshou fenfang de quanli" (Female employees must enjoy the right to be assigned housing). *ZF*, 2 (Feb. 1980), 29.

"China Advises Women on How to Prevent Rape." *Morning Call* (Easton, Pa.), May 10, 1985, A11.

The China Daily. Beijing.

China Report: Political, Sociological and Military Affairs. No. 434 (JPRS 83802), June 30, 1983, 66–69.

"China's Report on the Elimination of Discrimination Against Women." *Women of China*, 3 (Mar. 1984), special supplement.

Chow, Tse-tung. *The May Fourth Movement*. Stanford, Calif.: Stanford University Press, 1975.

Chu, David, ed. *Sociology and Society in Contemporary China, 1979–83*. Armonk, N.Y.: M. E. Sharpe, 1984.

Class of '77 Marriage Problems Investigation Group, Philosophy Department, Chinese People's University. "What Is the Divorce Situation after the Implementation of the New Marriage Law—An Investigation of Dongcheng District, Beijing." *In* Chu, 104–16.

Comaroff, J. L. *The Meaning of Marriage Payments*. London: Academic Press, 1980.

Croll, Elisabeth. *Chinese Women Since Mao*. London: Zed Books, Ltd.; Armonk, N.Y.: M. E. Sharpe, 1983.

————. *The Politics of Marriage in Contemporary China*. Cambridge: Cambridge University Press, 1981.

————. *The Women's Movement in China: A Selection of Readings, 1949–1973*. London: Anglo-Chinese Educational Institute, 1974.

Croll, Elisabeth, Delia Davin, and Penny Kane, eds. *China's One-Child Policy*. London: Macmillan, 1985.

Dai Anmin. "Qizi xian wo qianshao shi" (When my wife suspects I have little money). *Jiefang ribao*, Nov. 16, 1985.

"Dalian chuangban nüzi zhiye gaozhong" (A women's vocational upper middle school is established in Dalian). *Nü qingnian*, trial issue (1985), 46.

"Dalianshi diyige qizi jiazheng xuexiban chengli" (The first home economics class is established in Dalian). *ZFB*, June 5, 1985.

Dan Dan. "Nüxingde meili jinjin shi wenrou ma?" (Is meekness women's only charm?) *Fujian qingnian*, 7 (July 1985), 18.

Dang Chunyuan. "Ganqing polie jiushi panjue lihunde yiju" (The destruction of love is the basis on which to judge divorce). *MF*, 2 (Feb. 1981), 13–14.

"Dang fumu ganshe ni hunyinde shihou" (When parents interfere in your marriage). *ZQB*, July 20, 1982, 4.

"Dang yige xiandaide 'xianqi liangmu'" (Become a modern "virtuous wife and good mother"). *Funü zhiyou*, 7 (1985), 15–16.

Dangdai qingnian (Contemporary Youth). Xi'an.

Davin, Delia. "The Single-Child Family Policy in the Countryside." *In* Croll et al., 37–82.

————. *Woman-work*. Oxford: Clarendon, 1976.

De Yi. "Protect the Rights of Women and Children." *Women of China*, 7 (1985), 14.

Diamond, Norma. "Collectivization, Kinship, and the Status of Women in Rural China." *Bulletin of Concerned Asian Scholars*, 7, 1 (Jan.–Mar. 1975), 25–32.

"Ding qiaoji, la guanxi, fufu daoyan—'pohun ji'" (An artful scheme, establishing a relationship for one's own advantage, under the direction of husband and wife—"notes on a forced marriage"). *ZQB*, Mar. 15, 1981, 8.

Ding Yuan. "Zai 'zhenghun guanggao' de beihou" (Behind the "marriage solicitation advertisements"). *Shehui*, 3 (Mar. 1983), 32–34.

"Dinghun hou haineng jiechu hunyue ma?" (After becoming engaged, can one still renounce the engagement?) *Funü shenghuo*, 5 (May 1985), 19.

"Diyici fuyue" (The first date). *ZF*, 4 (Apr. 1985), 25.

"Do Not Start Making Love to Middle School Students Who Are Still Young." *Extracts from China Mainland Magazines*, 65 (Nov. 16, 1956), 16.

"Do Not Start Making Love Too Early." *Extracts from China Mainland Magazines*, 41 (Apr. 3, 1956), 23.

Dong Tian'en and Zhao Shiyi, eds. *Yuan nin qingchun geng jianmei* (Wishing you a more healthy and beautiful youth). Beijing: Zhongguo funü chubanshe, 1983.

Dong Weiling. "Creating Jobs for Displaced Women Workers." *Women of China*, 2 (Feb. 1986), 15–16.

Dong Ye. "Wuge shaonüde lianming konggao" (An accusation signed jointly by five girls). *Aiqing hunyin jiating*, 2 (1985), 23–25, 51.

Dongfang qingnian (Eastern Youth). Hangzhou.

Duan Yue. "Nüqingniande jiuye youshi" (The superiority of young women seeking employment). N.a., *Weini jiuye dang canmou* (Advice for those of you seeking employment). Beijing: Beijing chubanshe, 1984, 63–69.

Falü yu shenghuo (Law and Life). Beijing.

Fan Qingshan. "Shenghuo meirong huazhuang" (Makeup for improving your daily appearance). *Zhongwai funü*, 4 (Apr. 1985), 36–38.

Fang Xiang. "Jianyi guiding tongjianzui" (Suggesting that adultery be made a crime). *MF*, 3 (1984), 18.

Fausto-Sterling, Anne. *Myths of Gender: Biological Theories About Men and Women*. New York: Basic Books, 1985.

FBIS Daily Report—China. Washington, D.C.: Foreign Broadcast Information Service.

Fei Xiaotong. "On Changes in the Chinese Family Structure." *In* Chu, 32–45.

Feng Bian. "The Concept of a Good Wife and Mother in the 1980's." *Women of China*, 4 (Apr. 1985), 13–14.

Feng Xing. "Chinese Women Athletes on the Rise." *Women of China*, 7 (July 1984), 24–26.

"Fengyang zhaogong nügong duo yu nangong yibei" (In Fengyang twice as many women workers were hired as men). *ZFB*, Mar. 20, 1985, 1.

"Fujian Huian xian gebie xiang zhaohun yanzhong" (Early marriage is serious in individual townships in Huian county, Fujian). *ZFB*, 33 (May 15, 1985), 1.

Fujian qingnian (Fujian Youth). Fuzhou.

"Fujian qingnian nannü lunzheng 'nüren buyao tai weile'" (Male and female youth in Fujian are debating "Women should not be too powerful"). *Xinmin wanbao*, June 14, 1985.

"Fumu ganshe nüer lian'ai qingli nanrong" (Parents' interference in their daughter's love life is incompatible with the accepted code of human conduct). *Wenhui bao*, Apr. 19, 1981.

Funü (Women). Shenyang.

Funü gongzuo (Women's Work). Beijing.

Funü shenghuo (Women's Life). Zhengzhou.

Funü zhiyou (Women's Friend). Harbin.

Funü zhiyou zazhishe, ed. *Funü baike quanshu* (Women's encyclopedia). 2 vols. Jilin: Beifang funü ertong chubanshe, 1985.

Gao Yuan. *Born Red: A Chronicle of the Cultural Revolution*. Stanford, Calif.: Stanford University Press, 1987.

Gao Yuan and Zhuang Ze. "Qingshaonian qiangjian fanzui xingwei chuxi" (A preliminary analysis of the crime of rape among teenagers). *In Shehuixue wenji* (Essays on sociology). Shanghai: Shanghai shi shehuixue xuehui, 1985, 212–26.

Gei shaonü de xin (Letters to young girls). Shanghai: Shanghai renmin chubanshe, 1984.

"Gei 'shishen' nüqingnian dang canmou" (Adviser to young women who have lost their virginity). *Qingnian zixun*, 1 (May 1985), 22–24.

Gilmartin, Christina. "Gender Violence in Contemporary China." Unpublished ms.

———. "Mobilizing Women: The Early Experiences of the Chinese Communist Party, 1920–1927." Diss. University of Pennsylvania, 1986.

Gold, Thomas B. "'Just in Time!' China battles spiritual pollution on the eve of 1984." *Asian Survey*, 24, 9 (Sept. 1984), 947–74.

Gong Peide. "Diwuci yuehui" (The fifth date). *Jiefang ribao*, Sept. 6, 1985.

Gu Shulan. "Funü gong" (Women's palace). *ZFB*, May 22, 1985, 2.

"'Guanmi' pianhun ji" (Chronicle of a marriage fraud by a "person who craved office"). *Baokan wenzhai*, Feb. 11, 1986.

"Guanyu Wang Fengxiang canhai qizide diaocha" (Concerning the investigation of Wang Fengxiang's cruel injury of his wife). *Funü*, 1 (1984), 11.

Guo Liwen. "Chengshi jingji tizhi gaige gei funü gongzuo tichu xin keti" (New problems for women's work caused by the urban economic reforms). *Funü gongzuo*, 3 (1985), 9–10.

Guo Yuzhen. "Yiwo weijian" (Take a warning from me). *ZF*, 11 (Nov. 1983), 34–35.

"Guonei shouchuang fengruqi; gongxiao xianzhu su jianmei" (China pioneers a bust enhancer; remarkable results in achieving healthful beauty). *ZF*, 5 (May 1985), inside back cover.

Hai Gui. "Ganhuale lan zhangfu" (Helping a lazy husband change). *Qingnian yidai*, 5 (1982), 24.

"Haishi you suo zhuiqiude nüxing hao" (A woman who has her own goals is preferable). *ZF*, 11 (Nov. 1984), 24.

He Xiuping. "Jiejiede muguang shi dengguolaide" (Older sister was stared down). *Yunnan fazhi bao*, Jan. 13, 1984, 4.

He Yaqing. "Shijie guanjun de zuji" (The tracks of a world champion). *Funü*, 1 (Jan. 1984), 2–6.

Hershatter, Gail. "Making a Friend: Changing Patterns of Courtship in Urban China." *Pacific Affairs*, 57, 2 (Summer 1984), 237–51.

Hong Qin. "The Old Man under the Moon." *Women of China*, 1 (Jan. 1985), 15, 17.

Honig, Emily. "Private Issues, Public Discourse: The Life and Times of Yu Luojin." *Pacific Affairs*, 57, 2 (Summer 1984), 252–65.

———. *Sisters and Strangers: Women in the Shanghai Cotton Mills, 1919–1949.* Stanford, Calif.: Stanford University Press, 1986.

Hu Jian. "Disanzhe jiurude lihun'an zhongzhong" (Various kinds of divorce cases that are due to third party intrusion). *Funü shenghuo*, 12 (1983), 20.

Hu Jiang. "Zenyangde xiaohuozi you xiyinli" (What kind of fellow has appeal). *Dangdai qingnian*, 5 (May 1985), 21.

Hu Rong. "Dang hao 'yazhai furen'" (Do a good job of holding down the home front). *Qingnian yidai*, 5 (1982), 22.

Hu Tingyi. *Xing zhishi mantan* (An informal discussion of sexual knowledge). Nanchang: Jiangxi renmin chubanshe, 1980.

Hua Yi. "Cong Li Hui tan disanzhe" (A discussion of third parties based on Li Hui). *Shehui*, 1 (Feb. 1985), 35.

Huang Jingyao. "Dushen xianxiang fenxi" (An analysis of the phenomenon of singlehood). *Jiefang ribao*, Dec. 21, 1985.

Huang Mingzhan. "Zenyang zhidao guniang xihuan ni" (How to tell if a girl likes you). *Dangdai qingnian*, 5 (May 1985), 22.

Huang Shuze. "Peiyang nühaizide jianqiang xingge" (Cultivate a strong personality in girls). *Beijing funü*, 2 (Aug. 1983), 32.

Huang Yin. "Nü da dangjia bu yijia" (When girls grow up they should marry, but it's not easy to do so). *Jiating*, 5 (May 1984), 16–18.

"Huangse shukan dui wode fushi" (My corruption by pornographic publications). *ZQB*, Mar. 21, 1982, 1.

"Huyu jizao yifa zhicai canhai funüde xiongshou" (An appeal for swift punishment in accordance with the law for the assailant who caused injury to a woman). *MF*, 10 (Oct. 1984), 24–26.

Ji Shuhan. "Qiangsheng zai huidang" (Gunshots are reverberating). *Zhongwai funü*, 1 (Jan. 1985), 31–33.

Jian Shengyuan, Luo Shizheng, and Wang Xianwu. "Wei yige bei lingrude funü pa'an erqi" (Smiting the table and taking a stand on behalf of a woman who has been humiliated). *ZF*, 11 (Nov. 1983), 2–4.

Jiang An. "Ni juyou 'nanzihan' qizhi ma?" (Do you have a "manly" temperament?) *Jiefang ribao*, Nov. 22, 1985.

Jiang Yangming. "Ji yao xuxin, you yao zizhu" (Be both open-minded and in control). *Jiefang ribao*, Mar. 14, 1986.

Jiang Yongping. "Yu nüqingnian tantan jiuye wenti" (Discussing the problems of finding employment with young women). *In* Zhongguo shehui kexueyuan qingnian yanjiusuo (Chinese Academy of Social Sciences, Youth Research Institute) and Sichuan renmin guangbo diantai (Sichuan People's Broadcasting Station), eds. *Qingnian jiuye zhilu* (Youth's path to employment). Beijing: Zhongguo shehui kexue chubanshe, 1983, 87–95.

Jiang Yuanming. "Keyi de 'zhidao'" (Doubtful guidance). *ZQB*, Aug. 22, 1982, 1.

Jiang Yuanming and Li Tangzhen. *Xifu yu popo* (Mother-in-law and daughter-in-law). Taizhou: Jiangsu renmin chubanshe, 1983.

"Jiaru wo shi Xiao B . . ." (If I were Xiao B). *ZF*, 8 (Aug. 1985), 10–12.

Jiating (Family). Guangzhou.

Jiating yisheng (Family Doctor). Guangzhou.

Jie Zhuanguang. "Qizi de yingxiangli" (The influence of a wife). *Qingnian yidai*, 5 (Oct. 1982), 22–23.

"Jieda yige nüzhongxuesheng de nantai" (Answering the difficult question of a girl middle school student). *Qingnian yidai*, 1 (Feb. 1984), 58.

Jiefang ribao (Liberation Daily). Shanghai.

"Jiezhi de daifa" (Methods of wearing rings). *ZF*, 4 (Apr. 1985), 36.

Jilin qingnian (Jilin Youth). Jilin.

Jin Feng. "Mei de zhuiqiu he xiwang" (The pursuit and hope of beauty). *Zhongwai funü*, 2 (Feb. 1985), 4–6.

Jin Hua and Yan Wen. *Hunyin jiating wenti falü guwen* (Legal advice on marriage and family problems). Beijing: Qunzhong chubanshe, 1981.

Jin Jian. "Zenyang jiejiao nüqingnian" (How to make friends with young women). *Qingnian zixun*, 1 (May 1985), 25.

"Jin Xuerong nüedai popo bei panxing" (Jin Xuerong is sentenced for mistreating her mother-in-law). *Tianjin ribao*, July 3, 1980.

"Jinbi ji jingshen zhemo shifou goucheng baoli ganshe?" (Do confinement and spiritual torment constitute forcible interference?) *ZF*, 11 (Nov. 1983), 43.

Jing Ying. "Fuqi en'ai shiye fazhan" (If a husband and wife love each other their careers can develop). *Jiating*, 4 (1985), 14.

Jinse nianhua (Golden Years). Nanning.

"Jiujiu qingnian" (Save the young people). *Nüzi shijie*, 6 (June 1985), 19.

Johnson, Kay Ann. *Women, the Family and Peasant Revolution in China*. Chicago: University of Chicago Press, 1983.

Joseph, William. "Foreword." *In* Gao Yuan, *Born Red*.

Kallgren, Joyce. "Politics, Welfare, and Change: the Single-Child Family in China." *In* Perry and Wong, 131–56.

Kane, Penny. "The Single-child Policy in the Cities." *In* Croll et al., 83–113.
Ke Cunjie. "Jiechu shouyin exi" (Give up the bad habit of masturbation). *ZQB*, Feb. 6, 1982.
Ke Fu. "Gongkai zhenghun, libi jiancun" (Public marriage solicitation has both advantages and disadvantages). *Jiefang ribao*, Mar. 15, 1986.
Ke Wei. "In Our Families." *Women of China*, 2 (Feb. 1986), 2–5.
Lei Wenxian. "Shaonian xing chengshuqi de jiating jiaoyu" (Home education for the period of juvenile sexual maturation). *Zhongwai funü*, 1985: 4 (Apr.), 20–21; 5 (May), 44; 6 (June), 30.
"Let Them Marry Younger." *China Daily*, Jan. 7, 1984, 4.
Li Daowei. "Shui nenggan jiu bao shui" (Whoever is capable should take care of the other). *Shehui*, 1 (Feb. 1984), 36–37.
Li Feng. "Yu nüqingnian tan 'daomei'" (Some words to young women about the "curse"). *ZQB*, Sept. 11, 1982, 4.
Li Guangchun. "Jixiao zhaosheng hounan beinü baifen zhi cha tai bu gongping" (It is unfair that in recruiting students technical schools discriminate against women—they must get different scores). *ZFB*, Jan. 9, 1985, 2.
Li Li. "Yige lihun nürende fannao" (The worries of a divorced woman). *Xiandai jiating*, 5 (May 1985), 22–23.
Li Lie. "Funü zenyang fangwei qiangjian zuixing" (How women can defend themselves against the crime of rape). *MF*, 4 (Apr. 1985), 36–37.
Li Minghua, Wang Shengbing, Xiao Muhua, Tao Jianhuai. "Wuchangqu qinggong lian'ai hunyin xianzhuang diaocha" (An investigation of the current place of love and marriage among young workers in Wuchang district). *Shehui*, 6 (June 1983), 29–31.
Li Qian. "Dushen shenghuo shengyu buxing hunyin" (Single life is superior to unhappy marriage). *Qingnian zixun*, 1 (May 1985), 15.
Li Shaoqin. "Nüxingde meili" (The attraction of women). *ZF*, 5 (May 1985), 21.
Li Yuanzheng. "Ye tan 'nüzi yinggai rouxun'" (More on "Women should be meek"). *Fujian qingnian*, 6 (1985), 3.
Li Zengliang and An Huijun. "Tade huihen" (Her bitter remorse). *Nüzi shijie* (June 1985), 32.
"Lian'ai fangshi taolun" (Discussion of the form of love). *Jiating*, 1985: 5 (May), 24–25; 6 (June), 20–21; 7 (July), 26–27.
Liang Heng and Judith Shapiro. *Son of the Revolution*. New York: Knopf, 1983.
Liao Shijie, You Zhonglun, and Tang Xiaoqiang. *Lian'ai shujian* (Love letters). Chengdu: Sichuan renmin chubanshe, 1983.
Liaoningsheng Lüdashi zonggonghui he funü lianhui (The Federation of Labor and Women's Federation of Lüshun and Dalian in Liaoning province). "Buying qiangpo nügong 'liu zhi fang changjia'" (Do not force women to leave work and take prolonged maternity leave). *ZF*, 11 (1980), 29–30.
Lin Ling. "Nannü zhijiande xing chayi" (Sex differences between men and women). *Yuelao bao*, 7 (July 1985), 7, 4–5.
Lin Wanxiu. "Qinren zaodao wuru yihou" (After a family member suffers humiliation [sexual assault]). *MF*, 4 (Apr. 1985), 40.
Liu Chang. "Pianjian a, ni haikule wo" (Ah, prejudice, you harmed me and caused me suffering). *Dongfang qingnian*, 6 (June 1985), 18.
Liu Changlin. "Daxuesheng lian'aiguan wenti chutan" (A preliminary exploration of the question of the concept of love among university students). *Shehui*, 6 (June 1983), 32–33.

Liu Dalin. "Fouding zhencao, tichang zhongzhen" (Negate chastity, promote loyalty). *Nüzi shijie*, 5 (May 1985), 21.

Liu Enyu. "Dule 'Yiwei "daguniang" de dubai' yihou" (After reading "Soliloquy of an 'old maid'"). *Dongxi nanbei*, 1 (Jan. 1985), 30.

Liu Guanglun. "Shui shi 'funü huijia qu' wailun de famingren?" (Who was the inventor of the crooked theory that "women should return to the home"?) *Beijing funü*, 5 (Nov. 1983), 3.

Liu Hanhuai. "Lian'ai qinni judong zhi wojian" (My view on intimate love activities). *Fujian qingnian*, 5 (May 1985), 43.

———. "Zai danshen guniangde 'changlang'" (In the "gallery" of single girls). *Fujian qingnian*, 6 (June 1985), 36.

Liu Heng. "Qishi funü jiushi qishi ni ziji de muqin" (To discriminate against women is to discriminate against your own mother). *RMRB*, Jan. 19, 1984.

Liu Jianping. "Nüzi haoqiang bing fei buneng zuo 'xianqi'" (Strong women are not incapable of becoming "virtuous wives"). *Jiefang ribao*, Aug. 30, 1985.

Liu Jinbao. "Chaojia ji" (Record of a family quarrel). *In* Wang Fuchu, ed., *Daode fating* (The court of morality). Shanghai: Shanghai wenhua chubanshe, 1983, 71–74.

"Liu Shu tongzhi jianyi zhongshi nüzi peiyang" (Comrade Liu Shu suggests that attention be paid to the training of women). *Nü qingnian*, trial issue (1985), 46.

Liu Tong. "Yao ba xingzheng he falü shouduan jieheqilai" (We must unite administrative and legal methods). *Funü*, 1 (1984), 17.

Liu Xinwu. "The Overpass." *In* Helen Siu and Zelda Stern, eds., *Mao's Harvest*. New York: Oxford University Press, 1983, 29–90.

Liu Ying. "Yige bugan kongsude guniang" (A girl who did not dare to make an accusation). *Jiating*, 12 (Dec. 1984), 20–23.

Liu Yixian. "Guolai rende tanxi" (Sigh of one who has had the experience). *Fujian qingnian*, 7 (1985), 36.

Liu Zheng, Song Jian, et al. *China's Population: Problems and Prospects*. Beijing: New World Press, 1981.

Long Zhongmei. "Guzu shenghuode yongqi, kandao zijide liliang" (Gather your courage, become aware of your own strength). *ZF*, 11 (Nov. 1983), 32–33.

Lou Jingbo. "Danshen bu keqi" (Singles are not gullible). *Zhongwai funü*, 2 (1985), 20–21.

Lu Zhenqiu. "Dui yibaize 'zhenghun qishi' de fenxi" (An analysis of one hundred "marriage solicitation announcements"). *Jiefang ribao*, Oct. 19, 1985.

Lü Wende. "Zhiyin hunshi hefa bu heli" (Just because our wedding conformed to law but not to custom). *ZQB*, Apr. 17, 1985.

Luo Lu. "Shixian jiawu laodong shehuihuade xianshi kunnan" (The real difficulties of socializing housework). *Shehui*, 2 (Apr. 1984), 21.

Ma Xiaojun. "Yige touyue guojing guniang de chanhui" (Confession of a young woman who secretly crossed the border). *Funü*, 2 (Jan. 1984), 32.

Ma Xinfang. "Cong daniangzi hunyin wenti taolun xiangdaode. . . ." (Thoughts after a discussion of the problem of marriage for "old maids"). *Qingnian yidai*, 6 (June 1984), 37.

Ma Xuehong. "Yige daiye nüqingniande kunao" (The bitterness of a young woman waiting for employment). *ZFB*, Jan. 9, 1985, 2.

Ma Ying. "Ge Feng dajie bie renle" (Older sister Ge Feng, do not put up with it). *ZFB*, Apr. 17, 1985, 3.

"'Ma Zhuanyuan,' ni zai nali?" (Assistant Director Ma, where are you?) *RMRB*, July 11, 1983.

"Mama, bie zeguai ninde nüer!" (Mama, don't blame your daughter!) *Yuelao bao*, 7 (July 1985), 3.

The Marriage Law of the People's Republic of China. Beijing: Foreign Languages Press, 1982.

Mei Hongjuan. "What Does Killing One's Own Baby Girl Signify?" *In* Chu, 28–35.

"Meiguo qingnian dui 'xing jiefang' de chongxin renshi" (A fresh understanding of "sexual liberation" on the part of American youth). *Qingnian yidai*, 5 (Oct. 1984), 15.

Meihua shenghuo (Better Life). Shanghai.

"Meiyou jieju de aiqing gushi" (A love story without an ending). *ZQB*, June 27, 1982, 1.

"'Meiyou jieju de aiqing gushi' jiangyou jieju" ("A love story without an ending" will have an ending). *ZQB*, July 11, 1982, 1.

Meng Xiaoyun. "Dangdai Zhongguo funü mianmian guan" (Contemporary Chinese women viewed from several angles). *RMRB*, Jan. 8–10, 1986, 2.

Ming De. "Wo cong mituzhong fanhui" (I went astray and returned). *Funü*, 1 (1984), 15.

Ming Wen. "Woliang xuanzele xingfu" (The two of us chose happiness). *Jiating*, 6 (1985), 14–15.

Minzhu yu fazhi (*MF*; Democracy and the Legal System). Shanghai.

Minzhu yu fazhi bianjibu, ed. (Democracy and the legal system editorial bureau). *Hunyin anjian 100 li* (One hundred marriage cases). Shanghai: Minzhu yu fazhi zazhishe, 1981.

"Mo ba niaodao dang yindao" (Do not mistake the urethra for the vagina). *Jiating yisheng*, 1 (Jan. 1985), 45.

Mo Jun. "Hunqian jiancha chunmo zuihao neng quxiao" (The premarital examination of the hymen is best eliminated). *Zhongwai funü*, 5 (1985), 46.

"Mo wangle ni xinzhong de zhuiqiu" (Don't forget the pursuit of what is in your heart). *ZQ*, 3 (Mar. 11, 1984), 52–53.

Molyneaux, Maxine. "Mobilization without emancipation? Women's interests, the state, and revolution in Nicaragua." *Feminist Studies*, 11, 2 (Summer 1985), 227–54.

"Nan quan, nü wu" (Men box, women dance). *ZQB*, Aug. 1982, 7.

Ning Huaixin. "Zhizhi buwenmingde nao dongfang" (Stop the uncivilized practice of disrupting the bridal chamber). *ZQB*, Oct. 8, 1981.

Ning Qing. *Jiating wenti tongxin* (Letters about family problems). Changsha: Hunan renmin chubanshe, 1981.

Nü gongchengshi (Woman Engineer). Shanghai.

Nü qingnian (Young Women). Changsha.

"Nüer zhaoshou baoxing zhihou" (After your daughter is raped). *Jiating yisheng*, 6 (June 1986), 21–22.

"Nüxing xiuzhen zuotanhui" (A women's pocket-size discussion). *Fujian qingnian*, 6 (June 1985), 32.

"Nüzi chengcai xu kefude ruodian" (Weaknesses women need to overcome in order to make something of themselves). *Nüzi shijie*, 6 (June 1985), 39.

"Nüzi dushen wenti chutan" (A preliminary discussion of the problem of single women). *ZFB*, 15 (Jan. 9, 1985), 3.

Nüzi shijie (Women's World). Shijiazhuang.
Ou Yangman. "Xi 'toufa chang jianshi duan'" (An analysis of "long-haired, short-sighted"). *Zhongwai funü*, 5 (May 1985), 9.
Pan Yunkang and Pan Naigu. "A Tentative Discussion on Urban Families and Family Structure in China." *In* Chu, 46–68.
Parish, William, and Martin Whyte. *Village and Family in Contemporary China.* Chicago: University of Chicago Press, 1978.
Pasternak, Burton. *Marriage and Fertility in Tianjin, China.* Honolulu: Papers of the East-West Population Institute, 1982.
Peck, Stacey. *Halls of Jade, Walls of Stone: Women in China Today.* New York: Franklin Watts, 1985.
Pepper, Suzanne. *China's Universities.* Ann Arbor: Center for Chinese Studies, University of Michigan, 1984.
Perry, Elizabeth J., and Christine Wong, eds. *The Political Economy of Reform in Post-Mao China.* Cambridge, Mass.: Council on East Asian Studies, Harvard University Press, 1985.
"Pohun ji" (Notes on a forced marriage). *ZQB*, June 3, 1982, 2.
Population Census Office under the State Council and Department of Population Statistics, State Statistical Bureau, People's Republic of China. *Ten Percent Sampling Tabulation on the 1982 Population Census of the People's Republic of China.* In Chinese and English. Beijing: Zhongguo tongji chubanshe, 1983.
———. *The 1982 Population Census of China.* Hong Kong: Economic Information and Agency, 1983.
"Poxi buhe zenme ban?" (What should I do when my wife and mother don't get along?) *ZQB*, Jan. 1, 1980, 3.
"Protecting Infant Girls." *Beijing Review*, 5 (Jan. 31, 1983), 4.
Qiao Yan. "Zhidou qiangjianfande nügong—Zuo Lijun" (A woman worker in a battle of wits with a rapist—Zuo Lijun). *Beijing funü*, 5 (Nov. 1983), 20–21.
"Qing ting yige nüdaxueshengde kanfa" (Please listen to the view of a woman university student). *ZF*, 11 (Nov. 1984), 25.
"Qingchu baoban ganshe hunyinde jiu xisu" (Clear away the old customs of arranged marriages and interference in marriage). *ZQ*, 12 (Dec. 1983), 14–15.
"Qingchu wuran xuexiaode jingshen laji" (Clear away the spiritual garbage that is polluting the school). *ZQB*, Mar. 27, 1982, 1.
Qingnian yidai (The Young Generation). Shanghai.
Qingnian zixun (Youth Adviser). Beijing.
Qu Dashen. "Qiguanyan buzu weishun" (*Qiguanyan* should not be taken as exemplary). *Funü*, 3 (1981), 21.
Qu Hua. "Yige shou nüedai nügongde gongsu" (The accusation of an abused woman worker). *Gongren ribao*, Dec. 20, 1983, 3.
Qu Le. "Buyao qishi lilehunde funü" (Do not discriminate against divorced women). *ZF*, 11 (1983), 35.
"Quan shehui dou lai guanxin nüdaxueshengde fenpei wenti" (The entire society is concerning itself with the problem of work assignments for women university graduates). *ZFB*, June 5, 1985.
Renmin ribao (*RMRB*; People's Daily). Beijing.
Rind, Anita. "To Be a Feminist in Beijing." *In* Gregor Benton, ed., *Wild Lilies, Poisonous Weeds: Dissident Voices from People's China.* London: Pluto Press, 1982, 195–201.
Robinson, Jean. "Of Women and Washing Machines: Employment, Housework,

and the Reproduction of Motherhood in Socialist China." *China Quarterly*, 101 (March 1985), 32–57.

Rofel, Lisa. "Eating Out of One Big Pot: Ideology and the Economic Reforms in Post-Mao China." Paper prepared for the Conference on Anthropological Perspectives on China, University of California at Los Angeles, Nov. 22, 1986.

"Safeguarding Women's Rights." *Beijing Review*, 18 (May 2, 1983), 4–5.

Schwarcz, Vera. *The Chinese Enlightenment*. Berkeley: University of California Press, 1986.

Shan Guangnai. "Dui banhao chengshi hunyin jieshaosuode jidian yijian" (Several opinions about running the urban marriage introduction bureaus well). *RMRB*, July 5, 1984.

Shan Ren. *Miyue lüyou shouce* (A guide to honeymoon travels). Shanghai: Shanghai wenhua chubanshe, 1986.

Shanghai laonian bao (Shanghai Senior Citizens News). Shanghai.

"Shanghai youle baomu xuexiao" (Shanghai now has a school for maids). *Xinmin wanbao*, Sept. 19, 1985.

Shasha. "Wo koukaile ai de damen" (I knocked at the gate of love and opened it). *Qingnian zixun*, 1 (May 1985), 37.

"Shashi feichu fenfang 'yinan weizhu' louxi" (Shashi eliminates the ugly custom of giving priority to men in assigning housing). *ZFB*, June 12, 1985, 1.

Shehui (Sociology). Shanghai.

Shehui bao (Society News). Shanghai.

Shen Rong. "At Middle Age." *Chinese Literature*, 10 (1980), 3–63. Originally in *Shouhuo* (Harvest), 1 (1980).

Sheng Ping et al. *Xiandai nüxing shenghuo shouce* (Handbook for the contemporary woman). Beijing: Gongren chubanshe, 1985.

Shenghuo zhoukan (Life Weekly). Shanghai.

"Shenyang zhishijie nüyou lianyihui chengli" (The Shenyang Women Intellectuals' Friendly Society is established). *ZFB*, Apr. 24, 1985, 2.

Shenyangshi fulian (The Shenyang Women's Federation). "'Yi nanfang weizhu' fenfang buheli" (It is unreasonable to give priority to men in assigning housing). *ZF*, 2 (Feb. 1981), 11–12.

Shi Dezhao. "Fajun muqin youshi" (Promote the superiority of mothers). *ZF*, 3 (Mar. 1984), 40–41.

Shi Funan. "'Qiguanyan' de liuchuan shuomingle shenme?" (What does the spread of the term "*qiguanyan*" show?). *Beijing funü*, 2 (Aug. 1983), 20.

"Shi wo wuqing haishi ta budaode?" (Am I heartless or is he immoral?) *ZQ*, 1 (Jan. 1984), 12.

Shi Xingrong. "Buyao weida konghua yao shiji xingdong" (We want action rather than lofty words). *ZF*, 11 (1980), 2–3.

———. "Kandaole guangmingde qiantu he xiwang" (I have seen the bright future and hope). *ZF*, 11 (1980), 3.

"Shi zhende ai ma?" (Is this true love?) *Xiandai jiating*, 1 (Jan. 1985), 27.

"Shicong guniang sixiang hao" (Shicong is a clear-thinking girl). *Tianjin ribao*, Jan. 12, 1981.

Shizhuang (Fashion). Beijing.

"Shougang zhuanye peixunban luqu nüsheng guoban" (More than half the students admitted to the Capital Steel training class are women). *ZFB*, Feb. 13, 1985.

"Small Happiness." Directed by Carma Hinton and Richard Gordon. Long Bow Films, 1984.

Song Jie. "Wanbuhuide sunshi" (Irretrievable loss). *ZF*, 12 (Dec. 1980), 26–27.
Song Xiaoying. "Wo yao lihun" (I want a divorce). *Jiating*, 5 (May 1985), 17–18.
"Song Yuexia gaozhuang" (Song Yuexia brings a lawsuit). *ZQB*, Mar. 23, 1982, 1.
Spence, Jonathan. *The Gate of Heavenly Peace*. New York: Vintage Press, 1981.
State Statistical Bureau, People's Republic of China. *Statistical Yearbook of China 1983*. Hong Kong: Economic Information and Agency, 1983.
———. *Statistical Yearbook of China 1984*. Hong Kong: Economic Information and Agency, 1984.
———. *Statistical Yearbook of China 1985*. Hong Kong: Economic Information and Agency, 1985.
Su Haobin. "Zhongguo lihun xianxiang chutan" (A preliminary discussion of divorce in China). *Qishi niandai* (The Seventies), (Dec. 1982), 90–91.
Su Honglin. "Tao Chun huida buliao de wenti" (A question that Tao Chun cannot answer). *ZF*, 7 (July 1984), 17–18.
Su Shan. "Xie zai sanshi sui shengride shihou" (Written at the time of my thirtieth birthday). *ZFB*, 15 (Jan. 9, 1985), 3.
"Sun Jing de zaoyu shuomingle shenma?" (What did the bitter experience of Sun Jing illustrate?) *ZF*, 1980: 10 (Oct.), 9–12; 11 (Nov.), 4–8; 12 (Dec.), 24–27; 1981: 1 (Jan.), 36–39; 8 (Aug.), 27.
Sun Yi, "Aiqing de beiju" (Love tragedy). *Tianjin ribao*, Oct. 24, 1979, 2.
Sun Zhifeng. "Jiawu laodong xiandaihua shizai bixing" (The socialization of housework is imperative). *Shehui*, 2 (Apr. 1984), 20.
"Ta weihe zoushangle juelu?" (Why did she destroy herself?) *MF*, 10 (Oct. 1984), 24–26.
"Ta weishenme bianle xin?" (Why did he have a change of heart?) *Tianjin ribao*, Sept. 8, 1980.
"Talia weishenme bei chaisan?" (Why were the two of them split up?) *ZQB*, Jan. 17, 1980.
Tan Fuyun. "Funü yao you zhiqi zheng diyi" (Women must have the ambition to strive to be first). *Shehui*, 4 (Aug. 1984), 30–31.
———. "Funü zuzhi jianshe bixu shiying gaige xingshi" (The building of women's organizations must be appropriate to the circumstances of the reforms). *Funü gongzuo*, 3 (Mar. 1985), 22–23.
"Tan lian'ai shi buyao yingxiang bieren" (Do not disturb others when courting). *ZQB*, Apr. 20, 1982, 3.
Tan Manni. "Women: Fighting Discrimination in Jobs and Schooling." *China Reconstructs*, 35, 3 (Mar. 1986), 34, 39–41.
Tan Weiwen. "Jin 'niangjia' men" (Entering the door of my "parents"). *Jiating*, 5 (May 1985), 26–27.
Tang Liqin. "Yiwei 'daguniang' de dubai" (Soliloquy of an "old maid"). *Shehui*, 4 (Aug. 1984), 47–49.
Tang Min. "Yao tigao funüde zishen xiuyang" (Women's training must be improved). *Fujian qingnian*, 7 (July 1985), 19.
Tang Shaoyun. "Zenyang duidai zhongxuesheng de 'zaolian'?" (How should one deal with "premature love" among high school students?) *Wenhui bao*, June 14, 1985.
"Tangle yici fa, diule yitiao ming" (Getting a permanent and losing a life). *ZFB*, Feb. 13, 1985, 2.
"Tanguo lian'ai jiu bu chunjie ma?" (Is one impure if one has been in love before?) *ZQB*, May 9, 1982, 8.

Tao Kai. "Wo dui lihunde yidian kanfa" (Some of my opinions about divorce). *ZF*, 7 (July 1983), 15–16.

Tianjin ribao (Tianjin Daily). Tianjin.

"Tigao zerengan he zixinxin" (Increase the sense of duty and self-confidence). *Zhongguo funü*, 11 (Nov. 1983), 2–5.

Ting Lan. "Nüren bushi yueliang" (Woman is not the moon). *Nüzi shijie*, 6 (June 1985), 1.

Wang Anyi. "The Destination." *Chinese Literature* (Autumn 1984), 3–24.

Wang Fuchu. *Daode fating* (The court of morality). Shanghai: Shanghai wenhua chubanshe, 1983.

Wang Fuhua. "Si wen" (Four questions). *Renmin ribao manhua zengkan* (The People's Daily cartoon supplement), Mar. 5, 1983.

Wang Ge. "Da nianling guniang hunpei nande lishi yinsu kaocha" (An investigation of the historical factors making the marriage of older girls difficult). *Shehui kexue*, 2 (Feb. 1985), 33–34.

Wang Jingwen. "Nannü shengxue bili weihe ruci xuanshu?" (Why such a wide gap in the proportions of boys and girls entering the upper grades?) *ZF*, 9 (Sept. 1980), 40.

Wang Junhe. "Yinwei shi nüde jiu bu anpai gongzuo dui ma?" (Is it right to refuse someone a job just because she is female?) *ZFB*, Jan. 9, 1985, 2.

Wang Ping. "Bufang yishi: rang diannao hongniang wei nin qianxian" (No harm in trying: let the computer matchmaker act as go-between for you). *Jiating*, 11 (Nov. 1984), 16.

Wang Qiuliang and Zhu Wenjie. "Yixin yao dang mote'er de guniang" (A young woman who wanted to become a model with all her heart). *Xiandai jiating*, 7 (July 1985), 13.

Wang Ruichao. "Erjie a, ni mingmu ba!" (Rest in peace, second sister!) *MF*, 5 (May 1984), 30–33.

Wang Ruowang. "Hunyin yao zizhu" (One's marriage should be decided by oneself). *ZQ*, 1 (Jan. 1981), 9.

Wang Shanling and Lu Shucun. "Guanyu yanchang nüzhigong shengyu jia wentide diaocha" (An investigation of the problem of prolonging maternity leave for women employees). *ZFB*, June 5, 1985, 2.

Wang Wenbin, Zhao Zhiyi, and Tan Mingyuan. *Xingde zhishi* (Sexual knowledge). Beijing: Renmin weisheng chubanshe, 1980.

Wang Xinjuan. "Zhenjieguan" (The concept of chastity). *ZF*, 1 (Jan. 1985), 20.

Wang Yalin and Li Jinrong. "Urban Workers' Housework." *Social Sciences in China*, 3, 2 (1982), 147–65.

Wang Yanming. "Yizhuang duanming hunyin de shimo" (The whole story of a short-lived marriage). *Zhongwai funü*, 4 (Apr. 1985), 31–33.

Wang Yiling. "Qizi yinggai bao zhangfu" (Wives must take care of their husbands). *Shehui*, 1 (Feb. 1984), 36.

Wang Youqin. "Guanyu xing daodede yixie sikao" (Some reflections concerning sexual morality). *ZF*, 10 (Oct. 1985), 10–12.

———. "Yuan women you yige xinde funüguan" (Let us have a new concept of womanhood). *ZF*, 3 (Mar. 1984), 1.

Wang Yuxian. "Wo ceng chiguo 'zuojian zifu' de kutou" (I have tasted the bitterness of "becoming enmeshed in a web of my own spinning"). *Funü*, 12 (1984), 12.

Wang Zhou. "Danshen zhi wojian" (My views on singlehood). *Fujian qingnian*, 7 (1985), 36.

"Weile zhangfu ni yinggai dongde" (What you must understand for your husband's sake). *In* Funü zhiyou zazhishe, ed., 2, 299.

Weisskopf, Michael. "Abortion Policy Tears at China's Society." *Washington Post,* Jan. 7, 1985, A1, A20.

————. "China's Birth Control Policy Drives Some to Kill Baby Girls." *Washington Post,* Jan. 8, 1985, A1, A10.

Wen Jun. "Qiu'ai shi shenshengde" (Courtship is sacred). *Xiandai jiating,* 6 (June 1985), 13.

Wen Xianliang. "Nongcun guniang zenyang xuan qinglang" (How village girls choose a groom). *Jiating,* 11 (Nov. 1984), 17.

Wenhui bao (Wenhui News). Shanghai.

"Why Our Marital Relationship Has Broken Down." *Chinese Sociology and Anthropology,* 7, 3 (Spring 1975), *passim.*

Whyte, Martin, and William Parish. *Urban Life in Contemporary China.* Chicago: University of Chicago Press, 1984.

"Wo bei ta changqi qiling gai zenmeban?" (What should I do when I am bullied and humiliated by him for a long period of time?) *MF,* 7 (July 1985), 45.

"Wo didi zenma hui lunwei qiangjian fan?" (How could my younger brother be reduced to becoming a rapist?) *MF,* 4 (Apr. 1985), 38–39.

"Wo yiding dei yu ta jiehun ma?" (Do I have to marry him?) *Funü,* 12 (Dec. 1984), 15.

"Wode hua shi shanyide" (My words are well-intentioned). *ZF,* 11 (Nov. 1984), 24.

"Wode ze'ouguan" (My views on selecting a spouse). *ZF,* 7 (July 1984), 14.

"Woguo funü shiyexin qiang" (Women in our country are career-minded). *Shanghai laonian bao,* Mar. 4, 1986.

Wolf, Margery. *Revolution Postponed: Women in Contemporary China.* Stanford, Calif.: Stanford University Press, 1985.

————. *Women and the Family in Rural Taiwan.* Stanford, Calif.: Stanford University Press, 1972.

Women of China. Beijing.

Wren, Christopher. "Make Us a Match, Chinese Lonelyhearts Ask." *New York Times,* Sept. 30, 1984, A1, A8.

Wu chengshi jiating yanjiu xianmu zu. *Zhongguo chengshi jiating* (Urban families in China). Jinan: Shandong renmin chubanshe, 1985.

Wu Fengying. "Hehuanhua you kaile" (The flowers of reconciliation bloomed again). *Funü,* 1 (1984), 10.

Wu Jinbo. "Wo cuoguaile ta" (I mistakenly blamed her). *ZF,* 10 (Oct. 1982), 43.

Wu Mu. "'Sanzhang' xinü" ("Three heads" taking liberties with a woman). *MF,* 7 (July 1985), 20–21.

Wu Wenzao. "You guanyu lihun anjiande jige wenti" (Some problems concerning divorce cases). *Shehui kexue,* 5 (May 1982), 51–54.

Xiandai jiating (Modern Family). Shanghai.

"Xiang chengshi danan danü tigong yixie shuzi" (Some figures provided for urban older unmarried youth). *ZF,* 9 (Sept. 1984), 10–11.

"'Xianggang xiaojie' de beiju" (Tragedy of a Hong Kong miss). *Baoji wenhui gushi ban* (Dec. 1983), 1.

"Xiao meimei mo jinghuang" (Don't be alarmed, little sister). *Fujian qingnian,* 5 (May 1985), 46.

Xiao Ming. "Dalian's First Vocational School for Girls." *Women of China,* 1 (Jan. 1985), 6–7.

————. "Shouhui nide jiao ba!" (Butt out!). *Beijing funü*, 3 (Sept. 1983), 27.

————. "Wang ni cong wode guocuozhong xiqu jiaoxun" (I hope you will take a lesson from my mistakes). *Xiandai jiating*, 5 (May 1985), 13.

————. "Wo wei ni chengyao!" (I'll back you up!) *Beijing funü*, 2 (Aug. 1983), 4–6.

"Xiaomie zhe pohuai jingshen wenming de dahai" (Eliminate this great evil that destroys spiritual civilization). *ZQB*, Mar. 7, 1982, 1.

Xiaoshi. "Yu zhangfu tan nüxing jiefang" (Discussing women's liberation with my husband). *ZF*, 2 (Feb. 1986), 9.

"Xiaye lian'ai xuzhi" (Notice about love on summer nights). *Yuelao bao*, 7 (July 1985), 4.

Xie Bozhang. *Qingchunqi weisheng* (Adolescent health). 2d rev. ed. Beijing: Beijing chubanshe, 1983.

Xie Hua. "Pa 'xiu' dailai de houguo" (The consequences of feeling "shy"). *ZF*, 8 (Aug. 1982), 47.

Xie Wenliang. "Xinjiu jiaoti de hunsu tedian" (Old marriage customs being replaced by new ones). *RMRB* (overseas ed.), Feb. 3, 1986.

Xie Yong. "Danshen zhi wojian" (My view of singlehood). *ZQB*, Mar. 31, 1985.

Xin Bangxin. "Jiawu laodong shehuihua yu funü jiefang" (The socialization of housework and women's liberation). *Jiating*, 6 (1985), 16–17.

Xin guancha (New Observer). Beijing.

Xin Huan. "Liangge 'disanzhe' niangchengde yichu shehui beiju" (A social tragedy brought about by two "third parties"). *Shehui*, 1 (Feb. 1985), 29–31.

Xin Qin. "Liangge xin nüxing de duihua" (Conversation between two new women). *Qingnian yidai*, 3 (June 1985), 24–25.

Xin Zheng. "Yige guniang bei liangge pianzi roulin de shimo" (The whole story of how a young woman was ravaged by two tricksters). *Qingnian zixun*, 1 (May 1985), 47–48.

Xing Xiuling. "Longwu hede yuanfen" (The discontent and indignation of Longwu River). *MF*, 10 (Oct. 1983), 34–38.

Xinmin wanbao (New People's Evening News). Shanghai.

Xu Dian. "Buneng zai weihu fuquan" (The authority of husbands can no longer be defended). *ZF*, 6 (June 1984), 19.

Xu Feng. "Jiazhang huyu—xiwang shehui sheng'ai he zhichi" (We hope that society will support the parents' plea). *ZFB*, Apr. 17, 1985.

Xu Jin. "Ye yao xing jiaoyu" (Sex education is necessary). *Qingnian yidai*, 1 (1985), 56–57.

Xu Youhua. "Jinye xingguang canlan" (Tonight the stars shine brightly). *Jiating*, 12 (Dec. 1984), 18–19.

Xue Suzhen. "Shenme zai zu'ai daqingniande hunyin" (What is hindering the marriage of older youth). *Jiating*, 12 (Dec. 1984), 16–18.

Xue Suzhen, Wang Youzhu, and Wang Lijuan. "An Investigation of Some Marriage Cases in Urban Shanghai." *In* Chu, 82–98.

"Xueleide kongsu" (A denunciation in blood and tears). *Beijing funü*, 3 (Sept. 1983), 4.

Yan An. "Zifa hunyin jieshaosuo jianwen" (Information about spontaneous marriage introduction bureaus). *Qingnian yidai*, 5 (Oct. 1984), 24.

Yan Chengsheng. "Xiaoyuan gequ dailaide fannao" (Worries brought by songs on campus). *RMRB*, Dec. 30, 1985.

Yan Zhijiang. "Ta zishale!?" (She killed herself!?) *ZF*, 1 (Jan. 1985), 24–25.

"'Yanei' fanfa yu shumin tongzui" (A "government insider" who breaks the law commits the same crime as one of the common people). *ZF*, 3 (Mar. 1984), 18–19.

Yang Shanhua. "Fuqi xiangchu tantiaoshi" ([Problems caused by] different eating habits of a husband and wife). *Qingnian yidai*, 5 (Oct. 1984), 34.

Yang Xingnan. "Jushou nüdaxueshengde xianxiang yingdang gaibian" (The phenomenon of refusing to accept female university graduates must change). *ZFB*, Feb. 27, 1985, 1.

Yang Xiukun. "Yao tingzhi yaogan douzheng xingjin" (You must confidently struggle and march forward). *ZF*, 2 (Jan. 1984), 27.

Yang Yong. "Jiu weihu hunyin daode wenti fang Lei Jieqiong dajie" (An interview with Big Sister Lei Jieqiong on the question of upholding marriage morality). *ZF*, 10 (Oct. 1985), 13.

"Yao aihu nüqingnian mingyu" (Guard the reputations of young women). *ZQ*, 3 (Mar. 11, 1984), 58–59.

Yao Guochu. "Shehui ye yao guanxin dushenzhe" (Society must take care of single people). *ZFB*, 25 (Mar. 20, 1985), 3.

"Yige you jiejude aiqing gushi" (A love story with an ending). *ZQB*, July 11, 1982, 1, 3.

"Yimu pianhun chouju" (A marriage swindle farce). *ZQB*, Mar. 23, 1982, 3.

"Yindao chuzhong nüsheng shunli duguo qingchunqi" (Guide female junior high school students smoothly through puberty). *ZFB*, Feb. 6, 1985, 2.

"Yiyou hunyue, shangxuehou juede buchenxin zenmeban?" (If one is already engaged, but after attending school finds the match unsatisfactory, what should one do?) *Dangdai qingnian*, 5 (May 1985), 31–32.

Young, Marilyn. "Chicken Little in China: Some Reflections on Women." Paper presented at Duke University Conference on Chinese Marxism, Oct. 30, 1986.

Yu Luojin. "Wo weishenme yao lihun" (Why I want to divorce). *MF*, 1 (1981), 26–29.

———. "Yige chuntiande tonghua" (A spring fairy tale). *Huacheng*, 1 (1982), 141–221.

———. "Yige dongtiande tonghua" (A winter's fairy tale). *Xinhua yuebao*, 9 (1980), 94–127.

Yu Quanyuan. "Shenghuo buyinggai zheyang duidai ta" (Life should not treat her this way). *Dongfang qingnian*, 6 (June 1985), 19.

Yu Ronghe. "Qingchun jianying" (Youthful silhouettes). *ZF*, 2 (Feb. 1981), 42.

Yue Daiyun and Carolyn Wakeman. "Women in Recent Chinese Fiction: A Review Article." *Journal of Asian Studies*, 42, 4 (Aug. 1983), 879–88.

Yuelao bao (Matchmaker News). Fuzhou.

Zhang Cangniao and Zhan Yuanshui. "Women wei tai huyu" (We appeal for her). *Nüzi shijie*, 5 (May 1985), 22.

Zhang Gengsheng. "Hebi shi renminde youlü he xingfen" (The anxiety and excitement of the people of Hebi city). *MF*, 2 (Feb. 1984), 29–32.

Zhang Haidi. "Wo suo zhuiqiu de xingfu" (The happiness I seek). *ZQ*, 1 (Jan. 1984), 26–27.

Zhang Hongqiang. "Tongku de jueze" (A bitter choice). *ZF*, 6 (June 1985), 21–23.

Zhang Jie. "Fang zhou" (The ark). *Shouhuo* (Harvest), 2 (1982).

Zhang Ping. "Qing guanzhu nongcunde 'danan' wenti" (Please pay close attention to the problem of "older unmarried men" in the countryside). *ZF*, 9 (Sept. 1984), 11–12.

————. "Xiafang jingjiquan yihou" (After transferring my economic power). *Jiefang ribao*, Dec. 7, 1985.

Zhang Qingyun et al. *Nü qingnian shujian* (Letters from young women). Shenyang: Liaoning renmin chubanshe, 1982.

Zhang Shuyi. "Wo zhihaole qiguanyan bing" (I cured the henpecked disease). *ZQB*, Nov. 30, 1985.

Zhang Wei. "The New Health and Beauty Craze." *Women of China*, 12 (Dec. 1984), 40–41.

Zhang Xinxin and Sang Ye. "Beijing ren" (Peking man). *Shanghai wenxue*, 1 (1985), 4–27, 38.

Zhang Zhiguang and Wu Jing. "Ruhe zhengque duidai xing yishi" (How to deal correctly with sexual consciousness). *ZQB*, Dec. 4, 1980.

"Zhangfu youle 'waiyu' zhi hou" (After my husband had a new lover). *Jiefang ribao*, Nov. 23, 1985.

Zhangjiakoushi fulian (Zhangjiakou Women's Federation). "Yansu chuli shun yu minyi" (Handle it seriously, act in accordance with the popular will). *ZF*, 8 (Aug. 1983), 30.

Zhao Bingren. "Nüxingde zixinxin ying congxiao peiyang" (Female self-confidence must be fostered from childhood). *ZF*, 4 (Apr. 1985), 34.

Zhao Yanling. "Wei nüqingnian jiuye xiance" (Offering advice to young women seeking employment). *ZF*, 10 (Oct. 1980), 26.

Zhao Ziyang, Lü Xinkang, and Guo Zhanhua. "Lihunde yuanyin duozhong duoyang: dui Shenyangshi yiqian lihun anjiande zhonghe fenxi" (The variety of reasons for divorce: an analysis of one thousand divorce cases in Shenyang). *Shehui*, 2 (Apr. 1984), 22–26.

"Zhe posuide ai haineng gei wo xingfu ma?" (Can this tattered love still give me happiness?) *ZF*, 4 (Apr. 1985), 9.

"Zhelide xifu dou zhengda hongbian" (Daughters-in-law here hope to win red banners). *Nüzi shijie*, 6 (June 1985), 46.

Zhen Yi. "Tamen xinzhongde weinasi" (The Venus in their hearts). *Nüzi shijie*, 6 (June 1985), 22–23.

Zheng Mingming. "Jiefang ni neike aimei de xin" (Liberate that beauty-loving heart of yours). *ZF*, 4 (Apr. 1985), 36–37.

"Zhengque bawo qingchunqi jiaoyu de neirong he fangfa" (Getting a grasp on content and method of puberty education). *Shanghai qingnian bao*, 1757 (June 14, 1985), 2.

"Zhengque duidai cong nongcun laide 'xiao baomu'" (How to handle the "little housemaids" who come from the countryside). *Jiating*, 5 (1985), 36.

"Zheshi bukenengde" (This is impossible). *Fujian qingnian*, 5 (May 1985), 47.

"Zheshi 'jiating jiufen' haishi chufan xingfa?" (Is this a "domestic dispute" or a violation of the law?) *Zhongguo funü*, 12 (Dec. 1983), 37–38.

"Zheshi qizhuang yifu ma?" (Is this outlandish clothing?) *ZQB*, Aug. 1, 1982, 1.

"Zheyangde 'qinre' wo shoubuliao!" (I can't take this "passion"!) *ZQB*, Apr. 13, 1982.

"Zhezhong 'xianshi' jiu gaiguan" (We should poke our noses into "other people's business"). *Zhongguo funü*, 1 (Jan. 1981), 44.

Zhiyin (Understanding Friend). Wuhan.

Zhongguo funü (ZF; Chinese Women). Beijing.

Zhongguo funü bao (ZFB; China Women's News). Beijing.

Zhongguo qingnian (ZQ; Chinese Youth). Beijing.

Zhongguo qingnian bao (ZQB; China Youth News). Beijing.

"Zhongnan qingnü xianxiang youzeng wujian" (The phenomenon of regarding men as superior to women is increasing rather than decreasing). *ZFB*, Jan. 30, 1985, 1.

Zhongwai funü (Chinese and Foreign Women). Beijing.

Zhou Daoluan. "Lüelun qiangjian zui" (A brief discussion of the crime of rape). *MF*, 6 (June 1981), 10–11.

Zhou Guangyu and Cai Queyi. "Dui kaifa funü zhilide jidian yijian" (Some ideas about developing women's intellectual powers). *ZF*, 7 (July 1984), 4–5.

Zhou Jinde. "Disanzhe chazude zhuyao yuanyin" (The main reasons for third party involvements). *Shehui*, 3 (June 20, 1985), 38–39.

Zhou Yan. "Jiaru ni shiqule zhencao" (If you have lost your virginity). *Funü zhi you*, 7 (1985), 16.

Zhou Yinjun and Chen Rufeng. "Shanghaishi nüqingnian jiuye wenti chutan" (A preliminary discussion of the problem of young women finding employment in Shanghai). Zhongguo shehui kexueyuan qingshaonian yanjiusuo he Qingnian laodong yanjiushi, eds., *Qingnian jiuyede tansuo yu shixian* (Inquiring into and implementing employment for youth). Beijing: Zhongguo shehui kexueyuan chubanshe, 1983, 329–37.

Zhou Yuchang. "Xinli shehui yinsu he xing zhang'ai" (Psychological and social factors and obstacles to sex). *Shehui*, 2 (Apr. 1985), 45–47.

Zhu Guizhen. "Burying Old Grudges." *Women of China*, 1 (Jan. 1984), 40–41.

Zhu Jiaxiong. "Dang fumu fandui zinüde lian'ai shi" (When parents are opposed to their sons' and daughters' loves). *Xiandai jiating*, 7 (July 1985), 6–7.

Zhu Liangyu. "Bugai fashengde xue'an" (A murder case that should not have happened). *Falü yu shenghuo*, 5 (May 1985), 32–33.

Zhu Ying. "Wo ganyuan dang Tao Chun" (I am willing to be a Tao Chun). *ZF*, 6 (June 1984), 20.

Zhuang Guangze and Liu Xiaohe. "Daili quanxian yiwai de hua" (Some words outside the limits of a procurator's authority). *Qingnian yidai*, 5 (Oct. 1984), 23.

Zong Weizi. "Nüzi lianyihui bu yi duo" (The number of women's friendly societies should not increase). *Shehui bao*, June 13, 1985, 4.

Zou Nanrong and Cao Yang. "Sixing fan xiongdi he tamen shenhoude yinxiang" (Two brothers sentenced to death and the shadow behind them). *Fujian qingnian*, 7 (July 1985), 14–15.

———. "Yige jiatingde huimie" (The destruction of a family). *Fujian qingnian*, 5 (May 1985), 14–15.

Index